The Control of Drugs and Drug Users

The Control of Drugs and Drug Users
Reason or Reaction?

Edited by

Ross Coomber
University of Greenwich, UK

 harwood academic publishers

Australia • Canada • China • France • Germany • India • Japan
Luxembourg • Malaysia • The Netherlands • Russia • Singapore
Switzerland • Thailand • United Kingdom

Amsteldijk 166
1st Floor
1079 LH Amsterdam
The Netherlands

British Library Cataloguing in Publication Data

The control of drugs and drug users: reason or reaction?
  1. Narcotics, Control of
  I. Coomber, Ross
  362.2′936

  ISBN 90-5702-188-9 (Softcover)

For Liza and Jake

Contents

**PART THREE: CURRENT TRENDS AND POSSIBILITIES
FOR THE FUTURE**

Acknowledgements

First, I would like to thank Harwood Academic Publishers for their support through the duration of this project. Secondly, I would also like to thank each of the contributing authors who all did their very best to complete their work as quickly as they were able without compromising the quality of their contributions. Thirdly, I would like to thank the library staff at the Institute for the Study of Drug Dependence in London, especially John Witton, for all their help, not just in this project but at all times.

Preface

'Drugs are not bad because they are illegal, they are illegal because they are bad'
(Statement to Senate committee investigating drug legalisation by
John Lawn, former Director of the US Drug Enforcement Administration)

How, and even *if* currently illicit drugs and drug users should be controlled are questions which in recent years have been raised increasingly as an issue in the media and by other interested parties. These include many of those who have to actually enforce current controls, such as the police, and at the international level, bodies such as Interpol. In some arenas however, especially at the party political level, the issue has more often been about whether the debate itself is actually needed or is even considered to be appropriate. Individual politicians may feel the need to debate drug policy but this is widely perceived to be a political liability across the major political parties, potentially leaving the party vulnerable to the dreaded accusation of being 'soft on drugs'. Outright condemnation of drugs and their use remains the public Party political consensus – drugs are bad and dangerous and therefore little debate is needed except to agree newer and tougher measures. This is largely due to the broad acceptance of the rationale for existing drug controls, the direction of the approaches taken, and of their historical formation as a reasoned response to an accurately portrayed problem. There are however fundamental difficulties with each of these assumptions. There is a further problem such that for the most part these assumptions are also reliant upon a highly questionable scientifically progressive world view of rational and benevolent public policy.

Public policy regarding the Public Health is legitimised through recourse to scientific evidence demonstrating the need to control or manage a problem as it becomes evident. Unfortunately, in relation to drugs the assumed problem has never been a simple one, neither conceptually, nor indeed, pharmaceutically. A simple, chronistic reading of drugs control history can point to periods where drugs were increasingly becoming associated with overdoses and deaths (opium), with a growth in addiction (morphine, heroin, cocaine), with violent and criminal activity (opium, cocaine, heroin, even marijuana) and correspondingly point to the apparently rational controls which were then introduced in response to these public health concerns. It is deceptively easy, and of course both convenient and comforting, to read history in such a way. Once policy has been consolidated in history as essentially rational that attributed rationality can then feed into the current situation – if previous policy has a sound grounding then the same rationales and concerns must also apply today and consequently justify and legitimate current policy. Numerous historical re-evaluations of how particular drugs came to be perceived as problems are however, able to point to the complex interplay of political, circumstantial, racial, sectional interest, economic, social and cultural influences which gave rise to particular policy at particular times (Bean, 1974; 1993; Berridge, 1984; Berridge and Edwards, 1987; Bruun *et al.*, 1975; Harding, 1988; Kohn, 1992; Matthee, 1995; Musto, 1987; Reinarman, 1979; Saper, 1974; Smart, 1984).

Unlike the assumption expressed in the quote which heads this introduction, the attribution of 'badness' to a drug and the policy for its control does not simply relate to some objective potential for harm inherent in the drug as many drugs which are considered 'bad' present less danger to the user than many that are legally sanctioned (Gossop, 1996). The attribution of badness cannot be divorced from the range of colluding, and often interacting, sentiments (be they moral, racial, or a localised fear of the unknown) which, for whatever reason, pervades the understanding of particular drug use. In fact, much of the literature discloses that fears and related perspectives on a whole variety of 'bad' drugs has as much, if not more, to do with *who* is using the drug than it has to do with the drug itself. We have no reason to believe that, in the current situation, policy is any less problematic. That existing drug control policies may have developed from a drug-centric foundation of exaggeration and falsity, interrelated with notions of 'otherness' (xenophobia/racism) and misplaced (and essentially contradictory) moralities as well as international and national politics, amongst other biases, suggests that until these influences have been acknowledged and neutralised, rational debate on drug and drug use controls will remain difficult. This book, looking at the development of controls in Britain and the United States and how those controls have since fared, aims to contribute to the growing literature which aspires to provide a grounding from which such debate may be pursued.

In part one of this volume a number of the authors tease out and explore some of these influences which can be seen to have impacted on drug control policy. In chapters one, two and three we are invited to acknowledge the particular histories of drug control in Britain and the United States. In particular, the emphasis is on the impact of many of those forces mentioned earlier: morality, xenophobia, racism, sectional interest as well as international politics. Geoff Harding in particular (chapter one), treats us to an historical perspective on how both drug (opium and its derivatives) and drug user were attributed specific qualities which then had repercussions in the controls introduced. Without the development of particular discourses which (influenced by forces other than 'science') defined drug and drug user in the ways they did it is difficult to accept that the development and trajectory of drug control would not have differed significantly. Likewise, Michael Woodiwiss revisiting US influences usefully reminds us of how pliable and powerful even the most apparently innocuous policy can be. Combined with zealous prohibitionist activity the development and implementation of the 1914 Harrison Act reflects all that is problematic about the history of US drug controls. Infused with distortion, xenophobia, racism and moral crusading one is left to reflect that current controls in the US have a creaky foundation based less on rationality than on reaction.

Whilst most control issues appear to be relatively transparent as regards enforcement, the laws are there, the policy is clear, at least in theory. When it comes to issues of treatment and rehabilitation, notions of power and control are subtly diffused within broader conditions relating to medicine, pharmacology and how conditions such as addiction have been defined. Decisions on *how* to treat heroin addicts have often had as much to do with considerations external to the condition of addiction, such as controlling leakage of supplies onto the black-market and pseudo-medical positions, than whether abstinence or maintenance is appropriate as treatment. Decisions which appear to be essentially medical and thus free of moral/political positioning thus often, under further scrutiny, show themselves to be less obviously clear-cut. Complimenting Harding (chapter one) Rachel Lart (chapter four), utilises a Foucauldian framework to illuminate our understanding of the power relationship between medicine, and thus medics, to the drug user up to the early 1980s. Once again, *who* the addict/drug user was is elaborated as significant in how the problem was understood. In the late 1950s and 1960s in particular she argues that a shift in treatment practices based upon the type of addict rather than on the conception of addiction itself was instrumental in deciding and inculcating new and future treatment policy. The treatment of drug addicts, particularly that involving the prescription of opiates or other substitutes, and in what ways, continue to be issues of importance for many, particularly those being treated, and those doing the treating. That there are specific power relationships involved in the treatment of drug users not based purely on medicine and the 'facts' however, continues to elude some.

It is not unreasonable to allude to the distortion and exaggeration of drug effects/dangers which have impacted on drug policy, especially in its early formative stages and that are often present even in the contemporary media and images presented by politicians as these problems are well documented (Bean, 1993; Goode and Yehuda, 1994; Murji, 1995; Parssinen, 1983; Reeves and Campbell, 1994; Reinerman 1989). However, this position needs to be careful not to slip into a too simplistic and out-moded 'social control' framework, particularly when relying on notions of 'moral-panics' which are often fairly uncritically employed. In respect to understanding how media and other representations impact on policy this is of course of critical importance. In chapter five, Karim Murji, whilst not shying away from the idea that much media representation on drugs is unuseful, asks us to re-assess the notions of moral-panic and unreasonable representation which have been commonly applied. Simply 'de-bunking' media representations he argues often leads to the de-bunkers committing some of the same sins of those being accused of the unreasonable representation of drugs and drug users. A more contemporary understanding of media reaction and counter-reaction needs to acknowledge that the "more complicated, contradictory and messily fragmented patterns of real life are an inconvenience which both approaches prefer not to deal with". The 'one dimensional' picture presented in media reaction that Cohen (1972) drew attention to is replaced by an alternative, but equally one dimensional view in counter-reaction.

It must be conceded however, that even if controls over drugs *were* more directly related to some objectively reliable assessment of their dangers, it doesn't necessarily follow that the controls which have been implemented are either the most appropriate or effective even within the stated aims of those policies. In fact it is this very point, whether existing drug control policy works and therefore continues to be appropriate, that provokes most calls for debate rather than a concern for how the policy came into being in the first place. In the second part of this book the contributors look at current controls over drugs and drug users (both in the realms of enforcement and treatment) and seek to assess their efficacy and continuing relevance. Nigel South (chapter six) provides us with a lucid account of the problems faced by current enforcement policy in Britain. In an attempt to curtail an increasing supply, drug controls (enforcement) have become increasingly punitive and 'draconian'. The impact of this policy during the 1980s and '90s, South argues, has been "Almost without exception ... overwhelmingly negative, with rising numbers of drug users, offenders in prison, drug related crimes, [and] demand on enforcement resources". He also notes something about drug control policy which is taking on increasing significance; how policy is being implemented in practice may not conform to the principled and formal position of extant policy. Sometimes change in practice actually precedes policy. Thus, in Britain and some other European countries the handling of cases of simple *possession* of 'soft' drugs through cautioning as opposed to prosecution has *de-facto* decriminalised much use. In some hard pressed localities this has even been extended to drugs such as heroin where the police forces involved see little benefit to pursuing prosecution. In circumstances such as these debate and re-considered policy has been preceded by action which is seen as appropriate to the conditions at hand. Thus a situation is now occurring whereby drugs such as cannabis are prohibited but that prohibition is not being enforced as it once was.

While Nigel South can point to the anomalies of enforcement strategies, and to the failures of supply and demand reduction in Britain and Europe, Bruce Bullington (chapter seven) casts a longer shadow over current US policy. The War on Drugs in the US he concludes has not been a mere rhetorical device to galvanise public support or been carried out superficially but has been fought "with a vengeance". Extensively reviewing the impact of enforcement and other measures in the War on Drugs he reflects on how "One of the most puzzling features of this war is how it has been possible to go to such extremes to assure a victory against drug use and users, and yet to have come away with no clear cut beneficial outcome". Reviewing the costs of prohibition in the States, Bullington questions the practicality and the reasoning of those who argue that the answer to future drugs policy is more of the same, based on the same reasoning.

Susanne MacGregor (chapter eight) showing some continuity from Rachel Lart's earlier chapter, analyses policy manoeuvres in treatment and rehabilitation from the 1970s to the present day. In trying to assess moves in treatment away from prescribing towards abstinence and then towards harm reduction (and thus back to aspects of prescribing) she argues that the British system should be seen as characterised not by a coherent or even consistent strategy but by appropriate and pragmatic responses to a constantly changing problem. Such pragmatism, which differs from the more forthrightly penal approach of the US, is perhaps most visible in the response to the dangers of HIV. "Thresholds were lowered and there was greater emphasis on educating about injecting practices and about sexual behaviour. At times it appeared that the main activity of drugs agencies was to hand out syringes, needles and condoms. Rather than such activities being discussed as matters of principle, as is the tendency in the United States, on the whole the British approach was flexible, tolerant, pragmatic and adaptable". Current policy it would seem is at times a mish-mash of reasoned response (albeit within a pre-defined and often questionable set of assumptions about the user and the problem in hand) to particular circumstances whilst at other times it is defined and legitimated by unreasonable adherence to principles of 'what ought to be', such as a zero tolerance to drug use. Debate needs to tease out and establish that which is based on reason, what is effective and indeed, what is possible. Thomas Szasz (chapter nine), in more polemic form, continues a theme he has developed over many years. Drug prohibition is hypocritical, in contravention of our basic 'rights' as individuals, and based on the scapegoating of drugs for other ills. The War on Drugs he contends is unwinnable, has contributed more to America's ills than have drugs themselves, and is based upon a falsification of 'danger' in society – by obscuring the fact that 'life is dangerous' and suggesting that drugs can and should be reasonably separated from a conception of risks in everyday life.

In this sense it is unfortunate that where 'debate' *has* taken place it has often been disappointingly shallow, tending to concentrate on dichotomous argumentation. Thus, simple prohibition is counter-posed with simple legalisation, and vice-versa. Part of the problem encountered by those who wish to engage in debate concerning reform of drug control policy is that of transcending this simplistic policy framework. Policy is a multifaceted continuum. A continuum because between outright prohibition accompanied by outright repression to enforce it and outright laissez-faire legalisation there are a multitude of variations possible. Multifaceted because within this continuum a variegated mix of policies is possible. In reality of course this is exactly what we have and how policy manifests itself. Drug policy in the US is not a pure mix of extreme prohibition and enforcement but it does have, in general, greater levels of prohibition and enforcement than the UK. The UK by contrast has a heady mix of (slightly lesser) prohibition, (lesser) enforcement and many more consistently applied approaches to the reduction of harm associated with drugs. For some prohibition-ists in the US harm reduction strategies are tantamount to condoning drug use, whereas in the UK this policy distinction has been made more comfortably. The debate has to move beyond simple oppositions. In this light, part three of the volume seeks to explore some of the issues that may be part of future policy de-bate which are not reliant either on simple prohibition or outright legalisation. It does explore however the potentiality of a relatively more liberal approach in a number of areas. One area which is subject to much discussion in the supply reduction literature is that of crop substitution, the 'encouragement' and/or spon-sorship of substituting the production of drug producing crops with crops such as coffee, bananas or other such alternatives. Historically these programmes have had limited success for a range of reasons but continue to be advocated as a means to reduce supply, particularly by the US. David Mansfield and Colin Sage (chapter ten) reassess the potential role of alternative development in poor drug producing countries. Outlining the difficulties and shortcomings of current approaches to crop substitution they argue that until the complexity of the role that drug crops play in these drug source areas is acknowledged and until key issues such as poverty targeting, participation and environmental sustainability are addressed then they will be limited in their success. They argue that more appropriate policy in the design of 'alternative development' programmes would have an emphasis on 'appropriate development initiatives' which would be 'given precedence over those of drug crop reduction'.

One of the problems of conflating drugs into 'good' and 'bad', is that it sug-gests that the pharmacological effects of the drugs are easily understood in terms of 'health' and their general or potential utility as a therapeutic agent. That heroin is widely used for therapeutic reasons in the UK, and sometimes even as a prescribed drug of addiction, but is prohibited in the US however, shows that this simple distinction is useless for even one of the 'hardest' drugs. In the US cocaine and morphine are available to be used therapeutically (although cocaine use has been limited in recent years) whilst cannabis, the 'softest' of drugs (?), is not. In the chapter which follows, *Missed opportunities? Beneficial uses of illicit drugs*, Lester Grinspoon and James Bakalar develop this theme further with respect to other currently illicit drugs. Considering in turn cocaine, various psychedelics (including LSD, MDMA, Ibogaine, psilocybin) as well as canna-bis, they outline the various therapeutic potentials that these substances may pro-vide. Such potentials they argue are wide ranging and significant. By outlawing drugs in such a way that doesn't acknowledge the multifaceted nature of their pharmacology and stresses the demonised aspects, they suggest that real benefits are being lost which could reduce suffering and improve well-being.

Closer to home, it is a common suggestion that more liberal controls would result in increased uncontrolled drug use. This position is predominately located in the assumption that drug use, especially those drugs such as heroin and cocaine (powder and crack) among others, is largely uncontrolled drug use. Wayne Harding (chapter twelve) sets about presenting the evidence which counters this simple 'pharmacomythology'. Drawing on a body of research he has long been involved with, considering informal social controls of drug use, and controlled and moderated drug use itself, he questions the validity of a notion suggesting that illicit drug use would necessarily become more compulsive and excessive if current restrictions were lessened. Harding rightly contends that any liberalising of drug controls would not be in isolation from other harm reduction activities. Existing informal controls such as those applied around alcohol would increase but these would need to be bolstered by, for example, increased and improved secondary prevention education, the provision of needle exchange programmes, and appropriate information about recreational and controlled drug use which would encourage and embellish the types of social controls which can be effective in reducing compulsive and excessive drug use.

Earlier in this introduction I alluded to the fact that what happens 'on the ground' is not necessarily the same as that which is laid down in policy dictums. In a number of countries across Europe a more liberal policing approach to possession is increasingly occurring, especially in regard to drugs such as cannabis which makes up the vast majority of enforcement activity. In Britain this slackening in the policing of drug *use* has even (as it has in similar ways in other countries) coincided with a call by the Home Secretary for harsher, not more lenient penalties for such offences. Richard Hartnoll (chapter thirteen) in his overview of *International Trends in Drug Policy* pinpoints tensions such as these as of emerging importance when he says "that significant tensions are building up over the emphasis and direction of policy. The pressures for change are largely generated from the bottom up, whilst the tendency from the top down is to resist change and re-affirm the status quo". Such tensions however are evident not just between the local and national levels but also between the national and international levels. Providing an overview of policy differences, local, national and international tensions, Hartnoll maps out some of the broad trends that can be discerned in recent years and the trajectory of policies such as harm reduction within these contexts. With reference to the above and in keeping with the overall theme of this volume and its underlying concern, Hartnoll concludes by posing "whether reason, based on scientific evidence, day by day reality, and a willingness to think clearly and imaginatively about a complex issue can play even a slightly larger role than it has on a topic dominated by unthinking reaction based on moralistic rhetoric".

REFERENCES

Bean, P. (1974) *The Social Control of Drugs*. London: Martin Roberston.

Bean, P. (1993) Cocaine and Crack: The Promotion of an Epidemic. In Bean, P. (ed.) *Cocaine and Crack: Supply and Use*. London: Macmillan.

Berridge, V. (1984) Drugs and Social Policy: The Establishment of Drug Control in Britain 1900–1930. *British Journal of Addiction*, 79, 17–29.

Berridge, V. and Edwards, G. (1987) *Opium and the People*. London: Yale University Press.

Bruun, K., Pan, L. and Rexed, I. (1975) *The Gentlemen's Club: International Control of Drugs and Alcohol*. London: University of Chicago Press.

Cohen, S. (1972) *Folk Devils and Moral Panics: The Creation of the Mods and Rockers*. London: MacGibbon & Kee.

Goode, E. and Ben-Yehuda, N. (1994) *Moral Panics: The Construction of Deviance*. Cambridge, Massachusetts: Blackwell.

Gossop, M. (1996) *Living With Drugs*, 4th Edition. Aldershot: Arena.

Harding, G. (1988) *Opiate Addiction, From Moral Illness to Pathological Disease*. London: Macmillan.

Kohn, M. (1992) *Dope Girls: The Birth of the British Underground*. London: Lawrence & Wisehart.

Matthee, R. (1995) Exotic Substances: the Introduction and Global Spread of Tobacco, Coffee, Cocoa, Tea, and Distilled Liquor, Sixteenth to Eighteenth Centuries. In, Porter, R. and Teich, M. (eds.) *Drugs and Narcotics in History*. Cambridge: Cambridge University Press.

Murji, K. (1995) Drugs. In P. Neate (ed) *Scare in the Community – Britain in a moral panic*. London: Community Care/Reed Business Publishing.

Musto, D. (1987) *The American Disease*. Oxford: Oxford University Press.

Parssinen, T. M. (1983) *Secret Passions, Secret Remedies: Narcotic Drugs in British Society 1820–1930*. Manchester: Manchester University Press.

Reeves, J. L. and Campbell, R. (1994) *Cracked Coverage: Television News, The Anti-Cocaine Crusade, and the Reagan Legacy*. Durham: Duke University Press.

Reinarman, C. (1979) Moral Entrepreneurs and Political Economy: Historical and Ethnographic Notes on the Construction of the Cocaine Menace. *Contemporary Crises*, 3, 225–54.

Reinerman, C. and Levine, H. G. (1989) The Crack Attack: Politics and Media in America's Latest Drug Scare. In, Best, J. (ed.) *Images of Issues*. Aldine Press.

Saper, A. (1974) The Making of Policy through Myth, Fantasy and Historical Accident: The Making of America's Narcotics Laws. *British Journal of Addiction*, 69, 183–93.

Smart, C. (1984) 'Social Policy and Drug addiction: A Critical Study of Policy Development', *British Journal of Addiction*, 79, 31–9.

Foreword

Research in the area of illicit drugs is continuing to develop, as the range of this collection demonstrates. From sociology through to media analysis, social policy to development studies, the collection demonstrates the expanding remit of drugs related research. It also underlines the range of perspectives which can illuminate the drugs issue and which are seen to be relevant. Drugs has always been an area where the input can be as much from history as from psychopharmacology.

The title of the book gives the clue to this multi-disciplinarity. 'Reason or reaction?'; much research has been tied to policy debates. Analysis has supported policy activism, and researchers have often adopted overtly partisan positions on the wider policy stage. That combination of activism and analysis is represented in this collection; it remains a strong impetus behind much research in the substance use area in general and not just for drugs. But there is also a need to develop analysis a stage further. This collection does that in a number of different ways-through applying theoretical perspectives such as those of Foucault, which are not directly policy relevant; through mapping and analysis, as in Susanne MacGregor's valuable work on the development of British drug services; and through beginning to debate concepts which are uncritically accepted because they suit the concerns of the policy debates. One example in this book is the critique of the undiscriminating use of the term 'moral panic' in relation to the media and drug use, a theme I have also addressed in recent work on AIDS (Berridge, 1996). Another polemical view which is uncritically accepted is the condemnation of U.S. Prohibition of alcohol in the 1920's. Historians need perhaps to spread greater awareness of the implications of their research on this period which indicates a more complex situation. The 'received wisdom' of gangster-ridden failure seems not to have applied throughout the period of Prohibition (Burnham, 1968–9).

Through such serious research and the articulation of the understanding of policy formation can come indirect, but ultimately fruitful, insights into policy making and how policy changes. Authors in this book draw attention to the continuing importance of historical themes within drug policy. The pharmacist, for example, the fulcrum of opium control in the mid to late nineteenth century, remains the major distributor of needles for needle exchange today. History is represented, too, in the continuing importance of 'experts' in the formation of policy. So far as the British situation is concerned, and despite the sporadic high political profile of the issue, policy responses have continued to be defined by experts — although who can be termed a 'drug expert' has significantly changed over time. The policy community has widened over the past two decades.

The dual nature of drug policy — its high political and public profile, coupled with its 'in-house' expert policy making, has led to a gulf between the unspoken expert view of policy and the public and political view. That gulf may be narrowing. Certainly, as MacGregor perceptively comments, drugs post AIDS is no longer such a 'stand alone' issue. Policies link with those for crime prevention, health promotion and urban regeneration. The notion of 'community safety' in the recent policy document resonates with similar themes in those other areas as well; prevention is the key.

This is essentially also a locally based approach — and one key theme which emerges from the analyses is the continuing and historically determined tension between policy making at local, national and international levels. Policy has fed into practice, but also practice into policy in a symbiotic relationship.

The interest of this collection is in policy change, and here it attempts to move away from crude stereotypes and opposites. David Mansfield and Colin Sage show how crop substitution as a policy just simply will not work in terms of marginal economies in the third world. The international drug economy is a more complex entity. What types of different regulatory systems are we talking about? Do they in effect already exist through the non prosecution of small scale drugs offences in parts of the U.K. and the medical 'shopkeeper' role, revived post AIDS? How could change be effected? Wayne Harding argues that a new culture could be created, using alcohol and the changed response to that drug, as his model. Smoking would be another example — here the post war period has seen a remarkable culture shift, as least so far as middle class smoking is concerned. The culture change is towards greater restriction and public disapproval. Smoking and drug use in some respects seem to be on a policy collision course, in particular through the adoption of the concept of addiction. Where the balance will rest remains to be seen. But the historical and contemporary evidence on smoking and alcohol, their 'policy communities' and their different national regulatory systems should be brought more closely into the debates on illicit drugs.

Ultimately this collection does not, and cannot provide answers to the policy debates. But its content underlines the broadening and increased sophistication of the research which can inform them.

REFERENCES

Berridge, V. (1996) *AIDS in the UK: The Making of Policy, 1981–1994*, Oxford University Press, Oxford.

Burnham, J. (1968–9) 'New Perspectives on the Prohibition 'Experiment' of the 1920's', *Journal of Social History*, Vol. 9, No. 2, pp. 51–68.

Virginia Berridge.
London School of Hygiene and Tropical Medicine.

Contributors

James B. Bakalar is a Lecturer in Law in the Department of Psychiatry at the Harvard Medical School. He is co-author with Lester Grinspoon of *Psychedelic Drugs Reconsidered; Cocaine: A Drug and its Social Evolution; Drug Control in a Free Society*, and *Marihuana, the Forbidden Medicine.*

Philip Bean is a Professor of Criminology and Director, Midlands Centre for Criminology and Criminal Justice, Loughborough University. He is the author of a number of books on drug abuse. He is President of the British Society of Criminology.

Bruce Bullington teaches in the School of Criminology and Criminal Justice at the Florida State University, Tallahassee, Florida. His principal research interests are drug policy and related issues. He is currently editor of the Journal of Drug Issues.

Lester Grinspoon, M.D. is Associate Professor of Psychiatry at the Harvard Medical School. He is the author of *Marihuana Reconsidered* and co-author with James B. Bakalar of *Marihuana, the Forbidden Medicine.*

Geoffrey Harding is Senior Lecturer in Primary Health Care Research, Department of General Practice and Primary Care, St Bartholomews and the Royal London Medical and Dental School, Queen Mary and Westfield College, University of London. He has carried out research in a variety of areas, including addiction, inter-professional relations between Pharmacists and General Practitioners, and consumerism and health care. His recent publications include a jointly edited collection (with S. Nettleton and K. Taylor) *Social Pharmacy: Innovation and Development*, 1994.

Wayne Harding, is a founder of, and is Director of Projects for Social Science Research & Evaluation, Inc., Lincoln, Massachusetts. He holds academic positions as a Lecturer on Psychiatry at Harvard Medical School, Department of Psychiatry; The Cambridge Hospital, Cambridge Massachusetts; and as a faculty member of Norman E. Zinberg Centre for Addiction Studies, Harvard Medical School, Boston Massachusetts. He has over 25 years of experience conducting both basic and applied research. His primary research interests include patterns of substance use, alcohol and drug abuse prevention, and highway safety.

Richard Hartnoll has worked as a researcher in the drugs field in London, Barcelona and currently in Lisbon since 1972. Over the past 17 years, the main focus of his work has been on a wide range of epidemiological approaches to illicit drugs at both the local and national level, and especially on comparative European studies.

Rachel Lart is Research Fellow at the School for Policy Studies, University of Bristol. She has researched and published in the fields of community care and drug misuse services. Her most recent work has been on the mental health of prisoners and their access to mainstream services on release from custody.

Susanne MacGregor is Professor of Social Policy at Middlesex University, London. She has conducted numerous research studies of drug policy and practice in England funded by, amongst others, the Department of Health, The Home Office and SCODA. Her most recent book is *Transforming Cities* jointly edited with Nick Jewson, 1997.

David Mansfield is currently an independent socio-economist. He has worked with the Overseas Development Administration, the United Nations and independently on concerns with illicit drugs for six years. This work has entailed visits to a number of source areas, including Pakistan, Bolivia, Burma and Afghanistan. His other work has mainly focused on evaluation and impact monitoring methodologies.

Joy Mott was formally a Principal Research Officer in the Home Office Research and Statistics Directorate and Visiting Research Fellow to the Department of Social Sciences, Loughborough University.

Karim Murji is Senior Lecturer in Social Policy and Sociology at Roehampton Institute, London. His publications include *Traffickers: Drug markets and law enforcement* (1992, with N. Dorn and N. South) and *Drug Prevention* (1992, with N. Dorn) as well as a number of articles about drugs and policing.

Colin Sage is Lecturer in International Environmental Policy at Wye College, University of London. Besides an interest in illicit drug crop cultivation, his research covers global, national and local level policies for sustainable development. He has undertaken fieldwork in Bolivia, Mexico and Indonesia.

Nigel South is Reader in Sociology and Director of the Health and Social Services Institute at the University of Essex. He has published extensively on drugs issues. He is currently interested in crimes against the environment and public health consequences.

Thomas Szasz is Professor of Psychiatry Emeritus at the State University of New York Health Science Centre at Syracuse. He is the author of 24 books, among them *The Myth of Mental Illness* (1961) and, on drug policy, *Ceremonial Chemistry* (1974) and *Our Right to Drugs* (1992). His most recent work is *The Meaning of Mind: Language, Morality, and Neuroscience* (1996).

Michael Woodiwiss is Senior Lecturer in History at the University of the West of England where he teaches a course on organised crime. He is author of *Crime, Crusades and Corruption: Prohibition in the United States 1900–1987* and the co-editor (with Frank Pearce) of *Global Crime Connections: Dynamics and Control.*

PART ONE
THE EMERGENCE OF DRUG CONTROLS

CHAPTER 1

Pathologising the Soul: The Construction of a 19th Century Analysis of Opiate Addiction

Geoffrey Harding

Opium has been consumed wholesale, largely with equanimity, in Britain for centuries. In broad historical terms however, it is only relatively recently that the use of opium (and latterly opiates such as morphine) and it's attendant addictive properties emerged as a public health issue of concern, and became the subject of widespread vigorous debate. This debate originally resulted in compulsive opiate use being re-defined from mere bad habit, to that of a moral disease or "disease of the will", and latterly as a medically defined condition. Combined with other negative perspectives on drug use and drug users, this resulted in opiates being subject to increasing controls from the mid to late nineteenth century.

The aim of this chapter is to supplement existing accounts of the nineteenth century responses to unregulated opium use by approaching this development from a perspective derived from the work of the philosopher, Michel Foucault. This perspective is elaborated in Foucault's *The Archaeology of Knowledge* and is essentially a methodological treatise which attempts to provide a novel means of analysing historical knowledge. In applying it to the development of institutionalised responses to opiate use this analysis aims to explore the conditions in which compulsive opiate use could be know as addiction, and be spoken of as a particular type of problem.

As with all Foucaudian analyses, this analysis of historical responses to opiate use involves a rejection of objective concepts of knowledge and truth. Hence it is not assumed that addiction exists as an objectively given, self evident state which was simply discovered. Rather, the analysis is premised on the assumption that what constitutes addiction is a social construction. What distinguishes this approach from previous articulations of a social constructivist perspective is the claim that objects are constructed through what Foucault terms "discourses" and networks of "discursive practices" (Foucault, 1974).

It is through analysing discourses that we can move towards an understanding of **how** we know what we know — specifically, how the contours defining addiction could be known. The term discourse, in the Foucaudian sense, however is not equated simply with language. An analysis of discourse does not involve simply what was said, but rather how it was possible for what was historically documented to have been recorded. Discourses are not treated simply as if they were a descriptive record of an objective world, but are the embodiment of what are termed discursive practices. The concern is not with who said what, but rather the conditions under which those sentences of the discourse are capable of being uttered and have a truth value. Thus,

> ... the familiar objects of the social world ... are not "things" set apart from and independent of discourse but are realised only in and through the discursive elements which surround the objects in question. Things then, are made visible and palpable through the existence of discursive practices ... (Prior, 1989:3)

These discursive elements include the authority and status of statements which describe and refer to these objects, the concepts which formulate the object, and the theoretical viewpoint from which they are developed. This chapter then, examines the discursive elements which formed the conditions in which it was possible for opiate addiction to spoken of as a precise object during the late 19th century and be rendered susceptible to particular types of power and control.

A MORAL PATHOLOGY OF ADDICTION

From the stand point of conventional histories of the social response to opiate use in 19th century Britain, it may be considered as curious that this analysis starts several decades after the initial expressions of concern over opiate use were first articulated. The reason for this is that the task is not to re-establish that point in time when addiction first emerged as an issue of concern, but to establish how it was possible that opiate addiction could be analysed and understood in terms of a model which explained addiction as a result of an impaired moral faculty. This model, which was successfully promulgated within 19th century Britain, although premised on the concept of the individual addict's pathology, was not formulated within a bio-medical conceptual framework, although it could be, and was subscribed to within medicine as a legitimate analysis of addiction. Rather it resulted primarily from the analytic endeavours of a 19th century anti-opium movement: the Society for the Suppression of the Opium Trade.

In order to place this study into a wider context it is useful to briefly consider the social circumstances within which opiate addiction was understood and articulated within terms other than of the addict's underlying pathology. There are a number of accounts documenting the use of opiates in nineteenth century England. Of these the pioneering contribution by the social historian Virginia Berridge is particularly notable (Berridge, 1977a, 1977b, 1977c, 1977d, 1978a, 1978b, 1978c, 1978d, 1978e, 1982, Berridge & Lawson, 1979, Berridge & Edwards, 1981).

Berridge has observed that in England during the first half of the nineteenth century opium dependence was popularly known as a 'habit' rather than 'addiction'. Opium and opium based preparations such as laudanum — a mixture of raw opium, distilled water and alcohol — were cheap, widely available, and could be bought without restriction from pharmacists and general grocers. In the main they were consumed in quantity by the working classes as a culturally sanctioned practice restricted largely to self-medication. Consequently many people developed a dependence syndrome; but they remained unaware of the fact until their regular supply was interrupted or restricted. When their 'habit' was recognised it constituted nothing more than an unfortunate side effect of the drug or a concomitant of their poor social conditions (Berridge & Edwards, 1981).

The essentially relaxed attitude to opium consumption and acceptance of its use for non-medical purposes is illustrated in the response (or rather lack of response) invoked by a rash of scandalous confessions among the literary middle classes, of opium use, most notably those of Thomas DeQuincey. In 1822 DeQuincey's revelations were published under the title of *'Confessions of an Opium Eater'*, a development which marked the beginning of an awareness of the stimulant properties of opium. DeQuincey's *'Confessions'* met with mild protestations over his 'recreational' use of the drug — purportedly to induce a creative imagination conducive to writing — but overall the reaction remained merely one of mild curiosity. (Berridge, 1982)

However, after the mildness of public reaction to these scandalous confessions, the first significant development in response to opiate use was not concerned with whether it was consumed merely as a stimulant, but rather with the effects, if any, this practice had on life expectancy (Berridge, 1977b). Medical inquiries into the effects of opium grew apace during the 1820s. These led Robert Christison, Professor of Medical Jurisprudence at Edinburgh University, to judge that neither opiates themselves, nor their sustained consumption, produced any directly damaging condition. For the most part of the early nineteenth century regulation of the drug's use remained embedded in the culture of urban and rural working class communities (Berridge & Edwards, 1981).

By 1840 however, opium consumption, which earlier was an issue only in so far as its effects on longevity were concerned, had evolved a number of other facets. For example, a Dr Thompson (Thompson, 1840) writing in the *Medical Times* of the same year, was given to opine that opium when consumed as a 'stimulant' — i.e. for no recognisable medical complaint, — "… affected all that was good and virtuous in women, it acted as an aphrodisiac and subverted all morality". Responses provoked by opium consumption could also vary in accordance with the consumer's class. While middle class usage could be held to result from pressure from severe 'mental distress' (Medicus, 1851), working class 'stimulant' consumption was popularly attributed to poor housing conditions and the prevalence of fever (Parliamentary Papers, 1844).

The elevation of unrestricted opium use as a public health issue was resultant on developing class tensions. These tensions were evident in the nineteenth century Public Health campaign's enquiries into the consequence of unrestricted availability of opium. An image of working class use of opiates consumed gratuitously, as a cheaper alternative to alcohol, was fabricated by these enquiries. Fuelling the rising concern over the open availability of opium was the development of the medical and pharmaceutical professions in the mid-nineteenth century. Working class practices of self medication were diametrically opposed to the aspirations of the middle class medical and allied professions — to tighten their control over all forms of medical treatment. It was therefore in the interests of these professions to exaggerate the dangers of uncontrolled distribution and access of opium when called to give evidence to the various public health commissions (Berridge & Edwards, 1981). Support for initial regulatory control over the distribution and access to opiates then rested largely on a perception of who was using them and how they were being used.

Nonetheless, what ever the explanations for compulsive opiate consumption it was conceptualised as the product of an intrinsic pharmacological property of opium. People, therefore, did not addict themselves to opium; but rather it was opium's imputed pharmacological properties (as yet little explained and even less understood) that were thought to be responsible. Whatever the reason for taking opium — whether it was as a 'stimulant' consumed as a luxury, or for the relief of pain — in those cases where addiction ensued, it was perceived to result primarily from opium's properties and not from qualities inherent in the addict. Though the upper classes disapproved of opium consumption by the lower social strata, and made exaggerated claims of it's "stimulant" use among the labouring classes amidst emerging concerns over assumed links between opiate use and race (see Berridge & Edwards, 1981, Chapters 14, 15) to justify its control (while regarding such use among the upper social echelons as considerably less problematic) it was the drug's mode of use then — as a purported stimulant — that was the issue of concern, rather than a perceived state of addiction itself.

The anti-opium lobby therefore agitated for a response directed not at the addict but the addict's supply. The first legislative measure designed to regulate opium's availability followed, with the passage of the 1868 Pharmacy Act which allowed only registered pharmacists to sell opiates. Until addiction itself could be conceptualised, made visible and analysed as a pathological deviation from the normal — as an example of abnormality — the addict could not be responded to with either blame, moral indignation or medical treatment. Subsequent to the Act, however, a distinct model of addiction was evident, and by the turn of the century the addict could be cast, not as a victim of opium, but as an irresponsible individual wilfully adopting a course of self-destruction — fully aware of the probable consequences but unable to resist the drug induced craving. In other words, the addict was cast as a 'willing victim' whose condition was a symptom of a pathological breakdown or impairment of normal moral functioning, resulting in the addict irresponsibly denying his own morality: a moral pathology of addiction. Describing the moral-pathological model, however, does not explain how such a model came to be spoken of and invested with a truth value. To do so, the analysis now turns to the status and position of those who were authorised to articulate this model as an object of discourse.

THE SOCIETY FOR THE SUPPRESSION OF THE OPIUM TRADE

This model owes its existence primarily to discursive practices surrounding the founders of an anti-opium movement: the Society for the Suppression of the Opium Trade (SSOT). The Society is of particular significance not least because it was the most prominent organisation in the Victorian anti-opium movement, giving an organisational focus to the hitherto sporadic protests by the movement as a whole. Since its inception it had waged, for nearly fifty years, an unremitting and ultimately successful campaign against the British controlled Indo-Chinese opium trade. The Society's Quaker founders were strong moral enforcers, committed to using political practices to change what they perceived as social wrong-doings. Along with other moral reformers of the day they regarded the exploitative practices endorsed by British colonial policies as distasteful, and particularly abhorred the use of force to export opium to China. Their objection to the trade lay in the belief that opium, when consumed for non-medical purposes — i.e. gratuitously and not for a specific ailment — was evil; and that the Chinese government, recognising this, had a right to block its importation on moral grounds. Despite Chinese protestations the British opium trade continued. During the course of the Society's campaign it had sought to persuade the British public that consuming opium for other than medically defined ailments was in every form and every instance evil in the fullest religious sense.

The Society for the Suppression of the Opium Trade was founded in 1874 by Edward Pease — a wealthy northern industrialist and Quaker. Its impetus derived from a public meeting, held in the same year in Birmingham, organised by a local Quaker, Thomas Reynolds, with the intention of drawing public attention to a trade which hitherto had not aroused widespread public concern. The meeting resolved to form an anti-opium committee; and from it, in November, the London based Society for the Suppression of the Opium Trade was formed.

The Society gathered momentum in early 1875, the bulk of its initial funding coming from the Pease's Quaker family. The Society's forty-six man General Council, presided over by the Earl of Shaftsbury, included seventeen members of Parliament, eighteen ecclesiastical ministers and several other distinguished members: Thomas Barnardo, the London philanthropist; Edward Bains, the educational reformer; and Thomas Hughes, Liberal MP and author of Tom Brown's Schooldays.

In March 1875, the Society published the first issue of its monthly journal *'Friend of China'* whose masthead carried the epigraph *'Righteousness exalteth a nation, but sin is a reproach to any people.'* The Society published in the first issue its major lines of attack against the trade, claiming that (a) Britain forced opium on China, (b) Revenue was the sole reason for continuing the trade, (c) Prohibition except for medical purposes was the Society's long range goal, (d) Everyone (except the British Government's India Office) agreed that opium is evil, (e) Opium could not be consumed in moderation, and (f) Opium physically and morally destroyed the user. Following through these lines of attack with thirty years of anti-drug sermons, tracts and resolutions, the SSOT had by the early twentieth century worn down the defenders of the opium trade through attrition. Evidence of its success as a moral pressure group was provided in May 1906 by the unanimously approved passage through the House of Commons of a resolution calling for a speedy close of the Indo-Chinese opium trade; whereas similar motions in 1875 and 1883 had previously failed by a two to one majority. Its task near completed, the Society eventually disbanded in 1916.

While its successes may be attributed partly to the Society's extensive political activities — which included organising anti-opium meetings up and down the country and issuing countless memorials to the Government deploring the British opium trade — and partly to the development in 1909 of an international response towards narcotic control, these activities do not account for the conditions in which it was possible for their claim that opiate addiction resulted from an impaired moral faculty for which the individual was not directly responsible could be spoken of as having a definitive truth value. To understand the conditions in which such a model could possibly be described the analysis now turns to the discursive practices of those who defined the meaning, nature and aetiology of opiate addiction in such terms: the Society of Friends (Quakers).

THE SOCIETY OF FRIENDS

Central to Quaker doctrine, as with most traditional religious systems, was its authority to differentiate mystical from the material, the spiritual from the corporeal, the supernatural from the natural, and appeals to an incorporeal soul to describe and explain an individual's behaviour, instead of classifying behaviour within a set of observable actions and circumstances. Religious discourse for example, speaks of such objects as "soul" from a theological perspective, while religious status and authority ensure the "soul" as an object of religious discourse has a truth value.

Setting the Quakers apart from many other non-conformist sects was a conception of the spiritual domain occupied by the individual's soul, which Quakers conceived of, metaphorically, as being physically comprised of material constitution. That is, the spiritual domain — the soul — could be affected involuntarily by the material, corporeal world. The path to righteousness was marked, not just by prayer, as with many nineteenth century conformist religious sects, but by pursuit of those activities which nourished the soul's morality, and the avoidance of those which adversely affected it. Quaker doctrine directed its members to the avoidance of luxuries, exhibiting pride, undue expenditure and self indulgence; and it stressed the need for simplicity, industriousness, moderation in all things, and the recognition of one's material as well as spiritual responsibilities. So it was possible for Quakers to implicate the functioning of opium's pharmacological effects in a metaphysical, incorporeal realm.

Quakers spoke with a widely recognised social authority and legitimacy conferred partly internally, by criteria of membership, and partly externally, by the Quaker's functional integration in wider society. Nineteenth century Quakers derived their status in part by their corporate identity as members of their organisational body the Society of Friends. Membership was synonymous with meeting the criteria of competence and knowledge of the Quaker mission — qualities distinguishing the Quaker from the non-Quaker. Quakers (or 'friends' as they were known to their fellow Quakers) believed themselves to be a 'peculiar people' and maintained their differentiation through such practices as dress: men in their collarless coat and broad rimmed hat, and women by their "quaker bonnet" and plain, unornamented clothes; speech: "thee" in place of "you", First day in place of Sunday and so forth. The social status of "Friends" was further enhanced by a number of characteristics defining their function in relation to society. They were committed and strong moral reformers who, through their philanthropic support were instrumental in establishing such reformist movements as The Peace Society, Bible Society, Foreign School Society, Anti-Slavery Society and the National Temperance Society. In all the Society of Friends were a prosperous and respected community who enjoyed an elevated social position. Their qualifications of competence, their knowledge equipping them as divinely inspired spiritual guardians, their overt commitment to a devout life were all elements which endowed Quakers with a socially recognised prestige and sense of what they said was true. Their knowledge base however, was not simply based on theological doctrine, but on evidence recorded from their various missions and collated together through the organisational structure of the Society of Friends. Central to this structure was the business meeting.

During the nineteenth century, these meetings (distinct from their meetings for worship) formed the backbone of the Society of Friends organisation. With preparatory meetings, monthly meetings, quarterly meetings and yearly meetings, the Quakers were able to channel information between various Quaker congregations conveying information among other things, on the condition of Quakerism across the country. The Quaker's organisational structure functioned as an apparatus for surveillance of the society's moral order. Indeed it was the frequency with which objections to the Indo-Chinese Opium trade were reported to the Quakers Yearly meetings that first committed the Society of Friends to direct action in rousing anti-opium public sentiment. A three pronged campaign was launched by the society detailing the immorality of the continuing trade, the demoralising effects on the Chinese and the attendant effects of the trade on the morals of the British Nation. In all the organisational structure of the Society of Friends, provided the movement with an effective communications network. Moreover, it provided at each level of its meetings an institutional site which legitimated the claims of Quakers to know society's moral standards and that the trade in opium, by virtue of the drug's effects, offended these moral standards. Concomitantly, it was also possible for Quakers to propose a model of addiction that was premised on the concept of a moral faculty akin to the physical body, which like the physical body had a pathology of its own. According to Quaker doctrine opiates could be considered to have not only a pathological effect on the physical body, but also to pathologically impair people's moral faculty rendering them incapable of moral functioning.

Such a model of addiction, which presupposes the effects of non-medical opiate use on a metaphorically corporeal moral faculty is evident by the 1880's when conformist and non-conformist religious sects sought to identify and associate with the SSOT's aims and objectives. In 1881 a public meeting to discuss the opium trade was organised by the SSOT. It was held in London's Mansion House and chaired by the Lord Major. Significantly his two chief supporters on the platform were both clergy-men: the Archbishop of Canterbury and a Cardinal Manning. Further evidence of wider conformist and non-conformist affiliation to the Society emerged as the century progressed. An anti-opium meeting was organised by the society in 1890 at Newcastle upon Tyne under the chairmanship of the Lord Bishop of the Diocese — the Rt. Reverend Wilberforce (Friend of China, 1890). In the same year, the Major of Sunderland was moved to observe at another anti-opium meeting that he was glad to think there were gentlemen of all religious creeds present (Friend of China, 1890). Support by conformist religions continued: in the following year, at the SSOT's annual meeting, its president, Joseph Whitwell Pease, was supported on the platform by the Venerable Archdeacon Moule and the Rev Cannon Wilberforce. By 1897, the Society was able to count among its vice presidents, five Anglican Bishops (Friend of China, 1897a).

It is significant that the opium 'habit' had not appeared to register as an invariant 'evil' during the early nineteenth century where it might be most expected to — amongst the ardent moralists of the wider religious communities. DeQuincey's revelations had provoked some moral protestations but these were unco-ordinated and indicate a notable absence of institutionalised concern. Moreover it was a response which was qualitatively different from the Quaker's in one salient respect. Unlike the Quaker's response, it was authorised by a crude metaphysic. The inferred relation between DeQuincey's opium 'habit' and his intrinsic immorality sprang from unformulated moral intuition: it was not established by systematic analysis, as with the Quaker's model. Following hard on the heels of the SSOT's formation however, adherents to both orthodox and non-conformist religious persuasions alike clamoured to identify with the Society's apprehension of the 'habit' as a symptom of a pathologically debilitated will. The final decade of the nineteenth century also saw increasing support from the non-conformist sects. By 1892, representatives from the Baptist Church,

Wesleyan Church, the Primitive Methodists, Congregation Unionist Church, the Free Church of Scotland and the United Methodist Free Church could all be found supporting the SSOT's cause (*Friend of China*, 1891).

It was also possible within the 19th century medical profession for doctors to register the concept of addiction in terms of a "moral pathological state". Up until the third quarter of the nineteenth century, medical concern with addiction was not in terms of opium's effects on the addict's moral state, but with opium's properties and its physiological and pharmacological effects on the body. Failed attempts to locate a physiological basis of addiction (*Friend of China*, 1892) had sustained well into the 1860s the medical debate as to whether opium acted as a stimulant or sedative on the habitue's nervous system. Comparisons were even made to establish variations of opium's effects on persons of differing constitutions. In 1846, a London surgeon, F. Robinson (1846) opined that the speed and efficacy of opium was more pronounced on, "... a person of this spare habit and highly nervous temperament than a large robust individual lymphatic sanguineous temperament." Medical attention was also drawn to comparing the different effects of various opiate-based preparations. Dr J. Connolly, writing in the Lancet in 1845 noted, "With some patients laudanum acts with certainty, and like a charm; others derive comfort for long periods from acetate of morphia; to some the liquor *opii sedativus* is alone tolerable." (Connolly, 1845). Up until the mid-century, then, medical circles were concerned with addiction — but as an issue clearly bound up with the physiological and pharmacological effects on the body.

In the last quarter of the nineteenth century, however, the medical conceptualisation of the opium "habit" as comprised of its observed pharmacological effects was replaced by the opium "habit" as a definitive object — which referred specifically to the non-medical use of opiates. Eminent representatives of the medical profession were given to testify, not only to the pharmacological effect of opium, but also to the 'spiritual seat' of addiction. By defining addiction in such terms, the conditions were evident in which it was possible for medicine to affiliate itself legitimately to the concept of a metaphorical soul containing a moral faculty whose health, or ill-health, development or retardation could be analysed in material terms. Medical "treatment" for addiction underlined this concept. An 1877 issue of the *Lancet* reported in its editorial the belief that morphia addiction degraded the moral character and advocated that, "Moral treatment by urging them early to some form of steady work, is particularly to be insisted upon." (Quoted in *Friend of China*, 1877). At the SSOT's Annual General Meeting of 1886, speaking in his capacity as a medical authority, a Dr Foster was moved to argue that opium, "... saps the moral nature, deteriorates the moral character and one loses all sense of moral obligation". Similarly, in 1894, Dr Norman Kerr, founder and president of the Society for the Study of Inebriety argued that repeated indulgence in opium induced 'normal perversion' (Kerr 1894). Kerr advocated treatment within the confines of an institution — an asylum or nursing home — on the rationale that they provided, "... everything which can contribute to the improvement of the soul and the spirit." (*ibid*). Moreover, in a paper delivered to this Society in 1897, Dr William Huntley maintained, "... the longer the habit is continued, the more the will power is abolished, the moral judgement weakened." (*Friend of China*, 1897b).

Some doctors sought to offer an analysis of addiction by shrouding it in a cloak of medical respectability but which was ultimately premised on the concept of a moral faculty that could be directly subverted by opiates. For example, the nineteenth century physician and scientist, Lauder Brunton asserted that opium's physiological action is

> ... at first to stimulate and afterwards to depress; to remove this depression the individual must take another dose — a habit of taking the drug is thus established. The nervous system suffers, the mental powers enfeebled, the moral faculties perverted, and there is an inability to distinguish between truth and falsehood.
> (*Friend of China*, 1892).

Such an analysis was indistinguishable from that of the SSOT's, but more importantly, was possible because medicine in formulating it could affiliate to a distinctive feature of the Quaker's model — a moral faculty whose health or illness, development or retardation could be analysed as if it were constituted materially. Within medicine's normative structure, delimiting what could comprise 'normal' medical knowledge and practice, it was therefore possible to accommodate the Quaker's model of addiction, and moreover support its application in medical practice.

CONCLUSION

Undoubtedly, nineteenth century health professionals and public health officials were significantly influential in promoting the addicted state as one of a moral failing. Moreover, the significance of social tensions resulting from the link between class (and race), and the purported "stimulant" use of opiates were of crucial importance in the movement towards bringing opiates and their use under regulatory control.

What I have attempted to map, by way complimenting our understanding of the British historical response to opiates, are some of the discursive relations which form the conditions in which it was possible for a particular analysis of opiate addiction to emerge, and be spoken of with a "truth value". It was these relations (among others) which contributed to producing this moral-pathological model: so that it could be distinguished, described and discussed as an analysis of the addicted state, not just amidst the Quakers themselves, but among the religious communities of all denominations and the medical profession of the late nineteenth century. Thus while doctors and public health officials were undoubtedly influential in promoting addiction as a "moral failing", it was in a wider field of relations that the moral-pathological model was confirmed and consolidated and could exist as an objective reality.

REFERENCES

Berridge, V. (1977a) Our Own Opium: Cultivation of the Opium Poppy in Britain, 1740–1823, *British Journal of Addiction*, **72**: 90–4.

Berridge, V. (1977b) Opium Eating and Life Insurance, *British Journal of Addiction*, **72**: 371–7.

Berridge, V. Fenland (1977c) Opium Eating in the Nineteenth Century, *British Journal of Addiction*, **72**: 275–84.

Berridge, V. (1977d) Opium and the Historical perspective, *Lancet*, **2**: 78–80.

Berridge, V. (1978a) Working Class Opium Eating in the Nineteenth Century: Establishing the Facts, *British Journal of Addiction*, **73**: 363–74.

Berridge, V. (1978b) Victorian Opium Eating: Responses to Opiate use in Nineteenth Century England, *Victorian Studies*, **21**: 437–61.

Berridge, V. (1978c)War Conditions and Narcotic Control: The Passing of the Defence of the Realm Act Regulation 40b, *Journal of Social Policy*, **7**: 285–304.

Berridge, V. (1978d) Professionalisation and Narcotics: The Medical and Pharmaceutical Professions and British Narcotic Use, *Psychological Medicine*, **8**: 361–72.

Berridge, V. (1978e) Opium Eating and the Working Class in Nineteenth Century: Public and Official Reaction, *British Journal of Addiction*, **73**: 107–12.

Berridge, V. and Lawson, N. (1979) Opiate Use and Legislative Control: A Nineteenth Century Case Study, *Social Science and Medicine*, **13a**: 351–63.

Berridge, V. (1982) Opiate Use in England, 1800–1926, *Annals of the New York Academy of Sciences*, 398: 1–11.

Berridge, V. and Edwards, G. (1981) *Opium and the People*, London, Allen Lane.

Connolly J. (1845) *Lancet*, 526.

Foucault, M. (1974) *The Archaeology of Knowledge*, Trans. A.M. Sheridan, London, Tavistock.

Friend of China (1877) **Vol. II, 8.**

Friend of China (1890) **Vol. XI,** 6.

Friend of China (1891) **Vol. XVIII,** 3.

Friend of China (1892) **Vol. XIII,** 4.

Friend of China (1897a) **Vol. XVII,** 1.

Friend of China (1897b) **Vol. XVII,** 2.

Kerr, N. (1894) *Inebriety or Narcomania: Its etiology, pathology, treatment and jurisprudence.* 3rd ed. London H.K. Lewis: 117.

Kerr *ibid*: 298.

Medicus, Teetotalism and Opium Taking (1851) *Lancet*, **1**: 694.

Parliamentary Papers (1844) First Report of the Commissioners for enquiring into the State of Large Towns and Popular Districts. **XVIII.**

Prior, L. (1989) *Social Organisation of Death*, London, Macmillan.

Robinson, F. (1846) *Lancet*, 360.

Thompson, Dr. (1840) *Medical Times*, **1**: 162–3.

CHAPTER 2

Reform, Racism and Rackets: Alcohol and Drug Prohibition in the United States

Michael Woodiwiss

Campaigns to prohibit drugs and alcohol in the United States emerged as part of a much broader moral reform movement. From the early nineteenth century many native-born Americans joined societies devoted to imposing virtue and abstinence on their fellows. These groups of concerned citizens lobbied in city halls, state capitals and Washington DC for more laws prohibiting behaviour they considered to be unacceptable, notably gambling, commercialised sex, drinking liquor and the use of certain kinds of drugs. Demands for the total suppression of unacceptable activities increased in intensity towards the end of the century, partly justified by a perceived threat to Protestant morality and social order from newly arrived immigrants or African Americans.

By the first two decades of the twentieth century moral reformers could claim that much of their programme had become official government policy. Tens of thousands of federal, state and local laws had been enacted in an attempt to coerce Americans into a virtuous and healthy life-style by prohibiting gambling, prostitution, alcohol and other drugs. However, the crusaders' dreams of a new moral and prosperous era of clear thinking and clean living were soon to be disturbed. Problems emerged as soon as enforcement was attempted; new criminal occupations were opened up as the demand for prohibited activities was met. It transpired that statutory virtue was easily circumvented. This chapter examines the racist origins and racketeering consequences of drug and alcohol prohibition.

From the late nineteenth century moral crusaders exploited the country's endemic racism and xenophobia to spread the prohibition message. Prejudice against the Chinese, for example, was behind the earliest local, state and federal legislation prohibiting the smoking of opium. Propagandists, especially in the West, spoke of 'yellow fiends' or 'yellow devils' enslaving white women and

13

children with their 'seductive poison.' The idea was established that drugs encouraged sexual contact between the races and threatened the purity, even the survival, of the white race. In 1881 San Francisco police reported the existence of opium dens where they had found 'white women and Chinamen side by side under the effects of this drug — a humiliating sight to anyone with anything left of manhood.' The same year the *San Jose Mercury* demanded that the practice of opium-smoking has to be 'rooted-out' before it could 'decimate our youth, emasculate the coming generation, if not completely destroy the whole population of our coast.' California's state legislature responded by passing laws that outlawed the opium dens. In 1887, the federal government added legislation that outlawed opium importation and smoking among Chinese but, significantly, not white Americans (Woodiwiss, 1988, p. 3; Kohn, 1992, p. 2; Duke and Gross, 1993, p. 83; Lusane, 1991, p. 31).

In similar ways prejudice against blacks added fuel to the arguments of those seeking to suppress the use of cocaine. In 1910, for example, the *Report on the International Opium Commission* claimed that cocaine made rapists of black males and that blacks achieved immense strength and cunning under its influence. Dr Hamilton Wright, the man most responsible for this report and for much of the national and international anti-drug effort that followed, came to the conclusion that,

> this new vice, the cocaine vice, the most serious to be dealt with, has proved to be the creator of criminals and unusual forms of violence, and it has been a potent incentive in driving the humbler negroes all over the country to abnormal crimes (Helmer, 1975, p. 12)

Similar absurd and unsubstantiated claims were widely believed and circulated. In 1914, for example, the *New York Times* reported that some Southern police departments, fearing that cocaine made blacks capable of withstanding .32 calibre bullets, had felt it necessary to switch to .38 calibre. The headline for this article was, **Negro Cocaine 'Fiends' Are a New Southern Menace** (Lusane, 1991, pp. 33–34).

Exaggerated claims, hysterical language and racial stereotyping also featured prominently in the propaganda calling for an end to alcohol use and the adoption of a constitutional amendment to prohibit the manufacture, transportation, sale or importation of intoxicating liquor within the United States.

Richmond Pearson Hobson introduced the idea of alcohol prohibition to the House of Representatives. In 1903 Hobson had launched a career as a temperance orator, gathering crowds in churches and camp revival meetings to repeat his attack on what he called, 'The Great Destroyer.' He contended that alcohol killed five times as many people a year as all the wars ever fought and that half the country's economy and half its population were already vitiated by alcohol. Alcohol, according to Hobson's 'research', was also the main cause of feeble mindedness and sexual perversion in women.

As a fund raiser for the Anti-Saloon League, Hobson received percentages of the money he could persuade his audiences to give. In nine years this amounted to $170,000, and, not surprisingly, Hobson decided that moral crusading was a lucrative career to pursue (Kobler, 1973, pp. 199–200).

In 1914, Hobson as a Representative from Alabama, got a national stage for his theories when he introduced a prohibition resolution in the House. He provided the following arguments in support of it:

> ... *Liquor will actually make a brute out of a Negro, causing him to commit unnatural crimes ...*
>
> *The effect is the same on the white man, though the white man being further evolved it takes longer time to reduce him to the same level. Starting young, however, it does not take a very long time to speedily cause a man in the forefront of civilization to pass through the successive stages and become semicivilized, semisavage, savage, and, at last, below the brute ...*
>
> *Science has thus demonstrated that alcohol is a protoplasmic poison, poisoning all living things; that alcohol is a habit-forming drug that shackles millions of our citizens and maintains slavery in our midst; that it lowers in a fearful way the standard of efficiency of the Nation, reducing enormously the national wealth, entailing startling burdens of taxation, encumbering the public with the care of crime, pauperism, and insanity; that it corrupts politics and public servants, corrupts the Government, corrupts the public morals, lowers terrifically the average standard of character of the citizenship, and undermines the liberties and institutions of the Nation; that it undermines and blights the home and the family, checks education, attacks the young when they are entitled to protection, undermines the public health, slaughtering, killing and wounding our citizens many fold times more than war, pestilence, and famine combined; that it blights the progeny of the Nation, flooding the land with a horde of degenerates; that it strikes deadly blows at the life of the Nation itself and at the very life of the race, reversing the great evolutionary principles of nature and the purposes of the Almighty.*
>
> *There can be but one verdict, and that is this great destroyer must be destroyed...*
>
> *The final, scientific conclusion is that we must have constitutional prohibition, prohibiting only the sale, the manufacture for sale, and everything that pertains to the sale, and invoke the power of both Federal and State governments for enforcement. The resolution is drawn to fill these requirements.* (Musto, 1987, p. 305; Rumbarger, 1989, pp. 177–178)

Although Hobson's resolution failed to get the necessary two-thirds majority this time it helped to bring the 18th Amendment to the Constitution a step nearer. Hobson, as we shall see, went on to bring his talents and pseudo-scientific reasoning to the crusade against drugs.

America's ambitious programme of moral reform would have dwindled into insignificance without the support of the country's commercial and industrial leadership. Manufacturing and business interests had no greater desire than a sober, industrious and docile work force and many were therefore inclined to provide money and political influence to the morality campaigns. The business class saw gambling, prostitution, drinking and drug-taking as diverting wages from the purchase of manufactured goods; if wages were not spent on wasteful activities there would be less demand for wage rises. Alcohol and other drugs were seen as likely to hamper efficiency at work at a time when most managements were searching for ways to get more productivity out of their workers. For these and other reasons morality became an attractive investment (Sinclair, 1962, pp. 117–125).

While most business money and influence went to the Anti-Saloon League, at least some of the fortune first amassed by railroad baron Cornelius Vanderbilt and inherited by his son William went to the campaign against drugs. In 1912, William's wife was looking for an issue to boost her image and found that the repression of narcotic drugs fitted the bill. Mrs William K. Vanderbilt organised anti-narcotics committees, led marches up and down Fifth Avenue in New York and, with the help of unlimited funds, launched telegram and letter campaigns to lawmakers in Albany, New York and Washington D.C. on the theme that helpless people of the lower classes needed protection from 'this poison.' These campaigns helped towards the enactment of the Towns-Boylan Act that came into effect on 1 July 1914 and provided for substantial penalties for all nonmedicinal trafficking and use of drugs in New York state. The aim of this in part was to force addicts to receive treatment because as, Charles Towns, one of the sponsors of the act, fancifully put it, 'it takes only five or six days to cure a drug fiend in hospital' (King, 1972, p. 24; Musto, 1973 pp. 104–106).

Also in 1914, a more significant Federal act was passed. The stated intention of the Harrison Narcotic Act was 'to provide for the registration of, with collectors of internal revenue, and to impose a special tax upon all persons who produce, import, manufacture, compound, deal in, dispense, sell, distribute, or give away opium or coca leaves, their salts, derivatives, or preparations, and for other purposes.' According to Edward Brecher, the Harrison Act was not intended to be a prohibition law but, 'merely a law for the orderly marketing of opium, morphine, heroin and other drugs — in small quantities over the counter, and in larger quantities on a physician's prescription.' However, zealous Treasury agents exploited an ambiguity in the wording of the Act to prohibit opiates and other drugs totally. They began an intense campaign to prevent doctors treating drug users resulting in some three thousand doctors serving penitentiary sentences between 1914 and 1938. Doctors were thus effectively prohibited from dispensing heroin or morphine to addicts or to ease the pain of the terminally ill despite representations from the medical community that these drugs were most effective in doing so. Drug control therefore became a police problem rather than a medical problem in America (Browning and Gerassi, 1980, p. 467; Brecher, 1972, pp. 48–50).

In 1915 an editorial in *American Medicine* noted the immediate consequences of drug prohibition and foresaw much of the tragedy that would follow:

> *Narcotic drug addiction is one of the gravest and most important questions confronting the medical profession today. Instead of improving conditions the laws recently*

passed have made the problem more complex. Honest medical men have found such handicaps and dangers to themselves and their reputations in these laws ... that they have simply decided to have as little to do as possible with drug addicts or their needs ... [The addict] is denied the medical care he urgently needs, open, above-board sources from which he formerly obtained his drug supply are closed to him, and he is driven to the underworld where he can get his drug, but of course, surreptitiously and in violation of the law ...

Abuses in the sale of narcotic drugs are increasing ... A particular sinister sequence ... is the character of the places to which [addicts] are forced to go to get their drugs and the type of people with whom they are obliged to mix. The most depraved criminals are often the dispensers of these habit-forming drugs ... One has only to think of the stress under which the addict lives, and to recall his lack of funds, to realize the extent to which these afflicted individuals are under the control of the worst elements of society (Brecher, 1972, p. 50).

In New York the demand from users and addicts fed a fragmented and sprawling industry in cocaine, best described by Alan Block:

Cocaine was imported, wholesaled, franchised, and retailed: It moved from South America to New Orleans, Canada, Buffalo, Philadelphia, West New York, New Jersey, and so on. It travelled back and forth from Broadway and the Forties to the Lower East Side, Harlem, Brooklyn, back to Philadephia, and to Boston. It slid up and down the Bowery, Second Avenue and Third Avenue, across 14th Street where it circled Tammany Hall, then it slipped down the Mott and Mulberry Streets — perhaps ending up at the Essex Market Court on First Street and Second Avenue (where it was sold, not used for evidence) or at the Odd Fellows Hall at 98 Forsythe Street. It was sold many times over by a variety of dealers (who were also at times consumers) to show people, the military, newsboys, prostitutes, Jews, Italians, blacks and so on. It was traded in movies, theatres, restaurants, cafes, cabarets, pool parlors, saloons, parks, and on innumerable street corners. It was an important part of the coin of an underworld that was deeply embedded in the urban culture of New York: supporters as well as exploiters of the myriad establishments that made up the night life of the city. And finally, cocaine was something of a bonding agent bringing criminals together in a variety of ways (Block and Chambliss, 1981, p. 53).

The most notable New York criminal entrepreneur to be involved in the 1920s drug trade was Arnold Rothstein. Rothstein ran illegal gambling games, provided gangster services during industrial disputes, and imported Scotch whisky during Prohibition, and drugs were just another simple way for him to make an illegal dollar. Two of his associates, Yasha Katzenburg and Dan Collins, bought quantities of drugs in Europe and Asia; these were then smuggled into the United States and sold to retailers in New York, Chicago, St Louis and Kansas City by more Rothstein associates (Joselit, 1983, p. 146).

Rothstein, like most other traffickers, did not set up any formal criminal organisational structures — that would have increased the chances of prosecution. 'The strength of all his many separate partnerships and deals', according to

Robert Lacey, 'lay in their separateness. The failure of one did not jeopardise the others' (Lacey, 1991, p. 61). The success of Rothstein and others showed the way for many more to make deals or set up and run the many thousands of ventures and operations that provided Americans with illegal goods and services and effectively nullified all prohibitions.

Despite the involvement of Rothstein and his associates, the industry in cocaine and heroin remained small relative to that prompted by the adoption of alcohol prohibition. The Volstead Act, which was intended to enforce the 18th Amendment, came into effect on 16 January 1920 and immediately made problems of crime and corruption in the United States considerably worse. Within hours of the act taking effect there were liquor robberies and hijackings. On 19 February the first of many federal agents was arrested for liquor law corruption. At the same time the dockets of Chicago's federal courts were congested with over 500 prohibition cases awaiting trial. Two of the main features of alcohol prohibition were thus already apparent: the circumvention of the law and the overload of the American criminal justice system.

There were many ways to slake the country's thirst as bootlegging, the word used to describe the illegal trafficking in liquor, became one of America's leading industries. There was easy money to be made buying, selling, and distributing beer and spirits. Local, regional, national and international ties soon developed among bootlegging entrepreneurs. One reason for this, as the historian Mark Haller has pointed out, was that a large urban market could absorb not just vast quantities of liquor but also a large variety of types: beer, Scotch, bourbon, gin, wines, champagnes. No distributor of illegal beverages to speakeasies, roadhouses and other outlets could possibly manufacture or import such a variety. Therefore some organisations specialised for good economic reasons, and any large organisation necessarily had ties with other organisations (Haller, 1976, p. 115).

But competition in an unregulated market often became bitter and bloody. As in the early days of other American industries, the struggle for markets and territory was fierce and expensive. The New York and Chicago gang wars were particularly savage and thousands died because they were connected to the illicit liquor industry. The murder of a minor bootlegger became so ordinary that newspapers scarcely took notice. Police conducted cursory investigations and no one worried that they rarely got convictions. Being a gang boss was no protection as the deaths of the likes of Jim Colisimo, Dion O'Banion, Hymie Weiss, Dutch Schultz, Joe Masseria, and Salvatore Marazano demonstrated.

The laws of supply and demand rapidly overwhelmed the law that hoped to produce an abstinent and healthy population. The number of illegal drinking outlets soon approached and then overtook the number of pre-Volstead saloons. By 1925 there were at least 15,000 illegal drinking places in Detroit and by the end of the 1920s at least 32,000 'speakeasies' in New York. Countless establishments, such as grocers, drug stores and tobacconists, sold liquor as a sideline. They all made profits so long as they continued operations and this often required regular payoffs to police or protection racketeers, or both. It all showed the accuracy of former President William H. Taft's 1915 prediction: 'The business of manufacturing alcohol, liquor and beer will go out of the hands of the law-abiding members of the community and will be transferred to the quasi-criminal class' (Kyvig, 1979, p. 106).

In every large city and many of the smaller ones it was common knowledge that the police and politicians colluded with bootleggers and speakeasy operators, and that periods of genuine enforcement were exceptional and temporary. In January 1924, for example, an aggressive campaign by Philadelphia's police chief, General Smedley Butler, closed 600 speakeasies and resulted in 2,000 arrests. The campaign was soon sabotaged with high level police officials warning speakeasies of impending raids, politicians and city officials interceding for violators, and magistrates dismissing most of the charges. 'Trying to enforce the law in Philadelphia,' General Butler said, 'was worse than any battle I was ever in.' Only 212 liquor law violators were convicted in his second year of office out of 6,000 arrested. 'Enforcement,' according to Butler, 'hasn't amounted to a row of pins after the arrests were made.' An additional problem was that liquor held as evidence tended to disappear. As the historian Herbert Asbury pointed out, immediately following these losses a number of policemen resigned from the force and opened up speakeasies. Others found it more profitable to stay put. In 1928 it was revealed that Philadelphia policemen, on salaries of less than $4,000 a year, had bank accounts ranging from $40,412 to $193,553 (Asbury, 1950, p. 185; Merz, 1969, pp. 140–145).

From the beginning enforcement agencies were integral parts of the organised distribution of alcohol. The Federal Prohibition Unit (renamed the Prohibition Bureau in 1927) was a small group of low-paid and inefficient agents, numbering only about 1,500 for the entire country. Dry agents were known to escort liquor trucks, protect smugglers and even help them unload their cargoes, deal in withdrawal permits for alcohol, and give information about raids. Clean-ups were unusual and prohibition agents were known to buy country homes, town houses, real estate, speedboats, expensive cars, and a host of other luxuries on salaries averaging less than $3,000 a year.

While the rich could have liquor delivered to their homes, the poor drank spirits that were often poisonous. For example, 25 men died in a three day period during October 1928 through drinking wood alcohol in New York City and throughout the country thousands more suffered from an affliction known as 'jakitis', 'ginger-foot' or 'jake paralysis' — they had paralysed their toes and insteps through drinking Jamaica ginger. (Sinclair, 1962, pp. 222–223) In sum Prohibition had simply made consumption of alcohol more expensive, secretive, challenging and risky.

As the 1920s proceeded more politicians and commentators were pointing out the absurdities involved in attempting to prohibit liquor. In 1926 Fiorello La Guardia estimated that it would require a police force of 250,000 men to dry up New York alone, 'and a force of 200,000 to police the police' (Asbury, 1950, p. 210). Diligent state enforcement in New York, according to Governor Al

Smith, would require one-third of the state's citizens to apprehend another third who were violators, while the remaining third would be tied up serving on juries (Goshen, 1973, p. 34).

In 1929 the new president, Herbert Hoover, recognised the problems of prohibition enforcement by announcing the creation of the National Commission on Law Observance and Enforcement, to be headed by former Attorney General, George Wickersham. After two years investigation the Wickersham Commission's reports made it clear that Prohibition had failed to deliver. Instead of the controlled working class and healthy environment for business promised by the prohibitionists there had been a progressive breakdown of respect for law and order. In fact, so many people expressed opposition and resentment to the dry law that one consultant concluded that,

> *the prohibition laws, so far, have been detrimental and harmful to the workers and their families and that the situation as regards manufacturing, trafficking in, and drinking liquor is getting worse from day to day and has now grown to such proportions that real control of it or enforcement of the law against it ... is almost an impossibility.* (National Commission on Law Observance and Enforcement, 1931, Volume 3, p. 356)

The commission's evidence suggested that economic realities would always undermine prohibitionist ideals. Its conclusions about alcohol could equally be applied to drugs and drug prohibition:

> *The constant cheapening and simplification of production of alcohol and of alcoholic drinks, the improvement of quality of what may be made by illicit means, the diffusion of knowledge as to how to produce liquor and the perfection of organization of unlawful manufacture and distribution have developed faster than the means of enforcement. But of even more significance is the margin of profit in smuggling liquor, in diversion of alcohol, in illicit distilling and brewing, in bootlegging, and in the manufacture and sale of products of which the bulk goes into illicit or doubtfully lawful making of liquor. This profit makes possible systematic and organized violation of the National Prohibition Act on a large scale and offers rewards on a par with the most important legitimate industries. It makes lavish expenditure in corruption possible. It puts heavy temptation in the way of everyone engaged in enforcement and administration of the law. It affords a financial basis for organized crime.* (National Commission on Law Observance and Enforcement, 1931, Final Report, p. 51)

Although the commission did not recommend the repeal of the 18th Amendment, its findings made it very clear that Prohibition had created or worsened a situation of widespread and systematic lawlessness and thus strengthened the case for repeal.

By the early 1930s the tens of thousands of arrests, convictions and incarcerations for liquor law violations each year were costing ever-increasing amounts of money and were not making an impact on the traffic in liquor. More than 40,000 liquor law offenders overstretched federal prisons and so it was thought necessary to begin the building of six new institutions. Senator Robert Wagner of New York caught the mood of the nation when he asked what purpose would the hiring of more men and the spending of more money serve, 'Why heap more sacrifice upon the altar of hopelessness?' (U.S.A. Constitutional Documents, 1931, p. 23).

The 18th Amendment was repealed in 1933. Within a few months more than a million people were legally employed in brewing, distilling and related jobs, from serving drinks to making barrels and pretzels. Federal, state and local tax and licence receipts exceeded a billion dollars yearly by 1940 and there was no noticeable increase in drunkenness and alcohol-related problems (Kyvig, 1979, pp. 178–186).

By the end of the 1930s Prohibition was seen by most as a ridiculous and costly mistake, and an unacceptable intrusion by the government into personal behaviour. Americans could see that the remedy for the evils of drink had proved worse than the original problem. However, they were unable to reproduce this logic when other prohibitions were involved. Prohibition had not been, as was claimed at the time, a 'great experiment' or historical aberration. American moralists, including many wielding power and influence, still believed that governments were capable of imposing the same standards of behaviour on huge and diverse populations. Repeal of alcohol prohibition was therefore just a setback and America's ambitious programme of moral reform would continue. Most of the institutions that moulded public opinion such as newspapers, churches, chambers of commerce and civic associations were set against any more tampering with the morality legislation. During the 1920s and 1930s only alcohol prohibition was discredited, legions of moral crusaders still existed and turned out propaganda to make sure that support remained for the laws against gambling, prostitution and drugs.

The campaign against drugs during the 1920s was led by the man who had introduced alcohol prohibition to Congress, Richmond P. Hobson. Hobson founded a series of organisations with names that indicated a desire to globalise America's anti-drug crusade: The International Narcotic Education Association (1923), the World Conference on Narcotic Education (1926) and the World Narcotic Defence Association (1927). Backed by some of the top people in American society, he successfully transmitted his anti-drug message to millions of Americans through school textbooks, newspapers and radio programmes. Drugs, according to Hobson's new polemic, caused all kinds of crime and he likened heroin addicts to the 'Living Dead.' These, he told radio listeners in 1928, 'lie, cheat, steal, rob and, if necessary, commit murder' to get their supplies and continued:

Heroin addiction can be likened to a contagion. Suppose it were announced that there were more than a million lepers among our people. Think what a shock the announcement would produce! Yet drug addiction is far more incurable than leprosy, far more tragic to its victims, and is spreading like a moral and physical scourge.

There are symptoms breaking out all over our country and now breaking out in many parts of Europe which show that individual nations and the whole world is menaced by this appalling foe ... marching ... to the capture and destruction of the whole world.

Most of the daylight robberies, daring holdups, cruel murders and similar crimes of violence are now known to be committed chiefly by drug addicts, who constitute the primary cause of our alarming crime wave.

Drug addiction is more communicable and less curable than leprosy. Drug addicts are the principal carriers of vice diseases, and with their lowered resistance are incubators and carriers of the strepticoccus, pneumococcus, the germ of flu, of tuberculosis, and other diseases.

Upon the issue hangs the perpetuation of civilization, the destiny of the world and the future of the human race.

Hobson's primary concern, of course, was still for the white elements of the human race. In his book, *Drug Addiction: A Malignant Racial Cancer*, for example, the carriers tended to be black and yellow while those at risk tended to be young and white.

His claims about drugs now seem absurd but were taken seriously at the time. At one time he said that one ounce of heroin would cause 2,000 addicts and warned that, 'In using any brand of face powder regularly, it is a wise precaution to have a sample analysed for heroin.' And, in a 1929 radio broadcast he told listeners that drug addiction constituted 'the chief factor menacing the public health, the public morals, the public safety.' While an academic study of the extent of the drug problem in America put the number of drug addicts in the nation at 110,000, Hobson told his much larger audience that the number was more than a million (Musto, 1987, p. 190–194; Epstein, 1977, p. 23–34). He was thus an appropriate founding father of a crusade that continues to be fuelled by imaginative statements and exaggerated statistics.

In 1930 Hobson applied unsuccessfully to become the federal government's chief anti-drug enforcement officer as Commissioner of the Federal Bureau of Narcotics (FBN), but Harry J. Anslinger, the man who beat him, shared many of his opinions, racist assumptions, and ambitions for a toughened up national and global response to drugs.

Anslinger's background had given him the edge in the competition for the position and at the same time would condition his response to the problem of drugs. According to his most authoritative biographer, John C. McWilliams, Anslinger had dedicated his life to the US federal bureaucracy. In 1926 he joined the United States Treasury Department and, as head of the Division of Foreign Control in the Prohibition Unit, he dealt with the control of smuggling through international agreements and the exchange of information with other countries. In 1928 he wrote a paper for a national competition that argued that Prohibition could work with efficient administration and effective enforcement. The plan included ways to prevent smuggling, eliminate illegal manufacture, and co-ordinate government agencies more effectively. The ways to prevent smuggling involved Congress giving 'power to the President to employ the Navy to co-operate with the Coast Guard in the suppression of the liquor smuggling.' Anslinger's plan also recommended that more prosecutors and judges should be appointed to catch more violators and that buying alcohol for nonmedical consumption should be punished by heavy fines and prison sentences (McWilliams, 1990, pp. 32–33). Repeal of alcohol prohibition in 1933 effectively scuppered these plans but as Commissioner of Narcotics, Anslinger simply adapted them to the prohibition of drugs and thus helped establish the framework for present day US drug control policies.

Meanwhile more traffickers were exploiting the fact that drugs are less bulky than liquids and therefore much easier to smuggle, transport and distribute. Importation was also aided by the worldwide network of business and political contacts established by bootleggers. Although the drug traffic remained much smaller than the traffic in alcohol, the profits were probably greater for those involved and the chances of disruption just as slim.

During the 1930s Anslinger joined a campaign that sought to prohibit another substance by making possession or sale of marijuana subject to draconian penalties.

The campaign had the by now familiar ingredients of moral crusades: hysteria and racism. For example, the following letter was sent to Anslinger from the editor of the Alamosa, Colorado, *Daily Courier*:

> *Is there any assistance your Bureau can give us in handling this drug? Can you suggest campaigns? Can you enlarge your Department to deal with marijuana? Can you do anything to help us?*
>
> *I wish I could show you what a small marijuana cigarette can do to one of our degenerate Spanish-speaking residents. That's why our problem is so great: the greatest percentage of our population is composed of Spanish-speaking persons, most of whom are low mentally, because of racial and social conditions.*
>
> *While marijuana has figured in the greatest number of crimes in the past few years, officials fear it, not for what it has done, but for what it is capable of doing. They want to check it before an outbreak does occur.*
>
> *Through representatives of civic leaders and law officers of the San Luis Valley, I have been asked to write to you for help* (Musto, 1987, p. 223).

Anslinger's own testimony before Congress also showed that moralism still fed off racism, playing on and adding to the established racist associations mentioned previously. He claimed that marijuana made users promiscuous and violent and, to emphasise the dangers to whites, he tended to use descriptions of instances involving blacks and Hispanics. McWilliams quotes two examples from Anslinger's long list of 'horror' stories:

> *Colored students at the Univ. of Minn. partying with female students (white) smoking and getting their sympathy with stories of racial persecution. Result pregnancy.*
>
> *West Va. — Negro raped a girl of eight years of age. Two Negroes took a girl fourteen years old and kept her for two days in a hut under the influence of marijuana. Upon recovery she was found to be "suffering from" syphilis.* (McWilliams, 1990, pp. 52–53)

Members of Congress responded to such tales by passing the Marijuana Tax Act of 1937 and thus added plants which, in Anslinger's words, grew 'like dandelions' to the illegal market. By the following year a quarter of the FBN's arrests were for marijuana. From then on Commissioner Anslinger's budget requests reflected this extra burden. (Dickson, 1968, pp. 143–156; Woodiwiss, 1988, pp. 31–32; Musto, 1987, p. 222)

On the question of racism Anslinger had almost lost his job in 1934 when he circulated the following description of the height and colour of an informer in a letter to district supervisors: "'Medium and might be termed a 'ginger-colored nigger.'" There were calls for his resignation, but a number of powerful Anslinger-supporters ensured that they were ignored.

The pro-Anslinger lobby included moralist organisations like the General Federation of Women's Clubs and Hobson's World Narcotics Defence Association, the newspaper publisher William Randolph Hearst, and most of the large manufacturers of pharmaceuticals in the United States. These companies included: Merck & Company in Rathway, New Jersey, Mallinckrodt Chemical Works in St. Louis, the New York Quinine and Chemical Works in Brooklyn, Hoffman-LaRoche in Nutley, New Jersey, Parke-Davis & Company in Detroit, Eli Lilly in Indianapolis, Sharpe & Dohme in Philadelphia, and E.R. Squibb & Sons in Brooklyn.

Since one of Anslinger's duties was to monitor the internal control of manufactured drugs, these companies had an interest in his survival as head of the FBN. Anslinger authorised a limited number of pharmaceutical firms to import the raw opium that was used for the production of various medicines. The few favoured companies could exploit their exclusivity to make extra profits. As McWilliams, puts it, 'The arrangement was mutually convenient for both Anslinger and the manufacturers. The drug companies made money, and Anslinger was given control of a powerful lobby' (McWilliams, 1990, pp. 86–89).

Some efforts, however, were made to challenge the punitive approach to drugs favoured by Anslinger and his supporters. August Vollmer, for example, the foremost police reformer of the day, argued forcefully for a regulatory rather than a prohibitive approach to 'vice' of all kinds. Vollmer had drastically improved the efficiency and organisation of several police forces and then used this experience as the basis of a book called *The Police in Modern Society*, published in 1936. Vollmer argued that the policeman's duty was to protect society from criminals and not to try to control morality. Any other approach was dangerously counter-productive, distracting the police and fostering crime and corruption. He considered that the problems of gambling, prostitution and drug addiction could not be solved by regular policing. On the drug traffic he wrote:

> *Stringent laws, spectacular police drives, vigorous prosecution, and imprisonment of addicts and peddlers have proved not only useless and enormously expensive as a means of correcting this evil, but they are also unjustifiably and unbelievably cruel in their application to the unfortunate drug victims. Repression has driven this vice un-*

derground and produced the narcotics smugglers and supply agents, who have grown wealthy out of this evil practice and who by devious methods have stimulated traffic in drugs. Finally, and not the least of the evils associated with repression, the help-less addict has been forced to resort to crime in order to get money for the drug which is absolutely indispensable for his comfortable existence.

He warned that addicts were forced to resort to crime to pay inflated black-market prices and stressed that the profit motive had to be taken away by the medical dispensation of drugs to addicts before any progress could be made in dealing with the drug problem:

Drug addiction is not a police problem; it never has been, and never can be solved by policemen. It is first and last a medical problem, and if there is a solution it will be discovered not by policemen, but by scientific and competently trained medical ex-perts ...' (Vollmer, 1936, pp. 117–118).

Another critique of drug prohibition was put forward by Representative John M. Coffee of Washington State in 1938. In that year Coffee introduced House Joint Resolution 642 'to provide for a survey of the narcotic-drug conditions in the United States by the United States Public Health Service.' Coffee felt that the Harrison Act had been misinterpreted and that the responsibility for drug en-forcement should have been given to the United States Public Health Service rather than the FBN. He told fellow congressmen that:

In examining the Harrison Special Tax Act we are confronted with the anomaly that a law designed (as its name implies) to place a tax on certain drugs, and raise revenue thereby, resulting in reducing enormously the legitimate importation of the drugs in question, while developing a smuggling industry not before in existence. That, how-ever, is only the beginning. Through operation of the law, as interpreted, there was developed also, as counterpart to the smuggling racket, the racket of dope peddling; in a word, the whole gigantic structure of the illicit-drug racket, with a direct annual turn-over of a billion dollars.

Coffee noted that the problem of corruption was pervasive in the FBN, and felt that corrupt cops and drug dealers would be put out of business if drug addicts were treated on the same basis as nicotine addicts and alcohol addicts. But, he said, that prompted a question: 'Why should persons in authority wish to keep the dope peddler in business and the illicit-drug racket in possession of its billion-dollar income?' This was, for Coffee, the significant question at issue ...

If we, the representatives of the people, are to continue to let our narcotic authorities conduct themselves in a manner tantamount to upholding and in effect supporting the billion-dollar drug racket, we should at least be able to explain to our constituents why we do so.

Coffee's resolution did not make it out of the House's committee stage and was not even considered by the Senate (McWilliams, 1990, pp. 92–95). In this and other cases Anslinger's political lobby was powerful enough to ensure that the case against the punitive approach to drug taking was not taken seriously. John Coffee was defeated for re-election in 1946 and by then August Vollmer's book was long out of circulation. Few American politicians and police officials have since risked their careers by criticising a massively expanded drug control bureaucracy.

During the 1940s and 1950s Harry Anslinger continued to couch his anti-drug arguments in the racist and manipulative tradition of earlier prohibitionists. He asserted that the main peril faced by the country in the post-Second World War era were two foreign conspiracies — communism and the 'Mafia' — and both were misleadingly depicted as coherent and centralised international conspiracies of evil. Journalists were fed many stories about the FBN standing alone in brave defiance of the Mafia and a new 'yellow peril', the People's Republic of China. The stories suggested that the intention of both these foreign threats was to speed up the moral degeneration of the United States. Anslinger himself co-authored a book published in 1954 which claimed that most of the illegal drug supply was grown and processed in communist China, from where it was spread 'with cold deliberation' to free countries, notably the United States. He had previously provided a link between the two conspiracies by explaining that, although the Chinese Communists were making the major profits, the Mafia was distributing the Chinese manufactured heroin in the United States. Drug trafficking, it was said repeatedly, provided China with dollars for war, and weakened the health and moral fibre of its enemies (Kinder, 1981, p. 171). Few chose to challenge these absurd ideas at the time and newspapers repeated Anslinger's propaganda as fact despite all the evidence and logic that suggested that most drug trafficking routes followed the established trading routes of the U.S.'s friends and allies. His charges against the People's Republic of China were eventually repudiated by a series of statements issued by the US State Department in 1971 (Musto, 1993, p. 283).

Anslinger also claimed to have the name and address of virtually every drug addict in the entire United States. His estimates of the rate of drug addiction in the United States were never questioned and he could thus claim success for his Bureau in the war on drugs when the numbers went down. On 9 July 1962, for example, the New York Times reported that there was 'statistical evidence that the small and highly professional Bureau of Narcotics has done much to cut down the use of illicit drugs' and continued:

> The incidence of narcotics addiction in the United States today is estimated at one in 4,000 as compared with one in 2,100 in 1950, the peak of a brief post-war resurgence of drug addiction.
> *The decline coincides with two control measures enacted by Congress, the Boggs Act of 1952 [sic] and the Narcotics Control Act of 1956. Both increased sharply the penalties for illegal possession and sale of narcotics.*

In reality, America's draconian laws had failed to deter drug traffickers from exploiting the richest market in the world and an accurate estimate of the numbers of drug addicts could not possibly be made. It would also later be revealed that high-level operators had little to fear from an agency that was quite the opposite of 'highly professional' (Permanent Subcommittee on Investigations of the Committee on Government Operations, 1975, pp. 134–144).

It is also worth noting that Anslinger made a notable contribution to the deliberations over the appropriate global response to drugs after the war. This response was consolidated in 1961 when the United Nation's Single Convention on Narcotic Drugs brought under one instrument most of the prior international anti-drugs pacts. Thus, ironically, a man whose racist assumptions hardly fitted comfortably with the UN Charter influenced a convention often thought to be one of the international organisation's main achievements.

Anslinger headed the Federal Bureau of Narcotics until 1962 and during this time thousands of drug users and sellers served long sentences in federal and state institutions, most for selling minute quantities of drugs to informants or undercover agents. The majority of those convicted were black and Hispanic Americans, unable to afford lawyers capable of invoking constitutional safeguards as to forced confessions, entrapment and illegal search and seizure. Many small-time dealers were sentenced to thirty-, forty-, and fifty-year terms in prison while the more successful drug suppliers could afford to buy immunity from the law.

Many lies and distortions about drugs can be attributed directly or indirectly to Anslinger and his agents. Nothing, however, was more fraudulent than the image he cultivated for his agency. FBN agents in countless books and articles were usually portrayed as tough, dedicated and efficient professionals guarding against Mafia or communist plots to poison America. In reality the agency had to be abolished in 1968 when it was found to be riddled with corruption. Almost every agent in the New York office of the FBN was fired, forced to resign, transferred or convicted, and this constituted about one-third of the agency's total manpower — a staggering proportion. Most were veterans appointed during Anslinger's time. Congressional testimony later revealed that FBN agents had taken bribes 'from all levels of traffickers,' had sold 'confiscated drugs and firearms,' had looted 'searched apartments,' had provided tipoffs 'to suspects and defendants,' and had threatened 'the lives of fellow agents who dared to expose them' (Permanent Subcommittee on Investigations of the Committee on Government Operations, 1975, pp. 134–144).

This scandal received minimal media attention and there was no questioning of the effectiveness of drug enforcement. Instead, in September 1972, the administration of President Richard Nixon decided to declare 'a total war on drugs.' In words that echoed those of Richmond Hobson fifty years earlier he announced that those who deal drugs 'are literally the slave traders of our times. They are trafficking in death.' (Lusane, p. 77)

To fill the role of the FBN, a new agency, the Bureau of Narcotics and Dangerous Drugs, had to be created in the Department of Justice. In 1973, after another bureaucratic shake-up, the Drug Enforcement Administration was created and remains the federal government's chief anti-drug agency amongst a multiplicity of drug control agencies. By 1975 the new agency had a staff of more than 4,000, and it possessed, in Rufus King's words, 'every armament and prerogative that could conceivably be conferred on a peacetime domestic agency' (King, 1975, p. 319).

Despite and in many ways, because of, the stepped-up enforcement, the war on drugs has continued to produce a world of institutionalised greed, chaos, corruption, betrayal and terror, which is far beyond that experienced during alcohol prohibition. The main victims in this war are African and Hispanic Americans who are disproportionately more likely to be arrested, convicted and sentenced for drug offenses than whites (Bureau of Justice Statistics, 1994, p. 21; Gordon, 1994, p. 143). Given the racist and manipulative origins of drug prohibition, these damaging consequences are sadly appropriate.

The only major federal legislative reverse suffered by the USA's moral crusaders remains the repeal of the 18th Amendment in 1933. Significantly this followed the Wickersham Commissions's Report in 1931, which presented evidence about the enforcement of Prohibition and impartially reported both sides of the wet-dry argument. The wets, who supported repeal and a regulatory approach to alcohol control, argued that Prohibition was a failure. It failed to solve alcohol-related problems, it deprived governments of revenue and, in fact, only succeeded in enriching corrupt people. The anti-alcohol drys could only claim that things might get better with more effective enforcement. For most people the wets won the argument and their representatives acted accordingly.

However, in the case of drugs, the historical record has shown that representatives of the American people including every president since Nixon would rather tolerate corruption and racketeering on a massive scale than take part in a reasoned, well-informed debate that seriously considers alternatives to prohibition. Billions of dollars have been spent on enforcement but evidence of the corrupt and destructive consequences of drug prohibition continues to mount up. It seems therefore that the questions posed by congressmen Wagner and Coffee still need to be addressed: 'Why heap more sacrifice upon the altar of hopelessness?' and 'Why should persons in authority wish to keep the dope peddler in business and the illicit-drug racket in possession of its billion-dollar income?'

To sum up, early US drug and alcohol policy was influenced more by racism and sensationalism than by reason and realism. Alcohol prohibition was discredited during the 1920s but the country chose to continue with other aspects of its ambitious programme of moral reform.

The successful shift from prohibition to regulation of alcohol was not repeated for the prohibitions of gambling, prostitution or drugs. There was no serious re-examination of the other moral reform laws despite the arguments of Vollmer and others who understood that prohibitory approaches often caused more problems than they solved. Instead, the attempt to impose virtue and abstinence on Americans continued; alternative approaches to perceived problems were either ignored or discredited. The prohibition of drugs was a part of this much broader moral reform movement. Until the United States acknowledges that its early drug control efforts were based on prejudice, false representations of drug powers, and the manipulation of evidence, it is unlikely to find or accept ways that might reduce the damage. Other countries should take note and resist the trend towards an internationalisation of the US war on drugs. It is to be hoped that more might then base their own drug policies on a reasoned understanding of drugs and drug users and an acknowledgment of the limits of the possible.

REFERENCES

Asbury, H. (1950) *The Great Illusion: An Informal History of Prohibition*, Greenwood Press, Westport, Connecticut.

National Commission on Law Observance and Enforcement (1931) *Report on the Enforcement of the Prohibition Laws of the United States*, 71st Congress, 3rd Session, H.D. 722, Volume 5, U.S. Government Printing Office, Washington D.C.

Block, A.A. and Chambliss, W. (1981) *Organizing Crime*, Elsevier, New York.

Brecher, E.M. (1972) *Licit and Illicit Drugs*, Little, Brown and Company, Boston.

Browning, F. and Gerassi (1980) *The American Way of Crime*, Putnam's, New York.

Bureau of Justice Statistics (1995) *Drugs and Crime Facts*, 1994, ONDCP Drugs & Crime Clearinghouse, Rockville, MD.

Dickson, D. (1968) 'Bureaucracy and Morality: An Organizational Perspective on a Moral Crusade,' *Social Problems*, Volume 16.

Duke, S.B. and Gross, A.C. (1993) *America's Longest War: Rethinking Our Tragic Crusade Against Drugs*, Putnam's, New York.

Epstein, E.J. (1976) *Agency of Fear: Opiates and Political Power in America*, Putnam's, New York.

Gordon, D.R. (1994) *The Return of the Dangerous Classes: Drug Prohibition and Policy Politics*, W.W. Norton, New York.

Goshen, C.E. (1973) *Drink, Drugs and Do-Gooders*, Collier-Macmillan, London.

Haller, M. (1976) 'Bootleggers and American Gambling, 1920–1950,' in Commission on the Review of the National Policy Towards Gambling, *Gambling in America*, Government Printing Office, Washington D.C.

Helmer, J. (1975) *Drugs and Minority Oppression*, The Seabury Press, New York.

Inglis, B. (1975) *The Forbidden Game: A Social History of Drugs*, Hodder & Stoughton, London.

Joselit, J. (1983) *Our Gang: Jewish Crime and the New York Jewish Community, 1900–1940*, Indiana University Press, Bloomington.

Kinder, D. (1981) 'Bureaucratic Cold Warrior: Harry J. Anslinger and the Illicit Narcotics Traffic,' *Pacific Historical Review*, 50 (May 1981).

King, R. (1972) *The Drug Hang-Up: America's Fifty Year Folly*, W.W. Norton, New York.

Kobler, J. (1973) *Ardent Spirits*, Putnam's, New York.

Kohn, M. (1992) *Dope Girls: The Birth of the British Drug Underground*, Lawrence & Wishart, London.

Kyvig, D.C. (1979) *Repealing National Prohibition*, University of Chicago Press, Chicago.

Lacey, R. (1991) *Little Man: Meyer Lansky and the Gangster Life*, Arrow, London.

Lusane, C. (1991) *Pipe Dream Blues: Racism and the War on Drugs*, South End Press, Boston.

McWilliams, J.C. (1990) *The Protectors, Harry J. Anslinger and the Federal Bureau of Narcotics, 1930–1962*, University of Delaware Press, Newark.

Merz, C. (1969) *The Dry Decade*, University of Washington Press, Seattle.

Musto, D.F. (1987) *The American Disease: Origins of Narcotic Control*, Oxford University Press, New York.

Musto, D.F. (1993) 'The rise and fall of epidemics: learning from history,' in G. Edwards, J. Strang, and J.H. Jaffe, *Drugs, alcohol, and tobacco: making the science and policy connections*, Oxford University Press, Oxford.

Permanent Subcommittee on Investigations of the Committee on Government Operations (1975) *Federal Drug Enforcement*, 94th Congress, 1st Session, 9, 10, 11 June 1975, Part 1.

Rumbarger, J.J. (1989) *Profits, Power, and Prohibition: Alcohol Reform and the Industrializing of America, 1800–1930*, State University of New York Press, Albany.

Sinclair, A. (1962) *Prohibition: The Era of Excess*, Faber & Faber, London.

U.S.A. Constitutional Documents (1931) *Repeal the Eighteenth Amendment*, U.S. Government Printing Office, Washington D.C.

Vollmer, A. (1936) *The Police and Modern Society*, University of California Press, Berkeley.

Woodiwiss, M. (1988) *Crime, Crusades and Corruption: Prohibitions in the United States, 1900–1987*, Pinter, London.

CHAPTER 3

The Development of Drug Control in Britain

Joy Mott and Philip Bean

Control of 'dangerous drugs' at a national and international level is essentially a 20th century phenomenon. Until then in Britain there had been, on the whole, a tolerant attitude to the use of opium, and later to morphine and cocaine when these drugs began to be produced in the second half of the 19th century. During most of the 19th century opium was readily available and easily obtainable, although there was concern about the extent of working class use, the dangers of overdosing and suicide, and 'child doping'. But moves in the middle of the century to regulate the sale of opium, and other poisons, owed more to the development of the medical and pharmaceutical professional bodies than to concern about its use (Berridge and Edwards, 1987).

Between 1827 and 1900 most of the opium used in Britain was imported from Turkey (Berridge and Edwards, 1987) while during this period most of the opium produced in British India was exported, legally or illegally, to China (Rowntree, 1905).

DOMESTIC CONTROLS 1868–1908

The Pharmacy Act 1868 was the first attempt to regulate the availability of drugs in Britain by making it unlawful for any person to sell or keep 'open shop' for retailing, dispensing or compounding poisons unless he was a pharmaceutical chemist, or to sell any poison unless the container was clearly labelled 'poison' with the name of the substance and the name and address of the seller. The Act did not apply to wholesale supplying or the direct supply of drugs by doctors to their patients. The poisons covered by the Act were listed in a two part Schedule. Part 1 introduced the most stringent controls over poisons (such as cyanide of potassium and ergot), requiring that the purchaser should be known to the seller, or introduced by someone known to him. Importantly for the later development of controls the sale had to be recorded in a register giving the date, the type and amount of poison sold, the purpose for which it was required by the purchaser and their signature. 'Opium or all preparations of opium or of poppies' were included in Part II which only required that the container in which the substance was packed should be labelled with the contents. Patent medicines containing opium were not covered by the Act. Preparations of morphine were added to Part II in 1869.

The status of opium and cocaine was raised by the Poisons and Pharmacy Act 1908 which amended the Schedule of substances to the 1868 Act while making no changes to the controls introduced by that Act. Although morphine and cocaine were covered by Part 1 of the Schedule to the 1868 Act, by the inclusion of 'alka-loids, all poisonous vegetable alkaloids and their salts', the suggestion of the Phar-maceutical Society was accepted that these drugs should be specifically named in the amended Schedule. Part 1 of the new Schedule included 'opium and all prepa-rations and admixtures containing 1 or more per-cent of morphine' and 'coca, and preparations or admixtures of, containing 1 or more per-cent of the coca alkaloids.'

THE ORIGINS OF INTERNATIONAL CONTROLS

The Shanghai Commission 1909

Victory in the Spanish-American war of 1898 provided the United States with colonies, notably the Philippines, the moral duty to 'uplift inferior peoples', the opportunity to compete with the European powers in trade with the Far East, the view that opium use was one of the gravest problems in the area, and a voice in the international control of drugs (Musto, 1987). By acquiring the Philippines the United States had also acquired the local opium problem which was to be re-solved by the gradual prohibition of the sale of opium, except for medicinal pur-poses, over a three year period starting in 1904.

The United States government was persuaded by Bishop Brent (the episcopal bishop of the Philippines) that an international meeting with the European pow-ers with interests in the far east, and Japan, was needed to stop the flow of opium into China and to make effective the prohibition of opium in the Philippines. Britain was at first reluctant to join the meeting because the longstanding and profitable opium trade between India and China was coming to an end. The 1907 Anglo-Chinese Agreement committed the British government to reduce the ship-ment of opium to China by 10 per cent a year while the Chinese government undertook to decrease the cultivation of poppies and the consumption of opium by a similar annual amount so that the trade would end in 1916.

The Shanghai Commission was convened in February 1909 under the chair-manship of Bishop Brent. At the request of Britain and the Netherlands the meet-ing was a fact-finding body making recommendations which did not commit the participants. Nevertheless, the resolutions of the Commission laid the foundations for the international control of drugs.

The Commission was attended by thirteen nations. Of the major opium producers, Turkey did not attend and Persia was represented only by a local merchant. The delegates were not willing to agree with the United States view that opium smoking should be prohibited because 'there is no non-medical use of opium and its derivatives that is not fraught with grave dangers, if it is not actually vicious.' They did agree to urge on their governments the desirability of the gradual suppression of opium smoking with due regard to the varying circumstances in each country; to re-examine their own laws with regard to the regulation of the use of opium for other than medical purposes; that nations should not export opium to other nations whose laws prohibited the importation; that measures should be taken by each government to control morphine and other opium derivatives. The latter was a British resolution, amended slightly by the American delegation.

The Hague Opium Convention 1912

After the Shanghai Commission reported the Americans were anxious to call another international conference to formalize the resolutions and lobbied the other nations who were less enthusiastic. In 1911 the International Conference on Opium was convened in the Hague and attended by twelve nations with Bishop Brent again acting as chairman. The aim of the conference was 'to advance a step further on the road opened by the International Commission of Shanghai of 1909; determined to bring about the gradual suppression of the abuse of opium, morphine and cocaine ...'

The resolutions of the Shanghai Commission formed the basis of the International Opium Convention signed at the Hague on 23 January 1912 and then circulated for ratification to give it the force of international law. Two subsequent conferences at the Hague in 1913 and 1914 were concerned with the ratification of the Convention.

The main provisions of the 1912 Hague Convention were:

1. the production and distribution, including import and export, of raw opium to be controlled by national legislation,
2. opium smoking to be gradually and effectively suppressed,
3. the manufacture, sale and consumption of morphine and cocaine and their salts to be limited by national legislation to medical and legitimate purposes, and to be controlled by a system of licensing,
4. statistics relating to the drug trade, and information about national laws and administrative arrangements, to be exchanged through the Netherlands government.

Britain ratified the Hague Convention on 15 July 1914. At the time no government department was willing to take on the responsibility for controlling drugs and it remained with the Privy Council Office. The outbreak of war in August 1914 increased the need to control drug smuggling, particularly as there was evidence of British ships being used to smuggle cocaine to India, morphine to Japan, and opium to the Far East and to the United States. An interdepartmental meeting in June 1916 to discuss how to deal with this smuggling, as well as fears about cocaine use by the armed forces in London, decided that these matters could best be dealt with by the police and that the Home Office should be the central controlling authority. This decision has been interpreted as indicating 'Britain was set on the path to an overtly penal narcotics policy' (Berridge, 1984).

COCAINE IN BRITAIN IN 1916

While the pre-war international concerns were largely focused on the control of opium Britain was soon to have to deal with a domestic problem with cocaine (Berridge, 1978; Spear and Mott, 1993). Early in 1916 it had been found that cocaine was being peddled in London by prostitutes and that the drug was being used by Canadian soldiers. Under the Defence of the Realm Act 1914 the gift or sale of intoxicants (i.e. any sedative, narcotic or stimulant) to a member of His Majesty's Forces with intent to make him drunk or incapable was an offence punishable by a sentence of imprisonment up to six months; but the sale to, or possession of 'intoxicants' by civilians could not be dealt under the 1908 Act.

In May 1916 an Army Council Order forbade the sale or supply of cocaine, and other drugs, to any member of the armed forces unless ordered by a doctor on a written prescription which could be dispensed only once. But the order had little effect on the non-medical trade and in July 1916, at the instigation of the Commissioner of Police for the Metropolis, Defence of the Realm Act Regulation 40B came into force.

DORA 40B permitted only 'authorized' persons; retail pharmacists, medical practitioners, persons holding general or special permits issued by the Secretary of State, or persons who had received the drug on doctors' prescriptions; to possess cocaine or preparations containing more than 0.1 per cent of cocaine (the limit set by the Hague Convention). All transactions in cocaine were to be separately recorded and these records to be retained so they could be inspected by someone authorized by the Secretary of State. The Customs Consolidation Act 1876 was amended by Proclamation to prohibit the export or import of cocaine except under licence.

In December 1916 the Regulation was amended to give the Secretary of State power to issue licences for the manufacture of cocaine (used as a local anaesthetic by dentists and in ophthalmic surgery), to make it an offence for a medical practitioner to give a prescription other than in accordance with the conditions laid down in the Regulation, and to require that medicines and other preparations containing cocaine be marked with the amount of cocaine contained in them. In addition, the Secretary of State was given the power to direct that an 'authorized' person who had been convicted of an offence under the Regulation or Proclamation should cease to be authorized. In December 1916 an official of the Home Office was empowered to inspect all books and records to be kept under the Regulation, this authority was extended to police officers not below the rank of inspector in May 1917.

The death of a popular actress, Billie Carleton, after attending a Victory Ball on 27 November 1918, was initially attributed to cocaine. This, together with evidence of opium, heroin and cocaine use by her social circle prompted intense press coverage, and inspired popular fiction, which emphasised the depravity of drug taking and the corruption of young women by 'mixing together currents of dope, sexual perversion, fornication and miscegenation' (Kohn, 1992).

As a result of the Carleton case there were calls from the police to enact the provisions of DORA 40B into permanent legislation. In any case the government was preparing to honour its obligations under the Hague Convention which had been ratified under the terms of the Versailles Peace Treaty. These obligations were reflected in the Dangerous Drugs Act 1920 and subordinate regulations.

THE DANGEROUS DRUGS ACT 1920

The 1920 Act retained most of the provisions of DORA 40B and extended control to morphine. The Act prohibited the production, import or export, possession, sale or distribution of opium, cocaine, morphine or heroin except by persons licensed by the Home Secretary or otherwise authorized on that behalf and specified maximum penalties for offences under the Act. The prohibitions also applied to preparations containing 0.2 per cent of morphine or 0.1 per cent of cocaine.

There is little doubt that the cocaine scare of 1916, and the death of Billie Carleton and the attendant publicity, 'made the public and politicians more willing to accept the stringent controls' of the 1920 Act (Parssinen, 1983). The prewar discussions by government departments about the control legislation required by the Hague Convention had favoured an extension of the existing pharmacy laws and 'reliance on professional expertise' (Berridge, 1984).

Although the Ministry of Health had been created in 1919, the Home Office kept responsibility for 'dangerous drugs', and for administration of the control legislation, and has retained the lead responsibility to this day.

Regulations made under the Act were aimed at restricting the possession of drugs to authorized persons and for the keeping of records on transactions in the drugs. A medical practitioner was authorized to possess and supply drugs only so far as was necessary for the practice of his profession. The attempt to prohibit self-prescribing by doctors failed because of opposition from the medical profession.

THE ROLLESTON REPORT 1926

The Home Office had found two difficulties in the interpretation of the Regulations to the 1920 Act. The first, and most important, was whether the prolonged prescribing of morphine or heroin to addicts was accepted by the medical profession as 'legitimate medical treatment', and the second, whether doctors should be allowed to prescribe these drugs to themselves.

The Departmental Committee on Morphine and Heroin Addiction was appointed by the Ministry of Health in 1924 to advise on the answers to these questions. The Chairman of the Committee was Sir Humphrey Rolleston, then president of the Royal College of Physicians. The other eight members were physicians and much of the evidence considered came from physicians. The Committee reported in 1926 (Report of the Departmental Committee on Morphine and Heroin Addiction, 1926).

In their Report the Rolleston Committee gave detailed consideration to various forms of treatment for addiction. It was noted that 'some eminent physicians, especially in the United States, had expressed the opinion that persons who had become addicted to the use of drugs could always be cured by sudden withdrawal under proper precautions' but the Committee did not advocate the method.

The Committee considered that addiction 'must be regarded as a manifestation of a disease, and not as a mere form of vicious indulgence' and also that 'there can be no question of the propriety of continuing to administer the drug (morphine or heroin) in quantities necessary' for the relief of pain in ordinary medical and surgical practice. It concluded that there were two groups of persons 'who were already the victims of addiction' to whom 'administration of morphine or heroin may be regarded as legitimate medical treatment' and gave advice on the precautions to be observed. The two groups of 'victims of addiction' included, firstly, 'those who are undergoing treatment for the cure of addiction by the gradual withdrawal method' and, secondly, those

> for whom, after every effort has been made for the cure of the addiction, the drug cannot be completely withdrawn, either because complete withdrawal produces serious symptoms which cannot be satisfactorily treated under the ordinary conditions of private practice; or the patient, while capable of leading a useful and fairly normal life so long as he takes a certain non-progressive quantity, usually small, of the drug of addiction, ceases to be able to do so when the regular allowance is withdrawn.

The Committee recommended that medical tribunals should be created to assist the Home Office in dealing with cases when 'there were strong grounds for believing that a doctor was administering drugs for illegitimate purposes either to himself or to others.' It was not until 1974 that such tribunals, set-up under the provisions of the Misuse of Drugs Act 1971, were used.

There is still debate about the significance of the Rolleston report in the development of British drug policy. Some hail it as 'a victory for the medical profession ... they triumphed by imposing on the report both the medical definition and the medical solution to the problem of drug addiction' (Parssinen, 1983). One authoritative British historian sees it as the doctors saving 'Britain from the consequences of transatlantic style drug control by their resolute defence of maintenance prescribing and a medical approach' (Berridge, 1984) and the defeat 'of a consistent attempt by the Home Office to impose a policy completely penal in direction' (Berridge, 1984). Another sees it as simply providing the answer to the question whether the prescribing of morphine or heroin to addicts was legitimate medical treatment, as giving guidance to doctors for the treatment of addicts and providing a standard of professional conduct to which the physician treating such cases could be expected to conform (Spear, 1995).

INTERNATIONAL DRUG CONTROL 1921–1971

The League of Nations, of which the United States was not a member, was entrusted with the 'general supervision of the traffic in opium and dangerous drugs' as set out in the Hague Convention. The Opium Advisory Committee was created in 1921 to carry out this task. Sir Malcolm Delevigne, the British representative on the Committee, later described some of the major defects of the Hague Convention (Delevigne, 1934). One was the absence any machinery to ensure that drugs were only exported to persons duly authorized in the importing countries, another was the absence of an obligatory requirement to licence people engaged in the trade.

The Second Opium International Conference was convened in Geneva in 1924 to strengthen the provisions of the Hague Convention. The major provisions of the Geneva Convention of 1925 were:

1. all persons engaged in the trade in controlled drugs were to be licensed and to keep records of all transactions,
2. all imports and exports had first to receive the approval of the government of both the importing and the exporting country,
3. the Permanent Central Opium Control Board was to be created as an independent body to keep the international trade under continuous review to which parties were required to submit detailed statistics relating to their production, sales, imports and exports of controlled drugs,
4. coca leaves, crude cocaine and cannabis were brought under international control.

A proposal to control cannabis had been raised at the 1912 Hague Conference by Italy and it had been agreed to study the question of cannabis misuse. In 1923 the South African delegate proposed to the Advisory Committee that cannabis should be considered a habit forming drug and it was again agreed that more information was needed. The Egyptian delegate to the Geneva Conference submitted a proposal that hashish should be included in the Convention because 'there was great danger involved in the consumption of hashish' and 'the illicit use of hashish was the principal cause of most cases of insanity in Egypt.' He also suggested that if hashish was not brought under control '... Oriental peoples ... (will say) the question was not dealt with because it does not effect the safety of the Europeans ...' (Advisory Committee on Drug Dependence, 1968). The Conference agreed to bring cannabis under limited control by controlling exports and imports but not requiring governments to control production or domestic traffic or to prevent its non-medical use or to send statistics on production to the Central Opium Control Board.

An attempt to include in the Convention a provision that the manufacture of drugs by each country should be limited to the quantities it required for medical and scientific purposes failed but the essentials of the scheme were unanimously accepted six years later by another International Conference and formed the basis of the 1931 Limitation Convention (Delevigne, 1934).

In 1946 international drug control functions were transferred from the League of Nations to the United Nations and a Commission on Narcotic Drugs replaced the Advisory Committee. The 1961 Single Convention codified the eight previous conventions that governed international controls and created the International Narcotics Control Board (INCB). The World Health Organization advises the Board on amendments to the schedules of drugs to be controlled.

The central feature of the Single Convention is the requirement that each country should submit to the INCB annual estimates of the quantities of the drugs 'to be consumed for medical and scientific purposes' and details of the production and manufacture of the drugs as had been required by the 1931 Limitation Convention. The drugs are listed in four schedules with the most stringent controls to be exercised over those listed in Schedule I including heroin, methadone, morphine, opium, other powerful analgesics, and cannabis. The use of these drugs is to be restricted to medical and scientific purposes. But each party to the Convention could 'adopt special measures of control' to drugs listed in Schedule IV which are generally, but not universally, accepted as having no legitimate therapeutic use including heroin and cannabis.

Like the Single Convention the 1971 Psychotropic Substances Convention provides for controls to be exercised over drugs listed in four schedules with decreasing degrees of stringency which parties to the Convention should exercise 'as far as possible.' Many of the drugs listed in the Schedules were already controlled by the legislation presently in force in Britain, the Misuse of Drugs Act 1971, for example, the amphetamines and LSD. Following the ratification of the Convention the Schedules to the Act were amended in 1985 to include the barbiturates and the benzodiazepines.

International Conventions and Domestic Legislation

All the Dangerous Drugs Acts between 1923 and 1964 were passed to implement the international conventions and not because of domestic drug problems. The 1925 Dangerous Drugs Act, implementing the Geneva Convention, came into force in 1928 and amended the 1920 Act to include coca leaves, crude cocaine and cannabis. The 1932 Dangerous Drugs Act extended control to certain alkaloids of opium and cocaine as specified in the 1931 Limitation Convention. Following the 1961 Single Convention the 1964 Dangerous Drugs Act created certain offences in relation to cannabis, and making it illegal to cultivate. Like a longstanding provision about opium smoking, the Act also made it an offence for an occupier to permit premises to be used for smoking or dealing in cannabis and for any person to be concerned with the management of premises used for any such purpose.

INTERNATIONAL ATTEMPTS TO BAN HEROIN

The United States had prohibited the legitimate manufacture of heroin in 1924 but its delegation to the Geneva Conference in that year failed to persuade the other countries attending to follow suit. The Limitation Conference of 1930–31 decided that member countries should be invited to consider the feasibility of banning the legitimate use of heroin. In reply to an enquiry from the Opium Advisory Committee in 1934 the British government said, since medical opinion was in favour of retaining heroin, no steps would be taken to abolish or restrict its medical use.

There were further attempts by the international control body to ban the legitimate manufacture of heroin in 1949, 1954 and 1978. The most serious attempt to do so came in 1954 when, on the advice of the World Health Organization, the United Nations Economic and Social Council urged all governments to prohibit the legitimate manufacture and export of heroin except for scientific purposes. There is little doubt that the proposed ban was instigated by the United States, for example, the writer of a leading article in The Lancet (1955) commented 'In this difficult campaign the United States needs the moral support of all the principal countries.'

In order to implement the ban the Home Secretary announced on 18 February 1955 that no further licences for the manufacture of heroin would be issued after 31 December 1955. The Times newspaper and the British Medical Association (BMA) led the opposition to the ban. The BMA argued that doctors should not be deprived of the use of heroin, or of any other drug, for the treatment of their patients because 'For generations the doctor in Britain has taken it for granted that he can prescribe for his patients any drug of which, in his professional judgement, they stand in need' (Pringle, 1955). The BMA asked the government to provide 'any evidence that a ban on manufacture of heroin in Britain will help to reduce heroin addiction abroad' and wondered whether the ban had been introduced to 'make those countries with inferior control systems — notably France — feel uncomfortable.' It also pointed out that the ban would be useless since it did not extend to morphine and heroin can easily be manufactured from morphine 'by those with some basic equipment and modest knowledge of chemistry.'

The ban was withdrawn on 14 December 1955 on legal advice that while the Home Secretary had the authority to licence the manufacture of heroin he had no authority to ban its manufacture! In January 1956 the Home Secretary announced that the export and import of heroin would be prohibited while manufacture would be restricted to the amount required for medical treatment and scientific use in the United Kingdom. More recently, membership of the European Union means that the United Kingdom may be compelled to permit the importation of heroin manufactured by other member countries.

In 1978 and 1987 the United Nations Commission on Narcotic Drugs adopted resolutions urging governments that had not already done so to prohibit the use of heroin on human beings. In 1995 the Commission was again asked to consider prohibition of the use of heroin and the chairman of the Commission will report in 1996.

DRUG USERS AND DRUG POLICY 1916–1971

In 1916 it was concern over the use of cocaine by members of the armed forces which led to DORA 40B and the introduction of stringent controls on the availability of cocaine including the creation of the offence of unauthorized possession of the drug. Either the extent of cocaine use had been exaggerated or the implementation of DORA 40B was highly effective in dealing with both licit and illicit use. Six months after the Regulation came into force, in January 1917, all police forces were asked to report on the operation and effect of the Regulation. Their reports frequently noted that cocaine (and opium) was so little prescribed, and only on a reduced number of prescriptions, that many pharmacists had ceased to stock the drug. The Metropolitan Police were satisfied that the traffic in cocaine had been 'almost extinguished' in London (Spear and Mott, 1993)

But in 1919 the Billie Carleton case brought the use of cocaine, and of heroin and opium, in theatrical circles and the demi-monde to public attention again. During the early 1920s cocaine was the 'in' recreational drug with illicit supply 'in the hands of young street hustlers whose customers were prostitutes, actresses, criminals, well-to-do bohemians, night-club habitues and others on the fringes of London's underworld' (Parssinen, 1983). Most of the prosecutions arose from arrests made in the Soho-Leicester Square entertainment area. In 1922 the death of Freda Kempton, a West End night club dance instructress, from a cocaine overdose again led to public outcry with the popular press highlighting the involvement of Chinese men and other 'aliens' in cocaine trafficking. The trials of two notorious cocaine traffickers, in 1923 of Edgar Manning, a Jamaican musician, and in 1924 of Brilliant Chang, a Chinese restaurant owner, were given extensive press coverage.

Penalties for offences under the 1920 Act had been increased by the 1923 Dangerous Drugs (Amendment) Act. Convictions for offences under the Dangerous Drugs Acts, particularly those involving cocaine, declined after 1925 and only began to rise in the early 1960s (Spear and Mott, 1993).

In 1926 the Rolleston Committee considered that 'addiction to morphia and heroin is rare in this country and has diminished in recent years.' The Committee arrived at this conclusion largely on evidence about patients treated in private practice and found that many were 'persons engaged in occupations which entail much nervous and mental strain' as well as 'those who, by reason of their occupation or otherwise, have special facilities for access to the drugs', mainly doctors. One commentator suggests that the findings of the Committee might have been different if it had received evidence of the use of morphia and heroin by Chinese seamen, West End prostitutes and Soho night club habitues, people who were unlikely to come seek medical attention for their drug use even if they thought it merited treatment (Parssinen, 1983).

In 1934 the Home Office, for the first time, made an estimate of 300 addicts coming to notice during the year, revised to 700 in 1935. An, Addicts Index was started in that year including brief details of cases of addiction reported by Regional Medical Officers of Health, cases discovered by the Home Office drugs inspectors from their monitoring of pharmacists' registers and some addicts who reported themselves (Spear and Mott, 1993).

During the 1930s around 500 addicts were known to the Home Office each year, mainly of therapeutic origin, around 90 per cent were addicted to morphine with the sexes equally represented, and the majority aged 50 and older. Most of the remainder were 'professional' addicts, that is, people working in the medical and allied professions. The statistics did not indicate the annual number of new addicts coming to notice and it seems reasonable to assume that many were continuing cases. In the immediate pre-war years a few non-therapeutic heroin addicts came to notice in London (Spear, 1969). The Home Office was mainly concerned about a few doctor-addicts and the police about vice and heroin sniffing at 'snuff parties' associated with shady night clubs and drinking clubs in Soho and Mayfair. By the late 1950s a few of the pre-war addicts were still being treated and were described as 'coming from the higher social and economic levels' with relatively 'high intellectual achievements' who had taken to heroin 'to live life more fully' (Frankau and Stanwell, 1960).

Until 1950 cannabis, still known as Indian Hemp, was not much used in Britain with the majority of cases of illicit import involving small quantities brought in by Arab and Indian seamen. Then there was evidence that the traffic in cannabis had spread to those parts of the country where there was a large West Indian immigrant population and it had become popular in dance clubs in Soho (Spear, 1969).

The First Report of the Interdepartmental Committee on Drug Addiction 1961

There was no major public concern about drugs in Britain in the mid-1950s or about the operation of the drug control policy, which had been established by the 1920 Dangerous Drugs Act and extended only to take account of the international conventions. There was activity at the time in the international arena, the United Nations Commission on Narcotic Drugs was busy drafting the Single Convention and there was the attempt to ban on heroin in 1955. In the circumstances, the Home Office considered it was timely to conduct a review of British drugs policy which would also consider new drugs which might be liable to produce addiction and whether the advice on the treatment of addicts given by the Rolleston Committee almost thirty years ago needed to be revised (Spear, 1995).

An Interdepartmental Committee, under the chairmanship of Sir Russell Brain, then president of the Royal College of Physicians, was convened in 1958 to consider these matters and make recommendations. The Committee completed its report in November 1960 before the addict statistics for that year were compiled. It considered that the incidence of addiction to controlled drugs was very small although 'the choice of drugs had altered, the new synthetics taken orally being now more popular' and the number of doctors and nurses involved 'though small in number remains disproportionately high.' The popular new synthetic drug was pethidine.

The Committee found that 'traffic in illicit supplies is almost negligible, cannabis excepted' and made no recommendations to change the existing control arrangements or to revise the Rolleston Committee's advice on treatment of addicts. In stating that 'addiction should be regarded as an expression of mental disorder rather than a form of criminal behaviour' it reiterated the view of the Rolleston Committee (Interdepartmental Committee on Drug Addiction, 1961).

The Second Report of the Interdepartmental Committee on Drug Addiction 1965

The Committee was reconvened in July 1964 with terms of reference 'to consider whether, in the light of recent experience, the advice they gave in 1961 in relation to the prescribing of addictive drugs needs revising and, if so, to make recommendations.' The 'recent experience' was that the number of addicts known to the Home Office had increased from 454 in 1959 with 68 addicted to heroin, to 753 in 1964 with 342 addicted to heroin. The new heroin addicts were of non-therapeutic origin and most were also described as addicted to cocaine. There had been also been 'a significant change in the age distribution of addicts', with the proportion aged under 35 increasing from 11% in 1959 to nearly 40% in 1964, of whom 40 were aged under 20 (Second Report of the Interdepartmental Committee on Drug Addiction, 1965).

The sex ratio had also changed with males outnumbering females. During the period 1961–1970 the number of male addicts increased tenfold while the number of females only doubled (Bean, 1974). Most of the addicts were found in London although there were significant numbers of young addicts in several towns in south-east England and in Birmingham.

The Committee found that the source of the supplies of heroin and cocaine used by the new addicts had come from 'a very few doctors who, while acting within the law and according to their professional judgement, had prescribed the drugs excessively.' The Committee was concerned that 'the doctor's right to prescribe dangerous drugs without restriction for the ordinary patient's needs should be maintained' while 'achieving better control of prescribing and supplying' and discouraging 'the development of an organized illicit traffic.'

The major recommendations of the Committee were:

1. all addicts to dangerous drugs should be notified to a central authority in order to reduce their opportunities to obtain supplies of heroin or cocaine from more than one doctor,
2. advice should be provided to a doctor when there was doubt that a patient was addicted,
3. the provision of treatment centres especially in London,
4. the prescribing of heroin and cocaine to addicts should be limited to doctors on the staff of the treatment centres.

The Dangerous Drugs Act 1967 and Regulations introduced the procedure for notifying addicts to the Chief Medical Officer at the Home Office (on 22 February 1968) and from 16 April 1968 only doctors specially licensed by the Home Secretary could prescribe heroin or cocaine to addicts. Most of these doctors worked in the newly opened NHS drug treatment centres (now called Drug Dependence Units).

Until 1967 the main source of supplies of heroin were from doctors' prescriptions but in that year significant use of illicitly imported heroin occurred for the first time in London. Then 'Chinese heroin', which had been used for smoking by the local Chinese population since the late 1940s, started to be sold to white users who prepared it for injection (Spear, 1982).

The 1960s Heroin Users

In the late 1950s and early 1960s the small number of indigenous London addicts was swelled by the arrival of about 70 very experienced Canadian addicts who had come to take advantage of the prescribing of heroin in the treatment of addiction and because there were proposals in Canada to provide for indeterminate prison sentences for convicted addicts. Although there was no evidence that the Canadians proselytised, excess from their prescriptions of heroin undoubtedly found its way on to the local black market (Spear and Glatt 1971).

The established London heroin addicts at the time have been described as 'jazz junkies', often from comfortable middle-class homes, who belonged to a drug-using sub-culture sharing an interest in jazz (a number were jazz musicians), art and poetry and identifying with the United States drug sub-culture using its argot, and with Jack Kerouac, William Burroughs and Alexander Trocchi said to be among their favourite authors (Glatt *et al.*, 1967).

The new London heroin addicts who began to appear in the early 1960s have been described as 'part of a sub-culture that was unashamedly hedonistic' who 'wheedled, cheated and extorted excessive supplies of heroin from their physicians' and sold the surplus to supplement their unemployment benefits 'to maintain a style of life without work consistent with the values of the sub-culture' (Young, 1971). While this description of the lifestyle of addicts may have fitted some living in Notting Hill Gate it did not apply to the homeless young drifters in Soho (Leech 1991) or to the group in Crawley where heroin use passed along friendship networks of young people living in comfortable circumstances at home with their parents (Rathod, 1972).

The new 1960s heroin addicts, and other drug users, came from all sections of society and from a diversity of family backgrounds. It was the youth of the new addicts, as much as the increase in their numbers, which contributed to the major policy change brought about by the 1967 Dangerous Drugs Act, the restriction of the prescribing of heroin and cocaine to addicts to licensed doctors.

Other Drug Users

The early 1960s were also the years in which amphetamines and LSD and, above all, cannabis gave the British cause for concern. With the development of the beat and hippy counter-cultures, cannabis and LSD were used by some young people as a means of seeking self-discovery and self-expression and as a symbol of the rejection of the materialist values of the affluent society and the work ethic (Young, 1971).

Drug use has often been closely associated with developments in youth culture and trends in popular music (Shapiro, 1986). Other young people, in the 'never had it so good' years of full employment and swinging London of the 1960s, used amphetamines to keep awake over the weekend and cannabis and LSD to add to their appreciation of rock music in all-night clubs and the new discos and at rock concerts and pop festivals.

Cannabis and LSD had to be bought from illicit sources while the amphetamines were often the Drinamyl tablets (known as Purple Hearts or Pep Pills) prescribed to their mothers for minor depressions. The Drugs (Prevention of Misuse) Act 1964 made the unauthorised possession of amphetamines an offence (LSD was added to the Act in 1966) but did not include regulations for their safekeeping by manufacturers and pharmacists so that thefts from these sources continued to fuel the market until such controls were introduced in 1971 by the Misuse of Drugs Act. After that illicitly imported or locally manufactured supplies began to appear.

THE TREATMENT OF ADDICTION

In 1926 the Rolleston Committee considered that, in certain circumstances, the long term prescribing of morphine or heroin to addicts was 'legitimate medical practice', the so-called British System. Neither the 1967 Dangerous Drugs Act nor the current legislation in force, the Misuse of Drugs Act 1971 (which consolidated and tidied up anomalies in the previous drug control legislation), in any way restricts the prescribing of heroin by any physician to their patients suffering from severe pain from physical illness or injury, or by licensed physicians to addicts, if the physician considers it to be clinically appropriate to do so. Nor does the legislation place any limits on the length of time heroin can be prescribed. All physicians can prescribe methadone to their patients including addicts.

That the long-term prescribing of heroin in the treatment of addiction is now done so rarely is the problem, modern day physicians tend to regard it as not proper medicine although they are prepared to prescribe methadone on a maintenance basis. Patients attending the Drug Dependence Units nowadays will rarely be prescribed heroin let alone maintained on it, the very small numbers who are will often be prescribed part heroin and part methadone. Although a few physicians have held out against this trend and are prepared to engage in long-term prescribing of heroin this has been to their professional detriment and in the face of some public vilification. Our view is that, in spite of these changes in practice the British System remains; that it now hardly ever operates as Rolleston intended is because key members of the medical profession choose not to do so.

INTERNATIONAL INFLUENCES ON BRITISH DRUG POLICY

In Alfred Lindesmith's terms, international discussions on drug controls are 'often highly charged with emotion, filled with mutual recriminations, charges and counter-charges' (Lindesmith, 1965). High moral tones are adopted with self-righteousness being the order of the day. Discussions at the first three international conferences were characterised by a phenomenon common to the 1990s: countries in which there is an illicit traffic with supplies originating from outside the country invariably blame the country of origin. Little or no blame appears to be attached to countries providing the markets for the illicit supplies.

At the first two international meetings the nations represented all had axes to grind. The Americans convened the 1909 Shanghai Commission because, among other reasons, it wanted to stop the flow of opium from China to the Philippines. At the 1911 Hague Conference the British pressed for action against cocaine because of concern about smuggling of the drug to India while Germany wanted to protect its extensive cocaine manufacturing industry. Britain was the major manufacturer of morphine in the world and the Board of Trade wanted to protect the industry. The Americans tried, and failed, to persuade the 1924 Geneva conference to agree to limit the production of opium and coca leaves for 'strictly medicinal and scientific needs', or to ban the manufacture of heroin, and never signed the 1925 Opium Convention (Musto, 1987).

In the 1930s the Japanese invaders of China did all they could to encourage the opium trade there, which the Chinese government later described as a form of genocide. Up to 1956 China was regularly accused by the United States and Formosa of deliberately encouraging the production of opium for political ends. Similar accusations have been made since the 1980s about the illicit cocaine trade, which if governments in central South America and the Caribbean have not actively encouraged, some have propped up the trade for their own ends. The profits and politics associated with drugs produce their own brand of corruption.

American Influence

There exists a popular assertion that the United States has had a dramatic and less benign influence on British drug policy beginning as far back as 1920. This is based on the view that Britain somehow agreed to introduce national controls to conform with United States policies and to retain a positive relationship. There is no evidence to support this or, if there is, we have not been able to find any. The British medical profession has, so far, resisted all American sponsored attempts to prohibit the legitimate medical use of heroin.

It is true that the United States wished to assert influence on the international controls — which country does not — but during the important period between 1924 and 1930 it, and China, had withdrawn from the international control arena.

It is too easy to raise the spectre of American influence on British drug policy but much harder to find evidence to support it. And that is what one British commentator is so critical of, when policy analysts have produced explanations without bothering to undertake the hard slog of going through government papers and finding out what really happened (Spear, 1995). Or if they have, they have quoted selectively from them. Our view is that there exists in some historical accounts a strong resemblance to the classical form of rumour, when each interpretation builds a little on the one before and in doing so gets further and further from the truth.

Drug 'Legalisation'

One of us (PB) wrote in 1974:

> Britain as member of the United Nations is still a party to these (international treaties), and a unilateral decision to remove drugs from control in Britain would attack the very foundation of a system which has laboriously developed since 1909. At this stage there is no sign that Britain would make such a decision and it would certainly not be given world wide approval. For better or for worse it appears that Britain must accept the system irrespective of its defects and the attacks being made on it by those who want to legalise such drugs as cannabis.

We see little reason to change this view. Experience over the last twenty years or so suggests that no political party in Britain would support any move which weakened Britain's commitment to the international conventions. Nor can those who wish to ignore them and opt for a British 'go it alone' policy meet the obvious objections to such an approach. Assume Britain wanted to 'legalise' a drug, say cannabis or coca leaf, which is not produced domestically (at least not on any great scale in the case of cannabis) we would then have the curious position of a drug being carried illegally from the country of origin to be imported illegally into Britain. It would only become legal when it passed through HM Customs and Excise. Presumably other countries could intercept the drug at any point prior to its arrival in Britain and could confiscate it and prosecute its transporters. Such a 'go it alone' policy hardly makes sense.

REFERENCES

Advisory Committee on Drug Dependence (1968) *Cannabis*. London: HMSO.

Bean, P.T. (1974) *The Social Control of Drugs*. London and New York: John Wiley and Sons.

Berridge, V. (1984) Drugs and social policy: the establishment of drug controls in Britain 1900–1930. *British Journal of Addiction*, **79**, pp. 17–30.

Berridge, V. and Edwards, G. (1987) *Opium and the People*. New Haven and London: Yale University Press.

Delevigne, M. (1934) Some international aspects of the problem of addiction. *British Journal of Inebriety*, **32**, pp. 125–151.

Frankau, I.M. and Stanwell, P.M. (1960) The treatment of drug addiction. *The Lancet*, December 24, pp. 1377–1379.

Glatt, M., Pittman, D.J., Gillespie, D.G. and Hill, D.R. (1967) *The Drug Scene in Great Britain*. London: Edward Arnold (Publishers) Ltd.

Kohn, M. (1992) *Dope Girls: The Birth of the British Drug Underground*. London: Lawrence and Wishart.

Leech, K. (1991) The junkies' doctors and the London drug scene in the 1960s: some remembered fragments. In *Policing and Prescribing: The British System of Drug Control* (eds.) Whynes, D.K. and Bean, P.T. London: Macmillan Academic and Professional Ltd.

Lindesmith, A.R. (1965) *The Addict and the Law*. Bloomington: Indiana University Press.

Ministry of Health (1926) *Report of the Departmental Committee on Morphine and Heroin Addiction*. (The Rolleston Report). London: HMSO.

Ministry of Health and Department of Health for Scotland (1961) *Drug Addiction. Report of the Interdepartmental Committee*. London: HMSO

Ministry of Health and the Scottish Home and Health Department (1965) *Drug Addiction. The Second Report of the Interdepartmental Committee*. London: HMSO.

Musto, D. (1987) *The American Disease: Origins of Narcotic Control*. New York: Oxford University Press Inc.

Parssinen, T.M. (1985) *Secret Passions, Secret Remedies: Narcotic Drugs in British Society 1820–1930*. Manchester: Manchester University Press.

Pringle, J. (1955) *Heroin: The B.M.A. Case Against the Ban*. London: British Medical Association.

Rathod, N.J. (1972) The use of heroin and methadone by injection in a provincial town. *Alcohol and Drug Dependence*, **2**, pp. 1–21.

Rowntree, J. (1905) *The Imperial Drug Trade*. London: Methuen and Co.

Shapiro, H. (1986) *Waiting for the Man*. London: Quartet.

Spear, H.B. (1969) The growth of heroin addiction in the United Kingdom. *The British Journal of Addiction*, **64**, pp. 245–256.

Spear, H.B. and Glatt, M. (1971) The influence of Canadian addicts on heroin addiction in the United Kingdom. British Journal of Addiction, **66**, pp. 141–149.

Spear, H.B. (1982) British experience in the management of opiate dependence. In *The Dependence Phenomenon*, (eds.) Glatt, M.M. and Marks, J. Lancaster: MTP Press.

Spear, H.B. and Mott, J. (1993) Cocaine and crack within the 'British System': a history of control. In *Cocaine and Crack: Supply and Use*, (ed.) Bean, P.T. London: The Macmillan Press Ltd.

Spear H.B. (1995) Personal communication.

The Lancet (1955) Annotation. 3 December.

Young, J. (1971) *The Drugtakers*. London: Paladin.

CHAPTER 4

Medical Power/Knowledge: The Treatment and Control of Drugs and Drug Users

Rachel Lart

INTRODUCTION

This chapter examines the development of British drugs services between the 1920s and the early 1980s. A key feature of British policy (as opposed to North American policy, for example) is the way that, for much of this period, drugs and drug users have been regarded as essentially a medical problem, and the medical profession has set the terms of debate. The enduring issue of the practice of prescribing to drug users will be discussed in detail.[1] Perhaps because it is the one form of help sought by drug users over which the medical profession has sole control, it is central to the history of the relationship between drug user and doctor. Over the period, different functions have been ascribed to prescribing; that of a medical treatment to stabilise the addict and restore normal function, an explanation for the spread of addiction, and a means of undercutting the illicit drugs market.

The central argument of this chapter is that this history cannot be read as implying a simple dichotomy within British drugs policy between treatment and control. Rather, it will be argued from a Foucauldian position on power that the two cannot be separated. The chapter starts with a description of what is meant by power/knowledge, and of the wider context of medical discourse and practice within which the history of drugs services can be located. The discussion will then explore how medical power/knowledge has constructed drug use and the drug user, why changes in that construction have come about, and how the practices and institutional arrangements around drug users have both reflected and created the changes.

49

Power/Knowledge

This chapter employs a particular conceptualisation of power drawn from the work of Foucault (1974, 1979, 1984). In this analysis, knowledge *is* power, in the sense that the process of the construction of knowledge, through the disciplinary techniques, is the exercise of power. This is in contrast to theories which see knowledge as a commodity certain groups in society hold, and controlled access to which is the basis of their power.

What is meant by the disciplinary techniques is those practices developed over the last two hundred years as the basis of scientific methodology: bringing objects together and observing, measuring, recording and ranking them. Foucault's argument, developed further by writers such as Armstrong (1983) and Rose (1988, 1989) is that these techniques have also been used in relation to people. The public buildings of the eighteenth and nineteenth centuries afforded increasing opportunities for such observation or surveillance: the hospitals, schools, orphanages, asylums, workhouses, factories and housing estates all functioned in this way. In less tangible form the development of uniform systems of recordkeeping, registration of births, deaths and marriages, and the national census, captured the population on paper. These processes are both the exercise of power, and the construction of knowledge. From them emerge 'truths' about the population and about the individual. There are no judgements here as to validity or essential truth of knowledge, indeed the notion of essential, universal truth is irrelevant:

> Each society has its regime of truth, its 'general politics' of truth: that is the types of discourse which it accepts and makes function as true; the mechanisms and instances which enable one to distinguish true and false statements, the means by which each is sanctioned; the techniques and procedures accorded value in the acquisition of truth, the status of those who are charged with saying what counts as true. (Foucault, 1984:73)

In modern societies, a central characteristic of the regime of truth is that it is 'centered on the form of scientific discourse and the institutions which produce it' (Foucault, 1984:73). Those people authorised, within this regime of truth, to speak are those Foucault defines as the *specific intellectual*. He counterpoises this to the role of the *universal intellectual*, 'a universal consciousness, a free subject' (1984:68), which was to speak universal, eternal truths. The specific intellectual, by contrast, has a delimited domain of knowledge, but within that domain produces truths that are accepted and validated. The institutional sites for the production of those truths — the hospital, the laboratory, the 'documentary field' — are also the source of legitimation of the discourse and of authority for the speaker (Foucault, 1974:51).

So we have several things: discourse taken as 'truth' because it conforms to the general regime of truth; a speaker justified and authorised as an expert with the authority to produce that truth and an institutional site from which to produce it; a delimited domain within which that truth operates; and a set of practices which both produce the truth and are its effects.

Medicine, because it encompasses knowledge of bodies both singularly (clinical medicine) and collectively (epidemiology, public health) is central to the development of this disciplinary exercise of power. To talk of control is to talk of the exercise of power, and to talk of treatment is to talk of the exercise of medical power. Drug use and the drug user are objects constructed within medical knowledge. For most of the period under discussion here, they appeared in the discourse as addiction and the addict, and these are the terms employed in this chapter. As will be shown these constructions underwent changes as the interplay between discourse and practice produced shifts and discontinuities. These can be located in the wider context of medical discourse and practice over the period. The key elements of this wider context are now outlined.

MEDICAL DISCOURSE AND PRACTICE

Foucault describes how nineteenth century medicine directed its gaze at the body, employing the techniques of disciplinary power, and how the hospital and the laboratory became the key sites of medical discourse. The physical examination of the body, the careful noting of signs and symptoms, the recording of diagnosis and prognosis, the keeping of records of observations and of the course and outcome of disease and, finally, the dissection after death of the body, became the practice of medicine within hospitals, and the mode of production of medical knowledge (Foucault, 1974, 1976).

This form of medicine, practised on large numbers of people within hospitals, constituted disease in a particular way. Anatamo-physiological knowledge of the body allowed the construction of norms, standards of functioning and organic structure, against which deviations, in the form of disease, could be measured. The source of disease was understood to be directly related to abnormalities of function or structure within the body. This perception of disease as existing within, and coterminous with, the physical body, while familiar to us, has a short history; 'There have been, and will be, other distributions of illness' (Foucault, 1976:3). However, the point for the present argument is the way in which, through specific practices, nineteenth century clinical medicine constructed truths about the body and disease.

Taking Foucault's work as his starting point, Armstrong (1983) traces how medicine developed new ways of looking at illness and disease, in the twentieth century, out of new ways of practice. He describes how

> the medical gaze, which had, for over a century analyzed the microscopic detail of the individual body, began to move to the undifferentiated space between bodies and there proceeded to forge a new political anatomy. (Armstrong, 1983:6)

The challenges to health of the early twentieth century were contagious diseases like tuberculosis (TB) and venereal disease (VD). These were diseases of contact, of relationships between people, not between people and the environment as cholera and typhoid had been. Armstrong takes the *Dispensary* as emblematic of a diffused, open form of surveillance (1983:8). Dispensaries were special institutions for the diagnosis and treatment of TB, not on an in-patient basis like the nineteenth century hospital or the sanatoria, but as ambulatory care. The patient stayed in the community, but the condition was managed by the dispensary. Also undertaken were screening, contact tracing and the observation and monitoring of the course of the disease within the community.

> A single patient with venereal disease was simply a manifestation of a disease which in all probability had already moved on and was manifesting itself elsewhere ... Disease was constituted in the social body and it was the social movement of the disease as it traversed that body, which had to be observed, monitored and interpreted, thereby establishing by its analysis the very existence of that same social space. (Armstrong, 1983:18)

So 'a new way of seeing illness' (1983:6) emerged: no longer enclosed within the body, but existing between bodies; no longer enclosed within the hospital, but visible in the community. In the post war period, the new discipline of social medicine further extended the gaze into the general population. Screening, to identify the potentially ill, became both technically possible and medically desirable. Armstrong traces the growth of the use of the survey to examine whole populations and the discovery that physical signs, hypertension or glycosuria, for example, which had been regarded as abnormal and which were part of the definition of illness were in fact present in large numbers of the 'normal' population (1983:95–97).

In summary, this new discourse of health took as its object states of health and illness that were no longer fixed, and that were manifested in the social body rather than the individual body. The practices were those of preventive medicine; notification and case-finding, and the use of the survey to examine populations.

Psychiatric Medicine

Equally key is the development of the medicine of the mind: psychiatry. Part of the argument is essentially the same; that in the enclosed space of the nineteenth century asylum, knowledge of madness was constructed through the disciplinary techniques. The bodies of the mad were arranged, examined, subjected to normalising judgement. The development of instruments of psychological assessment in the early twentieth century then made possible the surveying of non-hospitalised, general populations, and therefore an extension of the psychiatric gaze out into the wider community (Armstrong, 1983:64–67). However, a key feature of the reconstitution of the psychiatric discourse is the move from a somatic basis for mental pathology to the discovery of psyche as a specific realm.

Both Prior (1993) and Rose (1986, 1988) describe the somatic focus of late nineteenth and early twentieth century psychiatry. This focus on the body was natural in a psychiatry seeking to establish itself within the wider medical profession. To be able to explain madness in somatic terms, linking pathologies of the mind to actual abnormalities of structure and functioning, and to prescribe somatic therapies, changed psychiatrists from merely the keepers of the insane to doctors.

Rose (1986) argues that the re-siting of psychiatry away from the body, and into the mind and social being, began with 'the discovery of a new range of objects of administrative concern and psychiatric attention — the neuroses' (1986:47). These were mental disorders not sufficiently grave to constitute madness, but enough to affect social efficiency and personal happiness — they were a way of conceptualising what was happening in the case of those individuals who failed to conform to normalising judgements:

> The problem of the neuroses emerged outside both asylum and consulting room, in all those sites where individuals could be seen to fail in relation to institutional norms and expectations — the army, the factory, the school and the courts. (1986:48)

In particular, the experience of treating 'shell shocked' soldiers during and after the first world war contributed to the development of a knowledge of 'the existence of unconscious mental processes, elements repressed from consciousness as an attempt to resolve some intractable mental conflict' (1986:49). This, of course, is the basis of Freudian psychoanalytic theory, but in the case of shell shock, the Freudian insistence that repressed elements were specifically to do with sexuality seemed irrelevant. Mental illness was potentially present in most people — the shell shocked soldiers did not have abnormal histories — and was both treatable and preventable. There was not a binary divide between the mad and the sane, but rather a continuum. However, it was not psychiatry that first constructed this new definition of mental illness, but general medicine (which included neurology). Armstrong traces the appearance of the neuroses in the text books of neurology through the 1920s:

> The appearance of the psycho neuroses in medical texts formalised an increasing concern of general medicine with the mind. The mind in all its detail had become important — not the diseased mind of the mad or insane but the ordinary mind of everyone. (1983:22)

Armstrong's argument is that at this time psychiatry was still concerned with the 'great binary division of madness from sanity', while:

> In contrast, the neuroses celebrated the ideal of a disciplined society in which all were analysed and distributed. (1983:22)

The sites for practices concerned with neurosis were not within the asylums, but in general practice and, increasingly from the 1920s, out-patient departments and private or charitable clinics (Rose, 1986:51; Prior, 1993:44). The paradigm of the Dispensary can be applied to these sites from which the extended disciplinary apparatus was concerned with minds, and which began to employ the survey to construct knowledge about how mental illness was distributed among the population. The second world war proved a further stimulus to concern with the mind and the inscribing of a 'neurotic topography of the population' (Rose, 1989:25). In the build up to the war, and the planning for the predicted airborne bombing of civilian populations, the assumption was made that there would be an epidemic of neurosis among civilians under stress. In the event, there was no such reaction, but the state of the population's mind was of concern, not only in terms of anxiety and stress, but also morale — how to maintain and strengthen the civilian's commitment to the war. Surveys, opinion polls, hospital admissions figures, all gave useful information, and further created the psyche as an accessible realm:

> The mental state of the population was beginning to be translated into a calculable form: inscribed, documented, and turned into statistics, graphs, charts, and tables that could be pored over in political deliberations and administrative initiatives. (Rose, 1989:25)

Psychiatry emerged from the war with a unified construct; the difference between the psychoses and the neuroses were seen as quantitative rather than absolute, and both were sited, at least to some degree, in the psyche, the proper object of psychiatric discourse. General medicine, or rather the speciality of neurology, on the other hand, began to withdraw from concern with the mind, rather than the brain. Just as in the 1920s chapters on the neuroses had begun to appear in the neurological texts, so in the 1950s and 1960s they began to disappear (Armstrong, 1983:68), leaving psychiatry in possession of the realm of the psyche. Psychiatry has, of course, never lost its use of somatic explanations and therapies. But within medical discourse, it is the speciality that claims knowledge of and expertise over, and hence the right to speak the truth about, the mind.

To sum up, the argument about medical discourse in the twentieth century is that we have seen the construction of the social body and the psyche as realms within which health and illness exist, alongside the individual body which had been constructed by nineteenth century medical knowledge. This is not to argue that illness had never been seen to exist in these realms before, but to argue that they re-emerged in this period, through specific practices linked to the scientific regime of truth: assessment tools, surveys, statistical analysis. Nor is it to argue that the individual body, and the practices and institutional arrangements associated with it, were replaced in the discourse, but to argue that these realms coexist. In what follows, the ideas outlined above are used to analyse the history of British drugs services between 1920 and the early 1980s.

DISCOURSE AND PRACTICE IN DRUGS SERVICES

The discussion is based on a division of this period into two main parts: first, the period between the 1920s and late 1960s, when the medical concept of 'addiction' was reconstructed from an individualised somatic condition, to a socially infectious psychiatric one, and second, the 1970s, when the definition returned to an individualised one, but still psychiatrised. Finally, brief mention will be made of the early 1980s, when the 'problem drug taker' emerged in the discourse, and new services were developed, working with this figure.

From Somatic Dysfunction to Psychiatric Contagion: Addiction 1920–1970

In the period between the Rolleston report (Departmental Committee on Morphine and Heroin Addiction, 1926) and the second Brain report (Interdepartmental Committee on Drug Addiction, 1967), the definition of addiction changed from an individual dysfunction of the body, to a socially infectious condition of the mind. That this shift took place is well documented. What is offered here is a theoretical explanation of this discontinuity in discourse, based on the following themes. Firstly, the role of surveillance in the construction of the objects of discourse; the Home Office Index was a form of surveillance which helped construct addiction, by the 1960s, as existing in the social body, and as a particular public health issue. Secondly, with the construction of the psyche, addiction was reconstructed in the mind, not the body, of the addict. Post-war psychiatry's claim to speak the truth on the mind, and its claim to the neuroses, meant that psychiatrists became the authorised speakers on addiction. The public health measures of specialist clinics, combined with psychiatry's move into out-patient care, provided a model with which to respond to the perceived 'epidemic' of addiction: the Drug Dependency Clinics. The practice of prescribing for addicts is central to this; the epidemic of the 1960s was perceived to be fuelled by the actions of doctors who were overprescribing heroin and cocaine for addicts. The illicit drugs market at this time in Britain was principally the market in excess prescribed pharmaceutical drugs, not in imported and/or illegally produced drugs. It was surveillance of prescribing which created the Index, psychiatry's definition of the prescribing practices of others as incompetent and dangerous that justified the limiting of the right to prescribe, and the siting of that limited right within the Clinics that gave a concrete expression to the changed discourse.

Smart (1984), also draws on Foucault's work to discuss this period, locating drugs policy in the process of regulation and disciplining of bodies by the application of rational scientific knowledge to human behaviour. However, she takes issue with analyses of drugs policy that define the Brain Report and the ensuing changes as representing a significant shift, saying that 'the conceptualisation of the addict as a sick person and threat to public health which emerged coterminously with the construction of addiction as a social problem in the nineteenth century remained the unshaken epistemological basis of policy in the 1960s'. Rather than as a break with existing policy, she sees the Clinics as the rationalisation of such policy, made possible by developments and applications of scientific knowledge. For example the introduction of methadone as a substitute for heroin, and the development of techniques of biochemical screening such as urine testing, made new forms of surveillance and control of the drug user possible.

While in most respects agreeing with Smart's argument, my main point of divergence is from the implication that there had been no change in the way addiction was perceived as a disease and a threat to public health, or indeed in the conceptualisation of public health itself. The nineteenth century sources she quotes define the addict as becoming a 'worse than useless member of society'. In this formulation the addict is a 'problem' because they are a waste of resources, an individual unhealthy member of the social body, unable to play their role in an increasingly organised society. Here I argue that in the 1960s the addict was seen as a single manifestation of contagion, and hence of a 'menace to the community' (Interdepartmental Committee on Addiction, 1965: para 18), and that this is a re-conceptualisation of public health itself, and of drug use as a public health issue.

Addiction as individualised pathology

The career of drug use during the nineteenth century from a habit to an addiction — a pathology of the soul and will — and then to a somatic entity in medical discourse, has been traced elsewhere (Harding, 1988). This analysis begins in the 1920s, by which time addiction was accepted as a disease entity by the British medical profession (Berridge, 1978, 1980, 1984; Parssinen & Kerner, 1980; Harding, 1988). Although the condition could not be linked to a specific lesion in the body, it was classed as one of the neuroses and seen as an area of legitimate concern for the profession; the major medical texts of the time included a chapter on the subject. At this time the authorised speakers on the neuroses were neurologists, physicians and general practitioners, and it was they who treated addiction.

For those addicts the medical profession was likely to see and treat, the disease model and classification as a neurosis fitted the epidemiological evidence. Most were either doctors or other professionals with access to drugs (the 'professional' addicts) or else had become addicted in the course of treatment (the 'therapeutic' addicts). In all, addiction represented a 'very minor problem indeed, a middle-class phenomenon confined to a large extent to the medical profession itself' (Berridge, 1984). Working-class use, of laudanum for example, was a matter for control via the restriction of sales, and was not seen as a medical issue (Berridge, 1978). The disease was an individualised pathology; some people (principally women and physicians) were believed to have a predisposition, and the stresses of modern civilisation were regarded as a trigger for these sensitive individuals (Parssinen & Kerner, 1980).

Outside Britain, most notably in North America, different views obtained. International conventions were agreed in the pre-war years to outlaw narcotic drugs, and there was pressure on Britain to conform. In the 1920s it was partly this pressure and the Home Office's wish to conform that put drug use and its control on the agenda. In the immediate post-war period, the extension of the wartime controls imposed on the military to the civilian population, the passing of the 1920 Dangerous Drugs Act and the attitude of the Home Office seemed likely to criminalise the field. Use of narcotics without medical validation was proscribed and the question became one of the delineation of acceptable medical practice. Berridge argues:

> The disease concept of addiction and all that it entailed was under serious attack. A prohibitionist policy, under which the state would decide treatment and where both doctors and addicts could incur penalties, was, as in America at the same time, in the process of establishment. (Berridge, 1978:369)

At stake was the right of the medical profession to autonomy in defining addiction as a disease and in the choice of treatment; was the prescription of drugs for known addicts a reasonable course of action and therapy? This issue was complicated by the question of professional addicts prescribing for themselves. The Rolleston Committee was set up in 1924 with a brief to advise the Home Office on the matter. Its role was to clarify medical opinion about the place of maintenance prescribing in the treatment of addiction. The Committee was entirely composed of medical men, mostly experts in the field of addiction, and the Report, in 1926, reflected foregoing medical opinion. It confirmed the status of addiction as a disease and the addict as sick, and asserted the right of the medical practitioner to use professional discretion in the choice of treatment in this, as in other illnesses.

While the Report advised that the treatment of choice in addiction was gradual withdrawal of the drug of dependence within an institution, reflecting a concern with treatment and cure, and the separation of the normal and the abnormal, there was also the recognition that this might not be possible for all addicts and so the use of maintenance prescribing was a legitimate course of action. The report used case studies of 'stable addicts' to show how maintenance allowed some individuals to lead 'normal' lives even though engaged in an 'abnormal' activity. As Harding argues, in the Rolleston report:

> The addicted state was considered basically as life under abnormal conditions, whereby the toxic action of the opiate produced changes in the conditions of normal physiological functioning. (Harding, 1988:80)

Treatment by maintenance prescribing accepted these physiological changes and sought to compensate for them by the introduction of the substance of the opiate into the addict's body. A similar model underlay the treatment of diabetes, just made possible by the discovery in 1923 of insulin (Bliss, 1982); the introduction of externally produced insulin returned the body of the diabetic to normal functioning.

The Committee rejected the idea of notification of addicts to the Home Office when the British Medical Association opposed it, on the grounds that it would damage the confidentiality of the doctor/patient relationship. The Report also recommended tribunals to deal with cases of over-prescribing, for self or others. This instituted a means of control, but kept its immediate operation in the hands of the medical profession, a situation that was acceptable to both the Home Office and the profession. In fact these tribunals were never used, and were officially abandoned in 1953 (Trebach, 1982).

Rolleston represented the medical concept of addiction, as it stood in the 1920s. The report looked back to the nineteenth century: the division of illness and health and the enclosure of the sick in institutions for treatment. It protected the privacy of the doctor/patient relationship and the professional right to clinical freedom within that relationship, subject only to the scrutiny of peers. It established what became known as the 'British System' of treatment of addiction, in the tradition of what Strong (1979) has called, in another context, 'bourgeois medicine': individualised and private.

However, it can also be seen as beginning a blurring of the line between the normal and abnormal; the concept of the maintained addict carries in it an idea that health and disease are not so easily distinguishable, and that what was termed 'ambulatory' care might be a means of what would now be termed management of a condition in the community.

Constructing an epidemic

So how, by the 1960s, had the perception of addiction changed from that of the Rolleston era, an individualised pathology, to the idea of a socially infectious condition, as manifested in the Brain Report? Over the period, the addict and addiction had been made visible by a form of surveillance, the expression of the overall Home Office control left intact in the 1920s. From the 1930s the Home Office Index, a working list of all addicts receiving prescriptions, was compiled by the Home Office Drugs Branch from police reports of the routine surveillance of pharmacists' records, from the Home Office's own inspection of these records and from information supplied by doctors, especially police surgeons. Also available from this scrutiny were doctors' patterns of prescribing, as an account of the period by Spear shows dramatically (Spear, 1994:10–12). At a time when even the black market was the overspill from prescriptions, this technique gave a picture of the course of the 'disease' of drug use through the social body. Knowledge of drug use was there in the observable facts of the prescription and dispensing of dangerous drugs. It was not so much the individual addict who was being observed (in spite of popular belief in the status of a 'registered addict') as the pattern of disease; the treatment of the addict was, as already discussed, a matter for the individual doctor.

A study by one of the Drugs Branch Inspectors demonstrates this (Spear, 1969). A young man, 'Mark', was arrested in September 1951 for theft from a hospital pharmacy in May of that year. Spear identified the links between 'Mark' and most of the new cases of 'non-therapeutic' addicts 'coming to notice' over the next four years. The story is told in terms of an infective agent arriving in ideal conditions for the spread of contagion. A major raid on a London nightclub the previous year, and preceding seizures of imports, had led to a scarcity of cannabis in London. The arrival of 'Mark' during this shortage, Spear argued, was the advent of heroin on the London scene, and the beginning of what one psychiatrist described as the 'case-to-case' spread of opiate addiction (Bewley, 1965a).

The report of the first Brain Committee (Interdepartmental Committee on Drug Addiction, 1961), briefed in 1958 to review the Rolleston Committee's advice, did not reflect this changing picture. The Committee saw no reason to change the framework set by Rolleston; while institutionalised treatment was the ideal, the numbers of addicts were not sufficient to warrant the establishment of special institutions, registration would serve no useful purpose and, in contradiction to Rolleston and perhaps most importantly, the Committee saw no need for tribunals to investigate or discipline individual doctors' prescribing practices. The Committee had convened and taken evidence before the Home Office figures for 1961 were available, and before there was an awareness, beyond those immediately responsible for the collection of the figures, of the changes which had started to take place.

By the time the report was published, awareness of the changing pattern of drug use was more widespread. Between 1959 and 1964, the number of addicts on the Index rose from 454 to 753. Most of this rise was accounted for by heroin addicts of non-therapeutic origin, that is they had not become addicted in the course of medical treatment. There was also a significant change in the age distribution. In 1959, nearly 90% of known addicts were older than 35. By 1964, this had fallen to just over half with the majority of the younger people using heroin. The Index charted the progress of addiction from a disease of rather sad middle-aged or elderly individuals, who had become addicted in the course of therapy or because of professional access to the drug, to a contagious condition of the young (Bewley, 1965b; Glatt, 1965; BMJ, 1967; James, 1971). The emergence of these young 'recreational' or 'non-therapeutic' addicts posed once again questions about the medical justification for prescribing. Was it right to prescribe for these young addicts in the same way as for the older 'stable' addict?

Responding to the epidemic: the second Brain Report

The Brain Committee was re-convened in 1964 to review their earlier advice 'in relation to the prescribing of addictive drugs'. The issue centred around a few doctors, mainly in London, who were regarded by their peers as being responsible for the supplies of prescribed drugs which constituted the black market at that time. The second Brain report stated that 'not more than six' doctors were responsible for the excessive prescribing and that 'they had acted within the law and according to their professional judgement'. The problem was constructed by psychiatrist witnesses to the Brain Committee as one of general practitioners, on the whole either ignorant or gullible, who were prescribing excessively and thereby creating networks of addicts. One psychiatrist concluded that 'if potential addicts had less contact with addicts and less ease of access to narcotics there would be less addiction' (Bewley, 1965a). In rejecting the idea of tribunals in 1961, the Committee had rejected the means of opening that prescribing practice to professional scrutiny. In its second report the Committee 'side-stepped' the issue by making the treatment of addiction a matter for specialist psychiatrists and removing the general practitioner's right to prescribe (Fazey, 1979).

The Committee's main recommendations were: the notification of addicts, the establishment of 'special treatment centres' with powers of compulsory detention, and the restriction of the prescribing of heroin and cocaine for addicts to the staff of the treatment centres. An advisory committee to 'keep under review the whole problem of drug addiction' was also recommended. The report constructed addiction as firstly a psychiatric entity, on which psychiatrists were the authorised speakers, and secondly as contagious, and therefore a public health issue. The word 'notification' was used deliberately to reflect the belief that addiction was a 'socially infectious condition'. The special treatment centres (whose establishment was now justified by numbers) were to have 'facilities for medical treatment, including laboratory investigation and provision for research'. It was suggested that 'the centre might form a part of a psychiatric hospital or of the psychiatric wing of a general hospital'. Although the report did not give details of how these centres were to be run, the Brain Committee's view contained elements of the binary divide, separating the ill addict who was to be institutionalised, compulsorily if necessary, for treatment, from the rest of the community to whom the disease could 'become a menace'. In fact, compulsion was not really taken up as an issue and when the treatment centres opened, out-patient or 'ambulatory' care was the dominant mode of delivery.

The Drug Dependency Clinics

The way that the Clinics eventually emerged was the result of debate within the medical profession. The Home Office had no wish to impose 'a massive treatment organisation' (BJA, 1988) or even to see addiction become the sole concern of psychiatrists (Trebach, 1982). Their worry had been the excessive prescribing, but Spear reports that a return to the Rolleston tribunals would have been a way of dealing with this (BJA, 1988). It was from the medical profession's new construction of the disease of addiction that the public health measures of specialist Clinics, notification and controlled prescribing emerged.

Four linked articles in the British Medical Journal in May 1967 by three psychiatrists, Thomas Bewley, Philip Connell and John Owens, and one general practitioner, Peter Chapple, all of whom were involved and influential in the field, dealt with options for policy following the third reading of the Dangerous Drugs Bill in the House of Commons. What the writers reveal are different ways of seeing disease and of responding to it.

The first, by Bewley and closest to the Brain Report in ideas, presented a model of centralisation and fairly overt control, focussed on the body of the individual addict. There should be a small number of units, in close contact to standardise treatment and practice. The notification system and exchange of information between Clinics would keep the addict visible to the Clinics (Bewley, 1967).

Between this and the view of the second psychiatrist, Connell, the emphasis shifted from the monitoring of the individual addict's body to a wider consideration of the 'field of drug dependency'. This presented a range of services as being necessary, talking about a 'therapeutic spectrum' and the necessity of developing a 'team approach'. The Clinics should be distributed between a large number of hospitals to 'spread the load', with addicts making fortnightly maintenance visits. The mechanisms of control, while still there in the standardisation of records, procedures for transfer between Clinics and uniform maintenance schemes, were lighter and more subtle; the case for compulsory treatment had 'not been made', and research into new techniques of more 'objective' monitoring (urine testing for example) and other biochemical measures of drug use were necessary (Connell, 1967).

In Owens' article can be seen most clearly the dual therapeutic and controlling roles of the treatment centres. He outlined a model of a centre, the role of which was both to treat clinically the individual addict, and to contain the number of established addicts in an area, an issue of 'community mental health'. While displaying 'maximum concern which one has clinically for the individual addict', the centre should also be fairly rigidly structured, as 'it is imperative for the successful containment of the heroin-addiction problem that there should be a maximum control of the amount of heroin available on prescription'. There was a need for a tight system of registration of addicts, for identification cards to stop addicts using more than one centre, for the allocation of addicts to specific pharmacists, and the creation in each area of a 'drug squad which would see its job in terms which one would call therapeutic, to identify cases of drug-takers and to prevent drug abuse' (Owens, 1967).

The gap between the perception of the specialists and that of Chapple, the general practitioner, reflects that between the perceptions of 'hospital medicine' and 'biographical medicine' (Armstrong, 1979). Focusing on the individual addict as a social being, Chapple started from the premise that institutionalised treatment was bound to fail because addiction was a disease which had to be dealt with in the world where the addict lived, and with the addict's cooperation. The appropriate site for treatment was 'in the community', by experienced practitioners who could provide a continuity of care and a 'human and friendly therapeutic atmosphere'. Monitoring by techniques like urine testing would be used, but the emphasis was on the patient as a person and the surrounding social networks. (Chapple, 1967).

From Social Control to Therapeutic Challenge:
The Clinics in the 1970s

When first set up, the focus of the Clinics, and the attention of those who both worked in and used them, was on the practice of prescribing due to the need to control the supply of drugs into the illicit market. Over the following decade, the aims ascribed to this practice changed as the sense of an epidemic passed and the Clinics' role in controlling that epidemic became less important. The gaze of the psychiatrists running them shifted from the wider scene, the social body in which the course of the epidemic had been traced by the Index and Home Office surveillance, to their own practices, and to the people who presented to the Clinics. By the end of the 1970s, the discourse had changed again, and addiction was contained within the mind of the individual addict in whom the disease manifested itself. The practice of prescribing remained central to the discourse. The scrutiny of prescribing practices produced 'truths' about how the Clinics should operate, and from the scrutiny emerged changed prescribing practices, reflecting the changing construction of the disease.

Controlling the epidemic

The first task of the Clinics was to control the epidemic of heroin use by taking over responsibility for those addicts who had been receiving prescriptions from the NHS and private general practitioners, and to end the excessive prescribing, while still offering enough to keep the individual addict away from acquisitive crime and to 'undercut the black market'. The illicit market was not yet consolidated and in the hands of organised crime, and a major concern was to prevent demand from enabling this to happen (Connell, 1969), but against this was the concern that the Clinics should not become 'merely prescribing centres' (Owens, 1967). Because of the comparative inexperience of many of the Clinic staff, regular meetings between those responsible for running the Clinics were established in the first year of operation, and have continued ever since. The majority of the Clinics when first established were in London, and so these meetings have always largely involved the consultant psychiatrists and others running the London Clinics. The dominance of the London based specialists has been central to the development of treatment policies and services ever since.

Stimson and Oppenheimer (1982) give a picture of how the relationship between Clinic staff and addicts in the early days was often one of conflict and confusion in which the usual norms of medical encounters could not be adhered to. The staff were unusually explicit about their role in controlling a social problem and there were coercive measures (contracts, negotiations and sanctions) used which would not be considered ethical in other medical settings. These were justified by staff as being 'reasonable' because of the nature of the patients. Addicts were seen as being disenfranchised in some way. They did not want to get better, did not seek help or cooperate with treatment and behaved as if absolved from their social obligations. They did not, in short, understand the sick role and the obligations it placed on them and so confounded staff's expectations of patient behaviour. This was explained in terms of psychopathology by the staff. The staff themselves were monitored, but this was not perceived as a threat to clinical freedom, reflecting the perception of the Clinics' role in controlling an infectious condition.

Establishing norms

After the first year or so, the Clinics settled down; staff were more experienced, the group of existing addicts were absorbed into the caseloads, and the panic about the epidemic began to pass. The balance of tasks of the Clinics changed from controlling the epidemic to treating the individual, and practices within the Clinics began to change. The regular meetings between the doctors running the Clinics established an informal code of practice for Clinic operation, and began to construct norms for treatment policies (Connell & Strang, 1994; Mitcheson, 1994; Connell, 1991; BJA, 1988).

The operation of this code and the construction of norms can be analysed in terms of Foucault's analysis of the workings of power. Practices were agreed between the Clinics which identified the individual addicts, and located them within the treatment population. That population was arranged to be visible to and manageable by the Clinics. There was close communication between the Clinics, and the Home Office Index was available for consultation about an individual's identity. Individual clients were required to come into the Clinic on a weekly or fortnightly basis for examination, interview and urinalysis. Although in the early days the practice in some Clinics was to dispense drugs directly and to provide 'fixing rooms' (Stimson, 1973), a technique was employed to shift the physical act of drug consumption out of the Clinics, while maintaining control over that act. Prescriptions would be posted to a given pharmacist, for daily dispensing, so that the individual would have to present at that place each day. The total population was dispersed over a number of pharmacists, to prevent addicts congregating in chemists' shops (Connell & Strang, 1994). As well as these operational practices, the meetings began to scrutinise prescribing practices. In Mitcheson's recent description of this can be seen the operation of an 'intentional and nonsubjective power' (Foucault, 1981:94):

> Statistical information was provided at these meetings, regarding the number of patients receiving prescriptions at each clinic and the total quantity of heroin and methadone prescribed from each clinic. Even prior to the advent of cheap pocket calculators it was relatively easy for doctors attending these meetings to calculate a mean dose of opioids per patient for each clinic. (Mitcheson, 1994:178)

The effect of this information was to lower the average dose of heroin prescribed across the Clinics, not by any edict from a subjective power, central government for example, but by each doctor adjusting the basis on which s/he calculated the rationality of each decision. Knowledge of colleagues' prescribing practices was not the only factor in the rational calculations individual practitioners had to make. Within the medical, and particularly the psychiatric, discourse around drug use was the view that prescribing, and in particular prescribing of injectable heroin, was not an appropriate task, but was one that had been undertaken by the Clinics in the face of the epidemic, and in fear of worse social consequences if individuals were not kept out of the illicit drugs market.

Changing the task of the Clinic

The control over prescribing that the Clinics had did control the flow of pharmaceutical heroin and cocaine that had been the responsibility of the medical profession. What it did not do was to prevent the growth of the illicit market in non-pharmaceutical drugs (Power, 1994:34), and this wider goal was abandoned as the Clinics became inward looking and focussed on their own practices (Strang & Gossop, 1994:346). The reception given to a piece of research carried out at one of the London Clinics, and first presented to staff of other Clinics in 1976, demonstrates the changed priorities in decision making about prescribing practices.

This research was a random controlled study comparing the outcome of prescribing patients injectable heroin with that of refusing heroin and offering oral methadone. Patients were followed up by a social researcher, away from the Clinic. What the study showed was that on many variables there were very different outcomes from the two treatments. Patients prescribed heroin attended the Clinic more regularly and showed some reduction in their criminal activities. On other variables, such as accommodation, employment or diet, they showed no change following treatment. Patients refused heroin and offered oral methadone instead, polarised into a majority who continued to inject illegal drugs and only used the Clinic for specific services, and a sizeable minority who either stabilised on oral methadone (one-fifth), or stopped all drug use (one-fifth) (Hartnoll et al., 1980; Mitcheson, 1994).

These findings, employing scientific means of establishing the truth, confirmed the parameters of decision making about prescribing that had been intuitively but explicitly drawn since the start of the Clinics. To prescribe heroin would stabilise and keep addicts in contact, but not change them, while to refuse heroin would be more challenging, and potentially more therapeutic, to the individual, but risked adverse social consequences and loss of contact with the addict. The authors of the study have always claimed that the findings were presented neutrally, and were not intended to indicate that

> one treatment was superior to the other. Nevertheless, [the] research was perceived by many staff in London clinics as clear evidence for replacing injectable heroin maintenance with oral prescribing. (Mitcheson, 1994:183)

Following this, in the mid to late 1970s the earlier downward pressure on average doses of heroin was joined by a shift right away from heroin and injectable methadone to oral methadone, with most London Clinics refusing to prescribe injectable drugs to new clients. Again, this has to be seen not as a decision made by some central holder of power, but as the exercise of a locally rational power, that of the London psychiatrists, with the effect of changed local practices. What had altered was the relative weight given to the Clinics' tasks. Epidemic and contagion had disappeared from the discourse, as the psychiatrists had focused their gaze on what was happening within the Clinics and to their own patients. Challenging those patients therapeutically, and perhaps changing some of them, controlling their drug use in order to 'cure' them of the disease of addiction, was more important than trying to control society's drug use.

The practices for this therapeutic intervention were prescribing to help with withdrawal symptoms (detoxification) and those of more normal psychiatry and psychology (counselling, psychotherapy and groupwork). Smart, reporting on a national survey of Clinics carried out in 1982, provides evidence of this reorientation of policy. Of the Clinics surveyed 90% described individual psychotherapy as 'important' or 'very important', and 87% gave help with withdrawal this importance. Conversely, 84% saw maintenance on injectable methadone as 'not important' or 'not [Clinic] policy', and 97% saw heroin maintenance in this light (Smart, 1985). By the end of the 1970s, the Clinics were principally services for the individual addict's mind; essentially geared towards the control of individual drug use through detoxification. The medical help offered was structured in this particular direction, and away from maintenance prescribing.

In the early 1980s, there was another reconstruction of the discourse about drugs use, and a corresponding shift in the sites of practice. There was again a panic about an 'epidemic' of drug use, but this time the term did not imply contagion. The new epidemic was not visible to the narrowed gaze of the psychiatrists in the Clinics, and the explanation of addiction in terms of individual psychopathology conflicted with the epidemiological evidence. New speakers began to emerge, with a new discourse on drug use. 'Addiction' did not feature in the new discourse, instead the problem was 'drug misuse' or 'problem drug taking', and its outcome 'harm'. 'Harm' was conceptualised as not just psychological and physical, but also social, legal and financial (ACMD, 1982). As in the case of illnesses such as coronary heart disease, the means of prevention of that harm was located in the behaviour and choices of the individual, and was amenable to education and advice.

This new, diffused epidemic needed new institutional arrangements. A nationwide structure of services began to be built, employing the reconstructed concept of 'problem drug taking' and staffed by a wider range of people: nurses, social workers, probation officers, and generic 'drugs workers' (MacGregor *et al.*, 1991). The new services provided sites throughout the country from which these groups began to speak their own discourse on drug use (Stimson & Lart, 1991), away from London and away from the specialist Clinics.

CONCLUSION

Looking at British drugs policy through the lens of an analysis of medical power/ knowledge moves the debate on from a dichotomy between treatment and control. The techniques and practices of treatment are also those which control the drug user and those which make the drug user known. Knowledge constructed through those practices creates the object of the drug user within medical discourse, and in turn informs the institutional arrangements and practices that are the response to drug use and the drug user. From the changing institutional arrangements of the early 1980s, and nearly a decade of concern over the transmission of HIV among injecting drug users, has emerged the discourse of harm mimisation within British, or at least English, drugs policy (Chapter 11, Stimson & Lart, 1991). However, the same tensions continue, in particular over the role, legitimacy and acceptable extent of substitute prescribing, in debates both within the medical profession and between the profession and those other groups who in the 1990s also have authority to speak on drug use.

NOTE

1. It is perhaps worth outlining the history of the legal position in Britain with regard to prescribing. Any medical practitioner may prescribe heroin (diamorphine hydrochloride) to any patient, in the treatment of organic disease. It is a mainstay of the medical control of pain, in particular but not exclusively, in the treatment of terminal illness. Prior to the legislative and policy changes following the second Brain report in the 1960s (Interdepartmental Committee on Drug Addiction, 1965), any medical practitioner could also prescribe heroin (and cocaine) for the treatment of addiction. This practice reflected what has been known as the 'British System' of drugs policy, based on the premise that addiction is a disease and therefore its treatment is the remit of the medical profession. In brief, following the Brain report the right to prescribe heroin and cocaine for the treatment of addiction was restricted to medical practitioners holding a licence from the Home Office — principally those consultant psychiatrists working in the specialist Drug Dependency Clinics.

REFERENCES

ACMD (1982) *Treatment and Rehabilitation: Report of the Advisory Council on the Misuse of Drugs*, London: HMSO.

Armstrong, D. (1979) 'The emancipation of biographical medicine' *Social Science and Medicine*, **13a**, 1–8.

Armstrong, D. (1983) *Political Anatomy of the Body: Medical Knowledge in Britain in the Twentieth Century*, Cambridge: Cambridge University Press.

Berridge, V. (1978) 'Professionalisation and narcotics' *Psychological Medicine*, **8**, 361–372.

Berridge, V. (1980) 'The making of the Rolleston Report 1908–1926', *Journal of Drug Issues*, Winter.

Berridge, V. (1984) 'Drugs and Social Policy: the establishment of drug control in Britain 1900–1930', *British Journal of Addiction*, **79**, 17–29.

Bewlay, T. (1965a) 'Heroin and cocaine addiction', *The Lancet*, **ii**, 808.

Bewlay, T. (1965b) 'Heroin addiction in the UK' *British Medical Journal*, **2**, 1284–1286.

Bewlay, T. (1967) 'Centres of Treatment for Drug Addiction: Advantages of Special Centres' *British Medical Journal*, **2**, 498–499.

BJA (1988) 'Conversation with H.B. Spear' *British Journal of Addiction*, **83**, 473–482.

Bliss, M. (1982) *The discovery of insulin*, Chicago: University of Chicago Press.

BMJ (1967) 'Drug Treatment Centres' (Leader) *British Medical Journal*, **2**, 455–456.

Chapple, P.A.L. (1967) 'Centres of Treatment for Drug Addiction: Treatment in the Community' *British Medical Journal*, **2**, 500–501.

Connell, P. (1967) 'Centres of Treatment for Drug Addiction: Importance of research' *British Medical Journal*, **2**, 499–500.

Connell, P. (1969) 'Drug Dependence in Great Britain: a challenge to the practice of medicine', in Steinberg, H (ed.) *Scientific basis of drug dependence*, London: Churchill Livingstone.

Connell, P. (1991) 'Treatment of drug dependent patients 1968–69', *British Journal of Addiction*, **86**, 913–990.

Connell, P. and Strang, J. (1994) 'The creation of the clinics: clinical demand and the formation of policy', in Strang, J. and Gossop, M. (eds.) *Heroin Addiction and Drug Policy: The British System*, Oxford: Oxford University Press.

Departmental Committee on Morphine and Heroin Addiction (1926) *Report*, London: HMSO.

Fazey, C. (1979) 'In the heroin trap *Guardian,* 30 October.

Foucault, M. (1974) *The Archeology of Knowledge*, London: Tavistock.

Foucault, M. (1976) *The Birth of the Clinic: An Archeology of Medical Perception*, London: Tavistock.

Foucault, M. (1981) *The History of Sexuality: An Introduction*, Harmondsworth: Penguin.

Foucault, M. (1984) 'Truth and Power', in Rabinow, P. (1984) *The Foucault Reader*, London: Penguin.

Glatt, M. (1965) 'Reflections on heroin and cocaine addiction' *British Medical Journal* **2**, 171.

Harding, G. (1988) *Opiate Addiction, Morality and Medicine: From moral illness to pathological disease*, London : MacMillan.

Hartnoll, R.L., Mitcheson, M. Battersby, A., Brown, B., Ellis, M., Fleming, P. and Hedley, N. (1980) 'Evaluation of heroin maintenance in controlled trial' *Archives of General Psychiatry*, **37**, 877–884.

Interdepartmental Committee on Drug Addiction (1961) *Report*, London: HMSO.

Interdepartmental Committee on Drug Addiction (1965) *Report*, London: HMSO.

James, I.P. (1971) 'The London heroin epidemic of the 1960s', *Medical-Legal Journal,* **31**.

Lart, R.A. (1992) 'British medical perception from Rolleston to Brain: Changing images of the addict and addiction', *International Journal on Drug Policy*, **3**, 118–125.

MacGregor, S., Ettorre, B., Coomber, R., Crosier, A. and Lodge, H. (1991) *Drugs Services in England and the Impact of the Central Funding Initiative*, ISDD Research Monograph One, London: Institute for the Study of Drug Dependence.

Mitcheson, M. (1994) 'Drug clinics in the 1970s', in Strang, J. and Gossop, M. (eds.) *Heroin Addiction and Drug Policy: The British System*, Oxford: Oxford University Press.

Owens, J. (1967) 'Centres for Treatment of Drug Addiction: Integrated Approach' British Medical Journal, **2**, 501–502.

Parssinen, T. and Kerner, K. (1980) 'Development of the disease model of drug addiction in Britain 1870–1926', *Medical History*, **24**, 275–296.

Power, R. (1994) 'Drug Trends since 1968', in Strang, J. and Gossop, M. (eds.) *Heroin Addiction and Drug Policy: The British System*, Oxford: Oxford University Press.

Prior, L. (1993) *The Social Organisation of Mental Illness*, London: Sage.

Rose, N. (1986) 'Psychiatry: the discipline of mental health', in Miller, P. and Rose, N. *The Power of Psychiatry*, Cambridge: Polity.

Rose, N. (1988) 'Calculable minds and manageable individuals', *History of the Human Sciences,* **1,** 179–200.

Rose, N. (1989) *Governing the soul: The shaping of the private self*, London: Routledge.

Smart, C. (1984) 'Social policy and drug addiction' *British Journal of Addiction*, **79**, 31–39.

Smart, C. (1985) 'Drug Dependence Units in England and Wales: the results of a national survey' *Drug and Alcohol Dependence*, **15**, 131–144.

Spear, H.B. (1969) 'The growth of heroin addiction in the UK, *British Journal of Addiction,* **64**, 245–255.

Spear, H.B. (1994) 'The early years of the 'British System' in practice' in Strang, J. and Gossop, M. (eds.) *Heroin Addiction and Drug Policy: The British System*, Oxford: Oxford University Press.

Stimson, G.V. (1973) *Heroin and Behaviour; diversity among addicts attending London clinics*, Shannon: Irish University Press.

Stimson, G.V. and Lart, R.A. (1991) 'HIV, Drugs, and Public Health in England: New Words, Old Tunes' *International Journal of the Addictions*, **26**, 1263–1277.

Stimson, G.V. and Lart, R.A. (1994) 'The relationship between the state and local practice in the development of national policy on drugs between 1920 and 1990' in Strang, J. and Gossop, M. (eds.) *Heroin Addiction and Drug Policy: The British System*, Oxford: Oxford University Press.

Stimson, G.V. and Oppenheimer, E. (1982) *Heroin Addiction: Treatment and Control in Britain*, London: Tavistock.

Strang, J. and Gossop, M. (1994) 'The British System: visionary anticipation or masterly inactivity?' in Strang, J. and Gossop, M. (eds.) *Heroin Addiction and Drug Policy: The British System*, Oxford: Oxford University Press.

Strong, P. (1979) *The Ceremonial Order of the Clinic,* London: Routledge and Kegan Paul.

Trebach, A. (1982) *The Heroin Solution*, New Haven CT: Yale University Press.

CHAPTER 5

The Agony and the Ecstasy: Drugs, Media and Morality

Karim Murji

Human life is bounded by two chasms: fanaticism on one side, absolute scepticism on the other.

Milan Kundera

This chapter is about the media and drugs[1]. Its inclusion in a book about the control of drugs and drug users presumes that there is a link between these things and the media. But what is that link? The dominant, conventional approach has seen the media as a key force in the demonisation and marginalisation of drug users, as presenting lurid, hysterical images and as a provider of an un-critical platform from which politicians and other moral entrepreneurs are able to launch and wage drug 'wars'[2]. The media is thus seen to comprehensively *mis*-represent drugs, their effects, typical users and sellers and indeed the whole nature of the drug market and the enforcement response to it. In many ways the media may even define what we 'see' as drugs because it concentrates on solvents, heroin, crack, ecstasy, etc. In contrast, alcohol and tobacco are rarely spoken of as drugs, thereby conditioning public attitudes about the 'drug problem' and what the response to it should be. Furthermore, media coverage is not just misleading it can also actually be harmful because it is implicated in the triggering of drug scares and moral panics which lead to 'knee-jerk' drug crackdowns and punitive responses.

Followers of this broad line of argument see their task as being to 'debunk' media misrepresentations, sometimes by recourse to the proposition that media reaction constitutes a moral panic, and to insert in their place a 'true' picture of drugs. This type of approach has been commonly employed in various radical or critical approaches to deviance and the mass media. In terms of media studies it fits within the continuum of 'effects' theories (related terms are the 'mass market' or hypodermic models). Generally, these concentrate on the production and

deployment of media messages and, it is assumed, that these have real consequences or effects. Because of its 'media-centricity', the role of the audience is
often left largely unexamined. In contrast an alternative approach in media studies has stressed the ability of audiences to filter, interpret, de-construct and even
re-construct media messages into something that can be very different from any
intention that the producers may have had (Morley, 1995). This is the 'laissez
faire' or commercial model — it has been much less prominent with regard to
drugs. It has however been used implicitly in studies of drug prevention (for a
review see Dorn & Murji, 1992) which suggest that prevention messages and
campaigns are resisted by the audience, or may even increase audience interest
in experimenting with the very drugs that they are being warned about and
against. Both models are problematic in various ways, not least in over-stating
the power of either the media or of individual consumers. Further exploration of
the ways in which media messages about drugs are interpreted by all kinds of
different people would be of interest.

However, my primary aim in this chapter is to take issue with the conventional
and familiar debunking approach. I do not seek to simply adopt an empiricist view
that media 'effects' are difficult to demonstrate, though this is a criticism that such
approaches can be weak at dealing with. Rather I will argue that the debunking
method is itself problematic and that the moral panics argument in particular has
become virtually discredited through over and misuse. While I will be critical of
the debunking perspective it is important to state that in, broad terms, I do not de-
mur from the view that media representations are problematic and that they may
be implicated in 'panicky' responses from officialdom. For example Reinarman
and Levine (1989), Bean (1993) and Reeves and Campbell (1994) have all
deconstructed the media scare or panic about crack in recent years. I have also
argued along similar lines, though focusing more on the racialisation of media and
law enforcement discourse in the linkage between crack and 'yardies' (Murji,
1995). But while I instinctively share much of the distaste for the exaggerated form
and context-less content of some media coverage of drugs, I do not want to simply
engage in another 'rubbishing' of media reaction. Instead, I aim to question and
take issue with the counter-reaction to media reaction in an attempt at what
Giddens (1987) called the 'disruptive evaluation' of the familiar. My argument is
mostly based around examples of reaction and counter-reaction in the media to the
case of Leah Betts, a teenager whose death in November 1995 was commonly
linked to an ecstasy tablet that she had taken. I will go on to discuss a series of
problems with the ways in which the term moral panic has come to be used. Before
that I will argue that one of the problems with the counter-reaction is the way that
it 'mirrors' certain features of the very view that it opposes.

SORTED AND DISTORTED?

In December 1995 a number of large advertising billboards were filled with a
photograph of a young woman against a black background. A single word:

'SORTED' appeared in large letters next to the photograph; below it were the words: 'Just one ecstasy tablet took Leah Betts.' The death of Leah Betts received prolonged media coverage, from the time it occurred, through to her burial as well as over two months later when an inquest returned a verdict of accidental death. During the most intense phase of media attention *The Sun* gave over its front page to the story. Underneath a bold headline: 'Leah took ecstasy on her 18th Birthday' was an almost full page photograph of her lying on a hospital bed with a respirator on her face. Below it was an earlier, smaller picture of her smiling, next to which were the words: 'Don't become another Leah'. In the following two months a couple of other cases kept the subject of young people and ecstasy in the headlines. In January 1996 Helen Cousins fell into a coma after taking ecstasy and water to combat the effects of dehydration. After recovering she appealed to other young people not to take the drug which she likened to a 'dance with death' (*The Independent*, 13 January 1996, p. 3). A few days later another teenager, Andreas Bouzis, died in a club in south London after the ecstasy tablet that he had taken was thought to have exacerbated a congenital heart defect (*The Independent*, 15 January 1996).

In the aftermath of two deaths and one temporary coma all linked to ecstasy it is hardly surprising that there was a strong emotional response from the parents of the young people concerned. The parents of Leah Betts appeared regularly in the media to warn of the dangers of ecstasy. Following her daughter's recovery Mrs Cousins said: 'I'm pleading to all young people, don't chance your life, it can happen to you. If you take ecstasy it can take your life. Nothing is worth that. Don't weaken, be strong and say, 'no'' (*The Independent*, 13 January 1996, p. 3). After the death of her son Mrs Bouzis said: 'Yesterday our son had a future, he had a life … Today he is dead. Families and their love are very precious. Ecstasy tablets destroy families' (*The Independent*, 15 January 1996, p. 3). Elements of the media treated the death of Leah Betts and the other cases as symptoms of a general social malaise. For instance the *Daily Express* declared that the death of Leah — a teenager from a respectable home, whose father was an ex-police officer and whose mother had worked as a drugs counsellor — revealed that drugs were present as a 'rotten core at the heart of middle England'. Other dramatic images were invoked by tabloid newspapers. *The Sun* spoke of how 'evil ecstasy pushers [are] cashing in on Leah's death' to promote sales of ecstasy, while the *Daily Star* reported its horror that 'ecstasy club kids [are] still dicing with death' by continuing to take the drug despite the recent cases. Accompanying such stories were exposé style articles castigating magazines that detailed the content and likely effects of different 'brands' of ecstasy. Also, and probably inevitably, the *Daily Mirror* urged an 'even tougher crackdown on pushers'.

REACTION AND COUNTER-REACTION

The intense media reaction about ecstasy at this time — with its elements of dramatisation, exaggeration and a general sense of excitability — provoked a counter-reaction from some who sought to present an alternative view of the drug in the media. I will take two articles, one in a left wing magazine, the other in a liberal/left broad sheet newspaper to illustrate my argument about problems with counter-reaction. In the former Steve Platt (1995), then the editor of the *New Statesman*, declared that media reaction to the case of Leah Betts signalled that 'we are in the midst of a moral panic'. In the latter, Alix Sharkey in *The Guardian* examined distorted media coverage of ecstasy following the death of Leah Betts. These articles have been selected for the purposes of elaborating the argument that follows not because they are being presented as 'representative' of media coverage at this time. While there is overlap between them in the ways that both unpack and seek to debunk media coverage, I want to deal with them separately for the purposes of this paper. My aim is not simply to try to 'debunk the debunkers', though in criticising them there inevitably are some elements of this. Rather, I argue that both of them contain a series of problems, some or many of which could also be found within more academic/social scientific texts. First it is necessary to outline the case presented by Sharkey (1996). I will then look at the ways in which this 'mirrors' aspects of media reaction. Sharkey's main points (from which all the quotations below are taken) were that:

- Media 'horror stories' about ecstasy pre-dated the death of Leah Betts. Her case merely provided a hook or peg on which to hang those stories.
- The picture being painted by the media was one of ecstasy as a 'child-killing drug, available on every street corner.'
- 'There exists a largely manufactured consensus that drugs are "evil", those who sell them are "monsters", those who take them are "victims"'.
- The death of Leah Betts generated 'an avalanche of emotive but essentially uninformative copy.' But, 'nobody asked whether the death would have received such widespread attention had it not involved a pretty, white, teenage girl.'
- The corrosive effect of this type of media coverage is such that 'even factual TV programmes now take their editorial lead from such reporting.'
- The death of Leah Betts 'was not due to the effects of Ecstasy but to water intoxication.' However if this was the case the Bettses seemed unwilling to make it public at the time, instead they championed the view that ecstasy itself led to their daughter's death.
- The risk of death from ecstasy has been greatly exaggerated. Official figures of some 60 deaths since 1987 placed against estimated consumption of a million doses a week puts the risk of death at one in 6.8 million. The statistically greater risk of death from aspirin, let alone amphetamines, has been largely or totally ignored. Even a Swiss skiing holiday carries a higher risk of death than ecstasy use.
- Similarly, the emphasis on ecstasy as a threat to young people's lives obscures the fact that car accidents are the major cause of death for 14–24 year olds, and

that the majority of drug related deaths are due to smoking and alcohol. Even when considering illicit drugs only, deaths linked to ecstasy make up only a tiny fraction.

I have taken space to outline this argument because it strikes me as a good example of the debunking of the media and the attempt to re-contextualise the issue or problem as one of media reaction (see also Saunders, 1995). It accuses the media of selective perception (why Leah Betts, when other cases did not receive similar coverage?), the promotion of folk devil images of drugs and drug sellers ('evil pushers' and innocent victims/users), misleading, simplistic and hysterical coverage (ecstasy 'caused' the death of Leah Betts, it is 'a child killing drug') and of ignoring rational evidence (the greater risk of death from different activities).

What is wrong with this? While Sharkey does not personally say so, the debunking approach can sometimes include a complaint about 'the media' itself, which is presented as going through periodic, inevitable and predictable phases of reaction in which crude stereotypes will be perpetuated. But, of course, the reaction that is being objected to obviously represents only some parts and sections of the media. The observation that the counter-reaction also takes place in and makes use of 'the media', which therefore can not be spoken of as an ideologically homogenous or un-differentiated whole, is certainly trite but while it remains unacknowledged the criticism will still need to be made. This is but one difficulty with the counter-reaction. It can contain an exaggerated tendency to see media coverage as hysterical and promoting an anti-drugs 'consensus' even when the existence of counter-reaction must signal, at the very least, a crack in any widespread consensus. None the less, the media's basic message, we are told, simply apes the government's already discredited and fatuous 'Just say no' policy. The likelihood that the nature of media coverage means that it can be seen as exciting interest in drug use even while it appears to be forbidding it, or that government policy, for all its simplifications, does amount to more than 'Just say no' (see Home Office, 1994; see also Pearson, 1991) are both inconveniences best left to one side. Consequently, reaction and counter-reaction can often appear to be merely different sides of the same coin, or to 'mirror' one another. Elements that are problematic in media reaction are no less problematic when they occur in counter-reaction. The mirroring of what appear to be opposite points of view has been observed before[3]. For example, in his discussion of the 'Conservatism of the Cannabis debate', Nicholas Dorn (1980) showed that both supporters and opponents of cannabis legalisation subscribed to a common 'demonic' image of other drugs such as heroin. Similarly, in a book review, Dorn and Murji pointed out that drug 'warriors' and 'legalisers' display and share an equal passion in hyping up the nature (or 'horribleness' as we called it) of the drug market[4]. Once things can be seen to have got 'so bad', it enables both sides to make their case that either even more and tougher enforcement is required, or that legalisation is the only option left.

MIRRORING

The first way in which reaction and counter-reaction mirror one another is in their view of social consensus. Media reaction assumes that there is a moral or social consensus which is under threat or breaking down. Increased drug use by young people is presented as a symptom of this decline, or as a contributory or principal cause of social decay. For the counter-reactors there is a consensus but it is one that has been manufactured by the media and other interested parties. The image presented is one of a monolithic control culture which sees the world in terms of a binary opposition of good versus evil. In this sense counter-reaction subscribes to a comforting, but simple, dualistic conception of power — a world divided into 'them' and 'us'. The object of critical analysis should then be to uncover this false consensus. What remains un-questioned is the nature and even existence of any consensus. It is simply assumed to exist, either as something to be defended or to be exposed. The contradictory and messily fragmented patterns of real life are complications that both approaches prefer not to deal with. The 'one dimensional' picture presented in media reaction which Cohen (1972) drew attention to, is replaced by an alternative, but equally one dimensional, view in counter-reaction.

Similarly, in its concern to expose media hype, counter reaction can also end up effectively substituting one over simple message for another. Either, as the advert would have it 'Just one ecstasy tablet took Leah Betts', or it was not ecstasy at all but death was actually caused by water intoxication, due to an excessive intake of water to combat the effects of dehydration. As the headline in *The Guardian* (1 February 1996) stated following the inquest verdict: 'Leah's ecstasy death caused by water'. Thus media misconceptions can find their mirror image in the counter-reaction to (which is also in) the media. It can hardly be a coincidence that both types of perspective are promoted in newspapers and other media, since they make equal use of simplification and lay claim to certainty. They exemplify the 'sound bite culture' (Schlesinger & Tumber, 1994) in which complexity has little place. In this world of opposites the possibility that it was *both* ecstasy and water that contributed to the death of Leah Betts fail to suit the preferred framework of either side. As Dr John Henry of the National Poisons Unit indicated: 'If she had just taken the drug alone she might have survived. If she had drunk the amount of water alone she would have survived' (in *The Guardian*, 1 February 1996, p. 2; see also *Druglink*, 1996).

Both perspectives also contain a broadly similar, strong view of media 'effects'. Either popular culture mediated through music, magazines, television, etc., is seen as promoting drug use and activities 'associated' with it. Or, on the other hand, over the top media coverage is seen as promoting a false social consensus which alienates those with experience of drugs and marginalises users. From both viewpoints the media is constructed as a powerful social force with determinate and undesirable effects.

There are a number of other similarities. One is that both perspectives can see drug users as 'victims' at the mercy of drug sellers. For one side, young people are seemingly seduced by 'evil pushers'; alternatively, young people are seen as prey to being 'ripped off' by unscrupulous dealers selling them something that is not really ecstasy. Another similarity is that both can treat the parents of the young people in the cases discussed at the outset as ciphers. Either the parents' grief can be vicariously used to promote a particular message about drugs, or the parents are virtually 'dupes' who are being used by the media to promote an ideologically loaded message. A third similarity can be seen in the view that both perspectives have about the extent of drug use. While media reaction might see increased use in terms of an 'epidemic', the counter-reaction concurs with the view that usage has increased dramatically — Sharkey for example refers to 'a million doses a week'. It is notable that there is no disputing (or debunking) of the claim itself, not even much attempt to put drug use in perspective by suggesting that, as all evidence shows, cannabis is the most widely used illegal drug. Thus there is agreement that drug use is on the increase, all that is at issue is whether the language and style of media reaction is appropriate or not.

Both perspectives can also be seen to have an implicit conception of the 'audience' that is being addressed, constructed and re-constructed in media discourse. Eco (1979, see also Sparks, 1992) saw 'closed texts' as ones that envisage an average addressee and aim to arouse a particular response. This is more likely to be successful if the text can appeal to an existing 'common frame' of which the audience has already been 'made fond'. In the mass market place of media consumption it could be argued that both media reaction, favouring the individualising 'human interest' approach to private troubles, and counter-reaction, with its use of exposé style journalism, are forms of closed texts that are accustomed to constituting their audiences in a particular frame of reference. But the common problem with effects models is revealed in the need to make allowance for the probability that audiences, because they remain regular readers and viewers, may also have got used to 'seeing' and constructing themselves within such a framework. Thus there is a dynamic and reflexive relationship or inter-play between media and audience.

A MORAL PANIC?

The second strand of counter-reaction that I want to examine bases itself upon the view that the media's response can be classified as a moral panic. Platt's (1995) argument that media reaction to the death of Leah Betts was a moral panic is substantiated by the use of Goode and Ben-Yehuda's (1994) five criteria of a moral panic: a heightened level of concern, increased hostility towards those associated with the activity, a high level of consensus that the activity is a real and serious threat, exaggeration of the nature of threat and the volatility of moral panics. From this perspective the media and self-selected moral entrepreneurs, in cahoots with the government, are seen as conveying a simplistic anti-drugs message which ignores the fact that more and more young people are trying drugs. Hence the reality of drugs and their effects are swept under the carpet by the dominant prohibitionist mentality. Because Platt and Sharkey make similar points about media coverage I am not going to spell out the former's argument in detail. Rather I want to examine the use of the moral panics argument since its appearance in counter-reaction acts as a pillar for the debunking of the media that probably all users of the term aim to accomplish.

Since Cohen (1972) the term moral panic has been widely used and abused, achieving the status of a sociological concept that has passed into everyday language. A moral panic has been held to be occurring in media and official reaction to street crime (Hall *et al.*, 1978), juvenile crime (Pearson, 1983, Hay, 1995), child abuse (Jenkins, 1992), as well as alcohol, solvents and all or particular drugs (Dorn, 1983, Ives, 1986, Young, 1971, Pearson *et al.*, 1986, Kohn, 1987, Reinarman & Levine, 1989, Parker *et al.*, 1988, Ben-Yehuda, 1990, Coffield & Gofton, 1994). I now consider some of the problems that arise from the use of the model or framework of moral panics.

Sparks points out that Cohen's use of the term was 'a modest and descriptive one'. But, while Cohen's original formulation:

> usefully [drew] attention to the recurrence of themes of social anxiety and their association with rhetorics of crisis, it elides all such 'panics' under a single heading, representing them as a consequence of some (hypothetically universal, endlessly cyclical) feature of social life, namely panickyness (Sparks, 1992, p. 65).

Cohen and Hall *et al.* (1978) did seek to carefully contextualise and theorise the model of moral panic. But this has not always been evident in the manifold uses of the term since then. As a result, moral panic has become a throwaway phrase, a 'catch all term for anything that we don't like' (Thompson, quoted in Jenkins, 1992), and 'a value laden terminology' (Waddington, 1986) revealing as much about the view of the user as the phenomenon itself. Whenever something is described as a moral panic the intention is always pejorative, there are no instances that I know of where the user does not seem to use it dismissively against the phenomenon depicted.

It is true that one can easily find newspapers and other media that present ecstasy and other drugs in apocalyptic terms and make use of individual and unrepresentative cases to address or represent the 'state of the nation', just as it is true that there are commentators and moral entrepreneurs who 'man the barricades' and call for more law, more punishment, etc. But this ease indicates that moral panics have become common-place and everyday, rather than exceptional (McRobbie, 1994):

> moral panics have become the way in which daily events are brought to the attention of the public. They are a standard response, a familiar sometimes weary, even ridiculous rhetoric rather than an exceptional emergency intervention (McRobbie & Thornton, 1995, p. 560).

For instance, at the time of writing there has been some fuss about the newly released British film *Trainspotting*. It has been criticised for virtually inciting people to try heroin and an insufficiently censorious view of drug-taking. In a similar way there was some controversy about the depiction of drug taking in the film *Pulp Fiction* for allegedly 'celebrating' drug use. Does this constitute a moral panic? The problem, it seems to me, is that to say it is (or that any one of a host of other issues are) makes little allowance for the possibility that audiences may well recognise there is more than an element of commercial hype in much of this type of coverage. The moral panic has become a 'routine means of making youth-orientated cultural products more alluring' (McRobbie & Thornton, 1995, p. 559). It has become part of a 'promotional logic' which business practice can play upon, as Cohen (1972) recognised in his discussion of the 'exploitative culture'.

The media may be able to generate such 'moral panics' and a panoply of new folk devils almost to order — for example, new age travellers, anti-road building protestors, campaigners against live animal exports, etc. But simply identifying their presence and existence in the media is hardly the same thing as saying that whatever 'views' are presented about such groups are widely shared. After all in the case of all of the 'new' folk devils just mentioned, there has been at least sufficient public support for them to make any claims about consensus, concern, hostility and the reality of the threat questionable at the very least[5]. Not each and every instance of exaggeration of the 'threat' posed by some group or activity can be regarded as a moral panic, unless the term is now being used so loosely as to refer to all and every social anxiety, however localised, and whether it is widely shared or not.

The un-covering of media over-reaction has been a key element of the moral panics framework. But the empirical basis on which this can be asserted is far from being as straight-forward as it may appear. Even one of the most sophisticated elaborations of a moral panic has been found wanting. Sumner and Sandberg (1990) have shown that, contrary to Hall *et al.*'s (1978) argument, 'mugging' was not the dominant issue in the news in 1973. Rather, their re-analysis of newspapers found that the prime news story concerned industrial relations and trade unions. Yet no one has argued that there was a moral panic about strikes. A similar argument could possibly be applied to more recent events. Around the same time as the Leah Betts case there was considerable media coverage about knives following the fatal stabbing of a head teacher outside a school in London. Despite the extensive coverage given to this incident and calls for increased police powers of stop and search, there has been no case presented that this was a moral panic about knives and young people.

Claims about media over-reaction run into further problems. To return to the example of 'mugging' again, it has been argued that the scale of the reaction to it was not, as Hall *et al.* (1978) argued, disproportionate to its actual occurrence (Waddington, 1986)[6]. Crucially, Waddington argues that there is no basis for identifying what the empirical criteria for a 'proportionate' response are (see also Reiner, 1988). Critics and counter-reactors asserting that the media over-reacts imply that news coverage is, or should be, governed by a quasi-actuarialism. An argument could certainly be made that media coverage of heroin, crack and ecstasy in recent years was 'out of keeping' with the actual usage of these drugs. But what is the 'right' or appropriate level of reaction? To illustrate the problem of establishing an answer to this question I will take a different example. Media coverage of HIV/AIDS in the late 1980s had many features of a moral panic when, for example, it was depicted as a 'gay plague' or as of concern to injecting drug users only (though see Watney, 1987 for a critique of moral panic theory as applied to this issue). But were those who called for more resources and attention to be given to harm reduction and prevention messages, and in the process warned about a potential 'epidemic' of HIV infection, irrespective of the actual prevalence of HIV, also engaging in a moral panic? After all, 'rational statistics' could be used to say that there are far more deaths from prostate cancer. Hence both approaches can be accused of 'sensationalism' and 'over reaction' in hyping up the problem in order to attract attention. Health educators and others involved in prevention could argue that a 'disproportional' reaction can be justified by an appeal to the 'hidden' scale of a problem or its potential as a 'future threat'. But such appeals are equally open to those who issued apocalyptic warnings about the addictive power of crack (see Bean, 1993, Murji, 1995). A more credible case could be made out for differences in the *style* and *content* of different warning messages, which would indicate that there are important political and qualitative differences between those who use terms such as 'gay plague' or a 'child killing drug' and others who want to promote harm reduction and safer sex and drug use messages. But, in formal terms the 'warnings' can appear similar enough to worry anyone who chooses to say that only one of these is disproportionate and an over-reaction and therefore part of a moral panic.

A further problem with users of the moral panic argument is a tendency to see panics as actively promoted by a particular group, or at least as being a peg around which powerful groups can hang their pre-set agenda. But in this instrumentalist conception there is rarely any acknowledgment that such groups may have something to lose from moral panics too[7]. For example, following their role in the spectacular representation of drugs as a problem and continuing evidence that usage has not declined, the police are faced with two possibilities — either to 'give up' and join the drug legalisation lobby, or to campaign for even more powers, a bigger net, more resources, etc. Both options position them in a posture of defeat: the 'problem' is either insoluble, or so overwhelming that only further special powers, the limits to which can never be specified, will do (Dorn *et al.*, 1991)[8].

Another example reveals a different problem with both the instrumentalist and disproportionality aspects of the moral panics argument. In the early 1980s there was a campaign by parents in Merseyside for more attention to be paid to the increase in heroin use by young people. Their complaint was that there was insufficient reaction by the media and the authorities. This local campaign for more action may have touched off the wider national campaign that brought publicity about heroin to areas where usage was much lower and to young people who may not have considered it before. But the parents may have felt that their (over?) reaction was necessary in order to get the authorities to respond. Hence the media and powerful groups are sometimes forced to follow rather than lead public opinion. And, as all the examples used suggest, exaggeration can be routinely used as a means of getting the media, politicians and the public to react in cases where they otherwise seem to show little interest.

Finally there is a problem with the periodization of moral panics. To return to Platt again, we might ask if there was a moral panic about ecstasy in 1995, when did it begin and end? Clearly for Platt (1995) and Sharkey (1996) the death of Leah Betts acted as the touchstone for the onset of a moral panic. But how would this view deal with the fact that the cultural industries associated with 'Acid House' and 'rave' culture were predicting that there would be a moral panic as long ago as 1988? Or that the music press were running exposés about ecstasy at that time and asking why the tabloids were ignoring the issue? There was eventually much press attention paid to the 'rave' scene in the summer of 1988 and throughout the early 1990s (see McRobbie & Thornton, 1995) just as, well before the death of Leah Betts, there was considerable news coverage of the deaths of young people being linked to ecstasy. As the headlines 'Alarm grows over rising death toll' and 'Ravers play 'Russian roulette' with ecstasy' (*The Independent*, 28 December 1991, p. 5) indicate, the themes of 1995 were in many ways a replay of a well established story. How does the proponent of the moral panic explain this? Goode and Ben-Yehuda (1994) have the catch-all answer since one of their criteria of a moral panic is that they are volatile. But, as a 'totalizing' or holistic conception of society, the media and social regulation has 'fissured' (McRobbie & Thornton, 1995), accounting for the persistence, residues and decline of moral panics requires a good deal more explanation than this (see also Watney, 1987). For all these reasons it seems to me that, to say that the media is involved in a moral panic about drugs in general or ecstasy in particular, raises a number of difficulties which are rooted in the way that moral panics and the role of the media have been theorised. These problems can not simply be dismissed in the way that Goode and Ben-Yehuda (1994) do in response to Waddington (1986) when they argue that the popularity of the term moral panics in journalism and social science establishes its verisimilitude and utility.

REASON AND EMOTION

The implicit or explicit use of reason as a key motif of counter-reaction raises a final set of problems. The play upon and with rationality takes two main forms. It is most evident in the appeal to rational statistics as well as the writing style and tone that is adopted. The statistics of death — the much smaller probability of death linked to ecstasy against the known deaths caused by less publicised activities — are used to highlight the media's emphasis on the former at the expense of the latter to reinforce the view that media coverage is ideologically loaded. The argument that the media constructs particular cases and deaths as exceptional and newsworthy while ignoring many others is plausible. It is certainly possible to find other cases that have not received as much coverage as that of Leah Betts. But, in the appeal to rational statistics the unstated implication in counter-reaction is that a moral calculus governs news coverage, or should do so. Yet the extent or amount of media reaction to death probably rarely corresponds simply to the numbers involved. As Kettle indicates, news coverage of a disaster is likely to emphasise 'six Brits' over '60 Frogs, and 600 more remote aliens' (cited in Walter *et al.*, 1995, p. 587). Pointing out the far greater number of deaths due to tobacco, alcohol, car accidents, etc., achieves the rhetorical effect of exposing media partiality. But it also glosses over the unexamined assumption that the ordinary and commonplace are the stuff of everyday news. While the question of how 'the news' is constructed is an important one, it is still the case that:

> The deaths boldly headlined and portrayed by the news media are extraordinary deaths. That is why they are so eminently story-worthy as news. They are also types of deaths which, unlike the majority of deaths, occur in a public place' (Walter *et al.*, 1995, p. 595).

Hence it is at least understandable why there was a lot of coverage given to the case of Leah Betts. The revelation that other deaths did not generate as much coverage does not go beyond what is already known: that news values shape and construct what becomes the news. It does not amount to a case against the media, particularly since counter-reaction is also part of the media circle. To put the case another way, I am arguing that it is not sufficient to uncover that the media is partial, since it is difficult to know what an 'impartial' media would like.

The second aspect of the use of reason is evident in the style adopted by the counter-reactors. Michael Keith (1992) has written about the ways in which academic writing masks its own rhetoric chiefly through the use of a dispassionate tone and style. These conventions, Keith argues, account for why writings that convey anger and emotion can be dismissed as not serious and disqualified from consideration. Though the writings I have been considering are journalistic it seems to me that they employ the same strategy and, I would contend, a close examination of other debunking texts would reveal much the same conventions commonly in play. Hysteria and emotion are taken as the hall marks of that which is to be debunked and this is best done with a 'cool', dispassionate and logical tone. Reason is, self-evidently, rational while emotion is irrational and therefore not to be trusted. Hence reasonableness marks another boundary between 'us' and the 'others'. But as Sparks pointed out, reason is not the opposite of emotion: 'Rather the opposites of emotion are the 'detachment and equanimity' of a spurious objectivism and the 'sentimentality' of inauthentic responses' (Sparks 1992, p. 75).

Rationality performs a key rhetorical role in counter reaction because it makes it possible to depict media reaction as moralistically pushing a particular agenda using emotional, even hysterical, language and images. It enables the creation of a dichotomy in which only one side is seen as engaged in rhetoric, as Sharkey (1996, p. 2) demonstrates: 'When drugs cannot be considered outside this simplistic rhetorical context, meaningful debate is impossible.' Reasonableness thus creates a space for counter-reaction to 'cloak' or suppress its own moral enterprise and rhetoric[9]. But opposing views about drugs can not be seen in terms of morality versus non- or a-morality. Paradigms of morality imbue debates about drugs, whether those views come from the most ardent 'warriors' or the most ardent libertarians (see Rouse & Johnson, 1991, Husak, 1992). Both perspectives contain moral positions in the struggle over definitions, lifestyles, etc., rather than morality being the preserve of one side only. This criticism of counter-reaction for its use of rationality is not intended to be read as a collapse into the post-modernist rejection of reason. Rather I am arguing that we need to pay more attention, as Garland (1990) has observed about punishment, to the 'sentiments and passions' that the subject of drugs can and does arouse. The use of reason, I have sought to argue, seeks to artificially disqualify emotion, even though there clearly are sentiments and passions that underlie counter-reaction too.

CONCLUSION

I have argued against the conventional debunking approach to some sections of the media's coverage of drugs. The counter-reaction contains ideas or themes that are just as problematic as the views to which it is opposed. Furthermore it can be seen as relying upon a rather out-dated vocabulary about moral panics and accused of deceitfully covering up its own moral enterprise. In taking issue with the conventional reaction to media coverage I have spent more time criticising the critics than the originators. This is not intended as a defence of any of the media's reporting of drugs. It is meant to indicate that theorising about drugs and the media requires more rigour than the examples of counter-reaction that I have used here. While the sociology of the media, youth cultures and deviance has moved on (Schlesinger & Tumber, 1994; Morley, 1995; McRobbie & Thornton, 1995) the terminology of moral panics remains stuck in a time-warp that requires a model of social consensus, a monolithic media and control culture and a seemingly gullible, or at least highly suggestible, public to work.

There are however a number of unresolved problems that require more attention than I have space to consider here. In drawing attention to equivalences between apparently contrasting perspectives, the differences between them have been under-played. I have mainly focused on the form and content of reaction and counter-reaction. But it is also worth asking *where* the different views are usually to be found. At some risk of overstating the case, it is probably true that drug scares and the most extreme forms of coverage are likely to be found in the mass market tabloid newspapers while the more 'reasoned' counter-reactions are to be found in broad sheet quality newspapers[10]. If these are taken as broad indicators of the sites of reaction and counter-reaction then the ways in which different sections of the media address and 'visualise' the audience is one difference that could be worthy of further exploration. A second difference is the possible presence in counter-reaction of multiple views about an issue, suggesting complexity and a degree of openness and debate, against the singular perspective that takes the form of a grand narrative adopted in reaction. A third issue is the question of weight and influence. The forces of reaction do not stand in an equal relationship to forces of counter-reaction. There are inequalities of access as well as resources (Schlesinger & Tumber, 1994). More over, the prevalence of political conservatism apparently makes it more acceptable to talk 'tough' about drugs (and crime and punishment) than to appear 'soft'. A recent example is the extensive coverage given to a Labour party shadow minister who called for a fresh look at the laws on cannabis. The response to even this modest proposal was a howl of protest by the media which eventually led the politician to apologise and retract. Hence it is more than likely that 'alternative' views get much less time and space in the media than 'main-stream' ones. In seeing similarities between reaction and counter-reaction we should be aware of de Certau's distinction between the strategies of the powerful and the tactics of the weak (in Morley, 1995).

Of course there are times when apparent media hysteria 'drowns out' any opposition to the orthodoxy, and the media literally circumscribe the limits of what it is possible to say in public. There is also a problem that many of the questions that journalists seek answers to are not answerable in the simple terms that are expected. Hence, there is every reason to question media representations about drugs, to ask what evidence the images presented are based upon and to challenge apparently dominant ideas. However, the simple replacement of these with equally one-dimensional views is not likely to achieve much beyond a sense of satisfaction that the 'control culture' has once again been exposed. Both reaction and counter-reaction need to be open to critical scrutiny. Ultimately the problem with both reaction and counter-reaction is that they construct a terrain in which each reader and viewer is invited to position her/himself as for one side and against the other. Thus there are apparently only two absolutist positions to select from, fanaticism on one side, scepticism on the other. But, as I have tried to argue, there is more than a bit of fanaticism and scepticism on both sides.

NOTES

1. I am grateful to Ross Coomber, Nigel South and, especially, Eugene McLaughlin for their comments on an earlier version. Steven Groarke, James Sheptycki and Kevin Stenson have helped to refine my thoughts on moral panics, though they have not commented on this paper directly.
2. The last point is well demonstrated by Reinarman and Levine (1989). They show how drugs came to be seen as the number one social problem in the USA, particularly in the years where politicians standing for election tried

to outbid each other in how 'tough' they were going to be on drug sellers and users.

3. Another aspect of mirroring has been observed in the rationale for changing the structure of law enforcement in relation to drug trafficking. The Broome report for the Association of Chief Police Officers (extracts from which are reproduced as the Appendix in Dorn *et al.*, 1992) successfully argued for enforcement to be organised on a three tier model on the basis that it should 'mirror' the organisation of drug trafficking itself (for a critique see Dorn *et al.*, 1991).

4. This was a review of R. Clutterbuck's *Terrorism, Drugs and Crime in Europe after 1992* (Routledge, 1990) that appeared in the *International Journal on Drug Policy* in 1992.

5. A significant change since the 1960s is that 'folk devils' and the pressure groups that represent them now produce their own newspapers and magazines, and provide spokespeople who are well versed in the ways that the media works (see McRobbie 1994, McRobbie and Thornton 1995).

6. There is a view that a moral panic is not about the 'objective' phenomenon but rather the ways in which 'social problems' are constructed (Jenkins, 1992). But even users of this approach have felt the need to compare the construction of problems with some evidence about their extent (e.g. see Reinarman & Levine, 1989). As Watney (1987, p. 41) has stated: 'Moral panic theory is always obliged in the final instance to refer and contrast 'representation' to the arbitration of 'the real', and is hence unable to develop a full theory concerning the operations of ideology within all representational systems.'

7. McRobbie and Thornton (1995) make a similar point by using the example of the government's ill-fated 'back to basics' campaign.

8. Nigel South has pointed out to me that there is a third option in which senior police officers seek to redefine the issue as a social problem linked to or caused by structural features such as poverty, unemployment, etc.

9. Becker (1963) saw moral enterprise as 'the creation of a new fragment of the moral constitution of society.'

10. My reservations about this are partly due to the fact that one of the most prolific proponents of drug legalisation, Dr Vernon Coleman, has written regularly for *The Sun*.

REFERENCES

Bean, P. (1993) 'Cocaine and Crack: The promotion of an epidemic', in P. Bean (ed.) *Cocaine and Crack: Supply and use*, Basingstoke: Macmillan.

Becker, H. (1963) *Outsiders*, New York: Free Press.

Ben-Yehuda, N. (1990) *The Politics and Morality of Deviance*, New York: SUNY Press.

Coffield, F. and Gofton, L. (1994) *Drugs and Young People*, London: IPPR.

Cohen, S. (1972) *Folks Devils and Moral Panics*, London: MacGibbon & Kee.

Dorn, N. (1980) 'The Conservatism of the Cannabis debate', in National Deviancy Conference (ed.) *Permissiveness and Control*, London: Macmillan.

Dorn, N. (1983) *Alcohol, Youth and the State*, London: Croom Helm.

Dorn, N. and Murji, K. (1992) *Drug Prevention*, London: ISDD.

Dorn, N., Murji, K. and South, N. (1991) 'Mirroring the market', in R. Reiner and M. Cross (eds.) *Beyond Law and Order*, Basingstoke: Macmillan.

Dorn, N., Murji, K. and South, N. (1992) *Traffickers: Drug markets and law enforcement*, London: Routledge.

Druglink (1996) 'The effects of E on harm reduction', January/February: 4.

Eco, U. (1979) *The Role of the Reader*, London: Hutchinson.

Garland, D. (1990) *Punishment and Modern Society*, Oxford: Oxford University Press.

Giddens, A. (1987) *Sociology and Modern Social Theory*, Cambridge: Polity.

Goode, E. and Ben-Yehuda, N. (1994) *Moral Panics: The Social construction of deviance*, Oxford: Blackwell.

Hall, S. *et al.* (1978) *Policing the Crisis: Mugging, the State and Law and Order*, London: Macmillan.

Hay, C. (1995) 'Mobilization through interpellation', *Social and Legal Studies*, 4: 197–223.

Home Office (1994) *Tackling Drugs Together*, London: HMSO.

Husak, D. (1992) *Drugs and Rights*, Cambridge: Cambridge University Press.

Ives, R. (1986) 'The rise and fall of the solvents panic', *Druglink*, July/August: 10–12.

Jenkins, P. (1992) *Intimate Enemies*, New York: Aldine de Gruyter.

Keith, M. (1992) 'Angry writing', *Environment and Planning D: Society and Space*, 10: 551–568.

Kohn, M. (1987) *Narcomania*, London: Faber.

McRobbie, A. (1994) 'Folk devils fight back', *New Left Review*, 203: 107–116.

McRobbie, A. and Thornton, S. (1995) 'Rethinking 'moral panic' for multi-mediated social worlds', *British Journal of Sociology*, 46: 559–574.

Morley, D. (1995) 'Theories of consumption in media studies', in D. Miller (ed.) *Acknowledging Consumption*, London: Routledge.

Murji, K. (1995) 'Drugs', in P. Neate (ed.) *Scare in the Community — Britain in a moral panic*, London: Community Care/Reed Business Publishing.

Parker, H. *et al.* (1988) *Living with Heroin*, Milton Keynes: Open University Press.

Pearson, G. (1983) *Hooligan*, London: Macmillan.

Pearson, G. (1991) 'Drug-control policies in Britain', in M. Tonry and N. Morris (eds.) *Crime and Justice*, vol. 14, Chicago: Chicago University Press.

Pearson, G. *et al.* (1986) *Young People and Heroin*, London: Health Education Council.

Platt, S. (1995) 'Moral panic', *New Statesman and Society*, 24 November: 14–15.

Reeves, J. and Campbell, R. (1994) *Cracked Coverage*, Durham, NC: Duke University Press.

Reinarman, C. and Levine, H. (1989) 'The crack attack', in J. Best (ed.) *Images of Issues*, New York: Aldine de Gruyter.

Reiner, R. (1988) 'British criminology and the state', in P. Rock (ed.) *A History of British Criminology*, Oxford: Oxford University Press.

Rouse, J. and Johnson, B. (1991) 'Hidden paradigms of morality in debates about drugs', in J. Inciardi (ed.) *The Drug Legalization Debate*, New York: Sage.

Saunders, N. (1995) *Ecstasy and the Dance Culture*, London: N. Saunders.

Schlesinger, P. and Tumber, H. (1994) *Reporting Crime*, Oxford: Clarendon.

Sharkey, A. (1996) 'Sorted or distorted?', *The Guardian*, 26 January: 2–3.

Sparks, R. (1992) *Television and the Drama of Crime*, Buckingham: Open University Press.

Sumner, C. and Sandberg, S. (1990) 'The press censure of 'dissident minorities', in C. Sumner (ed.) *Censure, Politics and Criminal Justice*, Buckingham: Open University Press.

Waddington, P.A.J. (1986) 'Mugging as a moral panic', *British Journal of Sociology*, 37: 245–359.

Walter, T. *et al.* (1995) 'Death in the news', *Sociology*, 29: 579–596.

Watney, S. (1987) *Policing Desire*, London: Methuen.

Young, J. (1971) *The Drugtakers*, London: Paladin.

PART TWO
THE CURRENT CONTROL CONTEXT

CHAPTER 6

Tackling Drug Control in Britain: From Sir Malcolm Delevingne to the New Drugs Strategy

Nigel South

'Action and reaction are equal and opposite'.
(Newton's Third Law of Motion)

INTRODUCTION

Great Britain has a new set of 'drugs strategies', one each for England, Scotland, Wales and Northern Ireland. Under titles such as 'Tackling Drugs Together' (the England strategy) and 'Drugs in Scotland: Meeting the Challenge', some old traditions, new problems and contemporary politics are brought together. The emphases and nuances of the strategies vary (Ashton, 1994, 1995, a, b) but whether with a harm minimisation slant (as in Scotland) or a community crime prevention emphasis (as in England), the bottom line is, in one way or another, drug *control*. The idea that a 'strategy' can answer policy and political needs in relation to drug issues is, of course, hardly new, although in the history of British policy it has some novelty — the evolution of the 'British System' was not, in truth, very systematic (Strang and Gossop, 1994, ch. 27 and *passim*). But in designing a strategy to answer the needs of policy and politics the needs of drug users do not *necessarily* figure too highly and the basic question about such strategies — 'can they work? — may be simply ignored or met with bullish assertions. Yet already there are forecasts that the current wave of strategies will face problems familiar from the past. Ashton's (1995 b) recent prognosis regarding the English strategy suggests that by the time of the strategy review in 1998, treatment and prevention are unlikely to have proven themselves a great success, funding will be as inadequate as ever, and drug use will have continued to rise despite the new 'coordination structures'. All of this will

87

leave a choice of declaring the policy a success because without it things would have been worse, a failure because the tide has not been turned, or a promising venture in need of adjustment or a greater impetus. Like the proverbial decision over whether the glass is half full, this choice will be determined as much by what the decision-makers want to see as by any scientific calculation. (Ashton, 1995 b: 6).

British control policy has been here before. The inherently indeterminate nature of its success or failure has been a long-standing characteristic: from the compromise that gave rise to the 'British System', through the bifurcation of 'treatment versus criminalisation' in legislation of the 1960s and 1970s, to the accomodation between tough enforcement policy and harm minimisation practices in the 1980s (cf Collison, 1993: 383; Henham, 1994: 224–5). In this chapter I shall first, briefly review aspects of this history relevant to contemporary concerns about drug control, then examine more recent developments in the 'get tough' decade of the 1980s and their follow-on into the 1990s, and conclude with some consideration of possible futures concerning legislation, drug control and the broader policy mix.

THE EARLY CONTROL DEBATE: ENTER
SIR MALCOLM AND SIR HUMPHREY

Famously, it was not through peace-time Parliamentary activity but use of emergency powers during the First World War, that the first significant legal measures of drug control were introduced in Britain[1]. Amidst national anxieties about any potential threats to the war-effort, a pro-control lobby was able to persuade the Home Secretary to employ emergency powers procedures to introduce the Defence of the Realm Act Regulation 40 B (1916) which controlled possession of cocaine (Spear, 1994: 4). Following the war, those favouring further control (among them Sir Malcolm Delevingne, a Permanent Under-Secretary at the Home Office), sought to take British policy down the penal road followed in the USA after the 1914 Harrison Act[2].

What actually came to pass seems to have been the rather British scenario of a 'gentlemanly confrontation' between the Home Office interests, led by Sir Malcolm, and representatives of the medical establishment who sought to retain and consolidate professional dominion over the treatment and maintenance of drug addicts. The very British compromise that resulted arose out of the deliberations on the desirable limits of medical authority (Spear, 1994: 5) published in the 1926 Report of the Ministry of Health' Departmental Committee on Morphine and Heroin Addiction — better known as the Rolleston Committee report, after its Chair, Sir Humphrey Rolleston. This was, by one reading, a framework for harm minimisation practice, and hence has been a highly symbolic point of reference for subsequent treatment and control debates. Rolleston was an explicit statement of policy and practice that said that if treatment aimed at withdrawal had not and did not seem likely to work for a dependent drug user then the 'medically advisable' intervention could reasonably be a professionally judged regime of maintenance prescribing of the required or substitute drugs, whether for the long-term or otherwise (Ashton, 1989: 13). In other words, that if a person could be seen to be capable of living a useful and productive life whilst being maintained — which would otherwise be denied him or her if they did not have legal access to drugs — then this could justify the maintenance approach which came to be called 'the British System'. In short, it justified an approach seeking to minimise harm to the individual, their family and society and to maximise the chances of the drug user being able to lead a 'normal' life.

There are many reasons why idealised accounts of this arrangement have been criticised, not least that as Ashton (ibid) observes, this was in large part a bid by the medical profession for the powers to deal with its own errant members. Many of the dependent users of the time were medical personnel who had abused their access to drugs. Others included those who had become dependent when pre-scribed drugs during the course of medical treatment. Hence, the medical pro-fession were defending both their own privileged status and that of the addict-patients in their care. It is open to speculation, whether such energy and principled argument would have been marshalled had the majority of dependent users resembled the working class 'new heroin users' of the 1960s and 1980s (on these groups and decades, see Spear, 1994; Pearson, 1987; Ruggiero and South, 1995, ch. 4)

Once in place however, through the following decades and right up to the late 1950s, this policy and practice based on maintenance and treatment seemed to work exceptionally well. Of course, this was for the rather simple reason that there was hardly any problem to treat. In David Downes's (1977: 89) memorable assessment, once examined in relation to its actual task, "the 'British System' [was] well and truly exposed as little more than masterly inactivity in the face of … an almost non-existent addiction problem". However, in the 1960s, and later the 1980s, new drug problems demanded rather more purposeful activity, and change and innovation were to follow (cf Strang and Gossop, 1994: ch. 27).

I observed above that 'by one reading' Rolleston represented an early statement of a form of harm minimisation. This by no means makes it irrelevant to my cen-tral concern here with control, for the other important point about the compromise that produced Rolleston was that while it was a victory *for* the medical establish-ment, the importance of treatment and their unchallengable authority in this regard (Spear, 1995: 13), it was not a victory *against or over* the Home Office, Foreign Office, legal control or penality. Indeed, an argument between the Home Office and "the recently established Ministry of Health over where responsibility for drug control should lie had been resolved in favour of the Home Office (Berridge, 1984: 23), it [then] fell to that [latter] Department to determine the extent to which medi-cal practitioners were following the guidance provided by Rolleston." (Spear, 1994: 6). Rolleston therefore provided much medical autonomy but its *framework* was *ultimately* regulated by the Home Office and the police; its parameters if not its everyday practice were, at the end of the day, marked out by criminal justice controls not treatment concerns. As Pearson (1991: 173) concurs, "It would be a mistake to see [here] the victory of the professional autonomy of medicine over state and police regulation. In spite of the acceptance of the Rolleston Committee's recommendations, the Home Office retained a major stake in the administration of the system, and unauthorized possession of defined substances remained a criminal offence." Furthermore, as Bean (1974: 35) has noted, while Britain's drug problems may have largely disappeared by the end of the 1920's, the political momentum of international control initiatives meant that between 1920 and 1964, all of the significant drugs legislation passed in Britain was less a response to any real domestic problem and more the result of willingness to meet national obligations set by international treaties (cf Ruggiero and South, 1995: 99–101; Bruun *et al.*, 1975). In other words, it is important to understand that while the 'British System' has had a *very* strong medical/treatment/social work dimension, "in so far as the 'British System' in its contemporary theory and practice goes beyond what is required internationally and beyond the control measures adopted by some other countries, it may fairly be characterized as a criminal-law based system of control of the user (as well as the trafficker)." (Dorn and South, 1994: 296). Historically, the 'British System' always has been a system of control. This does not, however, mean that it has in any way resembled the disastrous control regime pursued in the USA.

Before turning to the present, let us take a swift historical turn toward the enforcement side of the control equation. Here it is again interesting to find clear echoes of concerns of the present in the discourses of the past (cf South, 1994 b). For example, it has long been recognised that effective policing of domestic and international drug markets is a difficult if not impossible task. As one member of the international 'control community' wrote in 1931:

> The special features which characterize the drug problem and put it into a class by itself are: (i) The comparative ease with which the drugs can be smuggled — their bulk is small and there are endless ways of concealing or disguising them; and (ii) the insistent demand for them from those who are addicted to their use, and the high prices which these addicts are willing to pay for their supplies.
>
> The resourcefulness of those engaged in the illicit traffic is remarkable. When checked in one direction they find an outlet in another. When the control over drugs in their ordinary forms becomes too strict new forms are invented, which for the time being are not subject to the law, or operations are started in a new country where the control is less effective.

As the astute reader will have guessed, the author is our pro-control protagonist, Sir Malcolm Delevingne (Delevingne, 1931: 55–6). Elsewhere in his essay, Sir Malcolm may exaggerate the contemporary 'danger to civilization [posed by] the abuse of drugs' but his analysis of the responses of the drug market and traffickers to control measures is otherwise remarkably sound.

It was this 'innovatory dance'[3] between traffickers and legislators/enforcers that was central to new initiatives in control-legislation and enforcement in the 1980s (Dorn and South, 1990; Dorn *et al.*, 1992; Wright *et al.*, 1993). I shall turn to these recent developments next. However in reviewing these and finally commenting on future directions, I hope that I and the reader will recall the significance of 'the past' when we encounter declarations of 'the new'. Contemporary conditions and problems may be new but debates, philosophies and principles often have antecedents that are not acknowledged. Where 'we have been here before' but amnesia has set in, then policy and practice may be the poorer[4].

A DECADE OF DEVELOPMENTS: THE 1980S

The 1980s saw an unprecedented increase in the use of heroin, as well as several other drugs. The reasons for this are beyond the scope of this chapter and have been thoroughly analysed elsewhere (Auld *et al.*, 1986; Dorn and South, 1987; Pearson, 1991; South, 1994, 1994 a). In response, drugs in Britain became a political and highly politicised issue (Stimson, 1987), yet one which attracted a political consensus which persists (Berridge, 1991: 179; Ashton, 1995 b). Several cross-party Parliamentary committees (eg Social Services Committee, 1984–5; Home Affairs Committee, 1985) published Reports emphasising the serious threat posed by heroin and then cocaine trafficking[5]. The Government's 'strategy document' of this period *Tackling Drug Misuse* (1985) proposed five fronts for action:

1. Reducing supplies from abroad;
2. Making enforcement even more effective;
3. Maintaining effective deterrents and tight domestic controls;
4. Developing prevention[6];
5. Improving treatment and rehabilitation.

Significantly, the first 3 out of these 5 priorities are enforcement-led measures, and even the fourth — prevention measures — can be interpreted to include policing strategies designed to disrupt low-level markets, hence prevent supply, hence prevent use (cf Dorn and Murji, 1992). Coupled with the provisions of the 1986 Drug Trafficking Offences Act (hereafter DTOA) and the 1985 Controlled Drugs (Penalties) Act, all of this placed the police, customs, courts and prisons at the forefront of official rhetoric about responses in policy and practice[7]. Collison's (1993: 384) study of drug offenders nicely illustrates how, within this 'new' high profile 'enforcement climate' for policy and practice, the 'balance' between treatment and enforcement was weighted further toward the criminal justice scale:

> During the 1980s drug counsellors and doctors were busy attempting to encourage the
> new users (Pearson, 1987) of Class A drugs (particularly heroin) to come forward, be

counted, receive relevant harm reduction information (encouraging safer drug use and safer sex), and, when appropriate, to receive treatment. At the same time the criminal justice system was equally busy processing more and more drug users through the police station and court and on into the penal system. It is the latter process which is critical here, for it can be shown that the two parts of the 'system' have frequently been dealing with the same person(s). ... [Collison's] case study revealed that many of the individuals drawn into the criminal justice system as the result of low-level police surveillance and raiding of street-level drug markets were problem users and, once in the system, were likely rapidly to lose their victim status and be dealt with via the logic(s) of punishment and deterrence ideally reserved for the villains.

LEGISLATING 'NEW' ILLEGALITIES AND WIDENING LEGAL CONTROLS ON DRUGS AND DRUG RELATED CRIME.

Some of the significant legislation from this period had an unusual genesis. In the late 1970's, the 'Operation Julie' trial of manufacturers of LSD led to an appeal court decision that the Misuse of Drugs Act 1971 could not provide for the forfeiture of criminally generated assets. The liberally-inclined Howard League sponsored a Committee chaired by Sir Derek Hodgson to examine this quirky situation and make recommendations concerning a fair resolution. Convened in 1980 and reporting in 1984, the Committee supported the principle of forfeiture of criminal assets but also made the case that where money or property was forfeited this amounted to punishment that should be taken into account in calculating sentences. However, the 1985 Home Affairs Committee sought a rather more punitive resolution and emulation of 'American practice' "to give the courts draconian powers in both civil and criminal law to strip drug dealers of all the assets acquired from their dealings in drugs." (iv–vi; Stimson, 1987: 44). In the prevailing conditions of anxiety and consensus, the Government, politically predisposed toward the view of the Home Affairs Committee, was able to modify the liberal proposals of the Hodgson Committee and introduce the more punitive and far-reaching Drug Trafficking Offences Act 1986 (in force from 1987) (Dorn *et al.*, 1992, chapter 10; Dorn and South, 1991; Zander, 1989).

Coupled with upward revision of the sentencing tariff provided in the 1985 Controlled Drugs (Penalties) Act, this was all a dramatic assertion of penal power in drug control in Britain. The penal pressure has continued into the 1990s with the heavy penalties for trafficking made available under the 1991 Criminal Justice Act, the confiscation orders of the 1993 Act (Thomas, 1994) and the broad provisions affecting drug users, ravers, prisoners and other groups, in the 1994 Criminal Justice and Public Order Act (Malyon, 1994). Almost without exception, the impact of this unceasing punitive policy trend has been overwhelmingly negative, with rising numbers of drug users, offenders in prison, drug related crimes, demands on enforcement resources — the list goes on. At the bottom end of the tariff, recently proposed increases in fines for possession or supply of certain drugs (Druglink, 1994 a) will, with certainty, lead to an inability to pay and further imprisonment of more drug users for fine defaulting. At the top end of the tariff, it has become widely accepted that one of the main effects of the toughening of penal response, has been the hardening of the market: increasing criminals' attention to security, taking retributive action against informants, greater willingness to employ violence and firearms, development of more sophisticated organisational structures designed to distance the major players from enforcement attention and so on (Dorn & South, 1990; Dorn *et al.*, 1992). Some aspects of this process are illustrated by the increased sophistication of the money laundering business and enforcement efforts to target it (South, 1995).

'Going for the Money'

As the birth of the DTOA turned on the possibility of the sequestering of criminal profits, it is important to say a little more about this important new dimension of drugs policing — financial investigations. The drafting of provisions in the DTOA that would greatly empower financial investigations, reflected the belief of Government, Parliament and law enforcement bodies that Britain's financial system was (and is) facilitating a considerable amount of drug related money laundering. In response, as Levi (1991 a: 110) notes,

> Since 1984, when the Police and Criminal Evidence Act was passed, there has been a vast transformation in the range of legislation encroaching on the privacy of banking records. The movement in the direction of encouraging and, in an increasing range of cases, of requiring 'active citizenship' on the part of the banks has as its objectives (1) to prevent criminals from benefiting financially from the offences for which they have been convicted, and (2) to deter them and others from committing crimes for gain in the future.

Giving a higher profile to targetting money laundering, in both legislation and enforcement strategy, reflects earlier initiatives in the USA. In particular, it has been a position long held by the US Drug Enforcement Administration (since around 1978: US General Accounting Office, 1984: 5) that if traditional law enforcement efforts have so evidently had limited impact upon the organisation of drug trafficking, then a new strategy is called for. Pursuit of the **assets** of entrepreneurial crime may succeed in the destabilisation of trafficking networks where traditional emphasis on prosecution of the 'leaders' of 'organised crime' has manifestly failed (Dombrink & Meeker, 1986; Dorn, Murji & South, 1991). However, early evidence suggests that while the number of confiscation orders and the amounts forfeited have been rising (respectively, from 203 and £1.2 million in 1987 to 1,000 or so and £10.1 million at the beginning of the 1990s (Collison, 1994 a: 36)), so too have the scale and profits of the drugs economy (Ruggiero and South, 1995). As I described earlier, recent control policies have often had negative side-effects. In this case, going for the 'Big Money' and the 'Big Traffickers' has perhaps too often become a case of targetting those who are rather more visible and clearly more vulnerable. As Collison (1994 a: 36) notes,

> Zander has argued (confirmed in my [ie Collison's] own observation of drug detectives at work) that the police have used the actuarial skills prompted by the legislation to complement their detective skill in building up a supply biography for street level user-dealers so that they receive a substantial prison term and lose their car, video, furniture etc; that is the legislation provides extra penalty but also facilitates new approaches to case building (Zander, 1989). It is also important to bear in mind the fact that street level user-dealers are involved, through their dependency, in a business with a high cash flow but little or no long-term profit precisely because it has been smoked, snorted or injected.

Civil Liberties, Symbolic Power and Anti-Drugs Legislation

As Levi (1991 a) noted, the DTOA was a key piece of legislation in the setting of precedents for the erosion of banking confidentiality in Britain. It was also of considerable significance in terms of legal precedent and civil liberties implications, in two other respects. First, in the reversal of the onus of proof, (theoretically) placing this not upon the prosecution but upon the defendant when it comes to satisfying the court as to the source of identified funds. Second, and with particular relevance to the actions of the financial institutions affected, an offence created by s.24 occured if there was knowledge or **suspicion** of funds being the profits of drug trafficking. Traditionally 'suspicion' has not been sufficient grounds for action within the English criminal law. Rather 'knowledge' of, or 'belief' about, the fact of criminal activity has been required. 'Suspecting' an offence might normally be accepted as a subjective matter, unless it is argued that it is being used as an excuse to cover equivocation about reporting what **in fact** is knowledge of, or belief about, the perpetration of a crime. Again there is a reversal of the traditional expectation that the prosecution must prove the case; here it is for the defence to prove that there was neither knowledge or belief **nor** suspicion, or that there was an intention to disclose the relevant information to the police or other authorities (see eg. Samuels, 1986: 316). Provisions of the DTOA and subsequent legislation have had to respond to legal judgements and appeal court challenges, as well as refinements in drafting, but into the 1990s, the working principles and spirit of the original act remain in force. Thus, Henham (1995: 15) usefully brings this discussion up to date:

> Whilst there are several major erosions of due process discernible in the Drug Trafficking Act 1994 the most significant is that contained in s.2(8) of the 1994 Act which reverses the rule in R v Dickens [1990] by requiring [only] the civil standard of proof to determine whether a person has benefited from drug trafficking or the amount to be recovered. Sallon and Bedingfield [1993] have questioned the efficacy of a policy which drastically erodes some of the fundamental rights of an accused in a criminal

trial without establishing the potential for any perceptible reduction in drug use. (my additions in [])

Beyond the law court, these and other developments at domestic and international levels, are also intended to make powerful **symbolic** statements about Britain's stance on drug issues. Thus, in terms of its policy responsibilities as a 'good international citizen', the Government has publicised its' domestic efforts at the level of the international 'control community'. It has also been very active in European and Commonwealth bodies concerned with drug trafficking and money laundering. For example, promoting and initiating International Mutual Legal Assistance Treaties (which aid extradition of traffickers to the countries where they are wanted and also assist in financial investigations (Levi, 1991 b: 287–295)). Additionally, Britain has actively aligned itself with US policy, occasionally seeming to act as an ambassador for Washington DCs internationalization of its' 'War on Drugs'[8]. And finally and relatedly, the British Government and enforcement agencies have traded upon drug crime and associated 'threats' (arms, terrorism) *precisely as symbolic* issues. As noted, within the international community, highlighting contributions to cooperative action; and for domestic audiences, being able to show the tough line of action taken against an external threat. Again US influence and the real and symbolic (if waning) 'special relationships' between British and US Governments and enforcement agencies, have played their parts, although so too has the over-arching hegemonic 'internationalization' of US law enforcement (see Nadelman, 1993, for a brilliant review). Within this context of US internationalization and 'bilateralism', the US brings to bear continued pressure upon its various 'partners' to step up their contributions to the 'global war on drugs'[9].

THE 'INNOVATORY DANCE': THE MUTUAL INTERACTION BETWEEN TRAFFICKING ENTERPRISES AND LEGISLATORS AND ENFORCERS

The range of interventions, strategies and international agreements developed against national and international trafficking enterprises are now very wideranging and quite sophisticated — however **they are not working**. Or at least, not very well. To criminologists and sociologists, if not to regulators, this may be no surprise. Illegal markets may reflect many characteristics of legal ones but do not necessarily conform to the (often stereotypical) models of organization which regulators and law enforcers often adopt (Reuter, 1983; Ruggiero and South, 1995). For example, money laundering is **very big** business but it is not necessarily easily controlled by **'very big'** 'international agreements', 'enforcement stings' or 'revenue and taxation strategies'. It is an interstitial phenomenon and it takes advantage of, and integrates into, *legitimate* systems of commerce which are — from the parochial to the multi-national — necessary to the functioning of economic societies. Money laundering cannot therefore be controlled as if it were simply an unwanted slice of the pie that can be cut out and discarded. In relation to all forms of drug-related crime, it seems clear that tougher legislation without thoughtful analysis simply results in tougher barriers to investigation and tougher (and more violent) responses to detection.

Stepping up the War: Enforcement and Penalties

Enforcement changes

In a sense, like much else in the Thatcherite 1980s and on into the 1990s, drug control in Britain has been driven by market forces. On the one hand, enforcement-organisations have increasingly had to see themselves as 'internal markets' with a need to maximise resources and rationalise for 'efficiency gains' (cf Collison, 1994 a: 33, 37); and on the other hand, there has been the stimulus and pressure of the 'external market' — the drugs market that police and customs are supposed to be targetting. Both of these 'market forces' have been coming together since the early 1980s. A clear illustration was the restructuring of anti-drugs policing into the tiers recommended by the Broome Committee, a working group of the Association of Chief Police Officers (ACPO) (Dorn *et al.*, 1992: 152–8 and reprint of sections of the Broome report in Appendix; South, 1994 a: 409–10). This argued for a model of enforcement that would 'mirror' the supposed pyramidal structure of trafficking and distribution in Britain (Dorn *et al.*, 1991). Hence a pyramid of enforcement was to be established. At its apex was the then new National Drugs Intelligence Unit (NDIU), established at New Scotland Yard in 1985 as a joint Police and Customs services' 'clearing house'. This unit replaced the old Metropolitan police Central Drugs Intelligence Unit with the rationale that it should now become a more clearly *national* resource. Along with several other specialist intelligence units it has since been amalgamated into the National Criminal Intelligence Service. This became operational in 1992 (Dorn *et al.*, 1992: 154–5; Hebenton and Thomas, 1992).[10]

As a solid middle tier in the Broome Strategy pyramid, the Regional Crime Squads (RCS) created 'Drugs Wings' as attached but relatively autonomous units, to specialise in drugs cases and, in particular, undertake investigations that crossed local police force boundaries. At this third (bottom) level of force and divisional operations, there would be support for RCS operations as well as routine local policing of drugs. Interestingly however, it is perhaps here as much as anywhere else in policing, that some important developments have taken place. These involve the related increase in strategies of 'low-level policing' and referral schemes.

Street level — enforcement and diversion

At street-level, various police forces and strategy commentators have supported the idea of 'low level policing' aimed at disrupting street markets (Lee, 1995) and diverting users from criminalisation to counselling and treatment (Gilman and Pearson, 1991; Dorn and Murji, 1992). This is a development encouraged by recent policy recommendations (ACMD, 1991) and can incorporate the now-widespread use of 'Referral cards' or leaflets giving details of helping agencies, which police can hand out when cautioning or in other less formal encounters (Dorn *et al.*, 1990; Dorn, 1994; Barker, 1992). The rise of increased use of cautions and of referral to drugs agencies is of great significance because, as Henham (1994: 231) therefore observes,

> The dominant trend in simple possession cases is towards release with a caution, thus reflecting a trend towards general relaxation of penalties for soft drug use in European countries; ... It is apparent that *de facto* de-criminalization of soft drug use and possession has occured in certain European countries without necessitating deliberate sentencing policy changes.

It should be emphasised of course, that as these developments are *not* the result of centrally directed deliberate policy change, they are patchy: employed in relation to some drugs (eg cannabis, heroin) but not others (cocaine offences do not usually receive a caution (Collison, 1994 a: 28)). Similarly some police force areas (eg Merseyside, parts of London) have been more willing to pursue cautioning and referral schemes than others.

Sentencing trends

The courts and prison system have, of course, been as central to Government control strategies as enforcement, and it is perhaps particularly through the reality of sentencing that we can detect the impact of legislation and its interpretation. Overall, for those most vulnerable to the attentions of the law, if they are not cautioned or otherwise diverted from the system, then this has been a harsh experience. Once pulled into the system, it is harder to break free of it (Collison, 1994 b). At the same time, the 'Big Traffickers', against whom rhetoric has flowed most easily, have not, in general, been easily persuaded to take up Her Majesty's invitations to languish in her establishments.

While sentences under the 1971 Misuse of Drugs Act were generally of modest punitive proportions, the trend since the 1980s has been to longer and tougher sentences for drugs offences. From 1983, the courts were advised to refer to the Lord Chief Justice's guidelines (from R v Aramah; Kay, 1988) which suggested a raised tariff. The 1985 Controlled Drugs (Penalties) Act raised the maximum penalty for trafficking in Class A drugs from 14 years to life imprisonment, and with the 1987 implementation of the 1986 DTOA, such sentences could also include asset confiscation. The court's guidelines were amended upward as a result of R v Bilinski, 1987, (Dorn *et al.*, 1992: 185–6). These guidelines have recently been revised again, with higher penalties for the even larger seizures now being made. Interestingly and to reflect this increase in supply to the market, sentencing is to be based more on weight (and purity) than value at street level, as guidelines previously suggested. The Court of Appeal producing the guidelines argued that, the consequence of going by street value had been that "the sentencing level for like quantities of the drug became lower as the drug became more plentiful. It could not serve Parliament's purpose if the more drugs imported and lower the street price, the lower the sentencing level." (Henham, 1995: 17). The law has once again responded to changing market conditions, ensuring its principles of proportionality and retribution, and yet the most obvious question appears unasked. If past increases in penalty levels have so evidently failed to deter or break trafficking enterprises, to the extent that importation and distribution now produces seizures higher than ever, why should an automatic response of further increases in penalties be presumed to be any more successful?

In 1991, Home Office data on 'Offenders dealt with' in the late 1980s, showed a consistent rise in the number of persons 'found guilty, cautioned or dealt with by compounding for drugs offences' (ISDD, 1991: 26, tables 10, 11) and this trend continued into the 1990s (ISDD, 1994: 78, table 11). Yet, as Mott (1989: 32) observed of the limited research that has been done on the impact of sentencing on heroin users, "what [research] there is suggests that sentences of imprisonment may have little effect".

An interesting innovation of the 1991 Criminal Justice Act, (operating from October 1992) was that it allowed for sentencers to attach conditions to a standard probation order, requiring offenders to attend a drug or alcohol treatment agency or programme. After much debate about the desirable and undesirable features of this arrangement, many in the drugs field and probation service accepted that possible benefits might follow (Goodsir, 1992). In the event, recent research (Lee, 1993, Lee and Mainwaring, 1995) suggests that, for various reasons (including preference for the old orders available to the court), this option has rarely been taken up.

THE GOVERNMENT'S NEW STRATEGY DOCUMENTS

In recent years the Government has been criticised for appearing to have no coherent policy on drugs (Druglink, 1994 b). As in other areas of social policy (Samson and South, 1995), a high turnover of responsible Ministers and shifting Departmental priorities, have produced a number of changes, inconsistencies and controversies in recent British drug policy, (a sad history in which the influence of the fiscal priorities of the Treasury should be neither forgotten nor underestimated).

The issuing of the recent strategy documents is, in part, designed to silence critics about the lack of such strategy. So does Britain now have a coherent and fixed drugs policy? Well, on the one hand, formally speaking, policy *has* been stated. As Edwards and Arif (1980: 233) define the matter: policy can be represented by "a government statement that expresses a set of intentions which should guide the development of a programme". Such intentions have been set out for the different regions of Great Britain in different documents. This attention to regional diversity and accomodation of different policy platforms and priorities is, in many ways commendable, though it is not always logical and has clearly been subserviant to political negotiation, ideology and whim. The case for harm minimisation is a clear example: strongly endorsed in the Scottish document it is de-emphasised in the English strategy although it is grudgingly accepted if services can justify it as reducing health risks or under an umbrella of crime reduction. As Ashton (1995 b: 6) comments: "Though de-emphasised harm reduction is still alive in England: it's just that its clothes may need to be trimmed or adjusted." As has often been noted in the past, policy making is not a rational process! Blum *et al.* (1973: 285) observed of US drugs control policy some years ago that "policy decisions rest only partly on questions of fact, but are [also] heavily loaded with pragmatic, moral and political considerations".

Drug futures: Control issues

Howard Parker *et al.* (1995) have recently produced an important discussion of empirical data indicating that Britain (or at least the N.W. of England, from which it is reasonable to extrapolate) is experiencing the further 'normalisation' of drug use. This portrait of 'drug use futures' should clearly be accompanied by consideration of appropriate 'control futures'. In other words, if drug use is no longer definable as deviant, what is the argument for its criminalization; if it remains criminalized, how can drug use be *appropriately* regulated, policed and controlled?[11]

There are perhaps three routes that may be followed in present circumstances. For the pragmatic reason that full-scale legalization is unlikely in Britain in the immediately foreseeable future, I shall subsume elements of this possible fourth path within my discussion of the harm minimization approach.

One path is to simply look backwards to a mythical Golden Age, where ideals of discipline, morality, family values, hard work and so on (Pearson, 1983) 'naturally' prevented evils such as drug problems. This is the kind of approach favoured by the current Home Secretary, who has placed emphasis upon heavier fines, more imprisonment, more punitive 'get tough' measures and also issued a reproof to the police for adopting more liberal cautioning policies (Druglink, 1994, a).

The second path is that of consolidation, recently favoured in the 1993 ACMD report on *AIDS and Drug Misuse, an Update*. This has argued that while much has been achieved through innovation in harm minimisation approaches, it is now time to consolidate and reintroduce into the framework a 'back to basics' reminder about the importance of *preventing and stopping* drug misuse. The argument here is that past ACMD reports on responding to the problem of HIV/AIDS have been misread "as saying 'drug use no longer matters' " (Druglink, 1994 c). Here the 'bottom line' of drug control is reasserted, albeit in the language of treatment and prevention. However, and importantly, unlike the first path, this control concern is accomodated within the philosophy of the British tradition of compromise.[12]

A third and to my mind more desirable and constructive path is continued inno-vation on the ground as well as at policy level. Examples here would be extension of existing work with new groups (eg development of peer education among drug users (Bottomley *et al.*, 1995)), or new media, or in new geographical areas, or with new, previously uninvolved services (eg development of specialist 'Drug Courts' (Bean, 1995)), or even development of wholly new approaches. It must be admitted that I don't know what these new approaches would be — they're so new nobody's thought of them yet! But prior to the huge threats of the heroin and AIDS problems of the 1980s, many 'new' approaches that are now accepted orthodoxies were also unthought of, or at least undeveloped.

The sociology of science and of 'paradigm' changes (Kuhn, 1970), as well as many examples from the history of social policy (Samson and South, 1995) sug-gest that the second and third paths — of consolidation and innovation — may be a sensible and useful 'mix', meeting, as best they may, demands of the present and requirements of the future. A fourth path of full-scale legalization or even radical decriminalisation does not seem to be up for debate on the British control agenda — certainly not within the policy frameworks of either Conservative or Labour parties. However, Britain has already taken tentative steps down the road of *de facto, modest* decriminalisation for minor possession of some Class B and C, and even in some police force areas, Class A drugs. And this is happening within a broader framework of supportive harm minimisation approaches, Arrest Referral Schemes and so on. This mix of steps along the path of innovation, taken on ground made secure by a British 'tradition' of compromise and consoli-dation, may continue to produce many 'bad results' but it may also be our best hope of getting good ones.

CONCLUSION: J.S. MILL, SIR HUMPHREY, SIR MALCOLM AND BING SPEAR

In a free society, drug use by individuals will always raise the perennial John Stuart Mill 'On Liberty' type questions and debates. For Mill 'the only purpose for which power can be rightfully exercised over any member of a civilised com-munity, against his will, is to prevent harm to others. His own good, either physi-cal or moral, is not a sufficient warrant" (see Gossop, 1993: 151). As the American commentator Richard Blum and colleagues asked in 1973:

> Shall society decide that there is a 'right' to treatment for persons involved with drug problems? Is there a 'right' for people to use their bodies as they see fit? Is it wise for society to set forth criminal sanctions that punish persons for acting in ways that are detrimental solely to their own welfare and not that of others? (Blum *et al.*, 1973: 234).

One point that the harm minimisation framework of my third path clearly recog-nises is that this latter image of the drug user as harmful only to him or herself is naive and shortsighted — drug problems **do** cause harms for many others quite apart from the user. We should also be aware that in the laws of some of Britain's European partners, this issue is of more than philosophical importance, for these countries may uphold the *legal* principle that there can be no legal basis for prohibiting freedom of action in respect of an individual's own body (Leroy, 1992).

But all of this aside, the principal question put forward by Blum and colleagues, still stands : 'Would society be wise to respond to its drug problems by putting forward yet more criminal sanctions and punishing more drug users'? Despite recent criticisms of the 'treatment/enforcement' bifurcation of policy as largely mythical (Collison, 1993; Henham, 1994: 224–5), the early British tradition, epitomised by Sir Humphrey Rolleston's report, did provide a crucial and symbolic foundation for subsequent innovations 'in the name of' the chimerical 'British System'. The appropriate lesson of British history might therefore be that we re-think, re-appraise and re-value this history of pragmatism and compromise, innovation and consolidation. The Government's 'New' drug strategies do not seem to offer coherence, or the likelihood of delivering a better deal for drug users, or fewer drug problems for society. The ghost of Sir Malcolm Delevingne still haunts the Home Office. But the final word should rest with the late Bing Spear, who also did so much to shape Home Office policy albeit in a rather different direction to that favoured by Sir Malcolm. As Spear (1995: 13) recently argued — what we really need is "a fundamental rethink", instead "all we get from our current political masters is rhetoric" and "glossy government publications".

NOTES

1. Although, as Spear (1995: 13) notes "The UK's drug controls have their foundation in the 1913 Hague Convention, aimed at restricting the production and availability of certain drugs to 'legitimate and scientific needs'."
2. On control policy developments in this period and generally, see Berridge (1978, 1984); Kohn (1992); Pearson (1991); South, (1994 a, b).
3. A term suggested by Snider's (1991) idea of 'the Regulatory Dance' between corporate criminals and reform processes.
4. A good current example of ideologically self-induced, policy amnesia is Home Office insistence on pursuing electronic tagging and US 'Boot Camp-style' detention centres for drug- and other offenders. This, despite evidence of their past failures (all the way back to the Borstals in the case of tough youth punishment), cost and negative side-effects (Grewcock, 1995).
5. The British 'crack attack' panic of the late 1980s, and its failure, even by 1995, to become the major threat predicted is an interesting parable of the times (Shapiro, 1993; and see Silverman, 1994, for a somewhat sensationalist but informative account of the crack story and enforcement responses). This is not to deny the rather different experience of urban America.

6. This initiative included the designation of specialist teachers as Local Education Authority' Drugs Education (later Health Education) Coordinators. In the early 1990s funding for such posts all but disappeared although the new Government strategy documents reintroduce plans for schools to provide drugs education.

7. Of course, in the background and less well publicised by the political rhetoric of the day, there were other developments of equal significance. On the ground, the Department of Health was quietly endorsing the development of harm minimisation practice in the drugs agency field, and syringe exchange schemes and HIV/AIDS initiatives were being established around the country. However, these developments are considered elsewhere in this volume.

8. The argument put forward by Bullington and Block (1990: 39), that this war is a 'Trojan horse' that is really underpinned by traditional anti-Communist foreign policy concerns, is worth noting here. See also Levi (1991 b: 110, fn) on "the War on Drugs" as a "useful pretext for US involvement overseas" and also Dorn and South, 1993.

9. Though here, we might be forgiven for noting a degree of hypocrisy suggested by CIA use of 'front' banks for its own money laundering operations. On the BCCI affair, see Levi, 1991 a: 301, fn. 19; Passas, 1994: 75-76; and on other cases, see Chambliss, 1989: 189-90 on the Nugan Hand bank established in Sydney, Australia in 1976 and used by the CIA; and Robinson (1994: 40) on an even earlier — 1953 — case of CIA laundering in relation to plans to reinstate the Shah of Iran.

10. Some commentators have speculated that, building upon this kind of development, a national system of coordinating law enforcement efforts, (intelligence gathering *and operational*), could emerge, and in turn evolve into a national 'serious crimes' police agency — like the US FBI or a national CID (Greenway, 1994). Police supporters of such a proposal are less sanguine about the possibility that such an agency would have to dove-tail with an enhanced (post-Cold War) role for the Security Service in dealing with drug trafficking (if it were to be re-defined as posing a 'threat to the economic well-being of the country'). Relatedly, the development of intelligence and operational cooperation between European police forces, and the establishment of the Europol intelligence office concerned with drugs and terrorism, is of great significance (Hebenton and Thomas, 1995).

11. For a pragmatic consideration of some questions along similar lines, in the spirit of the British tradition he did so much to facilitate and improve, see the commentary by the late Bing Spear (1995).

12. The English strategy document combines some elements of both the first 'punitive' path (consider its' treatment of prisoners using drugs, discussed not in relation to harm minimisation as in the Scottish document, but under 'Crime' and in relation to new compulsory drug testing provisions of the most recent Criminal Justice Act) and the second 'consolidation' path.

REFERENCES

ACMD (Advisory Council on the Misuse of Drugs) (1991) *Drug Misusers and the Criminal Justice System, Part 1*, London: HMSO.

ACMD (1993) *AIDS and Drug Misuse — An Update*, London: HMSO.

Ashton, M. (1989) 'How the Rolleston report set the course of addiction treatment in Britain', *Druglink*, January/February, p. 13.

Ashton, M. (1994) 'New drug strategies for England and Scotland', *Druglink*, November/December, 6–7.

Ashton, M. (1995a) 'Strategic progress uneven across UK', *Druglink*, 10, 4, 5.

Ashton, M. (1995b) 'English national strategy goes live', *Druglink*, 10, 4, 6.

Auld, J., Dorn, N. and South, N. (1986) 'Irregular work, irregular pleasures: heroin in the 1980s' in R. Matthews and J. Young (eds.), *Confronting Crime*, London: Sage.

Barker, J. (1992) 'A positive bust: arrest referral in Southwark', *Druglink*, 7, 4, 15–16.

Bean, P. (1974) *The Social Control of Drugs*, Oxford: Martin Robertson.

Bean, P. (1995) 'Drug courts USA', *Druglink*, 10, 3, 13, 14.

Berridge, V. (1978) 'War conditions and narcotics control: the passing of Defence of the Realm Act Regulation 40 B', *Journal of Social Policy*, 7, 3, 285–304.

Berridge, V. (1984) 'Drugs and social policy: the establishment of drug control in Britain 1900–1930', *British Journal of Addiction*, 79, 17–29.

Berridge, V. (1991) 'AIDS and British drug policy: history repeats itself …?', in D. Whynes and P. Bean (eds.), 1991.

Blum, R. *et al.* (1973) *Drug Dealers — Taking Action*, New York: Jossey Bass.

Bottomley, T., Smith, M. and Wibberley, C. (1995) 'Peer education among crack users: not so cracked', *Druglink*, 10, 3, 9–12.

Bruun, K., Pan, L. and Rexed, I. (1975) *The Gentlemen's Club: international control of drugs and alcohol*, Chicago: University of Chicago Press.

Bullington, B. and Block, A. (1990) 'A Trojan-horse: anti-Communism and the war on drugs', *Contemporary Crises*, 14, 39–55.

Chambliss, W. (1989) 'State-organized crime', *Criminology*, 27, 183–208.

Collison, M. (1993) 'Punishing drugs: criminal justice and drug use', *British Journal of Criminology*, 33, 3, 382–99.

Collison, M. (1994a) 'Drug crime, drug problems and criminal justice: sentencing trends and enforcement targets', *Howard Journal of Criminal Justice*, 33, 1, 25–40.

Collison, M. (1994b) 'Drug offenders and criminal justice: Careers, compulsion, commitment and penalty.' *Crime, Law and Social Change*, 21, 49–71.

Delevingne, M. (1931) 'Drug addiction as an international problem', *British Journal of Inebriety*, 29, 2, 54–59.

Dombrink, J. and Meeker, J. (1986) 'Beyond "Buy and Bust": non-traditional sanctions in Federal drug law enforcement', *Contemporary Drug Problems*, 13, 4, 711–40.

Dorn, N. (1994) 'Three faces of police referral: welfare, justice and business perspectives on multi-agency work with drug arrestees', *Policing and Society*, 4, 1.

Dorn, N. and Murji, K. (1992) 'Low level drug enforcement', *International Journal of the Sociology of Law*, 20, 159–71.

Dorn, N., Murji, K. and South, N. (1990) 'Drug referral schemes', *Policing*, 6, 482–92.

Dorn, N., Murji, K. and South, N. (1991) 'Mirroring the market?: police reorganisation and effectiveness against drug trafficking' in R. Reiner and M. Cross (eds.), *Beyond Law and Order: criminal justice policy and politics into the 1990s*, London: Macmillan.

Dorn, N., Murji, K. and South, N. (1992) *Traffickers: drug markets and law enforcement*, London: Routledge.

Dorn, N. and South, N. (eds.), (1987) *A Land Fit for Heroin?: drug policies, prevention and practice*, London: Macmillan.

Dorn, N. and South, N. (1990) 'Drug markets and law enforcement', *British Journal of Criminology*, 30, 171–88.

Dorn, N. and South, N. (1991) 'Profits and penalties: new trends in legislation and law enforcement concerning illegal drugs' in D. Whynes and P. Bean (eds.).

Dorn, N. and South, N. (1993) 'After Mr Bennett and Mr Bush: US foreign policy and the prospects for drug control' in F. Pearce and M. Woodiwiss (eds.) *Global Crime Connections*, London: Macmillan.

Dorn, N. and South, N. (1994) 'The power behind practice: drug control and harm minimization in inter-agency and criminal law contexts' in J. Strang and M. Gossop (eds.).

Downes, D. (1977) 'The drug addict as a folk devil' in P. Rock (ed.) *Drugs and Politics*, New Brunswick, NJ.: Transaction Books.

Druglink (1994a) 'Home Secretary signals harder line on cautioning and raises fines', *Druglink*, July/August, 4.

Druglink (1994b) 'Labour offensive on drugs and crime', *Druglink*, March/April, 4.

Druglink (1994c) "Back to basics' report says cut drug use to curb HIV', *Druglink*, January/February, 4.

Edwards, G. and Arif, A. (eds.) (1980) *Drug Problems in the Socio-cultural Context*, Geneva: World Health Organization.

Gilman, M. and Pearson, G. (1991) 'Lifestyles and law enforcement' in D. Whynes and P. Bean (eds.).

Goodsir, J. (1992) 'A strategic approach to the Criminal Justice Act, *Druglink*, September/October, 12–14.

Gossop, M. (1993) *Living with Drugs* (3rd edn.), Aldershot: Ashgate.

Greenway, B. (1994) 'Gangland', *Police Review*, 9th December, 13–14.

Grewcock, M. (1995) 'Criminal justice policy: hostage to fortune?', *Criminal Justice, the magazine of the Howard League*, 13, 3, 1–3.

Hebenton, B. and Thomas, T. (1992) 'The rocky path to Europol', *Druglink*, 7, 6.

Hebenton, B. and Thomas, T. (1995) *Policing Europe*, London: Macmillan.

Henham, R. (1994) 'Criminal justice and sentencing policy for drug offenders', *International Journal of the Sociology of Law*, 22, 223–38

Henham, R. (1995) 'Drug offenders and sentencing policy', a revised version of a paper presented at the British Criminology Conference, 1995, and submitted for publication.

Home Affairs Committee (1985) *Misuse of Hard Drugs: interim report*, London: HMSO.

ISDD (1991) *Drug Misuse in Britain: National Audit of Drug Misuse Statistics*, London: Institute for the Study of Drug Dependence.

ISDD (1994) *Drug Misuse in Britain 1994*, London: Institute for the Study of Drug Dependence.

Kay, L. (1988) '*Aramah* and the street value of drugs', *Criminal Law Review*, December, 814–20.

Kohn, M. (1992) *Dope Girls: the birth of the British drug 'underground'*, London: Lawrence and Wishart.

Kuhn, T. (1970) *The Structure of Scientific Revolutions*, 2nd ed., Chicago: Chicago University Press.

Lee, M. (1993) 'The unspoken sentence?: Treatment conditions for drug using offenders under the 1991 Criminal Justice Act', *Criminal Justice Matters*, 12, Summer, 15.

Lee, M. (1995) 'London: community damage limitation and the future of drug enforcement' in N. Dorn, J. Jepsen and E. Savona (eds.) *European Drug Policies and Enforcement*, London: Macmillan.

Lee, M. and Mainwaring, S. (1995) 'No big deal: court ordered treatment in practice', *Druglink*, January/February, 14–15.

Leroy, B. (1992) 'The EC of 12 and the drug demand', *Drug and Alcohol Dependence*, 29, 269–81.

Levi, M. (1991a) 'Regulating money laundering: the death of bank secrecy in the UK' *British Journal of Criminology*, 31, 2, 109–125.

Levi, M. (1991b) '*Pecunia Non Olet*: cleansing the money launderers from the Temple', *Crime, Law and Social Change*, 16, 217–302.

Malyon, T. (1994) 'New law will hit homeless drug users and ravers', *Druglink*, 9, 5, 5.

Mott, J. (1989) 'Reducing heroin related crime', *Home Office Research Unit Buletin*, 26, 30–3.

Nadelman, E. (1993) *Cops Across Borders: The internationalization of US criminal law enforcement*, Pennsylvania: Pennsylvania State University Press.

Parker, H., Measham, F. and Aldridge, J. (1995) *Drug Futures*, London: ISDD.

Passas, N. (1994) 'I cheat therefore I exist?: The BCCI scandal in context' in W. Hoffman, J. Brown Kamm, R. Frederick and E. Petry (eds.) *Emerging Global Business Ethics*, Westport, Conn.: Quorum Books.

Pearson, G. (1983) *Hooligan: A history of respectable fears*, London: Macmillan.

Pearson, G. (1987) *The New Heroin Users*, London: Blackwell.

Pearson, G. (1991) 'Drug control policies in Britain' in M. Tonry and N. Morris (eds.) *Crime and Justice, vol. 14*, Chicago: University of Chicago Press, 167–227.

Reuter, P. (1983) *Disorganized Crime*, Cambridge, Mass.: MIT Press.

Robinson, J. (1994) *The Laundrymen: Inside the World's Third Largest Business*, London: Simon and Schuster.

Ruggiero, V. and South, N. (1995) *Eurodrugs: drug use, markets and trafficking in Europe*, London: UCL Press.

Sallon, C. and Bedingfield, D. (1993) 'Drugs, money and the law', *Criminal Law Review*, 165.

Samson, C. and South, N. (eds.) (1995) *The Social Construction of Social Policy: methodologies, racism, citizenship and the environment*, London: Macmillan.

Samuels, A. (1986) ''Dirty' drugs money and financial and business institutions', *Business Law Review*, December, 315–17.

Shapiro, H. (1993) 'Where does all the snow go? the prevalence and pattern of cocaine and crack use in Britain' in P. Bean (ed.) *Cocaine and Crack: supply and use*, London: Macmillan.

Silverman, J. (1994) *Crack of Doom: the extraordinary true story behind crack-cocaine*, London: Headline Books.

Snider, L. (1991) 'The regulatory dance: understanding reform processes in corporate crime', *International Journal of the Sociology of Law*, 19, 209–36.

Social Services Committee (1985) *Misuse of Hard Drugs: fourth report of the Committee*, London: HMSO.

South, N. (1992) 'Moving murky money: drug trafficking, law enforcement and the pursuit of criminal profits' in D. Farrington and S. Walklate (eds.) *Offenders and Victims: Theory and Policy*, London: British Society of Criminology and ISTD. pp. 167–93.

South, N. (1993) 'Criminal justice versus public health: decriminalisation, legalisation and harm reduction', *Criminal Justice Matters*, 12, Summer, 10.

South, N. (1994a) 'Drugs: control, crime and criminological studies' in M. Maguire, R. Morgan and R. Reiner (eds.) *The Oxford Handbook of Criminology*, Oxford: Oxford University Press, 393–440.

South, N. (1994b) 'Voices from the past: drugs and social history', *International Journal on Drug Policy*, 5, 4, 254–6.

South, N. (1995) "On cooling hot money': trans-atlantic trends in drug-related money laundering and its facilitation', *Criminal Organization*, 10, 1, 21–28.

Spear, B. (1994) 'The early years of the 'British System' in practice' in J. Strang and M. Gossop (eds.).

Spear, B. (1995) 'A personal account', *Druglink*, 10, 5, 12–13.

Stimson, G. (1987) 'The war on heroin: British policy and the international trade in illicit drugs' in N. Dorn and N. South (eds.).

Strang, J. and Gossop, M. (1994) 'The 'British System': visionary anticipation or masterly inactivity?' in J. Strang and M. Gossop (eds.).

Strang, J. and Gossop, M. (eds.) (1994) *Heroin Addiction and Drug Policy: the British System*, Oxford; Oxford University Press.

Thomas, D. (1994) 'The Criminal Justice Act 1993: confiscation orders and drug trafficking', *Criminal Law Review*, February, 93–100.

U S General Accounting Office (1984) *Investigations of Major Drug Trafficking Organizations*, Washington DC: GAO.

Whynes, D. and Bean, P. (eds.) (1991) *Policing and Prescribing: The British System of Drug Control*, London: Macmillan.

Wright, A., Waymont, A. and Gregory, F. (1993) *Drug Squads: law enforcement strategies and intelligence in England and Wales*, London: Police Foundation.

Zander, M. (1989) *Confiscation and forfeiture law: English and American comparisons*, London: Police Foundation.

CHAPTER 7

AMERICA'S DRUG WAR: FACT OR FICTION?

Bruce Bullington

INTRODUCTION

The twentieth century has been to a considerable extent a century of warfare, much of it derived from the inability of diverse ethnic and racial groups to co-exist. Think first of the two world wars with their toll of lives and property, the failed Russian revolution, the crimes of Japanese, German and Russian occupations; a myriad of smaller stories convey their own tales of destruction. As the century draws to an end the greatest threats to the well-being of humanity may be the specter of civil war in the former Yugoslavia and outbreaks of ethnically based hatred and violence in many other parts of the world.

In the United States it is comfortably believed that a "melting pot" has permitted, even facilitated, ethnic and racial harmony. There is, however, the disturbing rhetoric of a war of one group of Americans against another — a war on drugs. During the last twenty-five years this enduring civil war has intensified and its casualties have significantly increased, but the matter is as old as the century itself, and is rooted in America's seemingly intractable problem with race.

Casualties in the war on drugs continue to mount (and will for some time) on both sides. Among drug users and dealers there are high arrest rates, mushrooming proportions of America's incarcerated populations are offenders with drug violations as their principal or most serious offense; "enhanced" sentences for substance offenders have had devastating effects on young African-Americans and Hispanics living in America's inner cities. In the general community effects of the war on drugs have included increased crime and a staggering growth in rates of violence and the feeling of public insecurity.

Throughout this period, the nation has undertaken three or four declared drug wars. This began with the Nixon administration efforts in the early 1970s to force the Mexican government to bow to U.S. pressure (Operation Intercept) and the deal struck with the government of Turkey to terminate the growing of opium poppies in that nation. Then in the 1980s and early 1990s the successive administrations of Presidents Reagan and Bush embraced the rhetoric and policies of war, in the process committing vast new resources to the conflict. These truly remarkable expenditures resulted in breathtaking increases in the number of persons brought into the criminal justice system. They also provoked a host of seemingly intractable new problems.

Despite this there are a number of important policy makers and political leaders who argue that there has never been a serious war on drugs. For example, Congressman Charles Rangel, an outspoken critic of some aspects of present policy, says that the problem is that we have still not fought a real war (Rangel, 1989). In a similar manner, conservative columnist Thomas Sowell recently commented:

> Many of the people who write the laws, who sit as judges or who serve on parole boards are convinced they know so much better than the rest of us poor slobs how to handle criminals. Phony sentences keep the public happy, while reduced sentences and 'rehabilitation' through psycho-babble are supposed to deal with crime ...
>
> The anointed are going to believe any other explanations, however strained, before they believe that (that their moral preening has unleashed runaway crime). Far better to believe that crime is caused by the 'neglect' of 'society' than to believe that you have blood on your own hands. (Sowell, 1995:9A).

The extreme measures that some policy critics promote in order to end drug abuse and crime would, if implemented, make a shambles of our constitution and way of life. Despite such costs, these actions would not have their intended effect. The extraordinarily brutal punishments routinely meted out to offenders in Iran, China and elsewhere are offered up as examples of "what can be done" with the drug problem here if we are indeed serious about stopping it. However, these methods would be inconsistent with the traditions of western civilization.

Most recently, House Speaker Newt Gingrich told the Republican National Committee that we ought to "quit playing games" about illegal drugs. He called for a public vote to determine whether to legalize drugs or to adopt such severe penalties that people would no longer take them. His specific proposals called for the death penalty for those who import large quantities, other sanctions that he said would be "very Draconian, very real steps" and mandatory community service for users (Beamish, 1995:3A).

This paper examines the question of whether there has really been a war on drugs. Has there been only sound and fury signifying nothing? Has America made a real commitment to its war on drugs? Has the war been lost or never really fought? This paper describes several aspects of drug war policy: the promotion and enactment of legislation geared to enhancing punishments for drug offenders; huge increases in arrests, sentences, and correctional commitments for drug users; a half-hearted commitment to the funding of drug treatment efforts; and the war's devastating effects on the minority poor residing in America's inner cities. It concludes that the war has indeed been fought, and with a vengeance. Yet despite the huge commitments to the effort, its results provide little hope that there have been any significant breakthroughs, or even slight shifts in the desired direction. One of the most puzzling features of this war is how it has been possible to go to such extremes to assure a victory against drug use and users, and yet to have come away with no clearcut beneficial outcome.

COMMITMENTS TO THE DRUG WAR

The War Budget: Financing Antidrug Efforts

During the last two and one-half decades there has been a remarkable increase in the commitments of federal, state and local governments in the drug war effort. The federal government has led the way in these activities. President Nixon launched these programs during the early 1970s when he authorized the expenditure of about $200 million per year to expedite policies aimed at drug control (Currie, 1993:14). During the 1980s there was a massive increase in the federal commitment to antidrug programs, rising from approximately $1 billion in 1982, the year of President Reagan's first war on drugs, to a total of $20 billion spent during that decade by the federal government alone (Boaz, 1991:620)! During the 1990s these federal expenditures have continued to grow, the 1995 commitment by the Clinton Administration amounts to nearly $15 billion! (*National Drug Control Strategy*, 1995:111). After adjusting for inflation, the federal government is spending more than ten times as much on drug law enforcement today as it did on Prohibition enforcement in the 1920s (Boaz, 1991:629).

It is important to consider that these robust figures only account for the federal outlay in the war on drugs. States, cities and local governments are also spending immense sums to supplement the federal efforts. The effects of these obligations may easily be seen in terms of their disastrous consequences for the government structures that have supported them. Currie notes that in 1991 the state of California had accrued a $14 billion dollar deficit, largely attributable to the state's extraordinary outlay for prison construction and maintenance during the 1980s. The quintupling of California's financial commitments to prisons during that decade has had far reaching effects on other state programs, many of them directly linked to crime and drugs. Public schools have been starved for funds and a number of districts have been bankrupted. Mental health facilities have suffered severe cutbacks. Public health provision has been substantially weakened. Child protection agencies have had to reduce their activities. Libraries have been closed. Homeless shelters and programs have been eviscerated. A final irony is that even methadone maintenance programs have been curtailed in the interest of building more prisons to hold more drug offenders (Currie, 1993:18)!

Legislative Support for the Drug War

In order to support law enforcement efforts in the war on drugs, federal and state legislatures have taken unusual measures to ensure that drug offenders will be identified, arrested and severely punished for their misdeeds. The federal government passed ever more stringent legislation in 1984, 1986 and 1988: penalties for drug violations were significantly enhanced, even for first-time offenders. In many cases mandatory sentences were imposed in order to circumvent the discretion exercised by "soft" judges. In addition, expansion of both civil and criminal asset forfeiture programs was embraced, federal benefits were denied to convicted drug offenders and it was made possible for known users to be evicted from public housing (U.S. Department of Justice, 1992:184–185).

The states have followed suit, often exceeding the federal government in the extreme penalties they impose for drug offenses. One example may be seen in the case of the state of Michigan, which passed a special new drug law in 1978. Under this statute anyone found in possession of or attempting to sell a hard drug substance (heroin or cocaine) amounting to 650 grams or more (about one and one-half pounds, including the "cut" as well as the actual drug) would be forced to serve a life sentence without the possibility of being placed on probation or parole. This sentence was the same as that provided for a first-degree murder conviction in that state (Michigan abolished the death penalty more than one hundred years ago). Those caught with lesser amounts were treated little better; 225–650 grams brought a sentence of 20–30 years, and for 50–225 grams the sentence was 10–20 years. According to the bill's sponsor, the law was designed to get at and punish drug kingpins, rather than lower level couriers (Gordon, 1994:58).

By 1990 it had become apparent that the extreme penalties prescribed under this act were not having their intended effect. At that time a total of 138 people had been sentenced to life imprisonment under the act, 117 of them since 1986 when the crack scare first hit and drug enforcement was dramatically increased. The majority of those caught had not been high level traffickers but were low level couriers; more than one-half were first offenders and several were under 20 years of age. Only 50% of the lifers were white while 83% of the state population is white (Gordon, 1994:59, 60).

As it was learned that the law was not functioning as intended some judges began finding ways to mitigate the harsh sentences of those who were not hardcore drug offenders. In addition, it was found that a number of serious offenders, persons specifically targeted by the law for their high level dealing activity, had been able to evade the severe penalties by offering to provide "useful" information to prosecutors in exchange for a reduction in their charges. Those at the lower end of the distribution chain had no valuable information to offer, and therefore bore the full force of the penalty.

Two Supreme Court cases were initiated, and those finding difficulty with the law, including its architect, hoped that these decisions would resolve some of the provocative issues that had been raised. In *Harmelin v. Michigan* (111 S.Ct. 2680

1991), the U.S. Supreme Court refused to overturn the conviction and life sentence of the defendant for possession of 672 grams of cocaine. The case had been brought on the basis of an alleged violation of the cruel **and** unusual punishment clause of the 8th amendment to the U.S. Constitution. In reaching its decision to reject the argument, the Court stated that while the punishment may have been cruel, there was no constitutional requirement of "proportionality" in sentences (in response to the argument that this was the same penalty as that for first degree murder, and therefore disproportionate).

The following year in *People v. Bullock* (440 Mich. 15 1992) the Michigan Supreme Court disagreed with the federal decision, finding that mere possession of 30 pounds of cocaine did not warrant the mandatory life sentence. They based their decision on a unique wording in the Michigan constitution which forbids cruel **or** unusual punishment. In cases of simple possession (30 of the 160 persons then serving life sentences under this law had been convicted for possession only), the court determined that a parole review would have to take place after 10 years of the prescribed sentence had been served. This decision complicated matters even more, however, for now persons are serving longer terms under the other provisions of the act (possession of 225–650 grams) than for much larger amounts, such as the 30 pounds in the *Bullock* case (Gordon, 1994:62).

The situation in Florida reveals another egregious flaw in the stiff sentencing mandated under the drug law revisions passed throughout the 1980s. In the early 1980s Florida, along with many other states, developed a series of tough mandatory sentences for drug offenders. This legislation resulted in massive prison crowding and overwhelmed the authorities responsible for avoiding or eliminating such conditions (as a result of the drug wars most states are under court orders to reduce prison overcrowding). In response to this situation, Florida officials developed an early release policy for nondrug offenders in order to accommodate the influx of new drug commitments. This meant that very serious violent offenders were often being released from prison in order to make room for drug violators, many of whom had been sentenced for simple possession. Ultimately the average time served in Florida was reduced under the stiff new laws, with offenders completing about 35% of their prescribed sentences in 1989, as opposed to the 52% that inmates had served in 1987 (Rasmussen & Benson, 1994:75).

Apparently the Florida legislature has learned little from this experience, however, for in June 1995 they passed a bill mandating that **all** offenders serve 85% of their sentences. The governor allowed the bill to become law without signing it (he had wanted the legislation restricted to violent, repeat offenders rather than being applicable to everyone). In order to carry out this mandate, massive new spending ($1.8 billion) will have to be directed to cover the cost of building 60,000 new prison cells and to provide for the maintenance of offenders. The projected correctional budget for the state in 1996–97 will be at least $1.3 billion (Robertson, 1995:9A)! It is difficult to imagine where this money will come from, as the state is already experiencing substantial financial difficulty.

These are but a few examples of the legislative changes that the states have made in support of the war on drugs. In the name of these efforts we have seen the development of sentencing guidelines, extraordinary mandatory sentences, the elimination of probation and parole, a vast expansion of police powers and an easing of the search and seizure requirements. There has also been a sharp reduction in the "amenities" of life in prisons such as televisions, reading material and rehabilitative programs, reintroduction of chain gangs (The latest folly. A recent debate in Florida featured the architect of this new policy insisting that inmates be chained together, rather than individually shackled. Somehow the latter humiliation was not sufficient, yet the difficulties of working a group in concert or allowing them to use the bathroom facilities can only be imagined), and a host of other repressive provisions. Following the federal example, every state has felt the impact of the war and has committed scarce taxpayer resources to its conduct. In doing so they have simultaneously been forced to curtail or eliminate many other beneficial social programs, any number of which had the potential of actually contributing toward a reduction in drug use.

Police Activities

Now it is clear that the police have responded enthusiastically to the incentives provided under the aegis of the war on drugs. Arrests for drug violations have skyrocketed as police departments across the nation devoted and diverted significant resources to the targeting of these offenses. In 1993 alone, the FBI counted 1,126,300 drug arrests; this number, though high, was substantially below the peak level recorded in 1989 — 1,361,700. In 1993 drug arrests comprised 8%, and a growing proportion, of all arrests (*National Drug Control Strategy*, 1995:33).

Another way of looking at the arrest figures is to assess the rates of arrest for drug violations per 100,000 inhabitants. A review of the pattern of these rates from 1965–1992 reveals several points worth noting. First, the rates of arrest have climbed precipitously over the study period. The 1965 rate for adults was 36.4 per 100,000; by 1992 it had climbed to 554.7 per 100,000, an increase of more than 1500%! The same pattern may be found with drug arrest rates of juveniles, defined here as those under 18 years of age. In 1965 the overall rate for this group was 9.5%; in 1992 the comparable figure was 147.3%, an increase of 1550%! (*Uniform Crime Report*, 1992:190,202).

These data also reveal an interesting and important pattern with regard to the racial composition of drug arrestees. Regardless of which group one considers, in recent years the ratio of black/white arrests has remained at about 5/1 (*Uniform Crime Report, Ibid.*). Given that blacks comprise about 13% of the national population the arrest figures are, by any measure, extraordinary. We will return later to a more detailed analysis of the significance of race in the war on drugs.

When evaluating the involvement of different police groups it is learned that the federal drug enforcement apparatus is much less significant in making drug arrests than are state and local agencies. Given their relatively small number of personnel and the federal agencies' preference for targeting foreign operations and major interstate trafficking activities, this result is not unexpected. During fiscal year 1993 the DEA made a total of 21,231 arrests; 10% of these were for heroin, 52% for cocaine, 24% for marijuana and 14% for dangerous drugs (U.S. Department of Justice, 1993:465). However, during 1992 state and local police produced 1,066,400 drug arrests; 53% of these were for heroin and/or cocaine, 32% for marijuana and 15% for dangerous drugs. In that same year state and local police also made 3,091,623 alcohol related arrests (U.S. Department of Justice, 1993:448, 456, 458).

For the nation as a whole, state and local drug arrests increased 105% during the 1980–1989 period in response to drug war mandates (Currie, 1993:14). Most of these arrests focused on the users and sellers of harder drugs, although many marijuana offenders continued to be caught up in the enforcement net. Though the rate of arrests for marijuana offenses declined over this period, the rate for hard drugs grew precipitously. In 1980 the rate of drug arrests for heroin or cocaine sale or manufacture was 11 per 100,000. By 1989 that figure was 100 per 100,000, an increase in excess of 900%! (Currie, 1993:15).

A closer analysis of the practices of individual states reveals tremendous variability in terms of drug arrests. Rasmussen and Benson observed that these rates range from a low of 88 (per 100,000) in West Virginia to a high of 1,060 in California. They found too that eight states with a combined population comprising 36% of the U.S. total were responsible for 60% of all drug arrests. These states included California, Connecticut, Florida, Georgia, Maryland, Massachusetts, New Jersey and New York (Rasmussen & Benson, 1994:8). Currie notes that between 1983–1988, the California rates of felony arrests for narcotics offenses climbed 300% for adults and 600% for juveniles (Currie, 1993: *Ibid.*)!

Rasmussen and Benson found the cities are even more disparate in their drug arrest rates than are the states. Among those cities with populations between 100,000–499,000, tremendous variation was noted. In this group Madison, Wisconsin, had a low drug arrest rate of 57 (per 100,000), while Oakland, California had a rate of nearly 3,500! (Rasmussen & Benson, 1994:10).

Finally it is worth noting that despite the rhetoric of those sponsoring and directing the nation's war on drugs, the majority of drug arrests, whether federal, state or local, have been for simple possession offenses rather than the more serious crimes of sale or manufacture. This pattern predates the latest war efforts, for in 1981, 78% of the nation's drug arrests were for possession and 22% for sales. Today there has been a slight reduction in the proportion of drug offenses that are for possession only; in 1992, 68% of arrests were for possession and 32% for sales. (U.S. Department of Justice, 1993:458). One should note that some of those convicted for possession offenses were actually involved in higher level drug activity, but plea bargained the charges to lesser offenses. These reductions are not as common as has occasionally been suggested, however. A government study of the extent of plea bargaining in such cases concluded, "Drug defendants were more likely to be convicted of the same offense for which they were arrested than defendants arrested for most other felonies, except for those arrested for burglary." (U.S. Department of Justice, 1992:171).

It is evident that recent priorities have changed somewhat regarding the drugs targeted by enforcers. Marijuana has definitely been deemphasized in the most recent war on drugs, although it is still significant. In 1981 marijuana offenses (combining sales and possession) comprised 69% of all drug arrests. In 1992 only 32% of drug arrests were for marijuana violations (U.S. Department of Justice, 1993:458). The latter figure still constitutes a sizable, and inordinate, proportion of all drug arrests (given the drug's harm potential when contrasted with other controlled substances). No doubt this reflects the fact that many police agencies continue to energetically prosecute marijuana cases — as Rasmussen and Benson have suggested, they want a "piece of the pie", and can't find other kinds of drug offenders in their jurisdictions. These authors note that in 1989 marijuana arrests accounted for more than 50% of all drug arrests in twenty-four states (Rasmussen & Benson, 1994:181).

Based on the figures presented above and a great deal of other available data, it is clear that America's war on drugs has had a marked effect on the number and characteristics of drug arrests occurring across the nation. Police throughout the country have responded to the directives and incentives offered, such as the opportunity to share in the spoils of asset forfeiture provisions. The resulting record numbers of arrests have put intense pressure on other justice system components.

The Courts and the Drug War

As the police have flooded courts with drug violators, backlogs have mounted rapidly, clogging the system and forcing the development of innovative means to expedite the processing of these cases (Martin, 1990). Although court personnel and budgets have been supplemented to deal with the influx of drug cases, these enhancements have not been proportionate to caseload increases. For example, between 1989–1991 the federal courts were forced to handle a 600% increase in caseload, but were only granted an 80% increase in their budgets (Currie, 1993: *Ibid.*).

Many of the legislative changes adopted in the implementation of the drug war have been designed to minimize the discretion of judges. Critics have argued that judges have varied too greatly in their past sentencing practices. Discussions have focused on so-called concerns with equity, and mandatory sentencing policies have been adopted in response to these disparate sentencing practices. In reality, however, mandatory sentences have substantially increased the time that all convicted drug users and dealers must serve, while those convicted of other criminal offenses, and often very serious ones, get reduced sentences or none at all. Thus, in the name of equity we have extended the average time served by all drug offenders and made certain that few can avoid these sanctions.

Court room work groups (Eisenstein & Jacob, 1977) have learned to adapt their procedures to accommodate the new mandatory requirements. Charging decisions have taken on new meaning, for district attorneys can at their discretion determine the specific crime with which to charge a defendant. Those who are cooperative and who have valuable information to offer (serious drug offenders), are the ones most likely to receive breaks in terms of these charging decisions. The lower level user or dealer has nothing valuable to offer and therefore is made to suffer the full weight of the new sentences.

Sentencing decisions are made by the court, within the parameters of the law. Local jurisdictions can easily save huge sums of money by sentencing drug defendants to state institutions where the costs are spread out over the entire taxpaying group. If the offender were retained in the local jail facility, however, the entire cost would be paid by county residents. This problem, often referred to as a criminal justice "commons" concern, has lead to very uneven statewide sentencing patterns. Given the common pool of state resources shared by all jurisdictions, there is often fierce competition to place local offenders in available state prison slots, for this serves as a "no-cost" option to prosecutors and local judges (Rasmussen & Benson, 1994:191–199; Benson & Rasmussen, 1995:24–28). Without holding the counties financially accountable for these state placements, there may be no hope of easing the current overcrowding that is typically found in state facilities. Rasmussen and Benson have suggested that this reform would go a long way toward slowing down these past practices, for those jurisdictions that choose to incarcerate at a very high rate would then have to shoulder the full cost of doing so. Under those circumstances local taxpayers might think twice about who should be locked up if they are directly footing the bill for these actions.

Corrections: The End of the Line

The full impact of the decisions to aggressively pursue a war on drugs in the United States have been felt by correctional officials. While this country has always had a high rate of incarceration when compared with most other modern nations, the impetus of the drug war has pushed us head and shoulders above the others. During the early 1990s we surpassed South Africa and the Soviet Union with an incarceration rate of 426 per 100,000 persons. In the decade ending in 1990, U.S. incarceration rates had doubled; more than one million adults were then serving time in institutional settings. At the same time 1 out of every 46 adults was under some form of correctional supervision, whether in institutions, or on probation or parole (Irwin & Austin, 1994:3).

In terms of the huge outlays made for the drug war programs, correctional facilities and services have received a substantial portion of the total allocations. Between 1979–1988 government expenditures for the criminal justice system increased 101% for the police, 125% for the courts, 161% for the prosecution, 134% for the defense and 217% for corrections! The same pattern could be found in the numbers of employees hired in each component of the justice system between 1979–1990. During that period there was an increase of 28% in police personnel, 19% in court workers, 25% in the district attorney's office, 50% in the public defenders offices and 104% in correctional staffing (Irwin & Austin, 1994:14, 15)!

The dollar amounts allocated to these criminal justice agencies were staggering. In 1990 approximately $74 billion was spent to operate the entire criminal justice system in the United States. Twenty-five billion dollars of that money was spent on corrections, with 85% of that amount going to jails and prisons (Irwin & Austin, 1994:13). Given these figures it is easy to understand why so many American states are currently experiencing severe fiscal crises.

It is also important to note that we now find many impoverished communities actively bidding to have new prisons built within their boundaries. Prisons mean jobs and the cash they generate can stimulate local economies that have been down and out for some time. Not long ago these same communities would have been adamantly opposed to having a correctional facility located anywhere close by. However, the downturn in the economy and massive loss of unskilled and semi-skilled jobs over the last twenty-five years or so have provoked remarkable changes in attitude.

It should be apparent that drug users and dealers have been a major concern of American policy makers. The latter have made a heartfelt commitment in the attempt to force people to stop using condemned drugs, and to severely punish those who refuse to acquiesce. The various criminal justice components have all been significantly affected by these events as they have struggled to deal with huge increases in clientele while simultaneously managing their somewhat inadequate resources. We turn now to the question of how the war on drugs has impacted drug treatment in the United States.

DRUG TREATMENT AS A WAR CASUALTY

How has the war on drugs met the treatment needs of users? The answer is an ambiguous one, for there are major distinctions between user types, and the available services are not equally accessible to all who may need or request them. There are significant differences, for example, between private, for-profit, private, not-for-profit and public treatment programs. The private, for-profit treatment programs are abundant, well staffed and capable of delivering high quality care for substance abusers. The private, not-for-profit organizations are relatively small, poorly funded and can offer few forms of assistance. Finally, the public sector programs are inadequately funded, relatively few in number, have long waiting lists for admission, and are understaffed (their employees are overworked). We explore some of these concerns below.

Earlier there were few private, for-profit drug treatment providers, and apparently little need for them. One would find no more than a handful of such programs listed in the yellow pages of the phone book during the 1960s. Apparently those who could afford such treatment could find help through their private physicians.

During the last thirty years there has been a major change in the availability and range of private, for-profit drug treatment providers. Contemporary phone listings include page after page of hospitals, clinics and other facilities providing such care. This explosion in the availability of high-priced drug treatment programs may be attributed to the dramatic growth in the prevalence of drug use here in the 1960s and 1970s, and especially to the redefinition of what constitutes a drug problem. For example, simple use of the "wrong" substances is now categorically defined as problematic and indicative of some underlying disorder, even when such use has no measurable or obvious bad effects on the user. Or the popular "stepping-stone" notion predicts that there is no such thing as "innocent use", for it is thought that all can progress to more serious substances and use patterns.

Most of these relatively sophisticated drug treatment facilities cater to an upper middle class clientele, including those who can afford to pay directly for the help they receive, and a larger group of persons (mostly middle class) who have insurance coverage that will foot the bill for them. It is not coincidental that many of these programs specialize in 28 day treatments, for that is the maximum treatment stay that is reimbursable by many insurance companies. Another feature of these facilities is that they are extraordinarily expensive; it is not unusual for clients to have to pay as much as $750 per day just for the cost of a room, not including the charges for any specialized treatment that may be provided. Despite the exorbitant costs of such programs, there is little available evidence indicating that they are especially successful. While some users appear to be helped, others quickly regress, and over the long haul most experience continuing problems associated with their drug dependency.

It is now clear that the war on drugs has been a boon to those in the business of providing therapeutic services by effectively defining any use as problematic. Thus, the war has contributed substantially to the rapid growth in the number of such programs. There is of course fierce competition for clients among these facilities, and few have waiting lists. In fact, due to a shrinking middle class client base they often operate at 60% of capacity or less (Currie, 1993:229). In any event, it is evident that the well-off have access to a wide range of therapeutic interventions and are not likely to experience any criminal stigma associated with their drug use.

The private programs contrast sharply with those that are available in the public sector. Here we find few programs, little variability among them, inadequate funding, and a high concentration of especially problematic clients. Given these characteristics, it should come as no surprise that these facilities have not produced very favorable outcomes.

Unquestionably the one public program that has received the most attention of U.S. policymakers has been methadone maintenance. This chemotherapeutic approach provides heroin addicts with a cheap synthetic substitute for their preferred substance. Proponents argue that methadone clients are able to stabilize their lives (if they so choose), for they no longer find themselves driven by the demands of a habit that requires repeated injections (three to four times a day on average), and the necessity of obtaining the funds to sustain regular use. In theory then, methadone can allow for a relatively regular work and family existence and eliminate the need for committing crimes to support an expensive habit.

Despite its initial promise and the enthusiastic support of its backers, methadone maintenance has failed to be the panacea that many had claimed for it. When the drug is used carefully, with a specially selected group of heroin addicts, it can clearly be beneficial, sharply reducing their criminal activities and offering them the opportunity to bring some stability to their lives. In a number of instances, however, these programs have been poorly run. Some have not been selective with their clientele and have not had any salutary effect on their undesirable behaviors. A major reason for the failure of methadone to make a real dent in our contemporary drug problem is that it only works (when it does) with heroin users. Yet, according to most experts, since the mid 1980s cocaine has become much more popular and problematic than heroin ever was. At the present time (and in the foreseeable future), we do not have any similar substance that can be used to minimize the craving for cocaine, an especially reinforcing substance.

Other public programs include storefront operations and drug-free residential therapeutic communities (Gerstein & Harwood, 1990). These tend to be overwhelmed with clients, understaffed and starved for funds.

A third group of programs consist of private, not-for-profit efforts. Examples include Narcotics Anonymous, Alcoholics Anonymous, Teen Challenge and several others. Generally these rehabilitation programs receive little or no public funding. Participation in them is voluntary and they are staffed by ex-users. Surprisingly, these programs are often popularly thought to be especially helpful and successful, particularly when contrasted with some of the publicly funded efforts described above. This confidence in their potential appears to be based on the results of "in-house" evaluations, the testimonials of "recovered" users or on faith alone, for few have ever been subjected to careful external evaluation. These programs often refuse to provide outside researchers with access to their client populations, citing client confidentiality as the reason. In one comparative study that included control groups, the authors concluded that the group exposed to the therapeutic program did no better than the controls (Vaillant, 1983, cited in Coomber, 1995).

The U.S. record clearly reveals that drug treatment has not been a priority concern in the modern drug wars. Rather, treatment has been systematically downplayed, underfunded and relegated a relatively insignificant role in the antidrug battle. Several influential politicians, such as Congressman Charles Rangel and Senator Joseph Biden have repeatedly suggested that treatment has never really been tried yet and have urged their colleagues to "give treatment a chance". I believe that their assessment is correct.

At the present time adequate treatment facilities are available for those who are relatively well off. In most instances these are not people who are subject to much criminal justice attention. Therefore they often can discreetly obtain assistance without suffering much in the way of consequences.

The drug war has focused on a different class of user. In this conflict, minorities and the poor have been targeted for police attention, and the appalling statistics compiled in the war reflect this bias. For these users, many of whom are drug dependent, experiencing multiple problems in their lives, treatment programs are seldom available. Most must wait to gain admittance to the few programs that do exist. Given chronic fiscal shortages, these efforts have not been able to resolve the conflicts of more than a handful of those most in need of their services.

Publicly funded treatment service providers often find it difficult to attract problematic users who have not been referred through the criminal justice system. They are also frustrated when most of those who begin such efforts quickly leave to continue their drug use lifestyle on the streets. Mitchell Rosenthal (1991), the director of the Phoenix House Program in New York City, argues that largescale civil commitment is needed to force these recalcitrants into treatment, and then to keep them there for a sustained period of time "for their own good" (The same argument was used nearly forty years ago by psychologist David Ausubel and by officials associated with the implementation of involuntary civil commitment for addicts in California and New York.).

In summary, treatment has always been included in the rhetoric of the drug war, as if it were a priority concern of policy makers. The reality has been that federal, state and local budgets for fighting the war have systematically underfunded treatment in favor of law enforcement and criminal justice interventions. Those most in need of treatment are the least likely to be able to obtain it. On the other hand, the well-to-do who experience even minor difficulties associated with their drug use can easily find high quality facilities that will cater to their needs.

We must keep in mind that the majority of users only consume drugs, whether licit or illicit, occasionally and recreationally. Several writers have incisively challenged the notion that drug use, even addictive use, is a social issue that calls for forceful public resolution. For example, Thomas Szasz (1985) and Stanton Peele (1989) have presented cogent arguments that the drug prohibition policies pursued here are positively destructive of this nation's essential values regarding individual rights and freedoms. In this writer's view, any attempt to force treatment on users is inappropriate. Nevertheless, we have seen that given a drug war mindset, doing nothing is not an option when it comes to dealing with this problem.

Despite the reticence of the lawmakers to wholeheartedly support drug treatment, many experts believe these programs are a good investment. Fortunately the old "all or nothing" assumptions of the past no longer hold (the idea that a person must be permanently "cured" in treatment), and some enlightened treatment staff now have a much more realistic outlook about what can be expected. Studies have revealed that treatment can work by reducing the criminality of users both during and after they are involved in a program. Two very recent studies, one completed by the Rand Institute and the other by the state of California, both concluded that treatment efforts pay for themselves seven times over

(*Druglink*, 1994: 8). In addition, it is evident that these programs are often able to assist users to bring their habits under some semblance of control, perhaps not eliminating use entirely, but at least making it less problematic than it was before. Finally, these programs also work toward "normalizing" the user's life. In the end, particular treatment approaches may prove to be a good investment of public monies. Although there is little evidence that any dramatic changes can be expected from these efforts, they certainly can improve the life circumstances of problematic users. Our failure to invest more in these efforts is a direct byproduct of the drug war mindset. For these reasons I have called the current treatment dilemma a casualty of the drug war.

RACE, ETHNICITY AND THE DRUG WAR

Predictably, the effects of drug prohibition have been felt most keenly in the poorest sections of the country, especially among inner-city neighborhoods populated largely by blacks, Hispanics and members of recent immigrant groups. The reasons for this are not obvious, for according to the results of self report studies and a host of other data sources, these groups do not comprise the largest segment of the drug using population, nor even a particularly sizable proportion of it. Despite the claims that drug use is not particularly associated with social class, race or ethnicity, however, the poor and the minorities do comprise a disproportionate share of the problematic user population. The explanation most often given for the concentration of law enforcement efforts in ghetto communities is that these are the locales of the most visible illicit use, especially in and around the thriving open-air drug markets that operate there with impunity.

Ironically, both sides in the drug war have contributed to the rapid deterioration and destruction of these neighborhoods and the corresponding reduction in personal security and the quality of life experienced by inner-city populations. Ghetto residents are forced to cautiously move about in their own neighborhoods, constantly on the lookout for heavily armed youngsters on the prowl for rival gang members. The chilling account of L.A. gang life provided by Sanyika Shakur (Monster Cody Scott) in his book *Monster* reveals how these forays often result in the killing and wounding of innocents who simply happen to be in the wrong place at the wrong time (Shakur, 1993).

For their part, law enforcement troops maintain a more or less constant presence in the inner cities, yet they seem to be singularly unable to provide protection from the ongoing violence that has become a pandemic feature of modern American drug markets. Perhaps as important however, is the widespread belief among ghetto residents that the police are not only unable and unwilling to protect them, but are actually causing them harm through meaningless stops and other forms of harassment. The Rodney King affair in Los Angeles was only one example in a long list of "incidents" in which police have used excessive force when attempting to apprehend minority males.

The Decline of the Inner Cities

During the last twenty years America's inner cities have experienced a steady and dramatic decline. Consider the depressing trends that began in the 1950s with the flight of the growing middle class to the suburbs and the dramatic loss of jobs in the manufacturing sector of the economy. These events have been especially important to the poor because these occupations required relatively few skills and yet paid quite well. The groups most affected have been those left behind including poor blacks, Hispanics and several recent immigrant populations. While middle class America has enjoyed a steady (though recently diminishing) growth in their standard of living, those left to survive in the urban core have only slipped further and further behind.

These trends have been under way for some time. A number of factors contributed to the flight to the suburbs. Primary among these was the emergence of a sizable middle class in search of improved living conditions for their families. Government policies encouraging home ownership also served as a strong stimulus to the out-migration from the central cities. Finally, the funding and development of the interstate highway system facilitated travel in and out of the city core and between cities (Staley, 1992:10).

Major changes were also taking place within the civilian labor markets during this period. The most significant among these was the substantial reduction in the number of manufacturing jobs along with strong growth in the service producing industries. Between 1946–1993 the service sector has grown from about 58% of the total nonagricultural labor force to 80% of it (*Economic Report of the President*, 1994). Along with sharp reductions in the size of the manufacturing and goods producing industries there has been a marked change in the types of jobs now available within that economic sector. Since the early 1980s, most of the growth that has occurred in the manufacturing sector has been with small, high technology firms. Between 1972–1981 these high tech firms accounted for 87% of the growth in the manufacturing industries (Staley, 1992). Although the small companies offer new job opportunities, these positions require advanced education and specialized training. The current residents of America's inner cities cannot meet these standards and thus have been unable to take advantage of the few opportunities that are available.

The changes taking place in work opportunities have had a devastating impact on those residing in central city communities. These groups found themselves unable to move out of the city's core in order to follow the flight of manufacturing industries to suburban locations, other sections of the country (that offered a cheaper labor pool, tax benefits and other incentives to relocate), or to other countries. In addition, the few jobs that were being created called for skills they did not possess and for an education that they could not achieve. Even among the minority populations, those who were able to move out did so, leaving behind a growing concentration of very poor, troubled families (Anderson, 1994).

These trends have continued throughout the last decade as well. During this period there has been a continuing concentration of poverty areas in our largest cities, along with a steady, palpable, deterioration of neighborhood social conditions (Kasarda, 1993; Abramson, *et al.*, 1995). Kasarda states,

> there was not only a greater growth in the number of black poor in the cities during the 1980s than the 1970s, but also a growth in the percentage of blacks who were poor during the 1980s, in contrast to the 1970s ... the concentration of poor blacks in extreme poverty tracts increased considerably between 1980 and 1990 — from 33.8 percent to 41.6 percent. Thus, by 1990 more than two of five poor blacks in the 100 central cities resided in extreme poverty tracts (Kasarda, 1993:266).

Thus, although these bleak conditions have affected all groups living in these areas, blacks have suffered inordinately.

The social conditions that predominate in depressed communities are both well known and closely tied to crime, drug use and other indicators of social malaise. One concern that has been accorded a great deal of attention is the proportion of families headed by a single parent, most often the mother. In 1970 among America's 100 largest cities, 17.2% of households with children were headed by a female; by 1990 the comparable figure was 30.1% (the figures for whites was 18.8%, however, and that for blacks was 54.7%). When only considering the extreme poverty areas in these same cities, defined as tracts in which 40% or more of residents live in poverty, the differences are even more exaggerated. In 1990, 40.4% of white households located in severe poverty tracts were headed by a female, while 73% of black families were! The rate for blacks was actually twice that of Hispanics and three times that of whites (Kasarda, 1994:271).

A second important concern relates to the educational attainment of those residing in poor communities in the central cities. Here, too, the figures reflect a dismal reality; the condition of inner city residents has not been improving significantly, especially when considering the requirements for obtaining employment in modern, high technology industries. In 1990, for example, 36% of the urban black population and 54% of Hispanics aged 25 and above had not completed high school. In the extreme poverty areas the figures are 51% for blacks and 70% for Hispanics. While these figures only concern the adult population, the school dropout figures for youth do not offer much encouragement either. These rates improved only slightly between 1979–1990, from 16.8% to 14.6% (Kasarda, 1994:272–273).

Joblessness is a third key concern associated with the condition of today's urban poor. Without the opportunity to earn legitimate incomes, little can be hoped for with regard to improvement of the residents life conditions in these depressed communities. Unemployment is particularly problematic for high school dropouts. In 1990 the rates of joblessness among city residents aged 16–19 in America's 100 largest cities was 65%; in poverty tracts these rates ranged from 70–82%! (Kasarda, 1994:274). In a more recent study, Kasarda

(1994) found that the percentage of males aged 16–64 who were living in central cities in different regions of the country and not employed or in school ranged from 18–37% for whites, and 52–63% for blacks. Another way of viewing this concern is to look at labor force participation rates. Although white rates have remained quite stable over time, for minority groups there has been a decline in these figures. In 1960, for example, 70% of minority teenagers were working; in 1984 the figure was 55%, representing a 28% decline. The same trends were observed for young adults, with a 17% decline for those aged 20–24, and 9% for those 25–29. (Staley, 1992:22)

These three factors, single-parent households, poor educational achievement levels, and massive unemployment typify the life circumstances of those living in America's poorest inner-city communities. Although there has been some small improvement during the last twenty years with regard to the percentage of those completing high school, overall, life has become markedly worse for these urban residents. Given the changing job market with a shrinking industrial and manufacturing base, the movement of manufacturing concerns out of central city locations to other locales both here and abroad, and the level of preparedness required for those high-tech jobs that are now available, the future looks especially bleak for those living in inner-city America.

Drug Markets and the Informal Economy

As job opportunities began to disappear in the largest cities in America, an informal economy and labor market developed to cushion the blow to poor families. The informal economy is one that features cash transactions that go untaxed and business activities that are not controlled by government regulations. In many instances those who run otherwise legitimate businesses may believe that they can only survive by hiring people to work at low wages and without benefits. In the case of the apparel industry, for example, the number of sweatshops located in New York City increased from 200 in 1970 to more than 3,000 in 1981. At the time there were 50,000 workers hired in this manner in the shops and another 10,000 who were doing piecework at home (Staley, 1992:20). Unskilled workers participate in the informal economy because it offers them some income, although all would prefer a regular job with benefits and protected contracts.

Economists have attempted to estimate the magnitude of the informal economy, although doing so may be as difficult as measuring crime rates. The range of these estimates run from 3–30% of the Gross National Product. In 1987, a number of experts concluded that the informal economy amounted to approximately $450 billion (Staley, 1992:19)! In most cases these projections have only considered legitimate businesses that engage in illegal hiring and labor practices, although there certainly is a substantial informal economy in illegitimate businesses as well. For example, it is now widely believed that the drug business constitutes a very sizable component of the informal economy, involving upwards of $100 billion per year!

During the last fifteen years or so it has become evident that the drug economy is now a central feature of the depressed communities located in most large American cities. Many young men, and especially unemployed black and Latino youth find that participation in the drug trade can produce incomes well above what they ever could expect to receive in a legitimate job. Moreover, the work itself is exciting, interesting and allows for considerable free time in which to enjoy the fruits of their labors. Although there are certain risks involved in these occupations, they can be rationalized as a cost of doing business.

The cities serve as natural sites for the conduct of the drug business, for it is a service oriented concern. Wholesale and retail operations, financial support and distribution networks are all found in urban centers. Although the consumer group is not centralized in this way, the drug markets are (Staley, 1992:26).

It is now well known that most regular drug users are involved at some level in selling drugs to others. These activities may provide cash incomes, but in most cases simply allow the seller to help defray the costs of their own drug supply. Peter Reuter and his colleagues' study of drug dealing in the District of Columbia revealed that this activity can yield high returns for those with modest legitimate alternatives. Among those who reported selling on a daily basis, Reuter estimated they had median gross incomes of $3,600 per month and net incomes of $2,000 (not including free drugs). Most of the study subjects only sold on a part time basis, however. These people had median net monthly incomes of $721 from drug sales (Reuter, *et al.*, 1990:49).

Thus, it is evident that the rise of the drug economy in America's inner-cities may not be solely attributable to the addictive nature of the substances being sold there. Rather, general economic conditions have played a major role in promoting the growth and development of this illegal sector of the informal economy. As the available legitimate job base has dissipated in these central city locations, the drug economy has helped to fill the void by capitalizing the poorest sections of the inner cities (Staley, 1992:26).

Race and Drugs in America

Although no one has suggested that the war on drugs should have devolved into a war on the poor or on racial minorities, that has certainly been its outcome. The statistics generated by local, state and federal criminal justice agencies reflect a very one-sided war. Minorities stand out as disproportionately represented in all of these figures. This phenomenon is simply an extension of earlier drug wars, all of which have exaggerated the significance of minority use and targeted these groups for special attention. The record has now been well documented, beginning with xenophobic responses to early Chinese immigrants and their "special" problem with opium smoking. This was followed by hysterical accounts claiming that the use of cocaine lead black males to rape white women. Later the public was alerted to the dangers posed by Hispanic males use of marijuana and the violence it supposedly precipitated (Szasz, 1985; Morgan, 1978; Musto, 1987, 1989, 1991).

These are but a few examples of America's long history of claims of special concerns with threatening minority populations in the drug arena. Again and again moral panics have been induced by politicians and bureaucrats with vested interests, aided by distorted accounts in the media. These aroused concerns are then used to justify ever harsher responses to the escalating drug "crisis", on the basis of the public's demand that something be done about the problem.

The latest drug war has been no exception. The evidence is especially clear regarding the crack cocaine crisis of the mid to late 1980s. The decision to treat crack as an unusually harmful substance, and one categorically distinct from powdered cocaine hydrochloride, allowed federal lawmakers to justify adopting the "100 to 1 rule" (the 10 year penalty for possession of 5,000 grams of powdered cocaine is the same as that for possession of 50 grams of crack). Simple possession of crack also calls for a mandatory sentence under the federal statute, while possession with intent to sell is required to bring mandatory sentences for all other drugs. These laws appear to be racially neutral, for they make no mention of minority groups. However, it is well known now, and was then as well, that crack was a cheap form of cocaine that was used largely in very poor communities. Since blacks comprise a significant percentage of these populations, they naturally would suffer inordinately under the new provisions. And of course they have. In the federal system alone, 92% of crack defendants are black, while only 27% of powdered cocaine defendants are black (Chiricos, 1995:33).

The statistics regarding black male involvement in the criminal justice system because of drugs are beyond alarming. According to Jerome Miller, at the present time 56% of Baltimore's young black males are incarcerated or under probation or parole supervision. Black males are now five times more likely to be arrested for drug violations than are white males. While blacks comprise about 13% of the general population and 15% of the most age prone population (18–24), in 1991 they accounted for 41% of drug arrests (Gordon, 1994:143). The Washington, D.C. based Sentencing Project found that 25% of black males in their twenties are either in prison, on parole or probation: the figures for white males were 6% and for Hispanics 10% (Lusane, 1991:44).

CONCLUSION

The war on drugs, what Duke and Gross (1994) have called America's longest war, has accumulated a well documented track record throughout this century. Although recent commitments to continuation and escalation of the fight have been extraordinary when contrasted with earlier efforts, there can be little doubt that the nation's policy makers have been sincere in their attempts to curtail, even eliminate, illicit drug use here. Despite the tenacity of these convictions, however, serious drug use continues unabated and has in fact worsened. Our cities are much less safe and secure than they were before, and the lives of those living in America's inner cities have been made categorically worse. Meanwhile the "victories" claimed by the war's proponents have been slim at best and most appear, upon closer investigation, not to have been results of these programs at all.

So what has been achieved during the last fifteen years or so? The most notable accomplishment of this latest war effort has been the wholesale incarceration of young men, and especially minority males, at extraordinary rates for their involvement in drug use and sales. For some, these extreme measures could be justified if they resulted in diminished use of drugs and violence on our streets. Regretably, the opposite has occurred. Despite locking up a sizable proportion of the young black and Hispanic male population for drug offenses, the rates of problematic drug use have actually worsened considerably. In addition, street violence is much worse now than it was before the latest war effort began, and much of it can be directly attributed to the war's impact on inner city drug markets.

Our repeated efforts at drug interdiction have likewise produced few salutary results. Today the drugs we most fear are available nearly everywhere, and at quite modest prices. Moreover, the drug markets themselves have become increasingly dangerous for all concerned. Given the huge profits involved in the drug trade, the attempts to curtail these activities seem preordained for failure.

There has been a much ballyhooed reduction in the self-reported casual recreational use of substances throughout the 1980s and into the 1990s, although recent reports signal some possible reversals in these long term downward trends. Thus, a variety of government sources have indicated that many of the illicit substances are now markedly less popular and chic than they were in the 1970s and before. Both leaders and defenders of the war have been quick to claim the credit for these changes in attitudes and behavior, suggesting that their policies have established an inhospitable climate in which drug use is now popularly seen as morally unacceptable behavior.

Despite such puffery, a closer look at these trends reveals that the reported reductions in use actually began in 1980, well before the first modern Reagan war on drugs was launched in 1982 (not really taken up in earnest until 1986). Leaving aside the manifold criticisms that can be made regarding the validity of the surveys that have documented these changes in patterns of illicit drug use, it is clear that this war was never directed at casual use, but rather at the problematic use of hard drug substances, especially heroin and cocaine. All of the indicators of this type of use suggest that it has actually increased significantly throughout the war years.

Given the policy commitments established during the last fifteen years, it seems certain that Americans will be paying for the excesses of yesterday's and today's drug wars for years to come. Despite a recent slight reduction in drug arrest rates, our prisons are already filled to overflowing with drug violators. Most endure lengthy sentences imposed as enhanced penalties or as mandatory sentences for this special class of offense. The costs of building new penal institutions, staffing them and then paying the costs of housing prisoners is daunting, resulting in severe fiscal problems for most state and local governments. These costs will continue to grow for some time.

Throughout this period the American policy has seemingly been pieced together as a harms enhancement approach, in which every attempt is made to assure that those who indulge themselves in unapproved drugs will be harmed by doing so. This method stands in sharp contrast to the prevailing western European approach which emphasizes harms reduction, a policy that is designed to minimize the harms drugs do both to individual users and to the society generally. Our policies have magnified the harmful effects of drugs for several reasons. First, because we refuse to aggressively promote the dispensation of clean needles and syringes to users, we assure very high AIDS and hepatitis rates among intravenous users. Secondly, we encourage the substitution of harmful legal drugs such as alcohol for those which are illegal but less harmful, such as marijuana. Thirdly, we have made medical and other forms of assistance extraordinarily difficulty to obtain, thereby assuring the intractability of the miserable conditions suffered by users. Finally, we even punish casual use and force users to obtain their drugs in dangerous, underground markets.

Aggressive law enforcement efforts have also resulted in their own set of undesirable outcomes. By bringing extreme pressure to bear on drug markets police have escalated the levels of violence occurring in the drug trade as sellers compete with one another for territorial dealing rights. Police excesses in drug enforcement have always occurred, but these undesirable actions have increased precipitously in the latest drug war actions. It is now nearly a daily feature of American television news to observe police officers, armed to the teeth, invading "crack houses" in ghetto communities in order to assure that residents are not using the hated substance. Many popular "cops" television programs also document these actions as a uniquely American form of entertainment, featuring sparsely clad, spread-eagled minority residents surrounded by officers wearing bullet-proof vests and brandishing sufficient weaponry to conduct a real war.

Police enthusiasm for these tactics have been supported by the courts. Otherwise highly valued constitutional protections have been set aside in the drug war, assumably as a necessary tactic (many civil privileges must be waived during wartime). A recent example of this occurred in June 1995 when the U.S. Supreme Court acknowledged the right of an Oregon school to urine-test seventh grade athletes without any particular reason for doing so, other than the "good" of assuring that these young men and women are not using forbidden drugs (Epstein, 1995:4A). Urine testing has now become commonplace in American businesses and in public sector employment as well, although a generation ago these practices would have been unthinkable. Search and seizure regulations have also been significantly watered down in the interest of more easily obtaining convictions in the drug control effort.

Perhaps most importantly, the war on drugs has focused largely on young minority males. While it may never have been the intent of the designers of these policies or of those who implement them to discriminate against a particular racial group, the impact of the drug war has certainly been racist. And few seem to care about this deplorable situation. When questioned in opinion polls, both white and black Americans (the latter to a lesser extent) remain relatively unconcerned that the net effect of this war has been to single out blacks and Hispanics for special treatment under the law. In the interests of achieving a "drug-free society", most apparently do not care how this is accomplished, even if it means sacrificing some cherished constitutional protections.

Finally, we should note that the current war on drugs could never be successful in eliminating the drug markets that thrive in poor communities. As we have seen above, these markets provide, among other things, job opportunities for many thousands of minority males who otherwise have few options for legitimate, meaningful employment. The informal economy of the drug business has in effect provided capital for those mired in poverty, both jobs and cash with which to assure their very survival. It is now evident that the thriving open-air drug markets are at least partially a response to economic downturns and fragmented structural changes that have devalued the labor of those with few skills and little formal education. Should the war ever prove successful in eliminating this drug economy, the lives of these poor people could conceivably become even worse than they already are.

It may be encouraging to some that there has been diminishing enthusiasm for the drug war during the last few years under the Clinton administration. Based on our past record, however, it seems likely that the idea will be revised and recycled again, and probably quite soon. We Americans allow the drug issue to be politicized, shamelessly used by both major parties in their petty attempts to gain advantage over one another, rather than to discuss the matter rationally in a neutral context as many of the western European nations do. So long as we allow this to continue, we can rest assured that the drug demon will soon be unleashed again. The end results of these actions appear all too predictable in the mean streets of American cities.

And so, Mr. Gingrich, the evidence is in. Despite your recent posturing, it is clear that the U.S. drug war has been real, hard-fought and calamitous in its results. To call for a "real war" at this point is foolhardy, positively dangerous. Any honest assessment of what the past war has produced must lead to an outright rejection of the method, for it is extremely costly in both human and resource terms and has forced us to give up some very important protections in the process. Finally, to call for a public referendum on decriminalization seems disingenuous. This is due to the fact that you and your fellow politicians have for decades worked to create hysterical public reactions to drug use through campaigns of disinformation, knowing distortions of the truth and the like. Given the hostile environment that has been created in the wake of such tirades, calling for a public referendum on the issue at this point seems altogether too safe. And unfortunately, until the public reaches a point where they reject these divisive methods, no rational dialogue or discussion seems possible.

CASES

Harmelin v. Michigan. (1991) 111 S.Ct. 2680.
People v. Bullock. (1992) 440 Mich. 15.

REFERENCES

Abramson, Alan, Tobin, Mitchell and VanderGoot, Matthew (1994) The Changing Geography of Metropolitan Opportunity: The Segregation of the Poor in U.S. Metropolitan Areas, 1970 to 1990. *Housing Policy Debate.* 6:1 45–72.

Anderson, Elijah (1994) The Code of the Streets. *The Atlantic Monthly.* (May).

Beamish, Rita (1995) Legalize Drugs or Fight Serious War, Gingrich Says. *The Tallahassee Democrat.* (June 15).

Benson, Bruce and Rasmussen, David (1995) Tragedy of the Commons: The Origins of Failed Innovations in Criminal Justice Policy. (unpublished paper).

Boaz, David (1991) A Drug-Free America or a Free America? *U.C. Davis Law Review.* 24:3 (Spring). 661–637.

Chiricos, Ted (1995) Moral Panic as Ideology: Drugs, Violence, Race and Punishment in America. Forthcoming in Michael Lynch and E. Britt Patterson. *Race and Criminal Justice: A Further Look.* New York: Harrow and Heston.

Coomber, Ross (ed.) (1995) *Drugs, Your Questions Answered.* London: ISDD.

Currie, Elliott (1993) *Reckoning: Drugs, the Cities and the American Future.* New York: Hill and Wang.

Currie, Elliott (1994) *Druglink.* (November–December). London: ISDD.

Currie, Elliott (1994) *Economic Report of the President.* U.S. Government Printing Office.

Eisenstein, James and Jacob Herbert (1977) *Felony Justice: An Organizational Analysis of Criminal Courts.* Boston: Little, Brown.

Epstein, Aaron (1995) Drug Tests Allowed on Student Athletes. *The Tallahassee Democrat.* (June 27) 4A.

Gordon, Diana (1994) *The Return of the Dangerous Classes: Drug Prohibition and Policy Politics.* New York: W.W. Norton and Co.

Gerstein, Dean and Harwood, Henrick, ed. (1990) *Treating Drug Problems.* Institute of Medicine. Washington, D.C.: National Academy Press.

Hubbard, Robert, *et al.* (1989) *Drug Abuse Treatment: A National Study of Effectiveness.* Chapel Hill, N.C.: The University of North Carolina Press.

Irwin, John and Austin, James (1994) *It's About Time: America's Imprisonment Binge.* Belmont, CA: Wadsworth Publishing Company.

Kasarda, John (1993) Inner-City Concentrated Poverty and Neighborhood Distress: 1970 to 1990. In *Housing Policy Debate.* **4:3.** 253–302.

Kasarda, John (1994) Industrial Restructuring and the Consequences of Changing Job Locations. Unpublished paper. Chapel Hill, N.C.: Kenan Institute of Private Enterprise.

Lusane, Clarence (1991) *Pipe Dream Blues: Racism and the War on Drugs.* Boston, MA: South End Press.

Martin, John (1990) Drugs, Crime, and Urban Trial Court Management: The Unfortunate Consequences of the War on Drugs. *Yale Law Review.* **8:75.** 117–145.

Morgan, Patricia (1978) The Legislation of Drug Law: Economic Crisis and Social Control. *Journal of Drug Issues.* **8:1**. 53–62.

Musto, David (1987) *The American Disease: Origins of Narcotic Control.* New York: Oxford University Press.

Musto, David (1991) Opium, Cocaine and Marijuana in American History. *Scientific American.* (July), 40–47.

Musto, David (1989) How America Lost Its First Drug War. *Insight.* (November 20). 8–17.

Musto, David (1995) *National Drug Control Strategy: Strengthening Communities' Response to Drugs and Crime.* Washington, D.C.: U.S. Government Printing Office.

Peele, Stanton (1989) *Diseasing of America: Addiction Treatment Out of Control.* Lexington, Mass.: D.C. Heath and Co.

Rangel, Charles (1989) Our National Drug Policy. *Stanford Law and Policy Review.* **43:52**.

Rasmussen, David and Benson, Bruce (1994) *The Economic Anatomy of a Drug War: Criminal Justice in the Commons.* Lanham, MD: Rowman and Littlefield.

Reuter, Peter, MacCoun, Robert and Murphy, Patrick (1990) *Money form Crime: A Study of the Economics of Drug Dealing in Washington, D.C.* Santa Monica, CA: The Rand Corporation.

Robertson, Glenn W. (1995) Storm Warnings: Florida's Fiscal Future *The Tallahassee Democrat.* (August 2) 9A.

Rosenthal, Mitchell (1991) In Opposition to Drug Legalization. *U.C. Davis Law Review.* **24:617**. 637–654.

Shakur, Sanyika (1993) *Monster.* New York: Penguin Books.

Sowell, Thomas (1995) Criminals Get Better Treatment Than the Public. *The Tallahassee Democrat* (June 13) 9A.

Staley, Sam (1992) *Drug Policy and the Decline of the American Cities.* New Brunswick: Transaction Publishers.

Szasz, Thomas (1985) *Ceremonial Chemistry.* Holmes Beach, FL: Learning Publications, Inc.

U.S. Department of Justice (1992) *Drugs, Crime and the Justice System.* Washington, D.C.: U.S. Government Printing Office.

U.S. Department of Justice. (1994) *Sourcebook of Criminal Justice Statistics.* Washington, D.C.: U.S. Government Printing Office.

U.S. Department of Justice. (1992) *Uniform Crime Reports.* Washington, D.C.: U.S. Government Printing Office.

CHAPTER 8

Pragmatism or Principle? Continuity and Change in the British Approach to Treatment and Control

Susanne MacGregor

ANALYSING DRUGS POLICY

The aim of this chapter is to review and analyse current controls on drug users in Britain, especially as they operate through the treatment and care system.

'The most important lesson of the British system is the lesson of pragmatism' (Grant, 1994: vi). The British approach has never in practice been much like the coherent and self-contained orthodoxy it is imagined to be by overseas commentators. Rather it has always been 'a pragmatic and shifting response to a rapidly changing phenomenon' (*op cit.*:v).

In this chapter, I shall examine the shifts in policy and practice which have taken place in recent decades. I argue that changes can be understood, firstly, by looking at how the drug problem has been defined and re-defined; and secondly, through reviewing how key players perceived the range of choices open to them, where they saw their interests to lie and how they took advantage of the opportunities presented to them.

The focus will be on the British case but a complete understanding of the British experience requires some comparison with the situation in the USA. The influence of the United States on British drugs policy has long been a strong one. In the period under discussion, comparisons with the American experience were repeatedly invoked in discussions of the drugs and AIDS epidemics. And more generally in the wider context of social policy, as Britain moved to share common features of what came to be known as the Anglo-American model, direct policy borrowing (of ideas and practices — and in both directions) became a prominent feature of the period.

The main question addressed is why did the debate about drugs policy become framed in the way that it did? Why did certain policies and practices, which had previously been politically unacceptable, become suddenly acceptable again? For how long was this to last and how deep were the changes?

The contrast between abstinence-based and harm-minimisation policies formed the fulcrum of discussion. In typical British way, the issue was often fudged. Policies were articulated in such a way as to appear to provide support for both positions at the same time in order to obtain a working compromise, provide a base on which something could be done. The willingness of the parties involved to accept this fudge, not to insist on a rigid adherence to principle, is one of the continuities in the British system, reflecting a broader political culture which pervades drugs policy as much as other public policies.

'Politics is the art of the possible' said R A Butler, a leading post-war Tory politician. In the 1980s, despite this being seen generally as the decade of conviction politics, British drugs policy evidenced a sophistication of approach, a nice balancing of competing pressures, which indicated that the arts of negotiation and compromise remain central skills of the main players in this field.

A key theme of this chapter will be to show the power of history in spite of attempts at radical breaks (cf. also Berridge, 1991). Policy decisions taken previously, and the institutional arrangements which followed, laid down the parameters within which later choices would be made. Important in all this is the power of ideas. Certain sets of ideas, systematised especially in professional ideologies and codes, shaped views about the drugs problem and indicated the limits of appropriate policies. Within these arrangements, competing social groups each had their own particular interests. As policy developed in a changed situation, there would be shifting alliances and new players would enter the scene. These were to produce some changes of direction and changes in the relative influence and power of different interests but they did so within an overall frame which reflected certain broad agreements.

Over and above these particular interests stood the interest of government itself, especially for the maintenance of social order at home and good international relations with its allies. This determined its continuing acceptance that it had a responsibility to intervene to control the taking of illicit drugs. Although voices arguing a libertarian view were increasingly heard in this period, they had little direct influence on actual policies and practices.

During this period, there were also a number of innovations in service delivery and forms of control. Another aspect of this chapter will consequently be to explore the conditions which make for innovations and allow them to be developed.

The overall question addressed will be 'to what extent did developments in this period mark a decisive break with the past'? Did the period mark a sea change in policy, or were policy moves constrained by countervailing pressures?

It is concluded that the period saw more than an incremental shift in drugs policy. A transformation was begun which has not yet ended. This reflected wider changes going on in social and public policy which were in turn reflections of major social and economic transformations. Drugs misuse and drugs policy could not be immune to these developments.

Three major transforming forces coincided in the 1980s:

a) the arrival of a Radical Right reforming government determined to reshape political culture and the institutions of the welfare state;

b) the heroin epidemic, which encouraged a quantum leap towards embedding drug-taking within popular culture; and

c) the arrival of HIV and AIDS.

These three great waves, which happened to come together, may not have produced a sea-change but they certainly produced great turbulence. The storm has not yet settled.

One feature of this period was the stark contrast between the sensationalist discussion of drugs which dominated the media and political debates and the relatively calm and rational approach operating in services themselves. Most services were able to withstand these pressures towards extreme positions. One exception to this however was in the criminal justice and prison systems. The prominence of law and order in political rhetoric and as an issue in electoral politics impacted heavily and operated as a substantial constraint on the choices available in prison regimes and in the criminal justice system in general.

For a long time in Britain, the view of experts and practitioners has been that, if one is to develop sensible and practical policies which work, it is better to keep discussion out of the public eye. It is thought that once the public gets wind of what is going on, the pressure for drastic responses tends to build up. This is particularly the case when the wider public policy debate is dominated by populist and radical campaigning styles. In this period, the gap between informed opinion and public opinion grew in many policy areas. This partly seemed to reflect a deterioration in the standard of political debate (influenced perhaps by the soundbite culture of media-dominated politics). This was the case with regard to drugs: commercial pressures to produce a good story and increase the ratings led even previously serious television programmes to produce sensational and distorted analyses; and in attempts to appear more upright and decent than the next candidate, even centre-left politicians began to pander to stereotypes and prejudice and compete in offering simplistic, quick fix solutions to complex problems.

The heat generated by the issue of drugs has always been out of proportion to its real danger to society. The paradox has been that, for a neglected area of provision, this attention may not be unwelcome if it can be steered towards increased funding — so long as it is possible to so manage things that the established interests continue to influence the direction of policy. On the whole, this was done successfully in this period. This success was a result of the relatively small size of the drugs policy community, which was able to mobilise effectively (ride the waves). It was able at strategic moments to reach internal agreement, largely operating through its control of the main forums for discussion such as the: Advisory Council on the Misuse of Drugs (ACMD) — the main expert advisory body regularly consulted by government; the Institute for the Study of Drug Depёndence (ISDD) — a national institute particularly renowned for its library and information services; and the networks around the Department of Health and the Home Office; the Standing Conference on Drug Abuse (SCODA) — a largely government-funded national body co-ordinating voluntary projects in the drugs field, now spreading to include under its umbrella health and local authority community-based projects; the Local Government Drugs Forum and various other *ad hoc* or localised groups. This internal organisation and ability to mobilise gave it strength in its dealings with the relatively more diverse and poorly informed interests offering alternative approaches. These others (such as politicians, journalists and members of think tanks) tended to lose interest after a while and move onto other topics, leaving the experts to get on with the job of implementing policy. In the policy process, real long term power lies (as ever) in the detail of implementation rather than in the writing of grand 'mission' or policy statements.

The story told in this chapter thus follows directly from earlier ones. The development of policy can be seen to be a sequential process: one set of new initiatives creates boundaries that set limits on the shape of future innovations.

Important in this process is the definition of the problem to be solved. As important is the shape of the institutions developed from earlier initiatives. These then become vested interests and active participants in the next stage of development. Here it will be stressed that, although the Drug Dependency Units (DDUs — largely hospital-based clinics set up after the Brain Committee Report of 1965) are a central aspect of the institutions of the British system and other institutions cannot be understood other than in relation to them, they are not the only (nor even now perhaps the major) element in the British system of treatment, care and control.

The continuing tension between the separate spheres of influence of the Home Office and the Department of Health sets the boundaries within which policies develop. These are the major institutions at the central level. But again, they are not the only ones: other authorities have also to be seen as part of a growing array of bodies increasingly drawn into drugs policy and practice over this period. Relations between these various institutions changed as did the expectations of each. These shifts are important aspects of the overall shift in the shape of the system which the period under review was to witness. And as the system got bigger so it got harder to manage and to keep under control. Tensions between the rhetoric of local autonomy and the need for central control, especially on expenditure, are a marked feature of the period. For a time, more diversity and difference in the range of treatment and care options appeared but fairly soon attention was given to attempts to put the jigsaw back together again after the phase of profound restructuring. This led ironically to a greater standardisation of provision. Similar packages of care were offered and service delivery was increasingly dominated by large providers with a new professional and managerial style.

Finally the ubiquitous rubric of the 'partnership' principle was extended to drugs policy (see below). Partnership as the new mode of regulation appears at the end of our story as much in the drugs field as in other areas of British social policy. Here, we see drugs policy reflecting general and shared features of a move towards a new form of regulation in post-welfare state public policy.

Drugs policy, like all policies, is by definition about social control — it could not be otherwise. But what changes over time is the form of regulation, the manner in which it operates and thus how it impacts on different groups of people at different times. This is what is interesting about the policy process: it is in the interstices of regulation and resistance that the space for variation and political action can be found.

SOCIAL AND POLITICAL CONTEXT

Britain like other advanced capitalist countries has experienced acute social and economic changes in the past twenty years. Restructuring of economic life and social relations is now an accepted fact. Key aspects of these changes, which have impacted on the conditions which encourage or deter drug-taking and on the way in which drugs policies are formulated, are: the return of mass unemployment, with particularly high rates of long-term unemployment found among young people (under age 25), in certain regions and local areas and among certain ethnic groups; the increasing gap in life-chances between those with some educational or training qualifications and those without; changes in the public sector with the arrival of the mixed economy of care; the introduction of new systems of managerial control in private commercial, voluntary and public spheres, along with the development of quasi-markets, especially in the health service; a renewed interest in morals and values in social policy with greater emphasis on personal responsibility for failure, a revived division between the deserving and the undeserving; increased stress on consumer choice in human services and greater willingness to question and criticise previously highly regarded professions, including teaching, social work and medicine; increased poverty and inequality and correlation between social and spatial segregation; moves towards a more stratified form of service delivery, partly related to location, evident in social services, health services, housing and schooling; along with this arose the potential for new modes of regulation, with different forms for different strata of society — particularly significant here being discussion surrounding the prospects of the emergence of an 'underclass' excluded from primary labour markets and the call for a more punitive response to their misdeeds.

Features of the current cultural and social context often noted are diversity, differentiation and difference: these impact on forms of drug-taking as much as on other areas of social life. There is no longer, if ever there was, one drug problem or one form of drug misuser. Different styles and forms of drug-taking proliferate. Drug-takers are consumers *par excellence*. They similarly have different tastes and different needs when it comes to drugs services, requiring a mixed economy of care. On the whole, however, drug-takers have not so far mobilised effectively as a community of protest. Young recreational drug-takers have mobilised with other groups against the prohibitions of the Criminal Justice Act. But the most evident form of mobilisation of drug-users, which has impacted widely on society, has been in the form of criminality, where the crime-drugs linkage has become established. Some links between policing tactics, drug distribution networks and organisation, and riots and other disturbances were noted in this period.

THE DEVELOPMENT OF CURRENT POLICY FROM THE 1970S TO THE 1990S

In considering how the drugs problem was defined and redefined in this period and the policies and practices which followed from this, attention should be directed to three key elements: ideology (the stated policies); resources; and organisation.

The 1980s represented a watershed in social policy in both the United States and the United Kingdom, each under the influence of the dominant Reagan-Thatcher duo. In Britain, a particular form of social intervention developed — the 'initiative' — which involved the targeting of social programmes towards specific social categories for a time-limited period (MacGregor *et al.*, 1990). Considerable central control on the direction of policy was part of this social form together with a by-passing of the conventional social institutions traditionally concerned with social provision for these targeted groups. The assumption was that the established services represented producer interests and were unwilling to adopt new approaches to service delivery. At the same time, there was a reaction against institutionalisation and a move towards community care. However, for those who were defined as criminals and thought to pose a threat to conventional society, an increase in punitive responses was marked, with an increase in the use of imprisonment and in the length of sentences.

In the drugs field, the period was marked by a lessening of the dominance of the psychiatric specialists in the treatment system. Ironically, this did not mark the end of a broad medical dominance. The General Practitioner returned to play a role, not in the sense that most GPs wanted to get involved with what were seen as a deviant and unpleasant group of people, but rather in the form of a sub-specialism within General Practice of doctors with a particular interest in these problems (Glanz & Taylor, 1986). Similarly other para-medical professions became increasingly drawn into treatment, particularly notable being Community Psychiatric Nurses (CPNs) who were able to offer a combination of traditional counselling skills with knowledge of important physical and biological processes and conditions and ways to deal with these.

At the national level, the influence of the medical and allied professions continued. A major influence on the development of services in the 1980s was the Central Funding Initiative on the development of services for drug misusers (MacGregor *et al.*, 1990). This was directed by a small group of energetic and committed people within the Community Services Division at the Department of Health. The senior doctor civil servant involved played a dominant role in the development of services and the associated approach to treatment and care, along with colleagues in related professions of nursing and social work and administrative personnel. This continued a hallowed tradition in British social policy, involving a close alliance between the medical profession and the state.

Also influential in this period were the reports of the ACMD (ACMD, 1982; 1988; 1989), which continued to be dominated by medical personnel although increasingly joined by a larger group of experts drawn from a wider array of professional interests. A gradual evolution towards involvement of wider perspectives occurred but rarely in such a way as to disrupt the maintenance of a consensus view on policy matters (only when discussions of prevention arose did serious divergences of opinion seem to arise).

Changing Perceptions of the Drugs Problem

It has often been remarked that the early British system worked because there was no drug problem. The key principle of the British system, as in much else in British culture, has been the principle of containment. The DDUs were meant to fulfill this function but they soon proved inadequate to the task. Even in the days of the supposed British system, most medical professionals did not want to have much to do with addicts. When in the 1960s, following the Brain Committee's deliberations, the problem was perceived as a threat to social order, the peculiar specialism of psychiatry was encouraged to take control.

The DDUs might have worked if there had been more of them and they had been better resourced; if all addicts had behaved responsibly; if the clinics had always maintained good relations with their communities; if the doctors involved had been able to accept the paradox of prescribing dangerous drugs to patients in their care; and if there had not been an alternative source of supply. None of these conditions applied however.

The safe havens of the DDUs eventually proved inadequate as the size of the problem increased and its shape changed through the 1970s. Drug users were able to get supplies from other sources. Irresponsible and difficult clients (the 'chaotic' user) and those not using primarily opiates were rejected by the clinics and ended up in other places such as Accident and Emergency (A&E) departments and on the streets. Alternative services developed to meet their needs and these services agitated for a different approach to policy (Jamieson *et al.*, 1984).

While debates about policy continued at the top level, the voluntary sector got on and did things. It is impossible to appreciate the British system if the role of the voluntary sector is ignored. This grew up as a direct response and alternative to the clinic system. It met the needs not met by those services. It developed innovations when the clinics were becoming orthodox. The knowledge and experience contained within this sector was crucial to the later expansion of the system as a whole.

In the early seventies, particular problems were experienced by street agencies and by A&E departments in central London which were having to deal with chaotic and sometimes disruptive people, multiple drug misusers, whose behaviour and life chances were then very much affected by taking barbiturates. (A decade later the misuse of opiates and opioids was to become more prominent, following an upsurge in imports of heroin, influenced by revolutions and wars in other parts of the globe and increased facility of trade and transportation). At this time, the clinics, the main hospital-based service dealing with drug misusers, saw their waiting lists grow longer. GPs began to figure more as a source of new notifications of addicts to the Home Office (accounting for 15% of notifications in 1970 but 53% by 1981). It began to be recognised that a radical change in policy and resources would be required to meet the new situation. Illicitly imported heroin later accounted for another big increase in demand for services.

It began to be acknowledged that ease of access to services was of paramount importance. Services needed to be able to respond quickly and immediately to a request for care. Low-threshold services were the answer — ones which would take a person back several times until they were ready to make a significant change in their life-style. And a multi-disciplinary approach was recommended, drawing on the skills of diverse professions. The City Roads experiment showed what could be done, with nurses and social workers working in teams, supported by consultant psychiatrists and GPs. This type of service was provided mainly by the voluntary sector, which increasingly was called upon to fill the gaps and meet new needs. Yet the voluntary sector lived constantly in a precarious situation, fighting for survival and funds.

Debate at this time concentrated on three main issues: whether funding should be provided locally or centrally; the relative contribution of the statutory and non-statutory services; and the roles of different professions within the mix, social work versus medicine and specialists versus generalists.

The view of most people involved in the drugs field at this time was that central government should accept financial responsibility for provision of the core costs of specialist drugs services. The effect of local funding, where competition with more attractive client-groups was intense, would be to exclude drug users from care. There was a particular need for more detoxification services.

By the early 1980s, given the increased availability of imported heroin, the belief disappeared among most practitioners that it was possible to undercut the black market by legal prescription. It was also noted at the time that private, independent doctors were an option for the prescription of injectable opiates, which had largely ceased to be offered through the clinics as they had shifted to oral methadone regimes. Private doctors were again playing a substantial role.

At this time, the term 'problem drug-taker' entered the lexicon to describe what had formerly been seen as the 'addict' and later as the 'drug misuser'. This perception of the object of drugs policy was a person who experienced social, psychological, physical or legal problems related to intoxication and/or regular excessive consumption and/or dependence as a consequence of their own use of drugs or other chemical substances (excluding alcohol and tobacco). A multi-disciplinary approach was thought suitable to meet the broad range of needs implied by this definition.

Drugs policy was perceived to be directed towards problems in living rather than towards a craving produced by particular substances. However, just as this definition had attained establishment support, the heroin epidemic arrived and concentrated attention once again on the need for a medical approach to treating cases. Existing services were less able than ever to cope with the problems of drug misuse. Additional funding was required for an adequate response.

Changing Responses

Response came in the form of the Central Funding Initiative (CFI) which was to change radically the landscape of drugs services in England. This was part of the government's response to the ACMD Report of 1982 on Treatment and Rehabilitation, which had recommended the injection of new monies on a pump-priming basis to ensure the development of an adequate treatment and rehabilitation service. A comprehensive response involving both the statutory and non-statutory, the specialist and the non-specialist agencies was said to be needed. It was hoped that the CFI would be a way of remedying old problems such as lack of service co-ordination, inadequate treatment and rehabilitation resources, and absence of training for staff, while also rising to new challenges, such as providing a more comprehensive response, generating public awareness at the local level and promoting better joint planning. £17.5 million was provided to pump-prime new services or to develop further existing ones. Almost half of existing services received some additional funds and, in addition, a crucial new layer of services was developed — a layer of community-based services to complement hospital and residential rehabilitation provision. Services became more accessible and some major gaps were filled.

Prior to the initiative, the spread of services was sparse. The mainstay of the statutory system was the network of DDUs based in and around London. One-third of non-statutory services at that time were in and around London. After the initiative, 323 dedicated drugs services could be identified in England. The expansion developed services in areas which had previously been poorly served, especially through establishing community drug teams in many parts. Provision divided roughly evenly, half in the statutory and half in the non-statutory sectors. 71 per cent of all services in existence at the end of the 1980s had come into existence after 1984. A range of self-help organisations also developed in this period (MacGregor *et al.*, 1990).

Services which developed through the CFI reflected the new orthodoxy of the 1980s. Most bids for funds were for services characterised as multi-disciplinary, community-based and accessible. The attempt was made in this phase to encourage a move towards the involvement of more generalists rather than specialists in the provision of services (Strang, 1989). This was a realistic response to the fact of increased prevalence of drug misuse. Specialist services would be unable to cope alone. It was necessary to involve generalists — GPs, social workers, CPNs, and others — if the huge increase in demand was to be adequately met by a supply of services.

This was the thrust of the ambitions of most policy development in this period — to attempt to access other resources and bend them to meeting the increased need for services propelled by the increased misuse of drugs. In the end, the results were to be disappointing. The generalist remained as uninterested as ever. The main effect was to produce a new layer of drugs agencies and specialists.

The CFI was part of an increase in resources to extend and improve drugs services in England which characterised the 1980s. In addition, there were central government allocations to Regional Health Authorities based on the number of 15–34 year olds in their populations. And new money became available to meet the new needs associated with HIV disease (Strang & Stimson, 1990).

THE INFLUENCE OF THE AIDS EPIDEMIC ON DRUGS POLICY

The development of needle and syringe exchange schemes was a key feature of the British response to the link between drugs and HIV. From the mid-1980s onwards, influenced by the appearance of HIV, the importance of a harm-minimisation strategy came to be accepted within the British system for sound public health reasons. The aim was to contain the spread of infection and prevent its extension from the population of injecting drug users to the general population. This approach also involved increasing use of methadone prescribing. The gravity of the problem of the risk of HIV infection was such that the containment of the virus was accorded a higher priority than the prevention of drug misuse. The goal of harm-minimisation was accepted by the Minister of Health in a statement to the House of Commons on 29 March 1988. Decision-makers had been gradually persuaded that the policies associated with this approach were a lesser evil than spread of HIV to the general population. In 1988, an extra £3 million for the provision of services was announced, followed in 1989/90 with an extra £5 million available for the development of drug services. 'Coming on top of pre-existing AIDS allocations, the extra funding since 1986 gave health authorities at least £17 million to spend on drug services' (Berridge, 1991: 189).

Alongside these developments, a new public health approach to drugs services began to gain ground, supported by learning from the WHO Healthy Cities initiative (Ashton, 1992). In drugs policy as a whole, the prime aim was to extend the net of services to include as many as possible of the drug users, to help to contain the threatened epidemic and reduce its spread to the conventional population (prostitution was thought to be one important route). Thresholds were lowered and there was greater emphasis on educating about injecting practices and about sexual behaviour. At times it appeared that the main activity of drugs agencies was to hand out syringes, needles and condoms. Rather than such activities being discussed as matters of principle, as is the tendency in the United States, on the whole the British approach was flexible, tolerant, pragmatic and adaptable (Stimson, 1994: 250).

This shift in policy also brought new players into the drugs field — infectious disease specialists, public health specialists and general practitioners — further reducing the dominance of the psychiatrist in the treatment of drug misusers. Yet there remained, (some would say it was fortified), a stress on a concept of 'illness' in perceptions of the problem of drug misuse. Linked to the growing stress on prevention, (which has been influenced by thinking in the field of crime prevention), this may be leading, as Berridge has astutely commented, to the revival of 'social hygienist' concerns in this area of public policy (*op cit.*:195).

Some have gone so far as to say that AIDS saved the drugs services. It is certainly the case that the arrival of new money provided a real opportunity for precariously financed services to survive. By altering their range of provision to fit with the requirements of specific AIDS funding, drugs services were bent towards responding to this new need, while endeavouring to retain much of their previous provision. The effect was, however, to distort drugs service provision to concentrate on key areas related to the risk of HIV transmission — a focus on the route of administration (concentrating more attention on people who were injecting) and a focus on sexual behaviour (handing out needles and condoms). The needs of the large group of drug-takers dependent on other drugs and who did not inject were, some complained, being given insufficient attention.

Another reaction to this trend went further and argued that the stress on harm-minimisation contradicted the prime ultimate goal of abstinence and failed to meet the needs of those who would benefit from a more confrontational approach. Some even feared that open access and special provision of needles and condoms might actively encourage drug-takers to progress towards injecting or to become sexually promiscuous; it might even encourage prostitution.

On the ground, most drugs workers were aware of these contradictions and dealt with them by aiming primarily to provide services on an individual basis to each patient or client as appropriate to their needs. This clinical or case-work basis remains the dominant approach in most treatment or care, although it must be the case that increased case loads, under-resourcing and the pressures of the contract culture act against this ideal individualised response.

As it turned out, the expansion of these services was particularly important as part of the British response to the HIV/AIDs alarm. The syringe and needle exchange (Stimson *et al.*, 1988) above all symbolised the shift in ideology towards harm-minimisation, away from the challenging and confrontational style which had predominated earlier, especially in DDUs and residential rehabilitation (with one or two high profile exceptions). The voluntary sector had picked up the pieces of those who failed these challenges and tests. They were thus particularly well placed to respond when the call came for a more flexible response.

Thus one can see within the overall system that different professional and semi-professional groups developed to meet the needs of different sub-groups and styles of drug-taker. Similarly, different services orientated themselves towards different sub-groups of users. Each sub-profession developed their own rationale and mode of surveillance and control and each claimed superiority for their approach. While there was some variation in practice across the country, at the national level attempts were continually made to impose some order on this diversity. Guidelines on good practice were issued and circulars from the Department of Health encouraged practice to develop in ways favoured by a predominantly metropolitan elite.

One does not have to evoke notions of conspiracy to recognise the dominance of London and its hinterland in the formulation of drugs policy. The national capitol plays this role in many other areas of public life. However, some doctors based outside London resent this restriction and have argued that useful methods of treatment have not had a fair trial. In particular, this is the argument made by Dr John Marks, who for several years championed the prescribing of heroin over long periods and in unusual forms (such as reefers) to those unable to stop. In the mid-1980s in Liverpool (and later at Widnes and Warrington) in the north of England, he held posts where he was able to put these ideas into practice. The ending of his contracts provoked demonstrations, some publicity and claims that previously stabilised patients risked death and social disruption as a result. Marks correctly notes that despite there being over 100 psychiatrists licensed to prescribe heroin, less than a handful do so to any significant degree. This, he argues, pushes drug-takers into the hands of the illegal market, places them at the mercy of organised crime and encourages increased criminality among them. The counter-argument is that experience supports the view that it is good practice to concentrate on oral methadone on a reducing regime in most cases.

The 1980s thus saw a flurry of activity in response to the recognised facts of the heroin and the AIDS epidemics. The British response was built on what had gone before. While in other areas of social policy, the British were at a loss when confronted by new developments and sought to borrow ideas from other countries — principally, in such areas as urban policy, welfare and race relations, from the United States — in drugs policy, there remained a confidence that British ideas and knowledge were sufficient. This confidence relates very much to the continuing presence of eminent medical practitioners in the policy-making community. The existence of a body of knowledge in the alternative voluntary sector, on which the establishment was able to draw, was also important in developing a co-ordinated and relatively rational and pragmatic approach to this new problem.

COMPARISON WITH THE UNITED STATES

In the United States, the approach to drugs policy has shifted from an earlier libertarian one through the adoption of a medical conception to the current relatively unchallenged criminal conception: this latter has held sway for over forty years (Gerstein & Harwood, 1990: 3).

In both Britain and the United States, the balance between medical and criminal approaches to policy is the fulcrum of debate. But the two cases can be contrasted in terms of the relative weight given to medical and general health ideologies within the paradigm.

In the United States, methadone maintenance and therapeutic communities play a role. Twenty years ago, there was also a substantial build-up of a public tier of community-based drug treatment programmes. The idea was that these approaches would act in complement with criminal justice efforts. Later, federal support for these services declined. Some of the bill was picked up by the states but the result was a reduction in this provision. The country as a whole continues to see a phenomenal increase in the sway of the criminal justice system with many new prisons being planned to contain the casualties of what is feared to be a disintegrating social order.

There are two contrasting tiers of treatment programmes in the States — the public and the private. They are distinguished mainly by their mode of financing. The private tier treats those with insurance, the public those without. The public tier is under-resourced. The justification for public expenditure in this area (and for increasing it) lies in its effects on externalities, in reducing the social costs of drug use, such as crime and family dysfunction. The private or independent sector plays a large role in the American system with chemical dependency programmes having expanded particularly rapidly in the 1980s while at the same time the public sphere was relatively neglected. 'Outside of concern with isolating the growing acquired immune deficiency syndrome (AIDS) epidemic, public treatment was all but ignored' (*op cit.*:4).

It is estimated that 5.5 million Americans need treatment currently (something like 2% of the population over 12 years of age). About one fifth of these are under the supervision of the criminal justice system as parolees, probationers or inmates (*op cit.*:7). The indications are that while experimental, recreational or occasional drug use is becoming less prevalent in the USA, the problem of severe drug abuse. and dependence is growing larger, more difficult and more costly.

The goals of American treatment policy link closely to those of the criminal justice system. They have been summarised as: to reduce the overall demand for illicit drugs; to reduce street crime; to change users' personal values; to develop educational or vocational capabilities; to restore or increase employment or productivity; to improve the user's overall health, psychological functioning and family life; and to reduce fetal exposure to drug dependence (*op cit.*:8–9).

In the USA, the criminal justice system is the largest single source of pressure on individuals leading them to enter drug treatment. The social problems of increasing crime and of heroin and crack use have dominated discussion of social policy as a whole in the United States. In that country, race and racism are key organising principles for much debate and in the operation of policy.

THE IMPACT OF SOCIAL AND POLICY RE-STRUCTURING

Developments in drugs policy and practice in Britain have been influenced by the restructuring of services in health and social services consequent on the third term reforms of the Thatcher administration, especially as set out in the NHS and Community Care Act of 1990. This introduced new organisational and financial structures into the health service. The main element impacting on services was the distinction between purchasing services and providing them — henceforth these roles would be strictly separated. On 1 April 1993, new arrangements for community care were implemented in England. Among the services affected were residential services for people who misuse drugs. At the time, there were estimated to be 112 providers spread across the 108 local authorities in England, offering services to substance misusers (including provision for people with problems related to alcohol abuse). Some shift occurred between registered and non-registered beds as a result of the change in funding policy (MacGregor *et al.*, 1993).

The period marked the ascendancy of commissioning agents in drugs policy in Britain. These new players in the array of health and social services came to influence with the introduction of market principles into the operation of public services. The transition to the new system was marked by considerable confusion and disturbance but eventually things settled down. However, the nature of work changed as transaction costs increased: increased form-filling was noted with the requirement for greater accountability. In addition, accessibility to services decreased as a new barrier had been put in place — the requirement to assess each applicant on the basis of need and on financial grounds. The voluntary sector found itself having to engage in much more advocacy and liaison work in order to help drug users gain access to residential services. Particular concerns were raised that the new system deterred women with children, who feared that contact with the local authority would put them at greater risk of losing their children (since Local Authority Social Services departments were responsible for identifying children at risk).

The local authorities did not accept these criticisms. They were less persuaded of the importance of speed of access to services. They began to ask questions about the value of services. In negotiating contracts, they required services to demonstrate clearly that they were giving value for money. More stress began to be placed on the outcomes of service provision than had been the case previously in the drugs field (as in other areas of public policy). Efficiency and effectiveness were being taken seriously. The judgements of drugs workers were being questioned. They were no longer recognised as the authority on the needs of drug misusers: one local authority commissioner said, 'if we don't challenge their decisions on placements, there is a danger that the provider will be in the driving seat on community care'. Local authorities were sceptical about many of the claims made for services and were in general less sympathetic to the client group as a whole, when compared with more deserving cases, such as the elderly or people with disabilities.

The assumption of local authority responsibility for these clients introduced into service provision a new group of players who brought in different perceptions of need and good practice. They were willing to question established procedures and knowledges. They drew on different values and were working within a different culture from that which had previously set the tone of drugs policy. For example, the view that relapses are part of the pattern of recovery and that sporadic use of supportive residential care prevents deterioration, and may lead to later recovery, was little favoured by local authority assessment officers. While sympathetic to new and young clients, they were less willing to fund repeat attempts at cure.

In the first few weeks following the implementation of the new community care policy, project managers were intensely worried about the effect on their clients. Local authorities appeared to be taking too long in making assessments, assessors were difficult to track down and they were thought to lack the skills to deal with drug-takers. The main goals of community care were expected to be better access, more appropriate care, better value for money and stricter control on public expenditure. The effect of the transformation in the funding and organisation of drugs residential services was to reduce the number of people gaining access to residential services. Clients were being filtered out of the system as a result of a process which put up barriers to care. These barriers included fear of officialdom; distrust of local authorities; delays in the process — the time taken to organise an assessment; different assessments of need beginning to operate; different views on appropriate outcomes; financial constraints on local authorities; the rules on eligibility for funding; and criteria of residency in a local area. Problems were exacerbated where multiple agencies were involved, for example, where co-operation was required between health authorities, prison, probation or social service departments. The time of personnel was increasingly taken up with negotiations and administration. These barriers impacted particularly on women and on deviant and difficult clients; the homeless, who could less easily claim to belong to a particular local authority area were most affected by this (MacGregor *et al.*, 1993). Staff morale was badly dented.

A year later as a result of investigations, the Social Services Inspectorate was dismayed to find that little attention was being paid by many local authorities to developing services for drug misusers. A paragraph within a community care plan was as much as many had been able to produce. Yet the new commissioners, the purchasors of health and social services within both local authorities and health authorities, had assumed considerable powers over the shape of services offered by provider bodies in the new quasi-market structures of health and community care.

A PROFILE OF CURRENT TREATMENT PROVISION

In late summer 1994, a snapshot review of the extent and shape of the English drugs treatment system was conducted (MacGregor *et al.*, 1994). This project assumed that provision was best seen as a set of inter-related parts rather than as a collection of individualised and competing units of service, each of which could be evaluated in a straightforward way in terms of its specific outcomes without recognition of the way services work together. Any evaluation of outcomes would also have to utilise the concept of a drug-using career, in which a variety of services might attempt to intervene in different ways at different times and all might cumulatively play a part in the final outcome.

The drugs treatment system at this time was found to overlap considerably with provision for problems related to alcohol and with services focusing on HIV/AIDS and on young people in general.

The system could be seen to be composed of a number of key types of service: residential rehabilitation services; DDUs and clinics; in-patient treatment and detoxification in public hospitals and in private clinics; community-based drug treatment centres; community drug teams; drugs counselling and advice centres; needle exchanges; GPs and self-help groups. In addition, there were related services such as outreach activities, telephone help-lines, projects focusing on people with problems related to tranquillisers and prescribed drugs, and projects focusing on specific problems related to HIV disease.

The shape of services varied between different regions and local areas. The London Thames Regions continued to dominate service provision numerically and a number of national and internationally recognised centres of excellence are located there, as well as the headquarters of some of the large voluntary sector projects. Differences appear between rural and urban areas. Merseyside in the north of England (the Liverpool hinterland) has a distinct character and is notable for the attempt of services there to maintain contact with marginalised groups such as prostitutes. The involvement of local authorities and the role of GPs varied significantly between different regions and areas.

The main single source of funding for these services remains the health authority. Four out of ten services were funded solely by health authority funds while the others derived funds from more than one source. The main division between services continues to be between the statutory and the non-statutory services but, as each is under increasing pressure to compete for funds, some similarities in their operations are becoming apparent. Those who work within this system occupy a wide variety of roles and bring in perspectives from a range of professions, including psychiatry, community psychiatric nursing, social work, general nursing, general medical practice, outreach work and psychology, as well as there being managers, co-ordinators, secretaries and ancillary workers.

The pattern of interventions available in the system as a whole includes assessment, counselling and therapy, detoxification, prescribing, methadone maintenance, residential rehabilitation and adherence to the 12-step programme of recovery. Different services offer different packages of care made up of some of these interventions. The system in general is complex.

The main activities which appear to dominate the work of services are the provision of advice and information, referral on to other services, liaison with other services (including with the criminal justice system and the writing of court reports) needle exchange, social care, primary health care and outreach work.

Prescribing is a feature of service provision in about one half of services, this being a key feature of the divide between the statutory and the non-statutory sectors, although there are some overlaps.

The most common drug prescribed as part of treatment is methadone, which is most commonly taken orally with a small proportion of patients being prescribed injectable methadone. The main aim of prescribing is commonly reported to be stabilisation and detoxification, with an impact being noted individually in improvement in the health of the patient and socially in a reduction in crime. (This was in general asserted or based on anecdotal evidence rather than being the result of detailed evaluative research).

Prescribing for detoxification may be for a period of 6 to 8 weeks in a short-term reduction regime. For gradual withdrawal, the period may be over six months. Those for whom a maintenance regime is thought appropriate are prescribed drugs over a period of anything from 18 months to five years or more.

A rough estimate of the size of the population served by this system at any one time was of 84,000 people. (Other additional numbers would be in contact with GPs and with needle exchanges). Of this 84,000, about 10,000 would be cases new to that agency in any one month.

Two thirds of patients and clients were male and one third female. One half were in their twenties, one quarter in their thirties with smaller proportions aged over 40 or under 20 years. The vast majority of these patients and clients were reported to be white people.

The predominance of multi-drug use was stressed with the most common single drug referred to being heroin but within a pattern of multi-drug use.

Currently demand for treatment and care services exceeds supply. Access to residential detoxification is particularly difficult to acquire. Gaps were noted in day treatment services, provision for women and people from minority ethnic groups; after-care facilities and provision for day activities were also lacking. The lack of services for amphetamine users remained (as it had been for all the post-war years) a notable problem (MacGregor *et al.*, 1994).

The changing shape of all health and personal social service provision is the context within which demands on the drugs services must be viewed. A striking feature of the current drugs treatment system is the degree of change underway. The voluntary sector has altered the packages of services offered in response to the introduction of community care and the need to secure contracts or attract referrals from local authorities. In general there has been a move to offer integrated packages of care serving defined target groups of clients. Considerable restructuring is also going on in the health services. There have been mergers and amalgamations of services and diversification and decentralisation. The creation of Trusts has led to fundamental changes in the way services are organised and delivered. These health care provider services, like those in the voluntary sector, are responding to the need to secure contracts from purchasors. This has produced some uncertainty and some insecurity as power has moved to the new fundholders. There are some signs also of the entry of the independent sector into providing services in the drugs field. Agreed strategies are being developed across sectors. Managerialism has encouraged more explicit statement of aims and objectives.

The Government's Health of the Nation targets do not however focus particularly on drugs misuse. But HIV/AIDS and sexual health together do figure as one of the five priority areas of the national strategy. Authorities are encouraged to develop a comprehensive range of services to discourage drug misuse and to reduce risky behaviour, such as injecting, sharing of equipment and unprotected sex. The Government's target is to reduce the percentage of injecting drug misusers who report sharing equipment in the previous four weeks by at least 50% by 1997 and by at least a further 50% by the year 2000. This would indicate a reduction from 20% in 1990 to no more than 10% by 1997 and no more than 5% by the year 2000.

In our 1994 survey of the drugs treatment system (Middlesex University Census of Drug Treatment Services), we identified over one thousand pharmacy-based needle exchanges (1193) and more existed which were not caught in the first survey trawl. These form the most distinctive aspect of the provision which developed from the adoption of a harm-minimisation strategy. As well as pharmacy-based schemes, there are stand alone services, some are located within or proximate to another service such as a day centre; they may be mobile (using vans or other vehicles); they may be staffed by specific staff or by members of community drug teams or advice and counselling teams; and they may be co-ordinated by a special needle and exchange co-ordinator located within a public health department or health promotion unit. Practices vary widely around the country.

Over the years, various baits have been used to encourage drug users to remain in contact with agencies, (apart from the brief period of confrontational approaches when a virtual triage system operated in some of the clinics). The offer of heroin, reefers, injectable opiates, methadone, condoms, needles and syringes, a willing ear, advocacy and support when in contact with the police and courts, education and general advice — all have been used for this function.

Most people working in services at present in Britain describe their approach as being based on concepts of harm reduction but with abstinence being the ideal eventual goal. This is a pragmatic approach, recognising that success does not come quickly or easily in a field where users may begin drug use around the age of 14 and 10 years or so later experience considerable problems, psychological, social, with the law, with relationships, with employment, finance and so on.

Increasing attention is now being paid to the role of health care in prisons. It is widely recognised that prisons must play a part in collaborative arrangements designed to tackle drug misuse and contain the spread of HIV infection. One 1990 study of 450 people released from prison reported that many continued to inject drugs and have male homosexual unprotected sex while in prison. Those with a history of drug injecting continued to inject in prison and nearly three quarters of these shared syringes with other prisoners (AVERT, 1991). Attempts have been made to extend harm-minimisation practices into prisons, by providing clean needles and syringes for example. These invariably encounter hostile public comment when picked up by the press. Similar contradictions appeared when Ministers announced a crack-down on drug-taking in prison and introduced random testing. It has been argued that this may paradoxically encourage a switch from cannabis to heroin use as the latter remains for less time in the body's systems and is less likely to be detected. In the area of prison work, the conflict between principle and pragmatism is most acute.

RE-INVENTING DRUGS POLICY

The expansion of drugs services and the entry of new people into providing services has led to calls for more guidance from the centre. The centre in the Department of Health, Home Office and ACMD tries to hold the reins, to steer the forces along an agreed pathway and to develop links to hold them all together. It is a difficult task. A greater emphasis on prevention is now emerging in the drugs policy community, utilising the ACMD basic criteria of a) reducing the risk of an individual engaging in drug misuse; and b) reducing the harm associated with drug misuse (ACMD, 1984). This is in spite of the continuing stress on abstinence among politicians, journalists and the public. And now the precepts of the new managerialism are being offered as a way to hold together the pieces of a more diverse and potentially fragmented system.

Co-ordination and building partnerships are the methods proposed in this situation of multi-agency working (Howard *et al.*, 1993). These trends have crystallised in the new *Tackling Drugs Together* government strategy for the next four years (1995–1998). Its statement of purpose is to take effective action by vigorous law enforcement, accessible treatment and a new emphasis on education and prevention to:

- increase the safety of communities from drug-related crime;
- reduce the acceptability and availability of drugs to young people; and
- reduce the health risks and other damage related to drug misuse.

The three key areas for intervention are crime; young people; and public health.

A standard form of new regulation can be seen appearing within the human services. Similar approaches are being applied in drugs policy as in crime prevention, health promotion and urban regeneration. In these arrangements, more power is wielded by those able to talk the new language and to organise their work around principles of good management practice.

Throughout the 1980s, various calls had been made for better communication and collaboration and various devices were promoted to encourage this — such as drug advisory committees, which were to link with AIDS advisory committees.

Better training and sharing of good practice was also said to be needed. The range of agencies involved continued to spread, including a greater role for the probation service and for drugs prevention teams as well as for local authorities (especially local education authorities) — all these new agencies complementing the continuing work of health authorities and the voluntary sector.

More attention to links with local police has lately been encouraged as well as with parents' groups and self-help groups. The fragmentation of services brought about by the mixed economy of care has paradoxically produced a need for more attention to joint working, joint care planning teams, consultative committees and a whole range of devices for people to try to work in co-operation rather than in competition. Sometimes, professionals complain, they feel they are spending more time on the contracting process, justifying and accounting for their practice and attending meetings to find out what is going on, than they are in actually treating patients and helping clients.

Attempts to re-introduce planning under another name inform these attempts to establish partnerships. These partnership policies have borrowed substantially from American social policy in urban policy, crime prevention and now in drugs policy and practice. In 1990 and 1991, the Bush administration through the Office for Substance Abuse Prevention (OSAP) funded 250 communities around the country to develop broad based partnerships to combat the drug problem at the local level. The pace and range of change in society at large and in the erstwhile public sector forms the backcloth to these developments.

At the same time, there remain attempts to involve GPs more actively and more consistently in the provision of services for drug misusers. Yet there is evidence of continuing reluctance on the part of GPs to take on this role.

Above all, the criminal justice system is central to the British system of drugs control and care. There are signs of increased working together of the enforcement and treatment and care agencies. 'The boundaries of what constitutes enforcement and what constitutes prevention, treatment and care are being redrawn' (Howard *et al.,* 1993: 9).

While the focus of this chapter has been on treatment and care, one feature of developments in recent years has been the move towards closer links between the treatment and care and the criminal justice systems and prevention. In this respect, some move towards greater similarity with the American medical-criminal approach may be being observed. Greater stress on prevention and the spread of involvement even more widely to include responses from the 'community' is a feature of this trend. The attempt to involve the generalist continues — not only GPs but also schools, community police, tenants and residents associations and other local groups. These developments, as with the overtures towards the GPs, are often met by a rebuff and are thwarted by the different attitudes of experts and lay people (the public) when dealing with drug misusers. The public continues to see responding to drug misuse as principally a job for the police and rather than 'owning' the problem hope to eradicate it and run the drug pushers out of town. Principle not pragmatism tends to influence their perception of what is to be done.

The Home Office has developed a growing role in prevention activities, especially through the work of the Drugs Prevention Initiative. In 1989, the DPI was announced in response to fears of increases in drugs misuse, drug-related illness and crime. The initiative involved twenty drug prevention teams (DPTs) located in England, Scotland and Wales and focused on reducing the incidence of drugs misuse by preventing those people who had never used drugs or who use them experimentally from becoming or continuing as drug misusers. It aimed to encourage, inform and support the community in its response to drugs misuse. This is achieved by action at the local level involving professional statutory and voluntary organisations and individuals interested in playing a role. It assumes that the drugs problem will vary between areas and that local problems can only be solved by local solutions. It seeks to involve all sectors of the community in drugs prevention and emphasises including organisations and individuals who are new to drugs prevention but who have potential to play a role.

The Criminal Justice Act of 1991 also impacted on drugs policy by introducing major changes to the supervision and punishment of offenders in the community. It allowed for diverting less serious offenders from custody into community penalties. A specific provision enabled it to be a requirement that the offender should undergo treatment for alcohol or drug dependency. The Probation Service is playing a growing role in the referral of clients to drugs services. In addition, following riots in prisons and growing concern at the extent of drug misuse in prisons, there are calls for prisons to integrate their work more closely with the wider community. Many drugs misuse services are active in the prison system, providing advice and information and training prison staff. Such collaboration also comes from the desire to contain the spread of HIV infection and was encouraged by a Department of Health 1988 Circular on HIV and Drug Misuse. Other collaborative arrangements have included experimental arrest referral schemes (as in Southwark in south London) and agreements between police and agencies about police tactics in the areas around treatment centres and needle exchanges.

In spite of the fears of the established interests in the drugs field at the inclusion of more lay people in decision-making, especially through drawing them in to sit on Task Forces and committees, a dramatic shift towards a restrictive abstinence-based approach to treatment and care has not yet taken place. Through judicious persuasion and education, those who arrived with initially simple ideas and an attraction to quick-fix solutions have been won over to the pragmatic view.

CONCLUSION

The definition of the drug problem has changed over time, largely as a reflection of real changes in the shape and extent of the problem. As the system has expanded, a greater range of personnel in all parts of the country has been drawn in, bringing in different views and opinions. From the dominance of consultants in the 1970s to the power of the agencies in the 1980s, there has been a more recent shift of power to those who hold the purse strings in the health and local authorities. The pattern is one of constant evolution, discussion followed by the reaching of an agreement on what is the correct approach to a constantly changing phenomenon. Ironically, the tendency has been that just as such agreement has been reached, the system has been hit by another wave of change, challenging the agreed formulations. This sets off a new round of review and deliberation. Interested parties jockey for position — to maintain their share of provision or to exploit new opportunities provided by new money. Strong and persuasive voices are influential and in what remains a relatively small policy circle, particular individuals can exercise significant influence.

The British approach in the period under review can be seen as a rational one, involving debate among a restricted range of well-informed interest-groups. Such rational policy development depends upon there being a consensus of basic understandings about the nature of drug-taking and best practice. Shocks to this way of doing things occasionally arise when the issue is taken up in political circles, influenced often by electoral considerations or personal career ambitions. This is especially the case where law and order figures prominently in party politics and where politicians compete to hold the moral high ground. Media attention too encourages shock-horror approaches, which have to be calmly defused by informed experts working behind the scenes. To describe this as a pragmatic approach is perhaps to undervalue the character of this aspect of British public policy. What happens is not random or *ad hoc*. The development of policy has been pragmatic in the sense that the voices of both theory and experience are listened to and that decisions have tended to be made relatively free from fundamentalist pressure. The ability of the experts to retain their hold on decision-making and to resist the incursions of wider interests is one of the more notable features of the drugs field.

A cohesive policy community continues to tread a difficult path however as the drugs problem itself is very much influenced by wider events. Pressures on the financing of services also play an increasing role in explanations of policy and practice. With worries about social disintegration in some local areas and especially among some social groups, the link between drugs and crime has become more pronounced and the fear of lawlessness continues to lead to calls for more reactionary responses.

Before becoming too complacent about the smooth development of drugs policy, even in a period of intense turbulence in social life and social provision in general, we should note the blind spots which remain. The neglect of the very large numbers of amphetamine users is one major gap. Equally important is the race and gender blindness of existing provision. The failure to meet the needs of minority ethnic drug misusers, who are more likely to be found in the criminal justice system than in the treatment and care system, is a particular blot on British drugs policy. Similarly stereotypical images of women drug users and lack of attention to the needs of women with children continue to characterise the overall shape of the treatment and care system. For these groups, a little more principle and less pragmatism might be welcome.

REFERENCES

Advisory Committee on the Misuse of Drugs (ACMD) (1982) *Treatment and Rehabilitation* HMSO, London.

Advisory Committee on the Misuse of Drugs (ACMD) (1988) *AIDS and drug misuse* Part 1 HMSO, London.

Advisory Committee on the Misuse of Drugs (ACMD) (1989) *AIDS and drug misuse* Part 2 HMSO, London.

Ashton, J. (editor) (1992) *Healthy Cities* Open University Press.

AVERT (1991) *Prison, HIV and AIDS: Risks and experiences in custodial care.*

Berridge, V. (1991) 'AIDS and British Drug Policy: History Repeats Itself ...?' in *Policing and Prescribing: the British System of Drug Control* edited by D.K. Whynes and P.T. Bean pp. 176–199.

Department of Health (1984) *Guidelines on good clinical practice in the treatment of drug misuse* HMSO, London.

Gerstein, D.R. and Harwood, H.J (editors) Institute of Medicine (1990) *Treating Drug Problems* National Academy Press, Washington DC.

Glanz, A. and Taylor, C. (1986) Findings of a national survey of the role of general practitioners in the treatment of opiate use: extent of contact *British Medical Journal,* **293,** 427–30.

Glanz, A., Byrne, C. and Jackson, P. (1989) Role of community pharmacies in prevention of AIDS among injecting drug misusers: findings of a survey in England and Wales *British Medical Journal,* **209,** 1076–9.

Grant, M. (1994) What is so special about the British system? in *Heroin Addiction and Drug Policy* (edited by J. Strang and M. Gossop) Oxford University Press, pp. v–vi.

Home Office (1988) *Tackling Drug Misuse: a summary of the Government's strategy* (3rd ed.) HMSO, London.

Howard, R., Beadle, P. and Maitland, J. (1993) *Across the Divide: building community partnerships to tackle drug misuse* Department of Health.

Jamieson, A., Glanz, A. and MacGregor, S. (1984) *Dealing with drug misuse: crisis intervention in the city* Tavistock.

MacGregor, S., Ettorre, B., Coomber, R. and Crosier, A. (1990) *Drugs Services in England and the Impact of the Central Funding Initiative* ISDD, London.

MacGregor, S., O'Gorman, A., Cattell, V., Flory, P. and Savage, R. (1993) *Vulnerable Services for Vulnerable People: the impact of the transition to community care on the drugs and alcohol residential sector in England* Alcohol Concern and SCODA.

MacGregor, S., Smith, L. and Flory, P. (1994) *The Drugs Treatment System in England: report on a mapping exercise for the Department of Health Task Force to Review Services for Drug Misusers* Middlesex University, London.

Stimson, G., Alldrit, L. and Dolan, K. (1988) Syringe exchange schemes for drug users in England and Scotland *British Medical Journal,* **296,** 1717–19.

Stimson, G.V. (1994) Minimising harm from drug use in (Strang, J. and Donmall, M. [eds.]) *Heroin Addiction and Drug Policy: the British System* Oxford University Press pp. 248–256.

Strang, J. (1989) A model service: turning the generalist on to drugs in *Drugs and British Society* (ed. S. MacGregor) Routledge pp. 143–169.

Strang, J. and Stimson, G. (editors) (1990) *AIDS and drug misuse: the challenge for policy and practice in the 1990s* Routledge.

CHAPTER 9

The Perils of Prohibition*

Thomas Szasz

Virtually everyone now believes that certain drugs are "dangerous" and that it is the duty of the state to protect people from using them. From this point of view, the question is: What drugs should the state control and in what ways should it control them?

However, drug prohibition is also dangerous. In addition, it deprives Americans of the right to put into their bodies what they choose, a freedom they enjoyed from the founding of the Colonies until 1914. From this point of view, the question is: Do we have a right to eat shellfish, take an aspirin, or grow plants in our homes?

Inevitably, the way we pose the question prejudges the "problem." Talking about "dangerous drugs" does it one way. Talking about "rights" does it another way.

For millennia, persons had no rights. People who take the Judeo-Christian world view seriously regard God as the only Adult. Human beings are His children who must obey His rules, not question their legitimacy or rationality. The Bible regulates the minutiae of personal conduct. Rulers, acting as deputies of the divinity, treat people the way we treat minors. The result is absolute government.

In their effort to combat the abuses inherent in absolute rule, the Scottish and English Enlightenment philosophers turned this principle on its head. They "discovered" that the Creator endowed people with certain rights that the sovereign must respect. We call these rights "inalienable." When the United States gained independence from Great Britain, the American people appreciated that true liberty is freedom from the state, not freedom to control the state. The right to vote is not mentioned in the original Constitution of the United States. The Bill of Rights are restrictions on government power, not rights *to* things. Specifically, the First Amendment provides that "Congress shall make no law respecting the establishment of religion ..." The Framers could not have anticipated that, two

---

*This Chapter is an adaptation of the author's Preface to the paperback edition of his book *Our Right to Drugs*, Syracuse Press, 1996.

hundred years later, medicine would replace religion. Hence, the First Amendment's provisions do not prohibit Congress from establishing a regime of medicine, such as Adolfo Bioy-Casares (1986), the Argentinean novelist and poet, described as follows:

> Well then, maybe it would be worth mentioning the three periods of history. When man believed that happiness was dependent upon God, he killed for religious reasons. When man believed that happiness was dependent upon the form of government, he killed for political reasons. After dreams that were too long, true nightmares ... we arrived at the present period of history. Man woke up, discovered that which he always knew, that happiness is dependent upon health, and began to kill for therapeutic reasons.... It is medicine that has come to replace both religion and politics in our time.

Drug controls are but one element, albeit a very important one, in this development, to which I gave the name Therapeutic State (Szasz, 1963/1988).

Despite the evidence that bad habits are not diseases (Szasz, 1972), and that the War on Drugs is intrinsically unwinnable (Szasz, 1992), drug prohibitionists continue to try to control drug (ab)use by coercions rationalized as cures. In his book, *The Unmaking of a Mayor*, William F. Buckley, Jr. recalls that, in 1965, he wrote:

> And so the disease spreads in geometric proportion, and permits us to generalize that: *narcotics is a contagious disease.* ... [Hence,] it becomes necessary to treat it is a plague. New York should undertake to quarantine all addicts, even as smallpox carriers would be quarantined during a plague. The narcotics problem is properly a federal problem because the contagion is country-wide.

Buckley (1995) has since moderated his views, but has not abandoned defining the "drug problem" as a medical matter. Most other drug prohibitionists continue to act like Santayana's fabled fanatic who, after losing sight of his goal, redoubles his efforts. Exasperated by the failures of drug controls, A.M. Rosenthal (1995) — former editor of, and now a columnist for, the *New York Times* — denounces not only disapproved drugs but even disapproved debate about them. "The campaign for drug legalization," he declares, "is one of the most cruel and selfish movements in America." Gertrude Himmelfarb (1995), a respected neo-conservative historian, exhibits similar sentiments. She agrees with Senator Daniel Patrick Moynihan that "heroin in the 1960s produced the single-parent family," and that crack today "produce[s] the non-parent child." And she approvingly quotes columnist Mary McGrory that "An institution is better than a crack house or a life on the street." Himmelfarb's argument ignores that the crucial element in drug (ab)use is personal choice; that the coca leaf and the opium poppy have existed for millennia, without causing the effects she attributes to them; and that "crack houses" — unlike "coffee houses" — are the products, not of drugs, but of drug prohibition.

The War on Drugs has made our streets unsafe and our prisons overfull, but has not stopped people from using vast quantities of illegal drugs. According to conventional wisdom, that is the price we must pay to combat this "scourge"; without the War, things would be much worse. On a recent television program on the drug problem, former drug czar William Bennett proudly declared that the American people would not stand for any kind of "drug legalization." I am not sure that is true. But if it is, I am sure it is not something to be proud of.

If we do not want a person to do something, call it X, we can try to persuade him not to do X, or we can prohibit X and punish him if he does it and if we catch him. Persuasion may fail, of course. If it succeeds, however, the subject will control himself and become a "better" person. (The assumption is that he is being persuaded to become more, not less, self-disciplined.) Prohibition, of course, may also fail. Indeed, it is certain to stimulate interest in the prohibited act, incite defiance of the prohibition, generate an illegal market, and increase the amount of violence in society. And if the prohibition succeeds, it is only because the subject is rendered submissive to authorities he fears and loathes, making him a "worse" person.

Perhaps worst of all, calling certain drugs "dangerous" and prohibiting them obscures the fact that *life is dangerous*. Growing up means learning to cope with its dangers. Prohibition means being prevented from learning to cope with certain dangers intrinsic to life. The *external* prohibition of risks associated with self-regarding acts — epitomized by taking various substances into our bodies — does not reduce their dangerousness. It increases it. Only the *internal* prohibition of such risks reduces their dangerousness. These are commonplaces. But in the context of the debate on drugs it is taboo to mention them. Why? Because the proper thing to do is to detour the debate into the blind alley called "treatment" for "substance abuse."

So-called primitive people attribute all manner of calamities to angry gods — because they know, or they think they know, how to propitiate angry gods. We attribute all manner of (mis)behaviors to diseases — because we know, or think we know, how to treat diseases. So we declare that (ab)using drugs is a disease and that coercing people who do so into changing their behavior is a "treatment."

The Bible writers warned: "Woe unto them that call evil good, and good evil" (Isaiah 5:20). The War on Drugs has taught many children precisely that perverted lesson. In January 1995, *Time* ("Chronicles") magazine reported the case of a five-year-old boy in Mississippi who, home from school with the chicken pox, called 911 five times in a successful effort to have his mother arrested for smoking marijuana. The sheriff commented: "The boy was so proud of himself. He was tickled to death at what he had done."

As for adults, the War on Drugs has taught them that they are like (undisciplined) children, unable to resist the temptations of alcohol, cigarettes, drugs, food, and gambling, and that their inability or unwillingness constitutes a *bona fide* medical disease, requiring medical treatment. Blind to the implications of interpreting intemperance as illness, drug prohibitionist Morton B. Zuckerman (1995), editor of *U.S. News & World Report*, complains that drug addicts and alcoholics "qualify as disabled ... [and that] the federal government is paying some $1.4 billion annually to 250,000 substance abusers — who often spend the money on the substance, not on treatment."

One of the justifications advanced for prohibiting "soft" drugs is that their use leads to addiction to "hard" drugs. I doubt the validity of this so-called gateway theory. However, there is evidence that the prohibitionist's "habit" spreads from wanting to control recreational drugs to wanting to control recreational foods. Kelly D. Brownell (1994), a professor of psychology at Yale, proposes putting "a surcharge on foods with high fat and low nutritional value ... the true battle must be waged against an increasingly seductive environment" (*New York Times*, December 15, 1994). Note that Brownell blames the choice to ingest more calories than one burns, not on the failure of a particular actor to resist the temptation to overeat (or on his other reasons for behaving as he does), but on the "seductive environment" in which he is forced to live — in short, on our being blessed with an abundance of affordable good food.

Our drug laws are fundamentally flawed (Szasz, 1974, 1992). I say this because they treat adults as if they were children and seek to protect them from themselves; because they rest on the pretense that illegal drugs, officially classified as dangerous, are in fact more dangerous than legal drugs, not officially classified as dangerous (or even as drugs); and because they preclude entertaining the possibility that drug prohibition poses a greater threat to us than do drugs.

The legislator's task is to enact laws to govern the behavior of adults — not the behavior of children, whose management is primarily the responsibility of parents. Nevertheless, the War on Drugs has been characterized, and continues to be characterized, by a pervasive rhetorical preoccupation with "kids," exemplified by former First Lady Nancy Reagan's dimwitted slogan, "Just say no."

More importantly, prohibitionists maintain that if drugs were not prohibited, children would have even easier access to them than they do now. Whether this would happen, or whether the opposite would happen, depends on many other circumstances. For example, there is a gun in every Swiss household with a person of military age in it, but Swiss children do not have access to guns. The prohibitionists' scare-scenario of drug dealers plying their trade *legally* in the school-yard is objectionable because it obfuscates that most of our rights — for example, where to live, what religion if any to profess, and so forth — are contingent on these choices being denied to children. Once a person loses sight of this fact, it is easy to convince him that protecting children from "drugs" justifies making them illegal for adults. However, depriving adults of rights will not work as a substitute for disciplining children. On the contrary, it aggravates the problem and, in fact, has done so already.

Drugs, of course, are not the only cultural artifacts that can harm children. Fire, electricity, household appliances and cleaning products, over-the-counter drugs, and countless other products of human inventiveness endanger, injure, and kill children. We accept these risks that, in the long run, make our lives healthier and safer, and adapt to them by teaching children to cope realistically with the risks they pose.

In 1932, Karel Capek (1890–1938), the great Czech novelist and playwright, wrote a short satire titled "The Punishment of Prometheus" (Capek, 1932/1945). Replace fire by drugs, and Capek's cautionary tale becomes an unrivaled parody of the current medical incarnation of Leviathan.

Tried before a panel of Greek magistrates, Prometheus is accused of having "committed an act of criminal irresponsibility in bringing into the world so harmful a thing [as fire]." One judge declares: "I should describe his crime as the causing of grievous bodily harm and endangering the public safety." Another adds: "I accuse Prometheus of having entrusted this divine and irresistible element of fire to shepherds and slaves, to the first comer; I accuse him of not giving it up to authorized hands which would have guarded it as a treasure of the state and governed by its means."

Prometheus's crime was to place fire in the hands of everyman, instead of limiting access to it to agents of the state. Today, the person who opposes drug prohibition commits a similar offense, threatening the Therapeutic State's sacrosanct monopoly over the pharmacopeia.

REFERENCES

Bioy-Casares, A. (1986) "Plans for an escape to Carmelo," *New York Review of Books*, April 10, p. 7.

Brownell, K.D. (1994) "Get slim with higher taxes," *New York Times*, December 15, p. A29.

Buckley, W.F., Jr. (1965) "Narcotics as a plague", in *The Unmaking of a Mayor* (New York: Viking, 1966), pp. 216–219; p. 217, emphasis in the original.

Buckley, W.F. Jr. (1995) "Loony drug laws," *National Review*, February 6, p. 83.

Capek, K. (1932) "The Punishment of Prometheus", in *Apocryphal Stories* [1945], trans. by Dora Round (Harmondsworth: Penguin, 1975), pp. 7–12.

"Chronicles," (1995) *Time*, January 30, p. 20.

Himmelfarb, G. (1995) "The Victorians get a bad rap," *New York Times*, January 9, p. A15.

Rosenthal, A.M. (1995) "The cruelest hoax," *New York Times*, January 3, p. A19.

Szasz, T.S. (1963) *Law, Liberty, and Psychiatry: An Inquiry Into the Social Uses of Mental Health Practices* (Syracuse: Syracuse University Press, 1988), pp. 212–222.

Szasz, T.S. (1972) "Bad habits are not diseases: A refutation of the claim that alcoholism is a disease," *The Lancet* (London), 2: 83–84 (8 July).

Szasz, T.S. (1994) *Ceremonial Chemistry: The Ritual Persecution of Drugs, Addicts, and Pushers* (Garden City, NY: Doubleday).

Szasz, T.S. (1992) *Our Right to Drugs: The Case for a Free Market* (New York: Praeger).

Zuckerman, M.B. (1995) "Welfare's scandalous cousin" (Editorial), *U.S. News & World Report*, February 6, p. 102. 2.

PART THREE

CURRENT TRENDS AND POSSIBILITIES
FOR THE FUTURE

CHAPTER 10

Drug Crop Producing Countries:
A Development Perspective

David Mansfield and Colin Sage

1.   INTRODUCTION

Despite increasing recognition that the lack of rural development is a significant factor in the production of illicit drug crops, law enforcement still dominates the current drug control strategy of the United States Government (USG). At the same time development initiatives aimed at alleviating rural poverty have been marginalised in terms of budget allocations, undermined by the imposition of political and economic conditionalities, and deprived of popular support by the ever present threat of military and police intervention.

Meanwhile, use of the term 'Alternative Development' continues to confuse implying, as it does, that poor farmers are being invited to replace the production of coca and opium with highly remunerative and risk-free substitute crops in order to improve their socio-economic status. For the majority of drug-crop producing households, however, opium and coca offer a means of survival, acting as an insurance against food scarcity and other hazards. The failure of those responsible for the design of alternative development projects to recognise the important role these crops play in the livelihood strategies of the rural poor, has led to quite inappropriate interventions. Consequently, many of the currently recognised development priorities and elements of 'best practice' have been ignored in favour of attempts to achieve immediate but unsustainable reductions in drug crop cultivation.

This Chapter will initially provide a brief overview of source areas and the role of drug crops within the local economy and agro-environment. It will then discuss the current efforts of the USG as the main proponent of drug control policies, and introduce the concept of alternative development. The Chapter will focus upon the failure of policy makers and development planners to fully comprehend the multi-functional role drug crops play within the livelihood strategies of rural households and the wider community within source areas. Drawing upon a range of examples illustrating interventions in Latin America and South and South East Asia, the Chapter will discuss how key issues such as poverty targeting, participation and environmental sustainability have been overlooked in the design of alternative development interventions. It will conclude that there is a need for more appropriate development initiatives in drug source areas, where development objectives are given precedence over those of drug crop reduction.

2.   SOURCE AREAS

Although Thailand and Colombia have become synonymous with illicit drugs in the popular imagination, they are not the major producers of drug crops. In recent years these two countries have come to specialise in the value added activities of processing, trafficking and the laundering of profits while supporting only limited cultivation (see Table). In contrast Afghanistan, Myanmar, Laos and Pakistan cultivate the bulk of the world's opium and Peru and Bolivia are responsible for 90% of the world's coca supply. A range of development indicators, such as infant mortality, life expectancy, literacy and gross domestic product per capita, demonstrate that these are amongst the poorest countries in the world with high levels of rural deprivation. Afghanistan, for example, is ranked the world's third poorest country in the United Nations Development Programme (UNDP) Human Development Index, a composite measure of social and economic development (UNDP, 1994).

Estimated Worldwide: Production of Drug Crops for Major Source Countries (Metric Tonne)

Opium	1994	1993	1992	1991	1990	1989	1988
Afghanistan	950	685	640	570	415	585	750
Pakistan	160	140	175	180	165	130	205
Burma	2,030	2,575	2,280	2,350	2,255	2,430	1,280
Laos	85	180	230	265	275	380	255
Thailand	17	42	24	35	40	50	25
TOTAL	**3,242**	**3,622**	**3,349**	**3,400**	**3,110**	**3,575**	**2,515**
Coca Leaf							
Bolivia	89,800	84,400	80,300	78,000	77,000	77,600	78,400
Colombia	35,800	31,700	29,600	30,000	32,100	33,900	27,200
Peru	165,300	155,500	223,900	222,700	196,900	186,300	187,700
TOTAL	**290,900**	**271,600**	**333,800**	**330,700**	**306,000**	**297,800**	**293,300**

Source: U.S. Department of State, Bureau of International Narcotics Matters 1994, 1995.

Bolivia, meanwhile, is the second poorest country in the western hemisphere after Haiti, and has higher infant mortality rates than many Sub Saharan African countries (World Bank, 1994). Yet such rankings provide only an aggregate picture, whereas an analysis of specific source areas reveals greater levels of socio-economic deprivation and ecological vulnerability.

To date, the research that has been undertaken into the cultivation of drug crops has been highly impressionistic consisting of 'guesstimates' undertaken at the regional and national level. It has become increasingly clear, however, that coca and opium production are a function of marginal socio-economic and ecological conditions (WHO, 1992; Potulski, 1991; Hurd & Masty, 1990; Painter & Bedoya, 1991; Office of Technical Assessment [OTA] 1993). Hurd and Masty's study of Nangarhar, Afghanistan indicates that opium production tends to concentrate in the poorest areas. The size of landholding, access to irrigation, and population density were identified as important determinants in the level of opium cultivation. Potulski's research supports this claim, suggesting that source areas in South and South East Asia, as well as in Latin America, typically suffer from scarcities of land, water supply, and food, making them some of the most agriculturally underdeveloped areas of the world (Potulski, 1991 and 1992).

Yet, for source areas, opium and coca represent efficient cash crops well suited to these harsh local conditions. Opium, for example, will grow with little difficulty in conditions unsuitable for most other crops: it can be cultivated on either irrigated or unirrigated land at altitudes of up to 3000 metres, with farmers taking advantage of the variety of micro-climates found in the mountainous areas. Here, altitude is used to stagger planting dates in order to spread the demands upon household labour and to minimize risk of crop losses in the event of unseasonal weather and other hazards (Hurd & Masty, 1990).

Coca also shows resilience in a marginal environment, with different varieties suited to a range of altitudinal, climatic and soil conditions. It is a perennial which matures in only two years and which can be harvested 4 to 6 times per annum for up to four decades, although productivity does begin to dwindle after fifteen years. Moreover coca possesses some resistance to insect pests and diseases and is tolerant of acid soils, so that farmers need make only limited use of pesticides and fertilisers. Besides being well adapted to the local ecology, coca has enjoyed a high market value and fits well into the agricultural cycle of small-farm households. This has made it a popular crop, not only for the direct producers, but also for many thousands of poor migrant labourers who have found a source of seasonal wage employment in the harvesting of the coca leaves (Sanabria, 1986; Sage, 1989).

Both opium and coca are low input/high yield crops that produce non perishable, high value to weight products. The durability of opium means households can choose to store the product if market prices are deemed too low. In an effort to retain more added-value and to avoid the wild fluctuations in price, many coca producers in Bolivia refine the leaves into paste, a relatively simple operation requiring a few extra ingredients. This also reduces the bulk of, say, 500 kg of leaves to a more manageable 2.5 kg of paste. With many areas of cultivation lacking adequate infrastructure, the high value to weight ratio of coca paste and opium makes the transportation of relatively small amounts by mule or foot a profitable endeavour. Most importantly, both opium and coca yield products with almost guaranteed markets, high exchange value, and provide access to credit from merchants and intermediaries.

> Were it not for the undesirability of the end product, opium cultivation would be considered the ideal solution to the agricultural problems of Badakshan, and aid agencies would no doubt be heavily promoting its cultivation and introducing improved methods of production (Brailsford, 1989b:32).

Although the drug control strategy of the USG recognizes the marginal socio-economic and ecological environment of drug crop producers, it appears to place little emphasis on the alleviation of poverty (US Department of State 1987–1995). For political reasons priority has been given to a supply-side policy in which eradication at source and interdiction have been the principal tools and which, until recently, have accounted for at least 70 per cent of the Congressional budget for drug control (Jarvik, 1990).

3.   CURRENT POLICY

The USG has long been an active proponent of international drug control (Walker, 1989). The USG's estimation that approximately 80% of the narcotics consumed in the United States is of foreign origin has led it to believe that the control of production at source is essential to a successful drug control strategy (US General Accounting Office [GAO], 1990). Until the 1970s the emphasis of USG policy was on persuasion, but the failure of diplomatic efforts to yield quick results in the reduction of opium, coca and marijuana cultivation and a growing consumption problem at home, prompted a more interventionist approach, characterised by eradication and interdiction.[1] Moreover, the USG's perception of areas of cultivation as the easiest to detect and destroy, and therefore the most commercially vulnerable point in the supply chain, led to crop eradication and interdiction being acclaimed as the most cost effective and efficient strategy for drug control (Van Wert, 1988).

> Logic and common sense tells us that stopping coca in these valleys and countries may be cheaper and more effective than trying to do so once it arrives in the US. There are hundreds of thousands of street corners in America where crack can be sold. But there is only one Chapare and one Huallaga valley. (Senator S. Nunn cited in US Congress, Senate Committee on Government Affairs, Permanent Sub-committee on Investigations 1989:5).

Adopting such an approach has meant direct economic and military aid has become the defining feature of the USG's bilateral relationship with source nations. In 1988 the USG assisted crop eradication efforts in 23 countries and interdiction in around 70, a year when 91% of international narcotics control funding was allocated to these, and other law enforcement, activities (Wrobelski, 1988; US GAO, 1990).[2] This is a strategy which greatly conflicts with that of European governments who have channelled aid through the United Nations. The USG has tended to use multilateral assistance only where bilateral aid has been unacceptable to recipient governments, such as in Turkey in the early 1970s (Williamson, 1988). Consequently in 1988 only 1.7% ($3.4 million) of the USG's total expenditure on international drug control was directed through the United Nations (US GAO, 1990). By 1995, international organizations such as the UN Drug Control Programme (UNDCP) and the Organization of American States (OAS) were allocated only 5% of the United States' overseas narcotics budget (US Department of State, 1995).

By the 1980s compliance with the USG's eradication and interdiction efforts were integral to US foreign policy. Under the Foreign Assistance Act of 1961 and the Anti-Drug Abuse Act of 1986 and 1988 the USG defined and formalised 'cooperation' of source countries by law, and initiated punitive penalties for those which failed to comply. Under this legislation source countries are required to achieve 'the maximum reduction in illicit production determined to be achievable', enact legislation concerning extradition, money laundering and monitor precursor chemicals to gain a 'cooperative status' and, consequently, be eligible for aid. Failure to gain certification, in contrast, exposes source countries to a number of mandatory and discretionary sanctions.

For example, 'decertification' triggers the mandatory suspension of all US assistance for the current and subsequent fiscal years, until evidence of cooperation has been demonstrated. US representatives are also obliged to vote against the provision of loans considered by the multilateral development banks. At the discretion of Congress and the President, sanctions can also include: the denial of preferential tariff agreements for a country's exports; increased import duties of up to 50%; the curtailment of air transportation to the US; and the withdrawal of US cooperation in customs arrangements. Moreover, in order to be considered for future development assistance a country must establish drug control agreements with the US or with the United Nations.

Bolivia's failure to meet its coca eradication targets of 6,000 hectares per year in the late 1980s led to its decertification for non-performance and resulted in a loss of development assistance from the US of $9.5 million in 1986 and $8.7 million in 1987 (US GAO, 1988b). Yet project funding is subject to further conditionalities. The establishment of a drug law enforcement agency, the deployment of Drug Enforcement Agency (DEA) trained Bolivian forces and an approved eradication plan were all required as preconditions for US funding for the Chapare Regional Development Project in Bolivia. The tranching of Economic Support Funds according to predetermined eradication targets was also initiated for this project (*ibid.*).[3]

Yet in reality there is little evidence to suggest that these policies are either efficient, effective or economic in achieving their objectives in reducing either the production or the consumption of illicit drugs. In the United States indicators seem to suggest that the consumer of illicit drugs has never had so much, so pure and at such a low price (Boffey, 1988; McCoy & Block, 1992). Internationally, supply has soared. Coca production has increased from an annual harvest of around 20,000 metric tons in the late 1960s to an estimated 290,900 metric tons in 1994. Similarly, world opium production has experienced an almost fourfold increase, rising from 990 metric tons in 1971 to 3,409 metric tons in 1994 (McCoy & Block, 1992; US Department of State, 1995). Moreover, in the last decade production of opium has not only doubled, but more countries have begun to cultivate opium poppy. Indeed, US illegal heroin requirements could now be satisfied by opium production in the Western hemisphere alone (White House, 1994). Other commentators have indicated that opium production could in fact be far higher than the official figures suggest, with one source estimating that in 1992 Afghanistan was producing almost 2000 metric tons of opium, five times that estimated by the USG for the same year (Ferogh, 1992). Clearly the concentration of cultivation in politically disputed territories such as Afghanistan and the Shan State, Myanmar, not only makes estimates of production difficult, but thwarts efforts at crop control, interdiction and even the more progressive attempts at providing development assistance.[4]

4.   ALTERNATIVE DEVELOPMENT

It is said that the enforcement strategy increases lawlessness, forces consumers to switch to more potent forms of drugs and drives production to more distant regions. The development options, on the other hand, seek to restrict production through persuasion and cooperation and aim to strengthen law and order. The development options, while all still largely unproven and exploratory, are considered optimistic and humanitarian approaches which warrant serious consideration and support (Northridge, 1989:15).

The desired goal of alternative development is to create an appropriate economic environment in which households can attain an acceptable standard of living without the need for drug crop cultivation. Typically the entry point into source areas has been via efforts at research and extension. Later phases have adopted a more integrated approach: consolidating crop substitution initiatives with food for work schemes; encouraging income generation opportunities; fostering social development by widening access to education; improving health care through the installation of sanitation and drinking water schemes; and building roads to improve access to markets. Such efforts have begun to provide an indispensable infrastructure for the rural poor in facilitating a transition from illicit drug crops to the cultivation of legal and remunerative substitutes. Meanwhile, other policy initiatives have sought to integrate drug control into national development plans and encourage the revival and expansion of other sectors of the economy (Seyler, 1991).

Alternative development, via the introduction of substitute crops and other innovations, has disproved the myth that coca and opium will always offer the highest returns to small farmers (Potulski, 1991, 1992; UNDP, 1991; Smith *et al.*, 1992; Khan, 1991). For example, substitution efforts in Northern Thailand have shown that annual profits can be increased by over 50 times by replacing opium with flowers (Smith *et al.*, 1992). In the Bolivian Chapare rubber has been found to generate per hectare four times the returns of coca (UNDP, 1991). In Buner, Pakistan, household incomes were more than doubled through development efforts between 1976 and 1991, whilst opium cultivation had effectively been eliminated by 1983 (UNDP, 1991). Indeed, Thailand's success in reducing the level of opium production has proved what development efforts can achieve where decades of coercion have failed (Sharma, 1984). Current levels of opium production are half that produced in 1984 and only a quarter of the amount produced in the mid 1960s (McCoy & Block, 1992). Understandably, therefore, Thailand's programme of alternative development is considered one of the most effective in the world (US GAO, 1988a).

Yet, despite these positive results, the success of alternative development has largely been limited to reducing drug crop cultivation in specific local areas. Substantial and sustained reductions at national level have not been achieved, and in many source countries production continues to rise. In the case of Thailand, the long period over which it has maintained the strategy and the relative prosperity of the country, raises questions about the effectiveness of alternative development. It remains to be seen whether the Thai experience is a replicable model for countries such as Afghanistan and Laos where off farm income opportunities are currently extremely limited.

Experience has also shown that despite the availability of cash crops, small producers often continue to give priority to traditional cropping patterns that produce lower returns but offer greater security (Scott, 1976). This may be due to their recognition of the risks and uncertainties associated with the production of cash crops for domestic and export markets. The fluctuations in price of agricultural commodities (such as oranges, coffee, cacao, bananas and many more), have made farmers wary of becoming dependent upon a few commercial crops, particularly those that cannot be used for direct consumption by the household. Programmes of structural adjustment, which require countries to increase exports in order to raise foreign exchange to service their external debt, have also placed downward pressure on world market prices, as the supply of commodities has outstripped the rate of increase in global demand. Many alternative development projects are therefore promoting commercial crops in which profitability is at best uncertain, and in which other countries may already have established technical expertise and superior market access. The existing international division of labour and changing macro-economic conditions can consequently exacerbate the problems arising from poorly designed extension initiatives.[5]

Efforts to promote alternative development have failed to fully comprehend the multi-functional role drug crops play within the livelihood strategies of households and the wider community of source areas. Consequently, many current development initiatives aimed at drug crop control appear to have been designed in a vacuum. In an attempt to bring about quick and visible benefits in the reduction of drug crop cultivation, normal development criteria and 'best practice' are being ignored in favour of a rapid response. A consultant's report, prepared following an evaluation of a project in the coca-producing area of the Chapare in Bolivia, expressed concern about the cause of being seen to act and noted:

> The result is a process of shooting from the hip in which large, poorly-considered projects are thrown at complex situations. The approach of the agro-industrial projects, particularly, is evocative of 1960s development thinking, where it was felt that we had all the answers and simply had to 'transfer' them to the grateful peasantry. In short, the drug control imperative is being used to justify the worst features of naive top-down development (Dudley, 1991).

In order to support the argument that many of the conventionally accepted criteria of best practice in rural development are currently being overlooked in the battle against drug crops, the remainder of the Chapter examines three key issues. These are poverty targeting, participation and environmental sustainability, and an examination of these three issues will raise serious questions regarding the appropriateness and relevance of alternative development initiatives.

5.   KEY ISSUES

i)   Poverty Targeting

Currently, we have an inadequate understanding of decision making amongst drug crop producers at the micro level, with few indepth studies of the circumstances and priorities that influence the involvement of individual farmers in the cultivation of drug crops. This lack of detailed analysis at the household level means that current crop-substitution schemes tend to regard the producers of illicit drug crops as a homogenous group. The specific socio-economic, cultural and environmental circumstances that influence household production are consequently overlooked in project design. Rather, emphasis is placed on the high economic returns that opium and coca are reported to accrue per unit of land (Brailsford, 1989b; Hurd & Masty, 1991; Potylski, 1991, 1992; OTA 1993). This simplified model of human behaviour, which emphasises economic rationality over other motivations, is both inadequate and inappropriate given the variety of circumstances and opportunities facing drug crop producers.

Despite their suitability to the local environment, experience has shown that opium and coca are rarely monocropped. In the Chapare very few households grow in excess of 1.5 hectares of coca despite considerable variations in the size of land holdings. In the Upper Huallaga Valley of Peru, 76% of those households participating in an eradication programme were found to have less than 2 hectares of coca regardless of their total amount of land (Painter & Bedoya, 1991). Meanwhile in Turkey, where households had on average access to 5 hectares of cultivable land, a maximum area of 0.5 hectares under opium poppy was cultivated (Kumar *et al.*, 1986). Indeed, very few households have been found to dedicate more than 50% of their cultivable land to opium and coca, suggesting that they are generally grown as part of a diversified cropping pattern designed to spread risk while meeting food and income needs (Henkel, 1986; Hurd & Masty, 1991). This tends to counter the belief that drug crops are grown purely for their high returns to land (Painter & Bedoya, 1991). Moreover, rural households often face labour as well as land constraints, limited market opportunities and a preference for leisure (Goh, 1986). Given such conditions, it is not appropriate to assume that opium and coca production are determined entirely by simple economic rationalism — as current policy appears to suggest. Rather, the decision-making process of farmers that underlies the cultivation of drug crops is far more complex than this.

Coca and opium play a particularly important role where household access to land is acute. In Swabi, Pakistan the greatest proportion of land dedicated to poppy was found to be where household land holdings were less than 0.75 hectares (Khan, 1991). Similarly, in Achin, Afghanistan, where mean household land holdings are less than 0.5 hectares, 65% of cultivated land is dedicated to poppy cultivation. Yet in Sukhurd, Afghanistan, where the farmland is considered rich, crop yields are high and the population density low, only 10% of cultivated land was dedicated to poppy (Hurd & Masty, 1991). In the Chapare area of Bolivia the amount of land planted to coca as a percentage of total farm area varies considerably, although in general it is those households with the smallest farm area which have the largest proportion of their land under coca (Painter & Bedoya, 1991). Indeed, the smallest land holdings, where average size is 2–3 hectares of tillable land per household, are to be found in the Zona Roja (Red Zone) where coca predominates (Bostwick *et al.*, 1990).

The importance of coca as a safety net is perhaps best illustrated by the financial outlay resource-poor farmers are willing to undertake in order to establish production. For example, the labour required to prepare land and plant coca forces many households to hire casual field workers. However, once established, unremunerated family labour is usually sufficient to maintain and harvest the coca leaves and this, together with the long life cycle of the plant, allows coca to make an important and regular contribution to household income even when its price slips below theoretical costs of production (Painter & Bedoya, 1991). Indeed, for many households in source areas, drug crops generate the greatest proportion of total annual income — exceeding 90% in many of the poorest areas — enabling the rural poor to meet their basic needs (Potulski, 1992; UNDP., 1991; UNDCP., 1992b).

Consequently, coca and opium cultivation can be seen as part of a wider strategy aimed at achieving food and livelihood security, helping farmers to meet the uncertainties of the local environment and the consequences of commoditization of the rural economy. The emphasis on eradication within current programmes of alternative development is, consequently, inappropriate. Attempting to replace the income received from opium and coca with revenue from substitute crops is a necessary, but insufficient, condition for achieving reductions in levels of cultivation. This strategy will only satisfy those wealthier households that produce illicit crops for extra income. For the poor who are more vulnerable, however, current development efforts endanger the only buffer they have against food shortage. This is why programmes of alternative development need to recognise the high levels of socio-economic differentiation that exist in source areas, and target their initiatives accordingly.

For those most dependent on drug crops as a means of ensuring the survival of the household, for example, alternative development needs to create opportunities and encourage activities that contribute to livelihood security rather than simply to impose the speculative production of cash crops. In this respect, such programmes must begin by recognising the safety net that opium and coca provides, and work to establish a similar structure by strengthening the existing subsistence system and investing in small-scale food crop and livestock production. This would undoubtedly prove a less controversial and conflictive strategy than current priorities engender, and has the benefit of not exposing the most vulnerable farmers to the harsh realities of an incipient agro-export market. Given the failure of existing programmes to give adequate attention to the role that women play as generators of value and income in the production of coca and opium (OTA, 1993; Nicholl, 1988), together with prior eradication conditionalities and short term donor commitment, the poor associate current alternative development with increasing costs and risks. Only by allowing the genuine participation of the poor in the design and implementation of acceptable, truly "alternative" initiatives, can their needs and priorities be addressed and their livelihoods safeguarded.

ii)   Participation

Despite the rhetoric surrounding 'participation' and people-centred development, there has been little evidence of such an approach in current alternative development projects. Local institutions have been largely bypassed in drug crop producing areas despite their often long traditions of representative authority. Enforcement continues to dominate, with eradication regarded as a prerequisite in order to create the right conditions for successful alternative development (US Department of State, 1992). The basis for such action rests, as argued above, upon the erroneous assumption that households engage in drug crop cultivation to maximize profits, an assumption that has led to the exclusion of farmers and their organizations from consultative or collaborative participation in alternative development programmes.

Where eradication has been a precondition for financial assistance, farmers have usually opted to eradicate only a part of their crop. In the Chapare households destroyed 50 per cent of their coca in order to take advantage of the compensation of up to $2,000 per hectare. Yet while this demonstrated their willingness to cooperate with the crop substitution programme, US officials refused to allow compensation to be paid until 70% of the coca shrubs were eradicated — leaving the farmers without the money needed to plant other crops (Labrousse, 1990). Naturally, farmers were reluctant to embark upon the complete elimination of coca until they were assured that substitute crops were viable and remunerative (Bostwick *et al.*, 1990). Where complete eradication has been enforced without the prior provision of alternative sources of income it has had dramatic consequences for rural populations. In the Tekshan valley, Afghanistan, the loss of income incurred by households who complied with an opium ban introduced by their local commander, combined with limited access to irrigated land and the failure of substitute crops, led to a shortfall in food supply and the migration of 1,500 families (Brailsford, 1989b). A similar phenomenon was experienced in the Upper Huallaga Valley, Peru, where an uncoordinated approach of law enforcement and development interventions left households unable to meet their basic needs once eradication had occurred (Econsult, 1987). Moreover, eradication was quite unable to influence the underlying economic advantage of coca over the cultivation of substitute crops: indeed, quite the opposite. Consequently, small farmers whose coca had been eliminated simply left the project area and began planting coca in frontier zones as the only effective solution to safeguarding their livelihood needs (Painter & Bedoya, 1991; Econsult, 1987).

This experience is in stark contrast with Thailand where, despite USG insistence, the Thai authorities have allowed a four year grace period before embarking upon the forcible eradication of opium poppies. Building trust and having a flexible pragmatic approach have been essential preconditions, and enforcement has only been introduced once alternative income generation opportunities are in place. Here, eradication is viewed in terms of 'negotiated' law enforcement, in which the provision of basic needs is a necessary component part. Accordingly, "This participatory and contractual approach to the population represents a major element to ensure viability and sustainability" (UNDCP., 1993:18). This is an approach, incidentally, supported by UNDP who believe that "the idea is that development should precede or at least go hand in hand with enforcement … The development provides the sweetener to make the enforcement more palatable" (UNDP., 1991:10).

Elsewhere the imperative of law enforcement has not only undermined the credibility of development efforts in its presumption that eradication must precede the building of alternatives: it has also triggered massive resistance by target populations and fostered civil conflict. In Myanmar and Peru eradication operations have been used as part of an overall strategy of regional counter insurgency. Although 16,656 hectares of opium poppy were eradicated in 1988 in Myanmar with the assistance of the USG, this area has effectively become impenetrable (US Department of State, 1989). Meanwhile, the almost indiscriminate use of chemical and biological agents to eradicate coca in the Huallaga Valley during the late

1980s came to perfectly exemplify a style of enforcement that contributed to high levels of conflict between the Peruvian state and the guerrilla group, Sendero Luminoso (Sage, 1991). In Bolivia, too, the actions of the specialist anti drug police unit (UMOPAR) have resulted in increasing friction between the rural population of the Chapare and government agencies. Road blocks, occupations and demonstrations organised by the coca growers' unions to protest against the abuses of UMOPAR have occurred on a number of occasions, and resulted in the deaths of at least ten farmers in June 1988 (Painter, 1994).

The dominant paradigm of enforcement appears to view the entire rural population as guilty of criminal activity, whose cooperation is taken for granted and, if this is withheld, legitimises the use of force to ensure their immediate compliance. Local institutions have been largely bypassed due to the belief that they are controlled by drug trafficking organizations. This is ironic given the well-documented influence that major drug trafficking figures have had on senior government officials, police and military authorities.[6] In Achin, Afghanistan failure to fully involve the local population and their commanders in the design and implementation of an opium reduction programme led to a deterioration in the relationship between the target population and the local leadership (Brailsford, 1989a). In Bolivia, agreement between the government and the trade union movement, including the coca growers' federations, to work together towards a common programme of alternative development was seen as a very considerable achievement. However, Decree 22270 of July 1987 setting out this agreement and the procedures of consultation were rapidly overtaken by new legislation which placed greater emphasis upon eradication. Moreover, the failure of the international donor community to provide sufficient funds to create new economic opportunities as alternatives to coca, and the increasingly "heavy-handed" tactics of the authorities inevitably led to the collapse of the agreements.

Within this context of increasing socio-economic and political vulnerability it is understandable that producers treat alternative development projects suspiciously, taking advantage of the financial incentives and newly-installed infrastructure, but safeguarding their livelihoods through relocation to more inaccessible areas on a temporary or permanent basis. Indeed, it is argued that alternative development has systematically failed to acknowledge the mobility of rural populations in source areas, where migration has been a traditional response to changing opportunities and risks in the rural economy (Painter & Bedoya, 1991; Labrousse, 1990; Sanabria, 1986; Parnwell, 1993). In Bolivia the 1976 census revealed that more than one quarter of the population were found to be residing in a place other than that of their birth (Kraljevik, 1992). The Chapare in particular has been found to contain a particularly mobile population where a third of the population are thought to be transient and 10,000–22,000 families are said to have left the area in 1990. Inappropriate development interventions, and eradication in particular, can be seen to have played a major role in the relocation of producers to isolated areas free from state authority (Painter & Bedoya, 1991; Tullis, 1992; United Nations Economic and Social Commission for Asia and the Pacific, 1991;

Khan, 1991). Such migration can be viewed as a litmus test of unsuccessful development initiatives (Parnwell, 1993).

Consequently, it is apparent that there is a need for more appropriate interventions which would provide local people with the voice to influence the direction of their own development. The adoption of a more participatory approach, which would pay attention to local needs, household aspirations and community organisations, would assist in finding a more viable solution to illicit drug control and reduce the environmentally damaging consequences of relocation that have become synonymous with current alternative development initiatives (UNDCP., 1992a; Sage, 1994; Painter & Bedoya, 1991).

iii)   Environmental Sustainability

Alternative development has emphasised the need for alternative sources of income but has done so without giving due care and consideration to the environmental sustainability of such initiatives. Indeed, the environmentally fragile nature and limited land use potential of many source areas poses considerable constraints on finding substitute crops capable of generating adequate levels of income without undermining the long-term productive capacity of the resource base. In Afghanistan and Pakistan, for example, areas most closely associated with poppy cultivation are typically characterised by low agricultural potential. The staple wheat crop is sown on slopes which are shallow ploughed and which then revert to long fallow periods to restore soil fertility. The low productivity of pastures and other biomass leads to problems of overgrazing, while the fuel needs of local households account for trees and shrubs and result in the deterioration in the biotic composition of the rangelands, as well as an increased risk of soil erosion.

The Chapare region of Bolivia has been considered especially fragile and vulnerable from an ecological perspective. Indeed, it has been those interests most closely associated with eradication which have voiced most concern about the environmental damage caused by coca cultivation. This is ironic given that it is the high levels of rainfall in the Chapare which make it unsuitable for intensive agricultural production, yet agricultural intensification has provided the central element of alternative development.

Although coca is a perennial bush and in many ways ecologically preferable to annual crops, it is nevertheless a poor substitute for the forest canopy. As leaves are stripped from the bush four times or more each year, and with the clean weeding of coca fields, the soils are exposed to heavy rainfall and, without careful management, can result in erosion. However, reference to the Yungas region east of La Paz, where coca has been grown on terraced hillsides for many generations, demonstrates that under appropriate soil management practices coca is no more responsible for soil degradation than any other crop. One USAID-commissioned study concluded that "as a *crop* coca's effects on the environment seem average or even benign, especially in comparison with other crops grown in the (Chapare) region" (Tolisano *et al.*, 1989: F3).

One of the consequences of the dramatic expansion of coca cultivation has been widespread deforestation and the expansion of frontier areas by small farmers. In Bolivia there has been increasing encroachment into the National Parks of Isiboro and Amboro by coca producers with a consequent loss of forest cover and biological diversity (Calvani: pers. comm.). In Peru it has been estimated that about 700,000 hectares may have been deforested directly and indirectly due to coca, a figure which represents about ten per cent of the total deforestation in the Peruvian Amazon region this century (Alvarez, 1992).

The most environmentally damaging aspect of the drug trade results, not from the cultivation of coca, but from the dumping of toxic substances derived as by-products from processing operations. The disposal of sulphuric acid, ethyl ether, acetone, and other chemicals, together with kerosene, diesel and lime, all in substantial quantities, has enormous potential to create major pollution problems. The disposal of petroleum products in the river systems, for example, inhibits oxygenization of the water causing the asphyxia of fish life, and this may affect large riverside populations downstream which depend upon fish as a source of protein and income. It has been estimated that in Peru in 1986, in order to produce 6,400 tonnes of basic cocaine paste, the following quantities of precursor chemicals were used and discarded: 57 million litres of kerosene, 32 million litres of sulphuric acid, 16,000 tons of lime, the same quantity of toilet paper (used for drying the paste), and 13 million litres of acetone and toluene (Garcia-Sayan, 1989; Alvarez, 1992).

Yet serious ecological damage is also being caused by coca eradication schemes and the efforts of the USG to develop chemical and biological agents to attack and eliminate the shrub. This is being matched by a high level of vigilance on the part of coca producers, who continue to hold the Bolivian government to legal agreements enshrining the principle of voluntary substitution, and to ensure that forcible eradication does not proceed. Indeed, the use of the chemical defoliant 2,4-D in field trials in the Chapare in 1982 triggered a storm of protest from across the breadth of public opinion, and effectively brought to an end chemical testing in Bolivia.[7]

This is most unfortunate for those commentators who believe that "the last hope for winning the war against cocaine in South America is the large-scale application of herbicides against coca plants" (Lee, 1989: 206). The search for an effective herbicide looked to have ended in 1988 when the Eli Lilly company launched Tebuthurion (trade name "Spike"), a product designed to kill woody plants. Spraying in Peru's Huallaga Valley proved the product was effective, but the Environmental Protection Agency, while approving the product, warned that Spike was an extremely active herbicide which will kill trees, shrubs, and other desirable forms of vegetation, and should be kept out of ponds, lakes and streams.

Environmental scientists warned of the ecological devastation that could result from the use of Spike, and the Company itself recognised the product could cause irreversible harm to flora and fauna, and pulmonary and heart damage in humans. Yet the US Assistant Secretary for Narcotics Matters, Ann Wrobleski, described Spike as "less toxic than aspirin, nicotine, and nitrate fertilizers" (quoted in Lee, 1989: 206).

Eli Lilly's withdrawal of Spike from spraying programmes, for fear of legal and possibly other reprisals against its interests (Gladwell, 1988), set back the cause of chemical eradication of coca. But, undaunted, the USG has been supporting research into biological agents in its search for a "magic bullet" against coca (Kawell, 1989), experimenting in the Huallaga Valley with the larvae "Malumbia" (*Eloria Noyesi*) which is "seeded" from light aircraft over coca-growing areas. Peruvian and Bolivian peasants have long fought the voracious appetite of this larva on citrus crops, a possible commercial alternative to coca. Yet these examples of almost indiscriminate use of chemical and biological agents to eradicate coca exemplifies a style of intervention that not only has contributed to the high level of conflict in the region, but which demonstrates little real interest or concern in securing an environmentally-sustainable, long-term alternative to coca cultivation.

6. CONCLUSION

During recent years there has been increasing awareness of the serious consequences arising from the production, trafficking and consumption of illicit drugs for the social, cultural, economic and political development of source and transit nations. Indeed, framed within the context of increasing levels of addiction at source, the corruption of local, regional and national institutions by trafficking organisations, and the marginal socio-economic and environmental conditions which offer few alternatives to illicit crop cultivation, drug control represents one of the major development issues of the 1990s.

The Overseas Development Administration of the United Kingdom has recognised the importance of drug control as a development issue and designated it a 'policy objective'. More recently the USG has declared that drug control should be seen within a wider framework of sustainable development, and has called for greater involvement by the multilateral banks and international financial institutions (White House, 1994). Yet despite the rhetoric, financial aid for crop substitution and development assistance from the United States is still limited, amounting to 10.6% of the overseas narcotics budget, while law enforcement, military counter-narcotics support and eradication still command over 65% of the total budget (US Department of State, 1995). It seems that the USG will continue to favour the stick of enforcement as opposed to the carrot of development for the forseeable future.

It is the political and economic domination of source countries by the North, most especially the United States, which ultimately underlies the preference for militarising the control of drug crops and the failure to pursue an authentic strategy of alternative development. Nevertheless, it is also possible to highlight some of the principal shortcomings in the design and implementation of programmes of alternative development.

For example, many of the projects have proved too ambitious and unrealistic in their objectives, while the agencies responsible for implementation were unable to provide a focused and coordinated strategy (Painter, 1994; DeVincenti, 1991). The requirements of financial management have led donors to become victims of the project cycle, unable to offer the commitment needed to bring about a change in agricultural practice (OTA, 1993). By choosing not to recognise existing rural institutions, alternative development has also failed to promote the institutional change necessary to sustain initiatives. Priority has been given to establishing parallel institutions with little basis or legitimacy in the local community. Yet, elsewhere, experience has shown that genuine participation of local communities is essential for successful development (ODA, 1993). Participation is as relevant to development initiatives in drug crop source areas — such as Afghanistan, Laos and Bolivia where there is a long tradition of regional autonomy and strong local organizations — as it is in projects in rural Africa, or in urban South Asia. Indeed, alternative development has much to learn from many contemporary initiatives in the mainstream sectors of development.

Alternative development needs to promote a more flexible, and long term approach that builds on current development criteria and 'best practice', giving precedence to such key issues as poverty targetting and the needs of women, and not simply to eradication. Ideally, initiatives would be of a 10–15 year duration in order to create continuity, and to help reduce the sense of risk that rural communities associate with new agricultural innovations (OTA, 1993). Initially, small scale pilot projects would seek to collaborate with local communities through participatory appraisal and action research methods in order to identify the dynamics of drug crop cultivation, the level of interest in establishing alternative production systems, and priorities of local needs. Such an approach recognises and seeks to build upon rural people's own knowledge and promotes capacity building in local institutions. Attention would be given, for example, to establishing viable, locally-managed credit institutions in source areas, which are a prerequisite for the development of alternative economic activities (Painter & Bedoya, 1991; Tropical Research & Development Inc., 1992; Painter, 1994). Naturally, such initiatives would need time to become established, to have resulted in real improvements for local people who also exerted a high degree of "ownership" of the project, before crop eradication could remotely be enforced.

However, the failure of alternative development to reduce drug crop cultivation cannot solely be seen as a function of poor project design and implementation. Success in achieving sustainable reductions in opium and coca cultivation will continue to be localised unless the demand for their derivatives is reduced. This is hardly surprising; market economics dictates that where drug crop cultivation is squeezed in one area it will undoubtedly occur in another if the level of demand is maintained (Mansfield, 1993). Moreover, given that only 35 square miles of opium and 11 square miles of coca are required to satisfy the entire cocaine and heroin demands of the US, it is evident that policy alternatives to a single-minded strategy of supply-side control must be considered if a sustained reduction in the area under drug crops is to be achieved (British Agencies Afghan Group, 1990; Wisotsky, 1983).

Finally, there is an important issue of semantics. The term "alternative development" is misleading, implying that drug crops are bringing a type of 'development' to source areas that needs replacing by another. Yet, despite the rhetoric, there is little evidence to suggest that the 'lucrative trade' in drug crops has led to real social and economic improvements in source areas. The cultivation of drug crops is attractive to rural households because other crops cannot meet their basic needs in often marginal socio-economic and physical environments. Only by understanding and addressing the role that drug crops play in the survival strategies of the rural poor can interventions bring about sustainable improvements in the socio-economic development of rural households and thereby have any hope of displacing coca and opium cultivation. Consequently, alternative development is 'alternative' only in the sense that it contravenes the current priorities and best practice of rural development projects. These generally seek to respond to the needs of the poor and most disadvantaged populations, including women; encourage the participation of all stakeholders in the development process; and ensure the sustainable management of natural resources. It would appear that current efforts at "alternative development" fail badly by these criteria.

NOTES

1. Perhaps the best known example of this was Operation Condor, the aerial spraying of herbicides on opium poppy and marijuana crops in Mexico, financed and logistically supported by the USG. For further details see Walker 1989 and Gonzalez and Tienda 1989.
2. With the US Pentagon given a lead role in the "war on drugs", increased military aid overseas was directed, for example, to the armed forces of the Andean countries despite their having some of the worst human rights records in the world. According to Hargreaves,

   "Law enforcement assistance that had previously been given to Andean police forces was switched to military aid. Military aid to the Andes leapt from $22 million in the fiscal year 1989 to an unprecedented $131 million in the fiscal year 1990 and to $151 million in 1991. By 1991 the region had outstripped Central America to become the largest recipient of US military aid in Latin America" (Hargreaves 1992: 23).

3. The difficulties of meeting eradication targets in Bolivia can be briefly illustrated. According to Flavio Machacado (1992) in the 1987-88 eradication campaign, only 2,516 hectares of coca were substituted while 6,817 new hectares were planted, a net increase of 4,300 hectares in the total area under coca — and in the midst of an eradication programme! Yet of the Bolivian

government's request to the international donor community for $1.6 billion to finance a three year eradication programme, only $300 million was obtained, of which $15 million was disbursed.

4.   Indeed, the sheer difficulty of imposing controls over the production of drug crops in politically disputed territories cannot be exaggerated when one considers that more than US$118 million was spent on eradication efforts in Mexico between 1984 and 1987 but these were "unable to significantly reduce illegal cultivation" (US GAO., 1988c: 8).

5.   In Bolivia there have been serious problems in establishing the commercial viability of several crops being promoted as alternatives to coca. These included tea, ginger and tumeric which were being stockpiled in large quantities in the early 1990s without a ready market, with USAID underwriting costs by paying producers and providing grants and loans to foster small processing plants and export companies. The objective has been to identify niche markets in high-value, low-bulk goods but Bolivia faces competition from countries with much better infrastructure closer to major centres of consumption in North America (Sage, 1994).

6.   At the time of writing the Colombian defence minister, Fernando Botero, had just resigned over accusations that he had accepted millions of dollars from leading members of the Colombian drug cartels. President Ernesto Samper has also acknowledged that drug money may have been used to fund his campaign for office, enabling cartel leaders subsequently to blackmail the government (*The Guardian*, 3 August 1995).

7.   It was later alleged, maliciously or not, that the field trials may actually have been using the defoliant Agent Orange (2,4,5-T), a chemical closely associated with the brutality of American imperialism during the Vietnam War.

BIBLIOGRAPHY

Alvarez, Elena (1992) Coca Production in Peru. In *Drug Policy in the Americas*, P. Smith (ed.). Boulder, Co.: Westview Press.

Boffey, Philip (1988) 'Drug Users, Not Suppliers Key to Problem.' *The New York Times*, April 12th.

Bostwick, D., Dorsey, J. and Jones, J. (1990) *Evaluation of the Chapare Regional Development Project 511–0543*. Special Evaluation, USAID/Bolivia.

Brailsford, Guy (1989a) 'Opium Crop Substitution Programme: Achin District, Nangarhar Evaluation Report.' *Afghan Aid Evaluation Report*, Peshawar, Pakistan.

Brailsford, Guy (1989b) 'A Survey of Opium Cultivation in Badakshan Province, Afghanistan.' *Afghan Aid Evaluation Report*, Peshawar, Pakistan.

British Agencies Afghan Group (1990) 'The Involvement of Afghanistan in the Heroin Trade.' Discussion Paper.

De Vincenti (1991) Infrastructural Needs to Support Agricultural Alternatives to Coca. Report prepared for the Office of Technology Assessment, Congress of the United States.

Dudley, Eric (1991) Report prepared for the Overseas Development Administration, UK.

Econsult (1987) *Final Report on the Evaluation of Aid Project No. 527–0244: Development of the Alto Huallaga Area.* USAID, Project Evaluation Summary.

Ferogh, Abdul, A. (1992) 'Afghanistan's Future Narcotics Control Mechanism and Institutional Arrangements.' *Technical Consultation on Drug Issues in South West Asia*, Islamabad, Pakistan 21–23, Sept.

Garcia-Sayan, D. (1989) Narcotrafico y region andina: una visio general. In *Coca, Cocaina y Narcotrafico: Laberinto en los Andes*, D. Garcia-Sayan (ed.). Lima, Peru: Comision Andina de Juristas.

Gladwell, M. (1988) 'Coca war checked in pesticide debacle.' *International Herald Tribune*, 2 June.

Goh, Dieter (1986) 'How Subsistence Economies Work.' *Development: Seeds of Change*, 3:23–30.

Gonzalez, G. and Tienda, M. (1989) *The Drug Connection in US-Mexican Relations*. San Diego: Center for US-Mexican Studies.

Hargreaves, C. (1992) *Snowfields: The War on Cocaine in the Andes*. London: Zed Books.

Henkel, Ray (1986) 'The Bolivian Cocaine Industry.' *Studies in Third World Societies: Drugs in Latin America*, Ed. by E. Morales, (37): 53–80.

Hurd, Anne, E. and Masty, Stephen, J. (1991) 'Opium Poppy Cultivation Nangarhar Province Afghanistan.' Prepared for UNFDAC, Peshawar, Pakistan.

Jarvik, Murray, E. (1990) 'The Drug Dilemma: Manipulating the Demand.' Science, 250, Oct. 19th: 387–392.

Kawell, Jo Ann (1989) 'Going to the Source.' *NACLA: Report on the Americas*, XXII(6), March: 13–21.

Khan, Sahibzada (1991) 'Poppy Cultivation in Northwest Frontier Province: It's Past, Present and Future.' Rural Development Division, Islamabad, Pakistan.

Kraljevik, Ivo (1992) Migration, Social Change and the Coca/Cocaine Economy in Bolivia. Report prepared for the Office of Technology Assessment, Congress of the United States.

Kumar, Krishna, Carter, E. and Samuelson, S. (1986) *A Review of AID's Narcotics Control Development Assistance Program*, AID Evaluation Study No. 29.

Labrousse, Alain (1990) 'Dependence on Drugs: Unemployment, Migration and an Alternative Path to Development.' *International Labour Review*, 129(3):333–348.

Lee, R. (1989) *The White Labryinth: Cocaine and Political Power*. New Brunswick, NJ: Transaction Publishers.

Machicado, F. (1992) Coca Production in Bolivia. In *Drug Policy in the Americas*, P. Smith (ed.). Boulder, Co: Westview Publishers.

McCoy, Alfred, W. and Block Alan, A. (1992) *War on Drugs: Studies in the Failure of U.S. Narcotics Policy*. Oxford: Westview Press.

Mansfield, David (1993) *International Drug Control: The Application of Say's Law in an Attempt to Curb Domestic Drug Abuse*. Dissertation for MSc. (Econ.). The Centre for Development Studies, Swansea University.

Nicholl, Charles (1988) *Borderlines*. London: Picador.

Northridge, John (1989) 'Narcotics: Challenge to Extension.' *AERDD Bulletin*, 26, March: 9–15.

Office of Technology Assessment, Congress of the United States (1993) *Agricultural Alternatives to Coca Production*. Washington DC: US Government Printing Office.

Overseas Development Administration (1993) *Social Development Handbook: A Guide to Social Issues in ODA Projects & Programmes*. London: ODA.

Painter, James (1994) *Bolivia and Coca: A Study in Dependency*. London: Lynne Rienner Publishers.

Painter, Michael and Bedoya, Eduardo (1991) Institutional Analysis of the Chapare Regional Development Project and the Upper Huallaga Special Project. Report prepared for the Office of Technology Assessment, Congress of the United States.

Parnwell, Mike (1993) *Population Movements and the Third World*. London: Routledge.

Potulski, Nicole (1991) *Alternative Crops for Drug Growing areas in Asia (Pakistan, Afghanistan, Nepal, Thailand)*. Commissioned by the ODA from the International Centre for Underutilized Crops. Wye College, University of London.

Potulski, Nicole (1992) *Alternative Crops for Drug growing Areas in South America (Colombia, Ecuador, Peru and Bolivia)*. Commissioned by the ODA from the International Centre for Underutilized Crops. Wye College, University of London.

Sage, Colin (1989) Drugs and Economic Development in Latin America: A Study in the Political Economy of Cocaine in Bolivia. In *Corruption, Development and Inequality*, P. Ward (ed.). London: Routledge.

Sage, Colin (1991) The Discourse on Drugs in the Americas. *Bulletin of Latin American Research* 10, 3: 325–332.

Sage, Colin (1994) 'Coca, Development and the Environment in Bolivia. In *Strategies for Sustainable Development: Local Agendas for the Southern Hemisphere*, M. Redclift and C. Sage (eds.). London: J. Wiley & Sons Ltd.

Sanabria, Harry (1986) 'Coca, Migration and Social Differentiation in the Bolivian Lowlands.' *Studies in Third World Societies: Drugs in Latin America*, Ed. by E. Morales, (37):81–103.

Scott, James (1976) *The Moral Economy of the Peasant*. New Haven: Yale University Press.

Seyler, Daniel, J. (1991) *A.I.D. and Narcotics Control: An Issue Brief*. Washington DC: Agency for International Development Centre for Development Information and Evaluation.

Sharma, Yoyana (1984) 'Fighting Drugs through Development.' *Journal of Development and Cooperation*, (3):22–23.

Smith, Michael *et al*. (1992) *Why People Grow Drugs: Narcotics and Development In the Third World*. London: Panos.

Tolisano, J., Bossi, R., Henkel, R., Rivera, A., Seubert, C., Smith, D., Sutton, J., Swagerty, J. (1990) Environmental Assessment of the Chapare Regional Development Project, Bolivia. Development Alternatives Inc., Washington, D.C.

Tropical Research & Development, Inc. (1992) *Lessons Learned Evaluation conducted for the Selva Economic Revitalization Project 527–0348*. USAID, Project Evaluation Summary.

Tullis, Lamond (1992) *Handbook of Research on the Illicit Drug Traffic: Socioeconomic Consequences*. New York: Greenwood Press.

United Nations Development Programme (1991) *World Development: Special Report*. Vol. 4 (3).

United Nations Development Programme (1994) *Human Development Report*. Oxford: Oxford University Press.

United Nations Drug Control Programme (1992a) *Illicit Narcotics Cultivation and Processing: The Ignored Environmental Drama.* Vienna: United Nations Publications.

United Nations Drug Control Programme (1992b) 'Project Progress Summary Report 1991: Provision of Minimum Integrated Services for Basic Rural Sanitation (AD/BOL/88/411) April, Vienna.

United Nations Drug Control Programme (1993) Alternative Development as an Instrument of Drug Abuse Control. *Technical Information Paper No. 5.* Vienna: United Nations Publications.

United Nations Economic and Social Commission for Asia and the Pacific (1991) 'Proceedings of the Meeting of Senior Officials on Drug Abuse Issues and the Pacific.' Feb. 13–15th, Tokyo.

U.S. Congress, Senate Committee on Governmental Affairs, Permanent Subcommitee on Investigations (1989) *US Government Anti-Narcotics Activities in the Andean Region of Latin America.* Washington DC: Government Printing Office.

U.S. Department of State, Bureau of International Narcotics Matters (1987) *International Narcotics Control Strategy Report.* Washington DC: US Government Printing Office.

U.S. Department of State, Bureau of International Narcotics Matters (1988) *International Narcotics Control Strategy Report.* Washington DC: US Government Printing Office.

U.S. Department of State, Bureau of International Narcotics Matters (1989) *International Narcotics Control Strategy Report.* Washington DC: US Government Printing Office.

U.S. Department of State, Bureau of International Narcotics Matters (1990) *International Narcotics Control Strategy Report.* Washington DC: US Government Printing Office.

U.S. Department of State, Bureau of International Narcotics Matters (1991) *International Narcotics Control Strategy Report.* Washington DC: US Government Printing Office.

U.S. Department of State, Bureau of International Narcotics Matters (1992) *International Narcotics Control Strategy Report.* Washington DC: US Government Printing Office.

U.S. Department of State, Bureau of International Narcotics Matters (1993) *International Narcotics Control Strategy Report.* Washington DC: US Government Printing Office.

U.S. Department of State, Bureau of International Narcotics Matters (1994) *International Narcotics Control Strategy Report.* Washington DC: US Government Printing Office.

U.S. Department of State, Bureau of International Narcotics Matters (1995) *International Narcotics Control Strategy Report.* Washington DC: US Government Printing Office.

U.S. General Accounting Office (1988a) *Drug Control: U.S. Supported Efforts in Burma, Pakistan and Thailand.* Report to the Congress. Washington DC: US Government Printing Office.

U.S. General Accounting Office (1988b) *Drug Control: US-Supported Efforts in Colombia and Bolivia.* Report to the Congress. Washington DC: US Government Office.

U.S. General Accounting Office (1988c) *Drug control: US-Mexico Opium Aerial Eradication Program.* Report to the Congress. Washington DC: US Government Printing Office.

U.S. General Accounting Office (1990) *Drug Control: How Drug-Consuming Nations are Organized for the War on Drugs.* Report to the Chairman, Permanent Subcommittee on Investigations, Committee on Governmental Affairs, US Senate. Washington DC: US Government Printing Office.

Van Wert, James, M. (1988) 'The US State Department's Narcotics Control Policy in the Americas.' *Journal of Interamerican Studies and World Affairs*, 30(2&3), (Summer/Fall): 1–18.

White House (1994) *National Drug Control Strategy; Reclaiming our Communities from Drugs and Violence*. Washington DC: US Government Printing Office.

Williamson, Richard, S. (1988) 'The United Nations: Some Parts Work.' *Orbis*, 32(2), Spring: 33–45.

Wisotsky, Steven (1983) 'Exposing the War on Cocaine: The Futility and Destructiveness of Prohibition.' *Wisconsin Law Review*, (6):1305–1426.

World Bank (1994) *World Development Report 1994: Infrastructure for Development*. London: Oxford University Press.

World Health Organization (1992) 'Drug Demand Reduction: Challenges and Opportunities in Southwest Asia.' *Technical Consultation on Drug Issues in South West Asia*, Islamabad, Pakistan 21–23, Sept. 1992.

Wrobleski, Ann, B. (1988) 'Presidential Certification of Narcotic Source Countries.' Current Policy, No. 1061, April: 1–5.

CHAPTER 11

Missed Opportunities? Beneficial Uses of Illicit Drugs

Lester Grinspoon and James B. Bakalar

INTRODUCTION

No one needs to be told about the beneficial effects of legal drugs. It is almost too obvious to mention that alcohol in moderate doses is relaxing, relieves social anxiety, facilitates conversation, and promotes intimacy. There is also evidence that in small doses it has useful cardiovascular effects. Nicotine in the form of tobacco cigarettes is used as a mild stimulant or anti-anxiety drug, and very little tolerance to these effects develops. In some people it also enhances concentration, reduces boredom and depression, and sharpens visual reflexes (Schelling, 1992; Jarvik, 1991; Krogh, 1991). A much less familiar fact is that South American shamans (religious healers) use nicotine as a painkiller and take tobacco in large doses to induce a trance and communicate with the spirit world (Wilbert, 1991). Yet tobacco and alcohol are also highly addictive and can have devastating effects on mental and physical health — more devastating than the effects of some psychoactive drugs banned or severely restricted by law in modern industrial societies.

Many banned drugs also have significant medical and other beneficial uses. In the case of natural plant drugs like opium, coca, cannabis, mescaline, and psilocybin, this has been known for thousands of years in a variety of cultures. Historically, the uses of these drugs have been restricted as their dangers receive more emphasis and (at least in medicine) substitutes become available. Although the trend toward greater care in the use of drugs and a greater concern for safety has to be regarded as an advance, there is a considerable danger that legal and other restrictions are preventing the realization of genuine medical and other benefits. The proper balance has not yet been worked out.

Although most drugs are now, strictly speaking, illicit except when taken by prescription, the common understanding of the term "illicit drugs" includes only psychoactive drugs used for pleasure, most of which are covered by the criminal provisions of the federal Controlled Substances Act and similar state laws. It would be impossible to discuss all of them here. Some are among the most commonly used prescription drugs and have a variety of medical applications — notably the benzodiazepine tranquilizers, the barbiturates, and the synthetic and natural opioids. We will concentrate here on three classes of drugs that are placed in the two most restricted schedules under the Controlled Substances Act. Cocaine has legally accepted medical uses under federal law; marihuana and psychedelic drugs do not. We will explore the past and present, potential and actual, experimental and established, legal and illegitimate uses of these drugs.

COCA AND COCAINE

Cocaine is an alkaloid extracted from the leaves of the shrub Erythroxylum coca, which has long been cultivated in Bolivia and Peru. For thousands of years, inhabitants of the Peruvian and Bolivian highlands and the western Amazon region have been mixing coca leaves with ash or lime, putting the wad in a cheek, and letting the juice trickle into their stomachs. In many parts of the Amazon and the Andes today, coca is the everyday stimulant drug, used more or less as coffee, tea, chewing tobacco, and *khat* are used in other parts of the world.

In one study of a mountain village in Peru, coca was found to be the standard remedy for symptoms of hunger and cold and for two folk illnesses: *el soka*, a condition of weakness, fatigue, and general malaise; and *el fiero*, a chronic wasting illness. Coca was also the treatment of choice for stomach upset and stomach-ache and for colic, or severe gastrointestinal distress including diarrhea, cramps, and nausea (Fabrega, 1973).

In the form of leaf powder or tea, coca is taken for toothache, ulcers, rheumatism, asthma, and even malaria. Coca tea is often served to tourists arriving at hotels and inns in the high Andes as a remedy for the nausea, dizziness, and headache of *soroche* (altitude sickness). Unlike other stimulants, coca is also a local anesthetic. The juice of the leaf can be applied to soothe eye irritations or gargled for hoarseness and sore throat. Coca leaves are also used as a topical anesthetic for mouth sores. Coca contains minerals, vitamin C, and some B vitamins, and it is sometimes said to be an important source of these nutrients in the Andean diet.

Ever since the Spanish conquest there has been controversy about the health effects of habitual coca use. The evidence is unreliable, contradictory, and heavily colored by the political and social biases of observers. A number of studies have suggested that coca chewers are apathetic, of subnormal intelligence, or subject to various physical illnesses because they are weakened by the drug (Gutierrez-Noriega). But these findings are inconclusive and doubtful (Buck *et al.*, 1968;

Weil, 1978; Grinspoon & Bakalar, 1976). If coca users in the high Andes seem undernourished, demoralized, and unhealthy, that is easily explained by the miserable physical and social conditions under which many of them live — conditions for which coca use apparently gives them some relief. It is significant that many Indians in the Amazon who use coca are reported to be strong and healthy (Weil, 1981). In any case, the people of South America themselves, including those who do not use coca, usually reject the suggestion that it is a drug problem, a threat to health, or a danger to their community (Burchard, 1992).

Cocaine was isolated from the coca leaf in 1860. Throughout the late nineteenth century, both coca itself (that is, an extract from the leaf including all of its alkaloids) and the pure chemical cocaine were popular as medicines in Europe and North America (Park Davis & Company, 1974). In 1863 Angelo Mariani, a Corsican chemist, patented a preparation of coca extract and wine, which he called Vin Mariani; it became one of the most popular medicines of the era, and was used by such celebrities as Thomas Edison, Ulysses Grant, Henrik Ibsen, Pope Leo XIII, Emile Zola, Jules Verne, and the Prince of Wales. Mariani wrote several articles and monographs on coca in which he combined historical, botanical, and medical information with the promotion of his company's product; he could list thousands of physicians who recommended it (Mariani, 1974).

In 1901 the American physician W. Golden Mortimer published an encyclopedic volume, *History of Coca*, in which he recommended coca wine, coca extract, or cocaine for a great variety of purposes. In an appendix he cited the responses to a letter he had sent to "a selected set" of more than 5,000 physicians asking for their observations on coca. Of the 1,206 replying, 369 said that they had used coca in their own practices. They commonly observed that it increased appetite, raised blood pressure, stimulated circulation, strengthened the heart, improved digestion, stimulated the mind, and worked as an aphrodisiac. The most popular therapeutic uses were for exhaustion, overwork, and neurasthenia. Few thought there was a dangerous tendency to form a coca habit (Mortimer, 1901).

One of the most popular drinks containing cocaine was Coca-Cola, first concocted in 1886 by a Georgia pharmacist. The Coca-Cola Company was founded in 1892, and throughout the 1890s Coca-Cola was advertised as a headache remedy and stimulant as well as an enjoyable drink. In 1903 cocaine extract was removed from Coca-Cola and replaced with caffeine. A de-cocainized extract of the coca leaf is still used for flavoring.

In the medical use of coca and cocaine, it is hard to separate the central stimulant from the digestive, respiratory, vasoconstrictive, and local anesthetic effects. A singer or actor who drank Mariani's wine could hardly know how much of the improvement he or she noticed was caused by local anesthesia or constriction of blood vessels in the pharynx and how much by euphoria and a feeling of mastery. As for stomach and intestinal problems, the gastrointestinal system is probably the most common site of psychosomatic symptoms. The use of coca or cocaine in convalescence from long-lasting debilitating diseases represents a similar combination of central and peripheral effects.

The rediscovery of cocaine's local anesthetic properties by Karl Koller has proved to be of more permanent historical importance to medicine. Koller introduced topical cocaine in eye operations, and soon cocaine was being used in many other forms of surgery and dentistry. William Halsted of Johns Hopkins University invented nerve block or conduction anesthesia by injecting cocaine into nerve trunks. Soon regional anesthesia and spinal anesthesia were introduced. It was not until the early twentieth century that synthetic local anesthetics without the stimulant properties of cocaine were developed. Cocaine is still regarded as preferable to synthetic local anesthetics in a few circumstances (Schenk, 1979; Middleton, 1993).

Abuse and dependence became problems almost as soon as pure cocaine was introduced into medicine. Cocaine dependence first appeared in morphine addicts who took the cocaine cure recommended by Bentley and Freud. Halsted, the inventor of nerve block anesthesia, appears to have cured himself of a craving for cocaine by taking up morphine and paying the price of physical addiction. The growing fear of cocaine changed attitudes toward coca. Advocates of coca then began to fight a rear-guard action in its defense, insisting that coca never caused the kinds of problems that were ruining the reputation of cocaine. By 1900 public and medical opinion had begun to turn against both coca and cocaine. In 1906, following action by many states, the United States government passed the Pure Food and Drug Act banning food and drinks containing cocaine, although there had never been good evidence that oral coca and cocaine products were especially dangerous. Further legal restrictions soon followed, culminating in the Harrison Act of 1914, which regulated cocaine as well as opiates. Cocaine was still prescribed occasionally through the 1920s, although criminal laws and other restraints made it less easily available. But by 1930 it was rarely being used except as a surgical anesthetic.

Cocaine will probably never again be widely used in medicine, but a revival of interest in coca is possible. The American physician, Andrew Weil, has tried to promote such a revival. He believes that therapeutic uses of coca have been neglected because of the medical profession's fascination and subsequent disillusionment with the pure alkaloid cocaine. He has found coca useful in the symptomatic relief of indigestion, gastritis, constipation, motion sickness, laryngitis, and other ailments. He believes that it could serve as a substitute for coffee in persons who find that their stomachs are upset by that stimulant. He also proposes its use as an appetite-reducing drug and as an energizer for physical labor, and he suggests that it might serve as a relatively safe substitute in treating amphetamine and cocaine dependence. He points out that the coca differs from cocaine in several ways. It contains a number of related alkaloids rather than a single one, and it is less subject to abuse because it enters the body by the normal gastrointestinal route rather than intranasally, intravenously, or through the lungs. He believes that coca might best be administered in the form of a tea or chewing gum (Weil, *op. cit.*, p. 374). As Weil points out, chewing (or, more precisely, sucking) coca leaves would probably not appeal to North Americans.

Coca might be used as a mild stimulant or in the relief of minor discomforts if taken in the form of a tea or chewing gum. Beneficial uses of coca in South America do not fit into any western model of drug use as either recreational or medical. Cocaine has been used similarly. Despite popular myths, it is possible to control cocaine use, as several authors have pointed out in sociological studies (Cohen, 1989; Waldorf *et al.*, 1991).

PSYCHEDELIC DRUGS

The psychedelic ("mind-manifesting" or "mind-revealing") drugs have unusually wide-ranging effects that vary greatly depending on the setting and the user's personality and expectations. Because these effects are so difficult to define and describe, many names have been proposed: hallucinogenic ("producing hallucinations"), psychotomimetic ("mimicking psychosis"), psychodysleptic ("mind-disrupting"), and psycholytic ("mind-loosening"). These drugs have in common a capacity to produce vivid and unusual changes in thought, feeling, and perception without delirium or severe generalized toxic physical effects.

There are about a half dozen natural psychedelic drugs and scores of synthetic ones, most of them variants on a few chemical structures. The best known natural psychedelics are mescaline, derived from the peyote cactus, and psilocybin, found in over a hundred species of mushrooms. Among synthetic psychedelics, the best known and most potent is lysergic acid diethylamide (LSD), which is chemically related to certain alkaloids found in morning glory seeds, the lysergic acid amides. This class of drugs also includes the natural substances harmine, harmaline, ibogaine, and dimethyltryptamine (DMT), as well as a large number of synthetic drugs that are chemically described as tryptamines or methoxylated amphetamines. A few of these are diethyltryptamine (DET), 3,4,-methylenedioxyamphetamine (MDA), and 2,5-dimethoxy-4-methylamphetamine (DOM, also known as STP). Recently much attention has been focused on 3,4,-methylenedioxymethamphetamine (MDMA).

The natural hallucinogens have long been used by preindustrial cultures, especially in Mexico and South America, for magical, religious, and healing purposes. Religious use of *ayahuasca*, a substance containing harmine, is common and legal in the Brazilian Amazon. Today the peyote cactus is the sacrament of the Native American Church, a religious organization with branches in all western states of the United States (La Barre, 1964; Marriott, 1971). Peyote became known in industrial society toward the end of the nineteenth century, and many other plant hallucinogens have been discovered since. LSD was first synthesized in 1938 and its psychoactive properties were discovered in 1943; since then many other synthetic psychedelic drugs have been developed.

Ever since experimentation with these drugs began, some users and psychotherapists have maintained that psychedelic experiences can provide religious or emotional insight, heightened creative capacity, psychological insight, or relief from neurotic symptoms. From 1950 to the mid-1960s, psychedelic drugs — especially LSD, mescaline, and psilocybin — were used extensively in experimental psychiatry. They were first studied as chemical models for natural psychoses; little came of this line of inquiry and it was soon abandoned. But psychedelics were also used extensively in psychotherapy. More than a thousand clinical papers were published discussing forty thousand patients; there were several dozen books and six international conferences on psychedelic drug therapy. It was recommended for a wide variety of problems, including alcoholism, obsessional neurosis, and childhood autism. Beginning in the mid-1960s, with the increase of illicit use, it became difficult to obtain the drugs or get funding for research, and professional interest declined. There is now a growing interest in the therapeutic potential of this class of drugs, particularly some of the new phenethylamines. But because they are all in Schedule I, it is difficult to conduct clinical research with them.

One source of the therapeutic interest was the belief of some experimental subjects after taking a psychedelic drug that they were less depressed, anxious, and guilty, and more self-accepting, tolerant, or sensually alert. There was also interest in using the powerful psychedelic experiences of regression, abreaction, intense transference, and symbolic drama to enhance psychodynamic psychotherapy. Two kinds of therapy emerged, one making use of the mystical or conversion experience and the other exploring the unconscious in the manner of psychoanalysis. Psychedelic therapy, as the first kind was called, involved the use of a large dose (200 micrograms of LSD or more) in a single session; it was thought to be potentially helpful in reforming alcoholics and criminals as well as improving the lives of normal people. The second type, psycholytic (literally, mind-loosening) therapy, required relatively small doses and several or even many sessions; it was used mainly for neurotic and psychosomatic disorders. In practice, many combinations, variations, and special applications with some of the features of both psycholytic and psychedelic therapy evolved.

Complications and Dangers

The most common adverse effect is a bad trip, or hallucinogen hallucinosis, which occasionally produces a true psychotic reaction. Another common effect is the flashback, a spontaneous transitory recapitulation of drug-induced experience in a drug-free state. Prolonged adverse reactions, which are considerably less common, include anxiety reactions, depressive reactions, and psychoses. They are most likely to occur in schizoid and prepsychotic personalities with barely stable egos who cannot cope with the mind alterations produced by the drug trip. There is a close resemblance between people hospitalized for LSD reactions and those hospitalized for psychoses unrelated to drugs (Strassman, 1984; Grinspoon & Bakalar, 1979). Like any probing psychotherapy, psychedelic drug therapy presents the danger that material will come up and cannot be accepted and integrated. Psychosis and even suicide have been reported in the course of psychedelic drug treatment. On the other hand, some people who have worked with psychedelic drugs consider them more likely to prevent suicide than to cause it, and most studies questioning psychiatrists about adverse reactions to psychedelic drugs in experimental or therapeutic research have revealed a low rate of serious complications (Clark *et al.,* 1975; Cohen, 1960; Malleson, 1971).

All such studies have limitations. Some psychiatrists may have minimized the dangers out of therapeutic enthusiasm or reluctance to admit mistakes; some may have exaggerated the dangers under the influence of bad publicity; long-term risks may have been underestimated if follow-up was inadequate. The studies provide no basis for comparison with patients who were not treated with psychedelic drugs or not treated at all. The fact remains that psychedelic drugs were used for more than fifteen years by hundreds of psychiatrists who considered them relatively safe therapeutic agents.

Neurotic Disorders

In a book about her LSD treatment, one woman described the result this way:

> I found that in addition to being, consciously, a loving mother and a respectable citizen, I was also, unconsciously, a murderess, a pervert, a cannibal, a sadist, and a masochist. In the wake of these dreadful discoveries, I lost my fear of dentists, the clicking in my neck and throat, the arm tensions, and my dislike of clocks ticking in the bedroom. I also achieved transcendent sexual fulfillment.... At the end of nine sessions over a period of nine weeks I was cured of my hitherto incurable frigidity, and at the end of five months I felt that I had been completely reconstituted as a human being. I have continued to feel that way ever since (Newland, 1962).

These passages were written three years after a five-month period during which this woman took LSD twenty-three times.

The literature contains a number of such impressive case histories, but these anecdotal accounts can always be questioned; placebo effects, spontaneous recovery, special and prolonged devotion by the therapist, and the therapist's and patient's biases in judging improvement must be considered. The most serious deficiencies in psychedelic drug studies were absence of controls and inadequate follow-up. And psychedelic drug effects are so striking that it is difficult to design a double-blind study in which neither the person administering the drug nor the person taking it knows whether it is the active substance or a placebo.

Furthermore, psychiatrists did not agree about details. Should the emphasis be on expression of repressed feelings or on working through a transference attachment to the psychiatrist? How much therapy is necessary in the intervals between LSD treatments? There are no general answers to these questions. It appeared that LSD treatment sometimes produced spectacular improvement in symptoms, but no reliable formula for success was derived from these results. But in these respects psychedelic drug therapy seems to be in no better or worse position than most other forms of psychotherapy.

Alcoholism

Psychedelic therapy for alcoholism is based on the assumption that one over-whelming experience sometimes changes the self-destructive drinking habits of a lifetime, and the hope that psychedelic drugs can consistently produce such an experience. In one reported case, a 40-year-old unskilled laborer was brought to a hospital from jail after drinking uncontrollably for ten days. He had been an alcoholic for four years, and he was also severely anxious and depressed. He described his experiences during an LSD session as follows:

> I was afraid. I started to run, but something said "Stop! Stop!" ... then I felt as if ten tons had fallen from my shoulders. I prayed to the Lord. Everything looked better all around me.... I changed my mind from alcohol toward Christ and the rose came back into my life.... As I sat up and looked in the mirror I could feel myself growing stronger. I feel now that my family and I are closer than ever before and I hope that our faith will grow forever and ever.

One week later his score on a questionnaire testing neurotic traits had dropped from the 88th to the 10th percentile. Six months later his psychological tests were within normal limits; he had been totally abstinent from alcohol for all that time and despite a temporary relapse when he lost his job, he was still sober after twelve months (Kurland, 1967).

LSD undoubtedly produces powerful effects on alcoholics; the question is whether they can be reliably translated into enduring change. Early studies reported dazzling success. About 50% of severe chronic alcoholics treated with a single high dose of LSD were said to be recovered and sober a year or two later (Hoffer, 1967). But the early studies proved to be inadequate. When the patients were randomly assigned to drug and control groups it proved difficult to demon-strate any advantage for LSD treatment, even in studies conducted by advocates of the drug (Smart, 1966; Cheek *et al.*, 1966). The problem is that many alcohol-ics will improve, at least temporarily, after any treatment because excessive drinking is often sporadic and periodic relapses are common. The alcoholic who arrives at a clinic or hospital is probably at a low point in the cycle and has nowhere to go but up.

It would be wrong to conclude that a psychedelic experience can never be a turning point in the life of an alcoholic. As William James said, "Religiomania is the best cure for dipsomania." Unfortunately, psychedelic experiences have the same limitations as religious conversions. Their authenticity and emotional power are not guarantees against backsliding when the old frustrations, con-straints, and emotional distress have to be faced in everyday life. Even when the revelation does seem to have lasting effects, it might have been merely a symp-tom of readiness to change rather than a cause of change.

The fact remains that there is no proven treatment for alcoholism. Where so little is known, it probably does not make sense to give up entirely on anything that has possibilities. In the religious ceremonies of the Native American Church, periodic use of high doses of mescaline in the form of peyote is regarded as, among other things, part of a treatment for alcoholism. Both the Indians themselves and outside researchers believe that those who participate in the peyote ritual are more likely to abstain from alcohol. Peyote sustains the ritual and religious principles of the community of believers, and these sometimes confirm and support an individual commitment to give up alcohol. Even federal alcoholism clinics for Indians recognize that peyote might have some value (Albaugh *et al.*, 1974). If, for whatever reasons, psychedelic drugs work for at least some Indians some of the time, they might also help some non-Indian alcoholics.

Heroin and Cocaine Addiction

Ibogaine is a psychedelic substance derived from the roots of an African plant, Tabernanthe iboga. Apparently it allows the user to "play back" visual memories using the eyelids or any surface as a sort of movie screen. Ibogaine was briefly used to enhance psychotherapy in the 1960s (Naranjo, 1969), but is now receiving attention mainly because of the claim that it can interrupt chemical dependency, greatly diminishing withdrawal symptoms and drug craving in heroin and cocaine addicts, and allowing them an opportunity to free themselves from addiction at least for a time. The interest was generated by Howard Lotsof, a heroin addict who found that the ibogaine experience interrupted his addiction. A number of addicts have undergone this experience under the supervision of Dr. Hans Bastiaans in the Netherlands, where use of ibogaine is not illegal. Among this small group of highly motivated addicts, some have remained drug-free without craving for at least six months. For these patients, ibogaine compares favorably with other forms of addiction treatment. A larger number have had their addictions interrupted but need other support to remain drug-free (Lotsof, 1990). These results have generated interest, and other researchers are beginning to explore the therapeutic potential of ibogaine. It has been found to reduce withdrawal symptoms in morphine-dependent rats (Dzoljic *et al.*, 1988) and monkeys (Aceto *et al.*, 1990), and it causes rats to self-administer less morphine (Glick *et al.*, 1991) and cocaine (Cappendijk & Dzoljic, 1993). Animal studies have paved the way for clinical research that may determine whether or not ibogaine has the potential suggested by the anecdotal evidence.

Dying

There is a new consciousness today of the significance of dying as part of life. As we look for ways to change the pattern, so common in chronic illness, of constantly increasing pain, anxiety, and depression, the emphasis is shifted away from impersonal prolongation of physical existence toward a conception of dying as a psychiatric crisis, or even, in older language, a religious crisis. The purpose of giving psychedelic drugs to the dying might be stated as reconciliation: reconciliation with one's past, one's family, and one's human limitations.

Beginning in 1965, the experiment of providing a psychedelic experience for the dying was pursued at Spring Grove State Hospital in Maryland and later at the Maryland Psychiatric Research Institute. Walter Pahnke, the director of the project from 1967 until 1971, first reported on his work in an article in the Harvard Theological Review in 1969. When terminal cancer patients received LSD or DPT after appropriate preparations, about one-third were said to have improved "dramatically," one-third improved "moderately," and one-third were unchanged; the tests of improvement were reduced tension, depression, pain, and fear of death (Pahnke, 1969). Later experiments with terminal cancer patients produced similar results (Grof *et al.*, 1973). There were no control groups in these studies, and there is no sure way to separate the effects of the drug from those of the special therapeutic arrangements and increased attention that were part of the treatment. Nevertheless, the case histories are impressive, and it would be interesting to renew the research.

Mystical Experience

In the 1960s Walter Pahnke, a Doctor of Divinity as well as a psychiatrist, carried out an experiment designed to investigate the potential of psychedelic drugs to facilitate mystical experience (Pahnke, 1966). The study was designed as a controlled double-blind experiment. Ten seminarians from the Andover Newton Theological School took capsules containing psilocybin, while a matched control group of ten colleagues ingested a placebo just before entering the Marsh Chapel at Boston University to attend Good Friday services. Blind independent raters trained in content analysis procedures scored the descriptions of the experiences written by subjects shortly after Good Friday as well as transcripts of three separate tape-recorded interviews conducted immediately, several days and six months after the experiment. A 147-item questionnaire was administered to the subjects one or two days after Good Friday, and a 100-item questionnaire six months later.

Among other things, the experiment demonstrated how difficult it is to control a study of psychedelic drugs. Psilocybin's powerful effects were soon obvious to everyone who received it, even though most had not previously taken anything like it before. By the end of the day everyone knew whether he had received the psilocybin or the placebo. Thus the experiment cannot be said to be double-blind, and it is impossible to separate the relative contributions of psilocybin and suggestion in producing the subjects' reported experiences. On the other hand, the results are so striking it would be difficult to deny that psilocybin played a significant role.

On both questionnaires the experimental group reported a high degree of persisting positive changes. They wrote that the psilocybin experience helped them to resolve career decisions, increase the depth of their faith, recognize the arbitrariness of ego boundaries, increase the appreciation of eternal life, enhance their sense of joy and beauty, and heighten their sense of the meaning of Christ. Few such changes were reported by the control group.

In a long-term follow-up, Richard Doblin was able to interview 16 of the original subjects (nine control and seven experimental), a quarter of a century after the original experiment. Every member of the experimental group vividly remembered parts of the Good Friday experience; most of the controls could barely recall even a few details. The experimental subjects unanimously described this experience as having genuinely mystical features and regarded it as one of the high points of their spiritual lives. They were glad they had participated and believed their lives had been significantly affected in a positive way. They mentioned enhanced appreciation of life and nature, a deepened commitment to the Christian ministry or other vocations, and an enhanced sense of joy and equanimity in the face of crises. A representative description is the following:

> It left me with a completely unquestioned certainty that there is an environment bigger than the one I'm conscious of. I have my own interpretation of what that is, but it went from a theoretical proposition to an experiential one. In one sense it didn't change anything, I didn't discover something I hadn't dreamed of, but what I have thought on the basis of reading and teaching was there. I knew it. Somehow it was much more real to me.... I expect things from meditation and prayer and so forth that I might have been a bit more skeptical about before.... I have gotten help with problems, and at times I think direction and guidance in problem-solving. Somehow my life has been different knowing that there is something out there.... What I saw wasn't anything entirely surprising yet there was a powerful impact from having seen it (Doblin, 1991).

Several subjects reported a deepened involvement in politics as a result of their experience. They believe that feelings of unity led them to identify with and feel compassion for minorities, women, and the environment. For some, the feeling of timelessness reduced the fear of death and empowered them to take more risks in their lives, including participation in political struggles.

The fascinating and provocative results of this experiment strongly support the view that psychedelic drugs can help facilitate mystical experiences when used by religiously inclined people in a religious setting. The long-term follow-up provides further support for this conclusion. These effects have apparently persisted and sometimes deepened over time. As Doblin points out, "The overwhelmingly positive nature of the reports of the psilocybin subjects are even more remarkable because this long-term follow-up took place during a period of time in the United States when drug abuse was becoming the public's number one social concern, with all attendant social pressure to deny the value of drug-induced experiences" (Ibid, pp. 23–24). When it becomes possible to resume human research with psychedelic drugs, this kind of exploration will undoubtedly be pursued.

MDMA

There are now dozens of known psychedelic drugs, some of them synthesized only in the last twenty years. Few have been tested seriously in human beings. Their effects are sometimes different from those of LSD, psilocybin, and other familiar substances. These differences may be significant for the study of the human mind and for psychotherapy, but we cannot analyze them properly without more controlled human research. In particular, there are certain psychedelic drugs that do not produce the same degree of perceptual change or emotional unpredictability as LSD or psilocybin. They can in no way be regarded as hallucinogenic. Among these is MDMA (3,4-methylenedioxymethamphetamine), a relatively mild drug that is said to give a heightened capacity for introspection, insight, and intimacy along with temporary freedom from anxiety and depression, without distracting changes in perception, body image, and the sense of self (Naranjo, 1975; Greer, 1983). Its effect lasts two to four hours and is usually fairly subtle and controllable.

Although MDMA (also known as Ecstasy) was first synthesized in 1912, it did not begin to come into both therapeutic and non-therapeutic use until the early 1970s. What we know about it now is largely anecdotal, but enough has been written to give some confidence that the general nature of the experience can be accurately described. As compared with the more familiar psychedelic drugs, it evokes a gentler, subtler, highly controllable two-to-four hour experience that invites rather than compels intensification of feelings and self-exploration. The user is rarely forced into any mental or emotional state that is frightening or even uncomfortable. As one user put it, "I felt that my cognitive powers were unaffected. That is, except on the few occasions where the affective experiences were very strong (a minute or two, it seemed, at most), I could guide my thoughts to and away from whatever areas I chose."

Occasional physical side effects are mild nausea, jaw-clenching, muscle tensing, and blurred vision. Some users suffer from a hangover the day after with symptoms that include fatigue, anxiety, or headache. Psychotic reactions and prolonged adverse effects are rare; flashbacks have not been reported. Some studies suggest that at high doses or after chronic use MDMA is toxic to serotonergic brain cells. The issue is still in dispute. Tolerance develops quickly, and the drug is rarely used more than once a week. There is no craving and no withdrawal syndrome. The drug apparently becomes less interesting and attractive with repeated use, the experience loses its novelty, and the physical symptoms and hangover seem worse. Long-term heavy use is rare.

A few psychiatrists and other therapists in Europe and the United States used MDMA as an aid to psychotherapy for more than 15 years. It was taken in a therapeutic setting by thousands of people, apparently with few complications. Since 1985, when the drug was placed in Schedule I, therapeutic use and (for practical purposes) clinical research have been impossible in the U.S. Some research has continued in Switzerland and it may resume here soon.

MDMA is generally used once or at most a few times in the course of therapy. It is said to fortify the therapeutic alliance by inviting self-disclosure and enhancing trust. Some patients also report better mood, greater relaxation, heightened self-esteem, and other beneficial changes that last for several days to several months. Psychiatrists who have used MDMA suggest that it might be helpful, for example, in marital counseling and in diagnostic interviews, as well as in more traditional forms of psychotherapy. The reports of therapeutic results so far are anecdotal, mostly unpublished, and unverified, and require more systematic study for evaluation, but they are promising. MDMA creates very few of the problems that made it difficult to work with LSD in psychotherapy — the 8 to 12-hour duration of action, the possible loss of emotional control, the perceptual distortion, and the occasional adverse reactions and flashbacks.

Patients in MDMA-assisted therapy report that they lose defensive anxiety and feel more emotionally open, and that this makes it possible for them to get in touch with feelings and thoughts which are not ordinarily available to them.

One patient described his experience as "primarily an intense warmth and security about myself and other people." He added, "MDMA breaks down inhibitions about communication, making it easy to give or receive criticism or compliments that under normal circumstances are embarrassing."

Another patient put it this way: "I believe the most beneficial aspect of how I felt during the session was that I felt very little defensiveness. On my own and to myself during the session, I thought about things in myself that I didn't like. I was able to accomplish this without feeling guilty or defensive."

Another MDMA patient wrote "One of the major 'differences' [from a non-MDMA-assisted psychotherapy session] was the feeling of security and tranquillity. I had the feeling of being safe. Nothing could threaten me. I briefly tried to fantasize natural catastrophes, like an earthquake. I did not feel anxious or threatened." This patient also suggests that the effects of MDMA-assisted therapy may endure. Eighteen months after her third and last MDMA session, when she was asked whether she thought there was a lasting benefit, she replied, "I have been able to experience myself more fully ... to feel my feelings ... to be totally with myself ... to experience the ease of expressing myself when I am in touch with myself. The sessions enabled me to break through my defenses (rationalizing, analyzing, intellectualizing, etc.) that I used to win approval of myself and others ... to break through my facade and to go to the truth underneath.... At various times [that truth] meant grief, love, sadness, fear, humor."

MDMA might also help in working through loss or trauma. One patient described the effect as follows: "After a [MDMA-assisted therapy] session where I grieved the loss of [boyfriend] in my life, it surprised me that I felt so good about myself for having grieved so deeply ... for having been so deeply into my real self, crying my heart out, and how healthy it felt to know that I had really been there for those feelings rather than the facade I was living with — trying to be strong and get on with my life and unconsciously to avoid the pain, disappointment and sadness ... as well as my fear of being alone."

It is also said to help patients experience closeness and empathy. Nine months after his MDMA-assisted therapy session, a patient noticed "feelings of closeness and sharing with others — evaporation of the usual barriers to intimate communication." Another said, "I would say this is a heart drug, but not in the way I would have expected. I did not feel romantic love, strong feelings. I felt attention toward [the therapist and his co-therapist wife] and a concern for them and how they were. This feeling was one of compassion for their needs ... this feeling I have been able to carry over after the immediate MDMA effects have gone."

Many MDMA patients have claimed a lasting improvement in their capacity for communication with others. For example, one man who was asked about enduring effects five months after his sessions answered: "Communication is improved with [wife], less defensiveness between us, more leeway for diversity, desires, etc."

Interest in and capacity for insight is also said to be enhanced. Five months after one MDMA-assisted therapy session a patient reported: "Insights into problems have proven accurate and helpful in planning my private and personal life." Later he added, "I have a broader perspective on my life and activities; that carries on."

Many patients report strengthening of trust and increased capacity for intimacy. As one patient stated: "It was characterized by warmth ... although I was intellectually lucid and clear, the chief impact of the experience for me was in the heart, and not in the head. Fundamentally it seemed to facilitate intimacy. I found I could give and receive at very intimate levels without embarrassment or defensiveness."

Another patient put it this way: "I found it to be uncanny how easy it was to speak freely ... about feelings. I'm generally not very good at that but the MDMA apparently enabled me to let down the defenses and open up the offenses — but all in a gentle, matter-of-fact sort of way." And still another observed: "It breaks down the walls — relieves inhibitions — free thoughts escape — under a euphoric cloud that makes it okay to say anything and everything" (Greer *et al.*, 1986).

These features of the MDMA experience may account for the common observation that an MDMA-assisted therapy session can greatly enhance the therapeutic alliance. Many patients report how much more they trust the therapist and how much closer they feel to the therapist after one such session (Adamson, 1985). If, as many believe (Moras & Strupp, 1982), the strength of the therapeutic alliance is the best predictor of a good outcome in therapy, this characteristic of MDMA could be of very general usefulness. The same kinds of benefits reported in therapeutic use are also reported by many "recreational" users, who are actually taking the drug as a form of self-administered therapy (Eisner, 1989; Beck *et al.*, 1989; Peroutka, 1990).

At this time it is difficult to state precisely how MDMA may be helpful in psychotherapy, but the nature of the experience suggests that it could be useful in catalyzing the psychotherapeutic process irrespective of theoretical grounding; for example, it might be of interest to Freudian, Rogerian, and existential humanist therapists. It might also be helpful in marital counseling and diagnostic interviews as well as psychotherapy. Furthermore, the limited experience we have had with this drug is an indication that the development of drugs to facilitate psychotherapy is a path that should be explored (Grinspoon & Bakalar, 1986). The potential for psychotherapeutically useful phenethylamines has barely been tapped, although the FDA has recently given a favorable review to a study in which MDMA will be used to ease dying for patients with pancreatic cancer (Grob *et al.*, 1992).

CONCLUSION

When a new kind of therapy is introduced, especially a new psychoactive drug, events often follow a pattern of spectacular success and enormous enthusiasm followed by disillusionment. But the rise and decline of psychedelic drug therapy took a somewhat unusual course. From the early 1960s on, the revolutionary proclamations and religious fervor of the nonmedical advocates of psychedelic drugs began to evoke hostile incredulity rather than simply the natural skeptical response to exalted claims backed mainly by intense subjective experiences. Twenty years after their introduction, psychedelics were pariah drugs, scorned by the medical establishment and banned by the law. In rejecting the absurd notion that these drugs are panaceas, we have chosen to treat them as entirely worthless and extraordinarily dangerous. Maybe the time has come to find an intermediate position. If the therapeutic results have been erratic and inconsistent, that is partly because of the complexity of psychedelic drug effects. For the same reason, we may simply not yet have had enough time to sort out the best uses of these drugs. An informal kind of research continues anyway. Illicit psychedelic drug use is an underground spring that continues to feed the stream of interest in systematic, publicly controlled experimentation. Ironically, the illicit drug use that was one of the reasons for the interruption of legitimate research now serves to keep alive efforts aimed at resuming that research.

The claims for psychedelic drug use are subject to the same doubts as those of psychoanalysis or religious conversions. The mixture of mystical and transcendental claims with therapeutic ones is an aspect of psychedelic drug therapy troubling to our culture. The pronouncements of drug enthusiasts are sometimes too much like religious testimonials to please either psychiatrists or priests and ministers. Preindustrial cultures seem to tolerate more ambiguity in this matter, and there is now a growing interest in the ideas and techniques shared by primitive shamans, Eastern spiritual teachers, and modern psychiatrists. The word "cure," after all, means both treatment for disease and the care of souls.

The role of the guide on a psychedelic drug trip, which has both religious and medical aspects, is spontaneously reproduced in all cultures where psychedelic drugs come to be used. Much of the controversy about psychedelic drugs in the 1960s was in effect concerned with the question of who was qualified to be a guide. For the moment we have made the curious decision that no one in modern industrial society is qualified for this position. Nevertheless, serious psychedelic drug use continues underground in one form or another. Many have regarded it as an experience worth having, some as a first step toward change, and a few as a turning point in their lives. They might be deceiving themselves, but we do not know enough to be certain; the field has potentialities that are not being allowed to reveal themselves.

CANNABIS

Marihuana is derived from the cannabis plant. Its most important psychoactive chemical, delta-9-tetrahydrocannabinol, is contained in a resin that covers the flower clusters and top leaves of the plant; the resin also contains many chemically related substances with lesser effects. Cannabis preparations vary widely in quality and potency depending on the type of plant, climate, soil, and methods of cultivation and manufacture. The resin can be ingested in the form of a drink or in foods, but usually the leaves and flowering tops are smoked, either in a pipe or in a cigarette called a joint.

History

Like cocaine and other psychoactive drugs derived from natural plant sources, marihuana has been used for thousands of years as a medicine as well as an intoxicant. It was listed in an herbal published by a Chinese emperor that may go back to 2800 B.C. In Jamaica, where it was introduced in the 17th century by African slaves, it has become the most popular folk medicine. Cannabis in the form of an alcoholic solution was commonly used in 19th-century Europe and the United States as an anticonvulsant, analgesic, sedative, and soporific, and also for tetanus, neuralgia, uterine hemorrhage, rheumatism, and other conditions. It was thought to be a milder but less dangerous analgesic than opium, and it was also considered an appetite stimulant. Between 1839 and 1900 more than a hundred articles appeared in scientific journals on the therapeutic uses of marihuana. After the introduction of injectable opiates in the 1850s and synthetic analgesics and hypnotics in the early 20th century, the medical use of cannabis declined. But even as late as 1937, extract of cannabis was still a legitimate medicine marketed by drug companies.

The Marihuana Tax Act of 1937 imposed a registration tax and record keeping requirements that made medical use of cannabis so cumbersome that it was dropped from the U.S. Pharmacopoeia and National Formulary. This law was introduced under the influence of a growing concern about the use of marihuana as an intoxicant, especially among blacks and Mexican-Americans in the South and Southwest. The law passed after a strong campaign by the Federal Bureau of Narcotics, despite a lack of empirical evidence on the harmfulness of marihuana. The legislative counsel for the American Medical Association at the time objected to the law, saying, prophetically, that future investigations might show substantial medical uses for cannabis. But the AMA soon changed its stance and for the next 40 years maintained a position on marihuana very similar to that of the Federal Bureau of Narcotics. Recent years have seen some relaxation of legal restrictions and increasing clarification of the medical potential of cannabis and cannabis derivatives, but considerable obstacles remain and considerable research still has to be done (Grinspoon & Bakalar, 1993). Under federal and most state statutes, marihuana is listed as a Schedule I drug: high potential for abuse, no currently accepted medical use, and a lack of accepted safety for use under medical supervision. A synthetic form of THC is available as a Schedule II drug; such drugs are legally defined as having high abuse potential and restricted medical uses.

Safety

The greatest advantage of cannabis as a medicine is its unusual safety. The ratio of lethal dose to effective dose is estimated on the basis of extrapolation from animal data to be about 20,000:1 (compared to 3–50:1 for secobarbital and 4–10:1 for alcohol). Huge doses have been given to dogs without causing death, and there is no reliable evidence of death caused by cannabis in a human being. Cannabis also has the advantage of not disturbing any physiological functions or damaging any body organs when it is used in therapeutic doses. It produces little physical dependence or tolerance, and there has never been any evidence that medical use of cannabis leads to habitual use as an intoxicant.

Depression

Cannabis was first proposed as a treatment for depression by Jacques Joseph Moreau de Tours in 1845 (de Tours, 1857). During the next 100 years his proposal was supported and disputed in a number of medical papers. The most recent study on cannabis and depression was undertaken in 1973. Eight hospitalized patients were given either THC or a placebo for up to a week. The THC did not help them, and in four it produced discomfort and anxiety so serious it had to be withdrawn (Kotin *et al.*, 1973). But the patients were not prepared for the experience of an altered state of consciousness, and the brief duration of the trial must also be considered. Standard antidepressants often require three weeks or even longer to work. Today, among the minority of depressed patients who do not respond to any of the standard antidepressants or find the side effects unbearable, some have discovered that whole smoked marihuana is more useful than any legal drug (Grinspoon & Bakalar, 1993). This evidence is anecdotal and will eventually require large-scale clinical studies.

Pain

There are many anecdotal reports of marihuana smokers using the drug to reduce pain: post-surgery pain, headache, migraine, menstrual cramps, and so on. In particular, marihuana is becoming increasingly recognized as a drug of choice for pain that accompanies muscle spasm. This kind of pain is often chronic and debilitating, especially in paraplegics, quadriplegics, other victims of traumatic nerve injury, and people suffering from multiple sclerosis or cerebral palsy.

Many of these sufferers have discovered that cannabis not only allows them to avoid the risks of opioids for pain relief, but also reduces muscle spasms and tremors, sometimes allowing them to leave their wheelchairs (Petro, 1980). Cannabis may act by mechanisms different from those of other analgesics. Some new synthetic cannabinoid might prove to be especially effective as an analgesic — a possibility implied by the recent discovery of cannabinoid nerve receptor sites in the brain and other organs (Matsuda *et al.*, 1990; Munro *et al.*, 1993).

Seizures

About 20% of epileptic patients do not get much relief from conventional anticonvulsant medications. Cannabis has been explored as an alternative at least since a case was reported in which marihuana smoking, together with the standard anticonvulsants phenobarbital and diphenylhydantoin, was apparently necessary to control seizures in a young epileptic man (Consroe *et al.*, 1975). The cannabis derivative that is most promising as an anticonvulsant is cannabidiol. In one controlled study, cannabidiol in addition to prescribed anticonvulsants produced improvement in seven patients with grand mal (whole body) convulsions; three showed great improvement. Of eight patients who received a placebo instead, only one improved (Cunha *et al.*, 1980). While again the evidence is anecdotal, there are patients suffering from both grand mal and partial seizure disorders who find that smoked marihuana allows them to lower the doses of conventional anticonvulsant medications or dispense with them altogether (Grinspoon & Bakalar, 1993).

Asthma

Asthma is a breathing disorder that arises when bronchial muscles go into spasm and the pathway to the lungs is blocked by mucus and swelling. A number of antiasthmatic drugs are available, but they all have drawbacks — limited effectiveness or side effects. Because marihuana dilates the bronchi and reverses bronchial spasm, cannabis derivatives have been tested as antiasthmatic drugs. Smoking marihuana would probably not be a good way to treat asthma because of chronic irritation of the bronchial tract by tars and other substances in marihuana smoke, so recent researchers have sought a better means of administration. THC in the form of an aerosol spray has been investigated extensively (Tashkin *et al.*, 1975; Tashkin *et al.*, 1977). Other cannabinoids such as cannabinol and cannabidiol may be preferable to THC for this purpose. An interesting finding for future research is that cannabinoids may affect the bronchi by a different mechanism from that of the familiar antiasthmatic drugs.

Glaucoma

Cannabis may also be useful in the treatment of glaucoma, the second leading cause of blindness in the United States. In this disease, fluid pressure within the eyeball increases until it damages the optic nerve. About a million Americans suffer from the form of glaucoma (open angle) treatable with cannabis. Marihuana causes a dose-related, clinically significant drop in intraocular pressure that lasts several hours in both normal subjects and those with the abnormally high ocular tension produced by glaucoma. Oral or intravenous THC has the same effect, which seems to be specific to cannabis derivatives rather than simply a result of sedation. Cannabis does not cure the disease, but it can retard the progressive loss of sight when conventional medication fails and surgery is too dangerous (Hepler *et al.*, 1976).

It remains to be seen whether topical use of THC or a synthetic cannabinoid in the form of eyedrops will be preferable to smoking marihuana for this purpose. So far THC eyedrops have not proved effective, and in 1981 the National Eye Institute announced that it would no longer approve human research using these eyedrops (Roffman, 1982). Other natural cannabinoids and certain synthetic cannabis derivatives are still being studied. But smoking marihuana (six to ten times a day) seems to be a better way of titrating the dose than taking an oral cannabinoid, and most patients apparently prefer it.

Cancer Treatment

Cannabis derivatives have several minor or speculative uses in the treatment of cancer, and one major use. As appetite stimulants, marihuana and THC may help to slow weight loss in cancer patients (Regelson *et al.*, 1976). THC has also retarded the growth of tumor cells in some animal studies, but results are inconclusive, and another cannabis derivative, cannabidiol, seems to increase tumor growth (White *et al.*, 1976). Possibly cannabinoids in combination with other drugs will turn out to have some use in preventing tumor growth.

But the most promising use of cannabis in cancer treatment is the prevention of nausea and vomiting in patients undergoing chemotherapy. About half of patients treated with anticancer drugs suffer from severe nausea and vomiting, and for 30% to 40% of them, the commonly used antiemetics do not work (Roffman, *op. cit.*, pp. 82–83). The nausea and vomiting are not only unpleasant but a threat to the effectiveness of the therapy. Retching can cause tears of the esophagus and rib fractures, prevent adequate nutrition, and lead to fluid loss. Some patients find the nausea so intolerable they say they would rather die than go on.

The antiemetics most commonly used in chemotherapy are phenothiazines like prochlorperzine (Compazine) and the relatively new ondansetron (Zofran). The suggestion that cannabis might be useful arose in the early 1970s when some young patients receiving cancer chemotherapy found that marihuana smoking, which was of course illegal, reduced their nausea and vomiting. In one study of 56 patients who got no relief from standard antiemetic agents, 78% became symptom-free when they smoked marihuana (Vinciguerra *et al.*, 1988). Oral THC has proved effective where the standard drugs were not (Lucas & Laszlo, 1980; Sallan *et al.*, 1975.). But smoking generates faster and more predictable results in both glaucoma and cancer treatment, because it raises THC concentration in the blood more easily to the needed level (Chang *et al.*, 1979). Also, it may be hard for a nauseated patient to take oral medicine. In fact, there is strong evidence that most patients suffering from nausea and vomiting prefer smoked marihuana to oral THC (Grinspoon & Bakalar, 1993).

Oncologists may be ahead of other physicians in recognizing the therapeutic potential of cannabis. In the spring of 1990, two investigators randomly selected more than 2,000 members of the American Society of Clinical Oncology (one-third of the membership) and mailed them an anonymous questionnaire to learn their views on the use of cannabis in cancer chemotherapy. Almost half of the recipients responded. Although the investigators acknowledge that this group was self-selected and that there might be a response bias, their results provide a rough estimate of the views of specialists on the use of dronabinol (Marinol) and smoked marihuana.

Only 43% said the available legal antiemetic drugs (including oral synthetic THC) provided adequate relief to all or most of their patients, and only 46% said the side effects of these drugs were rarely a serious problem. Forty-four percent had recommended the illegal use of marihuana to at least one patient, and half would prescribe it to some patients if it were legal. On average, they considered smoked marihuana more effective than oral synthetic THC and roughly as safe (Doblin & Kleiman, 1991).

AIDS

The American AIDS epidemic first came to notice in 1981, and by now more than 311,000 Americans have died of the disease. Nearly one million are infected with the HIV virus, and perhaps as many as half a million are ill. Although the spread of AIDS has slowed among homosexuals, the reservoir is so huge that the number of cases is sure to grow. Women and children as well as both heterosexual and homosexual men are now being affected; the disease is spreading most rapidly among inner city black and Hispanic intravenous drug abusers and their sexual partners. The period of incubation (between infection and the development of symptoms) is variable, but averages 8 to 10 years. It appears that almost all infected persons will eventually become ill. No cure is known. Opportunistic infections and neoplasms (cancerous growths) can be treated in standard ways, and the virus itself can be attacked with anti-viral drugs, of which the best known is zidovudine (AZT). Unfortunately, AZT, along with other drugs used in the treatment of AIDS, sometimes causes severe nausea that heightens the danger of semi-starvation for patients who are already suffering from nausea and losing weight because of the illness.

Marihuana is particularly useful for patients who suffer from AIDS because it not only relieves the nausea but retards weight loss by enhancing appetite. When it helps patients regain lost weight, it can prolong life. The synthetic cannabinoid dronabinol (Marinol) has been shown to relieve nausea and retard or reverse weight loss in patients with HIV infection, but most patients prefer smoked cannabis for the same reasons that cancer chemotherapy patients prefer it: it is more effective and has fewer unpleasant side effects, and the dosage is easier to adjust.

Other Uses

The realities of human need may be incompatible with the demand for a distinction between medicine and all other uses of cannabis. Marihuana use simply does not conform to the conceptual boundaries established by 20th century institutions. It enhances many pleasures and has many potential medical uses, but even these two categories are not the only relevant ones. For example, it can be used to enhance creativity and productivity. A common problem in the treatment of manic depressive disorder with lithium is the complaint of patients that the medication robs them of some of their creativity, vitality, and enjoyment of life — one reason so many of them stop taking it even though they know the potentially disastrous consequences. Mild mood elevation (hypomania) often enhances creative thinking, and studies show that a better mood often produces more original associations and creative problem-solving. Speed of thought and an easy flow of ideas are associated with elevated mood in bipolar patients (Jamison, 1989). These are also common features of cannabis intoxication. People suffering from bipolar disorder have used marihuana both to preserve their creativity and to make continued use of lithium tolerable.

Experience over the last 20 years has compelled us to take much more seriously the claim that cannabis has useful properties that cannot be described as medical. There is no longer any doubt that marihuana can be an intellectual stimulant. It can help users to penetrate conceptual boundaries, promote fluidity of associations, and enhance insight and creativity. Some find it so useful in gaining new perspectives or seeing problems from a different vantage point that they smoke it in preparation for intellectual or creative work. Other non-medical uses of cannabis may have less to do with learning. It can enhance the appreciation of food, sexual activity, natural beauty, and other sensual experiences, and it can bring a new dimension to the understanding of music and visual arts. Under the right conditions and in the right settings it can promote emotional intimacy. For almost everyone it has the capacity to highlight the comical in life and catalyze a deep and salutary laughter.

As we noted, researchers have recently discovered nerve receptor sites stimulated by THC. This exciting discovery implies that the body produces its own version of cannabinoids. The first of these cannabinoid-like neurotransmitters was identified in 1992 and named anandamide (after the Sanskrit word for bliss) (Devane *et al.*, 1992). Cannabinoid receptor sites occur not only in the lower brain but also in the cerebral cortex, which governs higher thinking, and in the hippocampus, which is a locus of memory. These discoveries raise some interesting questions. Could the distribution of anandamide receptor sites in the higher brain explain why so many cannabis users claim that the drug enhances some mental activities, including creativity and fluidity of associations? Do these receptor sites play a role in marihuana's capacity to alter the subjective experience of time? What about the subtle enhancement of perception and the capacity to experience the physical world with some of the freshness and excitement of childhood? Perhaps further research on these receptors will also promote a better understanding of the remarkable medical versatility of cannabis. Such studies seem all the more promising now that cannabis receptors have also been found outside of the brain (Munro *et al., op. cit.*).

CONCLUSION

If any other medicine had shown similar promise, public and professional interest would be intense. But the government, in its zeal to prosecute the War on Drugs, has been doing everything it can to reduce that interest and prevent the fulfillment of marihuana's promise. Cocaine and morphine (Schedule II drugs) are legally available as medicines; marihuana is not. In 1972 an effort began to put marihuana in Schedule II, a classification that would allow doctors to prescribe it. Finally, in 1988, after years of hearings in which scores of witnesses presented impressive evidence of marihuana's medical usefulness, an administrative law judge recommended that it should be transferred to Schedule II. The Drug Enforcement Administration rejected the recommendation and was upheld on appeal.

Meanwhile the medical ban produces absurd and appalling consequences. A notorious example is the government assault on Kenneth and Barbra Jenks, a Florida couple in their 20s who contracted AIDS through a blood transfusion given to the husband, a hemophiliac. Both were suffering from nausea, vomiting, and appetite loss caused by AIDS or by the drug used to treat it, AZT; doctors feared that Barbra Jenks would die of starvation before the disease killed her. In early 1989 the Jenkses learned about marihuana through a support group for people with AIDS. They began to smoke it, and for a year they led a fairly normal life. They felt better, regained lost weight, and were able to stay out of the hospital; Kenneth Jenks even kept his full-time job.

Then someone informed on them. On March 29, 1990 ten vice squad policemen battered down the door of their trailer, held a gun to Mrs. Jenks's head, and seized the evidence of crime — two small marihuana plants they had been growing because they could not afford to pay the street price of the drug. Cultivation of marihuana is a felony in Florida; the Jenkses faced up to five years in prison. At their trial in July, they used the defense of medical necessity, which had succeeded only three times in the history of the United States. Their doctor testified that no other drug controlled the nausea, and that he would prescribe cannabis for them if he could. Since their March arrest both Jenkses had been losing weight again, and Mrs. Jenks had been hospitalized several time. The judge rejected the medical necessity defense and convicted the Jenkses. However, he imposed essentially no punishment; they were sentenced to a year of unsupervised probation and five years of "caring for each other."

The arrest of the Jenkses is just one unusually conspicuous result of a policy that is ordinarily disastrous in a quieter way. Sick people are forced to suffer anxiety about prosecution in addition to their anxiety about the illness, with therapeutically damaging effects. Doctors are afraid to recommend what they know to be the best treatment, because they might lose their reputations or even their licenses. Research is suppressed and medical wisdom ignored so that the government can enforce its views on the danger of recreational marihuana use.

The struggle over medical marihuana use illustrates some of the broader issues: self-medication versus government control, pure chemicals versus natural drugs, the historical direction of drug policy and the present minor challenges to it, the need to find a better balance in making rules about drugs. The potential dangers of marihuana when taken for pleasure and its possible usefulness as a medicine are historically and practically interrelated issues: historically, because the arguments used to justify public and official disapproval of recreational use have had a strong influence on opinions about its medical potential; practically, because the more evidence accumulates that marihuana is relatively safe even when used as an intoxicant, the clearer it becomes that the medical requirement of safety is satisfied.

Most recent research is tentative, and initial enthusiasm for drugs is often disappointed after further investigation. But it is not as though cannabis were an entirely new agent with unknown properties. Studies conducted in the past ten years have confirmed a centuries-old promise. As restrictions on research are relaxed, this promise will eventually be realized. The weight of past and contemporary evidence will probably prove cannabis to be valuable in a variety of ways as a medicine.

In any discussion of psychoactive drugs it can be difficult to draw a line between "therapeutic" and "recreational" uses or between normalizing uses and enhancing uses. The recent discussions about the significance of the popular antidepressant fluoxetine (Prozac) illustrate this problem. The uses of psychoactive drugs are assigned to various social categories in various cultures. These categories include religion as well as medicine and recreation. Because modern industrial societies consider it important to keep these categories separate, they have difficulty in regulating and controlling the use of psychoactive drugs. In these societies the distinctions between recreation, religious ritual, and medicine (or therapy) are reflected in separate formal and informal institutions.

It is so important for us to limit the purposes for which controlled substances are used that we tend to become suspicious of any proposal that leaves the purpose ambiguous or vague. Modern restrictions on what qualifies as religion make it difficult, with a few exceptions such as the Native American Church, to allow drug use for religious purposes. The same difficulty arises when anyone suggests a social arrangement for the use of psychedelic drugs, because they seem to involve a mixture of therapeutic with religious and other intentions. The proposals for psychedelic centers in which LSD and related drugs could be taken in a safe environment have often been met with suspicion, partly because it is hard to see whether these centers are analogous to resorts, religious retreats, psychiatric clinics, or scientific research institutions. But those distinctions have not always been so clear. The words health and holiness have a common root meaning "whole". In preindustrial societies medical diagnosis and prognosis have an aura of the occult, and disease is often considered an instrument of gods or evil spirits.

By the early 19th century, physicians in Europe and in the United States were convinced that most diseases had physical and chemical causes, but they knew too little to create a medical science with the intellectual authority and practical effectiveness of physics and chemistry. This uncertain situation, together with the growth of manufacturing, capitalist entrepreneurship, and the spirit of liberal individualism, made the nineteenth century a great age of self-medication and competing medical authorities. The patent medicine industry flowered, and many of its medicines contained psychoactive drugs — especially alcohol, opium, cocaine, or cannabis. Orthodox physicians used these drugs extensively as well; as late as 1910, morphine was the fourth most commonly used drug in the United States, and alcohol was fifth. These drugs were not specific cures for specific diseases, and little was known about how they worked, but they relieved suffering in a wide variety of situations. Opium, alcohol, or cocaine, like faith in a pharmacologically inactive nostrum, reduced the pain while nature took its course, often toward a restoration of health.

It was already well known that psychoactive drugs, like most strong medicine, could also be powerfully poisonous. Beginning in the later 19th century, chemists developed alternative drugs which were often synthetic, and at first at least appeared to have less abuse potential — aspirin, chloral hydrate, barbiturates, and (a little later) amphetamines. Meanwhile the public became more aware of the dangers of the familiar natural drugs. These dangers were magnified by the isolation of drug substances in pure form and the development of a new technology, the hypodermic syringe. The mistrust of the public and medical professionals was heightened because the indeterminate and apparently uncontrollable powers of psychoactive drugs seemed incompatible with scientific precision in their use. Alcohol, for example, lost its status as a medicine in the first two decades of the 20th century.

The impulse to clean up society and reduce disorder was hostile to self-medication and small-scale entrepreneurial competition in medicine. Just as professional hygiene required new standards for medical and pharmaceutical practice, intellectual hygiene seemed to demand clear and enforceable categories for psychoactive drug use. As synthetic chemistry, experimental physiology, and bacteriology advanced, the promise of a materialist medicine based on the recognition of specific agents for specific diseases seemed about to be fulfilled. Psychoactive drugs, with their nonspecific and merely palliative effects, became more suspect.

Psychoactive drugs had been used freely in the 19th century, and often the distinctions among categories of use were not clear. Doctors and the government had little legal control over the use of drugs. Sometimes there was little practical difference between a person drinking in a saloon and someone taking a "tonic" that contained alcohol as the main ingredient. This ambiguity now began to seem dangerous, just as the conflation of health and holiness had long been obsolete. Taking opium or alcohol to relax or taking cocaine to feel vigorous would no longer be regarded as a cure or treatment. The common man's or woman's right to make choices about these substances (even, for a time under Prohibition, alcohol) was repudiated. The government and organized medicine took control over their manufacture and distribution, restricting their medical uses and rejecting almost all other uses. This was part of the process by which 19th century liberal capitalism transformed itself into a state corporate system. At the same time the organized medical and pharmaceutical professions, sometimes in collaboration with drug companies, consolidated their power, incorporating more and more social functions in a process that has been labeled by hostile critics "medical imperialism." In what is now known as the Progressive era, the Pure Food and Drug Act, Harrison Narcotics Act, and Volstead Act were characteristic legislation as much as the Federal Reserve Act, which reformed the banking system.

Twentieth century societies have continually increased government control of therapeutic drugs. Psychoactive substances used as pleasure drugs were the first to be restricted, but all prescription medicines now have to undergo elaborate testing and certification before they are approved for medical use. Of all federal drug laws, only the first, the Pure Food and Drug Act of 1906, was designed to encourage free choice by consumers, because it was aimed at simple fraud — false statements about the contents of the package. Since the passage of the Food, Drug and Cosmetics Act of 1938, the power to decide the availability of most drugs has gradually been transferred, first from consumers to doctors and then (in part) from doctors to the government (Temin, 1980).

Although the system that began to establish itself in the Progressive era persists, in recent years the right of medical professionals to interpret the meaning of psychoactive drug use has been challenged by scholars and social critics as well as illicit drug users. In some cases they have advocated an openly religious conception of psychoactive drug use, in effect suggesting that we apply the standards of preindustrial cultures. Whatever the practical merit of this idea, it raises two interesting issues: the dangers of technological advance and the protective function of ritual.

Technical advances in science and manufacturing have increased the danger of drug abuse by producing chemicals in pure form and permitting their production on a vast scale. On the other hand, these products of modern industry have powers commensurate with their dangers: the face of Dr. Jekyll as well as Mr. Hyde. It could be argued that in modern industrial societies the medical profession has to provide the same kind of ritual or quasi-religious context that makes drug use relatively safe in preindustrial cultures. Although the priestly role of doctors in authorizing appropriate occasions for drug use and warning against possession by the demons in these drugs may sometimes seem arrogant, a return to 19th-century individualism or preindustrial technological and cultural forms may not be possible. But physicians should examine rationally how and when to use their authority in controlling psychoactive drugs. They do not have to regard the complex powers of these drugs as a challenge to their own domination of territory they have legitimately staked out. Psychoactive drugs are still an important part of the medical armamentarium, although most of those in use today are synthetic. The doctrine of specific etiology, based on infectious and dietary deficiency diseases, is the source of modern medicine's great triumphs, and yet it remains inadequate. For the vaguely defined functional problems that still account for many visits to doctors, we often still have no clear explanations and no better remedies than drugs that affect the mind.

This situation naturally causes much unease. Doctors are accused by lay people and accuse one another of using pills to resolve problems of living that demand more complex and difficult adjustments. On the other hand, there remains a large area in which diseases and problems of living overlap. Often a doctor's prescription of a tranquilizer is not very different from a lay person's self-prescription of a beer or a marihuana cigarette.

A World Health Organization report once defined health as "total well-being, physical, mental, and social" (World Health Organization, 1969). Others have recommended that drugs be used for positive reasons, to enhance life, rather than just to relieve boredom, pain, and misery. Yet the views on appropriate drug use held by the general public and most doctors are exactly the opposite. When talking about the dangers of non-medical drug use, we tend to use the broadest possible definition of health in order to justify the strongest restrictions; for example, we prefer to put more weight on the indeterminate notion of social well-being than on concrete and specific physical health problems. In establishing legitimate purposes for using drugs, of which health is obviously one, we define health narrowly, so that again severe restrictions can be justified. Protecting, preserving, or enhancing well-being in a broad sense is regarded as a legitimate reason for banning drugs, but not as a legitimate reason for using them.

We must learn to live with the ambiguity of drug effects and use these substances in ways that promote the highest and most harmonious development of human powers. This can be difficult given the circumstances of complex modern society, the powers of modern technology, and the growth of disposable resources, along with the conflicting influences of a decline in enforceable moral authority and a heightened awareness of the need for public protection against common risks.

But modern industrial societies do not handle drug problems nearly as badly as is sometimes thought. Most people have no trouble exercising self-restraint. Attitudes toward tranquilizers, for example, are conservative in all racial, social, and economic groups, but especially among the poorest and least educated. Most people disapprove of using drugs to enhance normal functioning (Manheimer *et al.*, 1973). Drug problems also limit themselves biologically, since many of them belong to a certain stage of life — late adolescence and early adulthood. There is a natural human desire to alter consciousness. Our primate curiosity makes us seek new things to see, feel, and think. It would be a mistake to use public health or social cohesion as an excuse to impose an impoverished conception of naturalness or normality on the search for new experience by changing consciousness.

We are not likely to see either a drug-using utopia or a drug-free society, so we have to become more flexible. Once an illicit drug like marihuana has been used by tens of millions of people, it can no longer be relegated to a small criminal or pathological category, and we must make distinctions among kinds of use and users. If the law and public language simplify and stereotype experience too much, they will defeat their own purposes.

Sigmund Freud said that the palliatives needed to make human life bearable include intoxicants that render us insensitive to our miseries, and for that purpose he even put them on a par with art (a "substitute gratification") and science (a "powerful diversion"). Baudelaire wrote in his essay, "On Wine and Hashish": "Wine is like man; we will never know to what extent it should be esteemed and scorned, hated and loved, nor how many sublime actions or monstrous misdeeds it is capable of. So let us not be more cruel to it than to ourselves, and let us treat it as our equal" (Baudelaire, 1851). He added that the disappearance of wine would produce a void more frightful than all the excesses for which it is responsible. Another great writer, G.K. Chesterton, said that the alcoholic and the abstainer both made the mistake of treating wine as a drug rather than a drink. But alcohol is, among other things, a drug. Most drugs are capable of "sublime actions or monstrous misdeeds," as well as many intermediate effects. We will never be able to regulate consciousness-altering drugs effectively until we recognize this fact and break the habit of dichotomizing and demonizing that makes it impossible for us to realize potential benefits of these substances.

REFERENCES

Aceto, M.D. *et al.* (1990) Dependence studies of new compounds in the rhesus monkey, rat, and mouse. *NIDA Research Monograph #95*, p. 607.

Adamson, Sophia (ed.) (1985) *Through the Gateway of the Heart: Accounts of Experiences with MDA and other Empathogenic Substances*. San Francisco: Four Trees Publications.

Albaugh, Bernard, J. and Anderson, Philip, O. (1974) Peyote in the treatment of alcoholism among American Indians. *American Journal of Psychiatry*, **131**:1247–1251.

Baudelaire, Charles (1974) *Les Paradis Artificiels*. Paris: Livres de Poche, p. 72 (orig. 1851, 1960).

Beck, Jerome *et al.* (1989) *Exploring ecstasy: a description of MDMA users: final report to the National Institute on Drug Abuse*. Grant No. 1R01DAO4408. San Francisco Institute for Scientific Analysis.

Buck, Alfred, A. *et al.* (1968) Coca chewing and health: an epidemiological study among residents of a Peruvian village. *American Journal of Epidemiology*, **88**:159–177.

Burchard, Roderick, E. (1992) Coca chewing and diet. *Current Anthropology,* **33**(1):1–24.

Cappendijk, S.L.T. and Dzoljic, M.R. (1993) Inhibitory effects of ibogaine on cocaine self-administration in rats. *European Journal of Pharmacology,* **241**:261–265.

Chang, A.E. *et al.* (1979) Delta-9-tetrahydrocannabinol as an antiemetic in cancer patients receiving high-dose methotrexate: a prospective, randomized evaluation. *Annals of Internal Medicine,* **91**:819–824.

Cheek, Frances, E. *et al.* (1966) Observations regarding the use of LSD-25 in the treatment of alcoholism. *Journal of Psychopharmacology,* **1**:56–74.

Clark, Walter Huston *et al.* (1975) Psychedelic research: obstacles and values. *Journal of Humanistic Psychology,* **15**:5–17.

Cohen, Peter (1989) *Cocaine Use in Amsterdam in Non-deviant Subcultures.* University of Amsterdam Institute of Social Geography.

Cohen, Sidney (1960) Lysergic acid diethylamide: side effects and complications. *Journal of Nervous and Mental Disease,* **130**:30–40.

Consroe, Paul, F. *et al.* (1975) Anticonvulsant nature of marihuana smoking. *Journal of the American Medical Association,* **234**:306–307.

Cunha, J.M. *et al.* (1980) Chronic administration of cannabidiol to healthy volunteers and epileptic patients. *Pharmacology,* **21**:175–185.

Devane, W.A. *et al.* (1992) Isolation and structure of a brain constituent that binds to the cannabinoid receptor. *Science,* **258**:1946–1949.

Doblin, Richard (1991) Pahnke's "Good Friday experiment": a long-term follow-up and methodological critique. *Journal of Transpersonal Psychology,* **23**(1):1–28.

Doblin, R. and Mark Kleiman (1991) Marihuana as anti-emetic medicine: a survey of oncologists' attitudes and experiences. *Journal of Clinical Oncology,* **9**:1275–1280.

Dzoljic, E.D. *et al.* (1988) Effect of ibogaine on naloxone-precipitated withdrawal syndrome in chronic morphine-dependent rats. *Archives of Internal Pharmacodynamics,* **294**:64–70.

Eisner, Bruce (1989) *Ecstasy: the MDMA Story.* Berkeley, CA: Ronin.

Fabrega, Horacio and Manning, Peter, K. (1973) Health maintenance among Peruvian peasants. *Human Organization,* **31**:243–256.

Glick, S.D. *et al.* (1991) Effects and aftereffects of ibogaine on morphine self-administration in rats. *European Journal of Pharmacology,* **195**:341–345.

Greer, George (1983) MDMA: a new psychotropic compound and its effects in humans. *Unpublished.*

Greer, George and Tolbert, Requa (1986) Subjective reports of the effects of MDMA in the clinical setting. *Journal of Psychoactive Drugs,* **18**:319–327.

Grinspoon, Lester and Bakalar, James, B. (1976) *Cocaine: A Drug and Its Social Evolution.* New York: Basic Books, pp. 120–129.

Grinspoon, Lester and Bakalar, James, B. (1979) *Psychedelic Drugs Reconsidered.* New York: Basic Books, pp. 163–166, 168–171.

Grinspoon, Lester and Bakalar, James, B. (1986) Can drugs be used to enhance the psychotherapeutic process? *American Journal of Psychotherapy,* **50**:393–404.

Grinspoon, Lester and Bakalar, James, B. (1993) *Marihuana, the Forbidden Medicine.* New Haven, CT: Yale University Press, pp. 1–23.

Grob, Charles *et al.* (1992) Anesthetic efficacy of 3.4-methylenedioxymethamphetamine (MDMA) in modification of pain and distress of end-stage cancer. *Draft of protocol for an experiment dated July 14.*

Grof, Stanislav *et al.* (1973) LSD-assisted psychotherapy in patients with terminal cancer. *International Pharmacopsychiatry*, **8**:129–141.

Gutiérrez-Noriega, Carlos (1948) El cocaísmo y la alimentación en el Perú. *Anales de la Facultad de Medicina*, **31**:1–90.

Hepler, R.S. *et al.* (1976) Ocular effects of marihuana smoking. In M.C. Braude, S. Szara (eds.). *Pharmacology of Marihuana*. New York: Raven Press.

Hoffer, Abram (1967) A program for the treatment of alcoholism: LSD, malvaria, and nicotinic acid. In Harold A. Abramson (ed.). *The Use of LSD in Psychotherapy and Alcoholism*. New York: Bobbs-Merrill, pp. 353–402.

Jamison, K.R. (1989) Mood disorders and patterns of creativity in British writers and artists. *Psychiatry*, **52**:125–134.

Jarvik, Murray, E. (1991) Beneficial effects of nicotine. *British Journal of Addiction*, **86**:571–757.

Kotin, J. *et al.* (1973) Delta-9-tetrahydrocannabinol in depressed patients. *Archives of General Psychiatry*, **23**:345–348.

Krogh, David (1991) *Smoking: The Artificial Passion*. New York: W.H. Freeman.

Kurland, Albert, A. (1967) The therapeutic potential of LSD in medicine. In R. DeBold, R. Leaf (eds.) *LSD, Man, and Society*. Middletown, CT: Wesleyan University Press, pp. 20–35.

La Barre, Weston (1964) *The Peyote Cult*. Hamden, CT: The Shoestring Press.

Howard Lotsof (1990) *Interrupting Drug-Dependency: A Summary of Nine Case Histories*. New York: International Coalition for Addict Self-Help.

Lucas, V.S. and Laszlo, J. (1980) Delta-tetrahydrocannabinol for refractory vomiting induced by cancer chemotherapy. *Journal of the American Medical Association*, **243**:1241–1243.

Malleson, Nicholas (1971) Acute adverse reactions to LSD in clinical and experimental use in the United Kingdom. *British Journal of Psychiatry*, **118**:229–230.

Manheimer, Dean, I. *et al.* (1973) Popular attitudes and beliefs about tranquilizers. *American Journal of Psychiatry*, **130**:1246–1253.

Mariani, Angelo (1974) *Coca and Its Therapeutic Applications*. New York: Stonehill, p. 144.

Marriott, Alice and Rachlin, Carol, K. (1971) *Peyote*. New York: New American Library.

Matsuda, Lisa, A. *et al.* (1990) Structure of a cannabinoid receptor and functional expression of the cloned cDNA. *Nature*, **346**:561–564.

Middleton, Robert, M. and Kirkpatrick, Michael, B. (1993) Clinical use of cocaine: a review of the risks and benefits. *Drug Safety*, **9**:212–217.

Moras, K. and Strupp, H.H. (1982) Pretherapy interpersonal relations, patient's alliance, and outcome in brief therapy. *Archives of General Psychiatry*, **39**:405–409.

Moreau de Tours, Jacques Joseph (1857) Lypemanie avec stupeur; tendance a la demence — traitement par l'extrait (principe resineux) de cannabis indica — Guerison. *Lancette Gazette Hôpital*, **30**:391.

Mortimer, W. Golden (1901) *History of Coca*. New York: Vail, pp. 491–509.

Munro, S. *et al.* (1993) Molecular characterization of a peripheral receptor for cannabinoids. *Nature*, **365**:61–65.

Naranjo, Claudio (1969) Psychotherapeutic possibilities of new fantasy enhancing drugs. *Clinical Toxicology*, **2**:209–224.

Naranjo, Claudio (1975) *The Healing Journey*. New York: Ballantine.

Newland, Constance, A. (1962) *My Self and I.* New York: New American Library, pp. 20–47.

Pahnke, Walter, N. (1966) The contribution of the psychology of religion to the therapeutic use of psychedelic substances. In H. Abramson (ed.). *The Use of LSD in Psychotherapy and Alcoholism.* New York: Bobbs-Merrill, pp. 629–649.

Pahnke, Walter, N. (1969) The psychedelic mystical experience in the human encounter with death. *Harvard Theological Review,* **62**:1–21.

Parke Davis and Company (1974) Coca erythroxylon and its derivatives. In Robert Byck (ed.). *The Cocaine Papers.* New York: Stonehill, p. 144.

Peroutka, Steven, J. (1990) Recreational use of MDMA. In Steven, J. Peroutka (ed.). *Ecstasy: The Clinical, Pharmacological, and Neurotoxicological Effects of the Drug MDMA.* Boston: Kluwer Academic Publishers.

Petro, D.J. (1980) Marihuana as a therapeutic agent for muscle spasm or spasticity. *Psychosomatics,* **21**:81–85.

Regelson, W. *et al.* (1976) Delta-9-tetrahydrocannabinol as an effective antidepressant and appetite-stimulating agent in advanced cancer patients. In Braude, Szara (eds.). *Pharmacology of Marihuana,* New York: Raven Press, pp. 763–776.

Roffman, Roger, A. (1982) *Marihuana as Medicine.* Seattle: Madrona, p. 99.

Sallan, S.E. *et al.* (1975) Antiemetic effect of delta-9-tetrahydrocannabinol in patients receiving cancer chemotherapy. *New England Journal of Medicine,* **293**:795–797.

Schelling, Thomas, C. (1992) Addictive drugs: the cigarette experience. *Science,* **225**:430–433.

Schenk, Nicholas, L. (1979) Local anesthesia in otolaryngology: a reevaluation. *Annals of Otology, Rhinology and Laryngology,* **84**:65–72.

Smart, Reginald, G. *et al.* (1966) A controlled study of lysergide in the treatment of alcoholism. *Quarterly Journal of Studies on Alcohol,* **27**:469–482.

Strassman, Rick, J. (1984) Adverse reactions to psychedelic drugs: a review of the literature. *Journal of Nervous and Mental Disease,* **172**:577–595.

Tashkin, D.P. *et al.* (1975) Effects of smoked marihuana in experimentally induced asthma. *American Review of Respiratory Diseases,* **112**:377–386.

Tashkin, D.P. *et al.* (1977) Bronchial effects of aerosolized delta-9-tetrahydrocannabinol in healthy and asthmatic subjects. *American Review of Respiratory Diseases,* **115**:57–65.

Temin, Peter (1980) *Taking Your Medicine: Drug Regulation in the United States.* Cambridge, MA: Harvard University Press.

Vinciguerra, V. *et al.* (1988) Inhalation marihuana as an antiemetic for cancer chemotherapy. *New York State Journal of Medicine,* **88**:525–527.

Waldorf, Dan *et al.* (1991) *Cocaine Changes: The Experience of Using and Quitting.* Philadelphia, Temple University Press.

Weil, Andrew, T. (1978) Coca and brain damage. April, *unpublished.*

Weil, Andrew, T. (1981) The therapeutic value of coca in contemporary medicine. *Journal of Ethnopharmacology,* **3**:367–376.

White, A.C. *et al.* (1976) Effects of delta-9-tetrahydrocannabinol in Lewis lung adenocarcinoma cells in tissue culture. *Journal of the National Cancer Institute,* **56**:655–658.

Wilbert, Johannes (1991) Does pharmacology corroborate the nicotine therapy and practices of South American shamanism? *Journal of Ethnopharmacology,* **32**:179–186.

World Health Organization (1969) *Technical Report Service 407.* Geneva, p. 84.

CHAPTER 12

Informal Social Controls and the Liberalization of Drug Laws and Policies

Wayne M. Harding

Debate about repealing the legal prohibition of illicit drug use inevitably raises questions about the impact repeal would have on the prevalence and incidence of use. How many more users of marijuana, cocaine, psychedelics, heroin and other illicit drugs would there be? Another equally important, though less often carefully considered, question concerns the impact of liberalizing legal controls on the consequences of use. Would illicit drug use become more compulsive and excessive or more controlled and moderate?

This chapter explores the second question by considering how informal social controls (norms and rituals) influence the consequences of illicit and of licit drug use. The chapter begins by discussing the prevailing cultural belief that the legal status of a drug and the consequences of its use depend almost exclusively on its pharmacology. I will argue that, contrary to this pharmacomythology (Szasz, 1975), social norms and rituals exert a powerful influence over the ways in which drugs are used and the likelihood that their use will lead to harmful consequences. The controlled use of alcohol and controlled use of opiates will be used to illustrate how norms and rituals affect drug use. The chapter closes with suggestions for changes in drug treatment, prevention, laws and enforcement, and research. These changes are presented as initial steps in a gradual process of liberalizing drug laws and policies. Focusing on this process is a productive alternative to continuing the polarized debate about maintaining legal prohibitions versus legalizing illicit drugs.

DRUG-CENTERED MYTHOLOGY ABOUT INTOXICANTS

In the United States, there is a widespread belief that the current system of drug controls rests on sound scientific evidence about the chemical nature of the drugs being regulated. Caffeine and alcohol are legally available, according to popular opinion, because they are comparatively benign drugs. They are "good" drugs. They possess some potential for harm when used to excess, but they can be used moderately (at least by adults) without significant risk. With alcohol, this view is abetted by the conventional wisdom that alcoholism is a disease, and that people who become alcoholics have some biological or psychological predisposition to its abuse. Put another way, alcoholism is attributed to defects in the drinker rather than the drink. With caffeine, most Americans would be hard pressed to name any harmful effects, and most do not regard it as a psychoactive substance. Few children drink coffee or tea, but this does not seem related to a belief that caffeine might harm them, since there are few qualms about children consuming caffeine in chocolate and carbonated beverages.

According to this cultural mythology, illicit drugs are prohibited because they are inherently much more dangerous. They are "bad" drugs for two reasons. First, even their occasional use is seen as likely to produce serious adverse physical and psychological harm, such as psychosis, overdose, impaired memory, etc. (The list of adverse effects is long and changes over time with new dangers replacing older, less credible ones.) The second reason illicit drugs are "bad" is that their regular use leads quickly to compulsive use and addiction, which cause more physical and psychological damage.

Tobacco use may seem an exception to this admittedly simplified description of cultural myths about good and bad drugs. After all, most Americans, including most smokers, acknowledge that although smoking cigarettes is legal, tobacco is a bad drug, a drug that cannot be used in moderation and leads to emphysema, lung cancer, and other grave health problems. But, most Americans would have no trouble explaining the apparent contradiction between tobacco's nature and its legal status as an anomaly created by the fact that the dangers of cigarette smoking were not known until comparatively recently. In addition, most Americans foresee the possibility that cigarettes will be prohibited in the future and are not opposed to this change.

THE IMPORTANCE OF INFORMAL SOCIAL CONTROLS

Evidence for the importance of social rather than pharmacological factors in determining which intoxicants can be used, how they are used, and the consequences of use come from several sources. Other chapters in this collection offer anthropological and historical evidence about the wide variability in drug use. This chapter focuses upon the extent to which informal social controls, norms and rituals, influence how drugs are used and the consequences of use.

This psychosocial approach begins with the observation that any drug can be used as well as abused. It does not, however, dismiss pharmacology. Although any drug can be used, some are harder to use moderately than others. Cigarettes are a good example. Most people who smoke with any regularity become compulsive, pack-a-day users. Regular, but occasional tobacco users, such as an individual who smokes one or two cigarettes a day after dinner, exist, but are very rare. Neither does this approach ignore the fact that drugs pose different health risks. It does distinguish, however, between risks that are inherent in the chemistry of the drug, such as the fact that heroin can produce physical addiction, and risks that can be modified, such as the risk of contracting AIDS/HIV by injecting heroin.

Alcohol use is probably the best example of the power of informal social controls to mediate a drug's pharmacological potential for harm. Alcohol is clearly a very dangerous drug. Physical addiction to alcohol can develop within a few weeks, and alcohol use is associated with dozens of physical and psychological problems, and with motor vehicle crashes, falls, and other accidental injuries. Despite all these dangers, most Americans who drink do so without experiencing serious problems. There are a painfully large number of alcoholics, between 10 and 20 million, but there are over 100 million social drinkers (National Institute on Alcohol Abuse and Alcoholism, 1994, pp. 3–22). Also, there is evidence that alcohol use has become more moderate over approximately the past decade. Per capita consumption of alcohol has declined from 2.76 gallons of pure alcohol in 1980–81 to approximately 2.43 gallons in 1989 (National Institute on Alcohol Abuse and Alcoholism, 1994, pp. 3–4). Although alcohol-related mortality accounted for about 5% of deaths in 1988, since 1979 there has been a decline in deaths attributed to alcohol (National Institute on Alcohol Abuse and Alcoholism, 1994, p. 29). For example, the proportion of traffic fatalities in which alcohol is involved (BAC of the driver or non-occupant was .10 percent or higher) has dropped from 46% in 1982 to 39% in 1989 (National Highway Traffic Safety Administration, 1991).

In short, while there is considerable room for improvement, Americans seem to be doing a better job controlling their alcohol use. Current drinking practices are clearly now far more moderate than at other times in American history. For example, during the early 1800's per capita consumption was as high as 7.1 gallons, laborers customarily consumed alcohol twice daily instead of coffee breaks, and "alcohol was a basic part of the diet and most people thought that whiskey was as essential as bread" (Lender & Martin, 1982, p. 46).

If the pharmacology of alcohol does not account for the fact that controlled alcohol use is the predominant using style, then what does? In large part, it is the informal social controls that promote social drinking while discouraging abuse. Pervasive norms and rituals define acceptable and unacceptable alcohol use, and many are so familiar that they can be readily articulated. Norms such as "don't drink and drive," "don't drink before sundown," "don't mix drinks," "hold your liquor," and "use a designated driver" proscribe drunkenness, excessive use, and risky behavior while intoxicated. Rituals define what is acceptable: a few beers at a baseball game, a drink with a business lunch (three martini lunches are no longer an acceptable ritual), a drink before dinner, wine with a meal, a few drinks at a cocktail party, a beer with the boys after work. Two important features of these rituals are: that alcohol use is treated as a part of a social activity rather than its main focus, and that drinking is generally treated as a leisure activity. These features communicate the message that alcohol should be used in a way that complements rather than disrupts social relations and should not interfere with work or other obligations.

Assimilation of informal social controls begins in the family as children see their parents and other adults drink. In some families, the socialization process includes allowing children to consume small quantities of alcohol. Children may taste a parent's drink or sip alcoholic beverages on religious occasions, at weddings, and during other special events. Rituals and norms are also reinforced for children and adults by portrayals of social drinking and unacceptable drunkenness in television shows, movies, magazines, novels and other media.

Many adolescents violate these informal social controls, by drinking to get drunk when they are outside the surveillance and moderating influence of their parents. However, during this period of experimentation and testing, many adolescents place some limits on their use. For example a 1992 survey of drug use among high school students in a Massachusetts community, found that: 42% "set a limit before they started drinking" that they then followed, 50% left a situation because drinking or drug use "seemed to be getting out of hand," 53% decided not to go somewhere "because there would be lots of drinking and/or drug use," 65% never rode with "a driver who was high, stoned, or loaded on alcohol or other drugs," and 79% never "take more than one drug at a time or mix alcohol with other drugs," (Harding & Apsler, 1994). At age 21, drinkers come under the scrutiny and influence of adult drinking companions, most of whom are committed to moderate use and reinforce the norms and rituals for controlling alcohol. Eventually, the drinker evolves a personal, but culturally approved, pattern of drinking and "social reinforcement for controlled use continues through adult life" (Zinberg, Harding & Winkeller, 1977).

Socialization in controlled use can break down. People grow up in families where one or both parents are alcoholics or neither parent drinks, and in both cases the probability of their having a problem with alcohol is higher than in the general population. There are some groups and subcultures that lack appropriate norms and rituals, such as strong sanctions against drunkenness. Biological or psychological factors predispose some people to problem drinking. Situational factors, such as severe stress, may overwhelm the cultural constraints on use. Although things do go wrong for individuals, social learning and reinforcement for controlled use exert a substantial influence on the way in which most Americans drink.

Formal social controls, the laws and regulations governing alcohol use, tend to buttress the norms and rituals that support controlled use. These laws and regulations prohibit drunk driving and public drunkenness, require training for servers in drinking establishments, limit the hours that establishments can serve alcohol, restrict the number of drinking establishments and liquor stores, and forbid drinking establishments to serve obviously intoxicated patrons. These laws owe their effectiveness to the fact that they are consistent with informal social controls. Put another way, we avoid being drunk in public not so much because it is against the law, but because it is socially unacceptable.

SUBCULTURAL NORMS AND RITUALS AND CONTROLLED OPIATE USE

Informal social controls that encourage control and discourage abuse also operate within the subculture of illicit drug users. Data to support this contention come from a series of studies of controlled marijuana, psychedelic, and opiate users conducted between 1972 and 1992 by this author with Dr. Norman Zinberg and other colleagues. Here, I will limit discussion to controlled opiate users, because their existence poses the most direct challenge to cultural myths about good and bad drugs.

The prevailing view of opiates, and heroin in particular, is that they are so powerful that only a few occasions of use lead quickly to addiction and to profound harm. Virtually any use nonmedical use of opiates is regarded as synonymous with drug abuse. All heroin users are seen as junkies (Harding, 1992). It was in part to test the accuracy of these beliefs that we undertook a study to identify controlled opiate users and compare them with compulsive users.

The findings presented here are from initial interviews with 61 controlled and 30 compulsive opiate users. These subjects were recruited through advertisements in newspapers, personal contacts with friends and colleagues, posters placed in the community, referrals by subjects, and by indigenous data collectors hired because they were familiar with the subculture of drug-takers. The subjects were paid a small fee for participating in a semi-structured confidential interview that lasted one to two hours. The interview topics included: demographic information, family history, relationships with others, history of and attitudes toward illicit drug use, psychological functioning, and drug-using practices. The validity of the subjects' responses was assessed by comparing data elicited by similar questions asked at widely spaced intervals during the interviews, by comparing responses among a subset of subjects who knew one another, and by interviewing friends of a subset of subjects. These and other procedures indicated that nearly all the subjects were truthful. We found evidence of inconsistent responses in only three cases, and omitted them from the analyses.

Subjects were assigned to a "controlled" or "compulsive" category based on a complex set of criteria. Neither controlled nor compulsive subjects could have been enrolled in drug treatment for longer than one month during the two years preceding the interview. This criterion eliminated controlled subjects whose use was being moderated by treatment. Controlled subjects were also required to have used opiates at least ten times per year during at least two of the previous four years. This eliminated candidates whose use was too infrequent to provide a reasonable test of their ability to control opiates. To make a clear case for the existence of controlled opiate users, we required that controlled subjects be moderate users of all the drugs they used (except tobacco). Controlled subjects were allowed to have many occasions of opiate use, but few periods of daily use. For example, in the two years preceding the interview, they could have had no more than three instances of from 4 to 15 days of consecutive use, nor could they have used an opiate more days than not in any 30-day period. In contrast, compulsive subjects were required to have had several long periods of frequent use. For example, in at least one of the two years preceding the interview, they had to have had at least two 30-day periods in which the number of using days exceeded the number of abstinent days, or to have met other criteria defining frequent use. Details about these criteria and study methods are available elsewhere (Harding, 1992; Zinberg, 1984).

The demographic characteristics of the controlled and compulsive subjects were very similar. The mean age for both was 26 years. Seventy-seven percent of the controlled subjects were males as compared to 67% of the compulsives. Eighty-two percent of the controlled subjects and 83% of the compulsives were "white." Twenty percent of the controlled subjects and 17% of the compulsives were married. Controlled subjects completed an average of 12.9 years of school, compulsives completed 12.2.

The study showed that controlled opiate use could be sustained for long periods. The mean period of controlled use was 4.5 years. Some subjects had been stable controlled users for as long as eight to 15 years. These data indicated that controlled use is not simply a brief transitional stage leading to compulsive use or to abstinence. However, this data did not rule out the possibility that, although they had been controlled users for several years, these subjects still had not yet reached the point in an opiate-using career when compulsive use typically begins. To test this, we compared the duration of the current using styles of the controlled (4.5 years) and compulsive (5.0 years) and found no significant difference. Nor was there a significant difference in the total lengths of the using careers of the controlled (7.2 years) and compulsive (8.4 years) subjects. Controlled users, then, had as much opportunity to become compulsive users as did the compulsive subjects.

Other analyses also contradicted the idea that opiate users progress through stages from minimal to controlled to compulsive use. For example, about half of the compulsive subjects had never had a period of controlled or less frequent use. They were classified as compulsive for every year that they had used opiates.

The findings indicated that controlled users can manage their opiate use. Although our classification criteria allowed controlled subjects to use opiates as often as every other day, in practice this did not occur. Forty one percent used an average of twice a week in the two years preceding their interview, 35% used one to three times per month, and 23% less than once per month. Only 26% of the controlled subjects had periods (4 to 15 days) of spree use as allowed by the classification criteria. Compulsive subjects used much more frequently (in part, this is an artifact of our classification criteria). For example, 46% used opiates one or more times a day or more. A significantly larger proportion of controlled users than compulsives (59% versus 17%) were able to keep opiates on hand without using them up. Controlled subjects were significantly more likely to be employed full-time (38%) than compulsives (10%), and less likely to have few friends or to be loners (20% versus 44%).

One goal of the study was to explore factors associated with controlled use. A variety of hypotheses were tested including several related to drug and personality variables. We hypothesized, for example, that controlled subjects had limited access to opiates that kept their use in check. However, no significant differences were found between controlled and compulsive subjects on variables measuring the ease of obtaining opiates, current dealing of any drug, current dealing of opiates, number of drug types ever used, number of drug types currently used, and history of a reduction in opiate use due to lack of availability. Also, no differences were found between the types of opiates used. Heroin was the opiate used most often and the drug of choice for controlled and compulsive subjects.

Quantitative and qualitative analyses indicated that the differences in these using styles were primarily associated with subcultural norms and rituals. Controlled subjects adopted a significantly greater number of rules and practices that operated to reduce the risks of opiate use than did the compulsives: 4.3 rules for controlled subjects, 2.7 for compulsives. Many controlled subjects, for example, never used opiates alone and explained this practice in terms of the need to have someone with them who could help if they experienced negative effects. Others never shared their works in order to avoid contracting hepatitis and other diseases. A few users spoke about keeping an extra set of works on hand for using companions. Many had rules about obtaining opiates, such as purchasing only from someone they knew well. Controlled users also tended to schedule use so that it would not interfere with work or other obligations. A typical choice was a weekend evening. One subject arranged to have her child cared for before using opiates, because she felt she might not be able to respond to an emergency effectively when she was "high." Controlled subjects were rigid about their patterns of use, and used less often than was necessary to avoid addiction. One used every Friday evening, and at no other time, for years. Another subject who ordinarily used opiates less than once a month, increased his use to as much as every other day during brief vacations. After a vacation, he abstained for a few weeks before reverting to once a month use. Another subject's rule about spree use was to use "no more than three days in a row." Some subjects made efforts to titrate their dose by injecting a small amount of heroin and waiting to gauge its effect before using more. Many controlled subjects had strict budgets for purchasing drugs, another way to limit use and avoid adverse consequences.

Controlled subjects acquired these norms and rituals gradually over the course of their drug-using career, but a crucial element in this process was joining a group of other controlled users. Controlled subjects were significantly more likely than compulsives to have known controlled opiate users and to use opiates in the company of controlled users. Only 8% of the controlled subjects did not use with controlled users as compared to 47% of the compulsives. Although controlled subjects tended to know compulsive opiate users, and many relied on these contacts to obtain opiates, they also tended to avoid administering opiates with compulsive users.

THE IMPACT OF PROHIBITION ON NORMS AND RITUALS SUPPORTING CONTROLLED USE

Given the lack of broad cultural support for controlled illicit drug use, controlled opiate users are doing a better job at managing their use than might be expected. The subcultural norms and rituals that guide their drug-taking are not learned in the home. Most parents have not used illicit drugs. Those that have cannot talk about their experiences with their children without running enormous risks. Offering a child a taste of wine is one thing, offering them a taste of marijuana quite another.

Illicit drug users are also denied the pervasive and ongoing support for controlled use outside the home that exists for alcohol. Subcultural norms and rituals that shape controlled use are a comparatively weak and uncertain sources of reinforcement for controlled use. New users may find it difficult to find and join using groups dedicated to control. We found this was a more serious problem for opiate users than marijuana and psychedelic users. Heroin and other opiate use is so widely disapproved that controlled subjects found it necessary to keep their use a secret even from users of other illicit drugs. This secretiveness makes it hard for new opiate users to locate experienced controlled users who can help them learn how to avoid addiction and other adverse effects. It is easier to find compulsive users because they are much less secretive about their use (perhaps because they have less to lose by revealing it.) Compulsives, however, offer little instruction or encouragement for controlled use. Those we studied tended to follow norms and rituals, like sharing needles, which increased rather than decreased the risks of use.

The dangers and inadequacies of relying solely upon the subculture of users for help in controlling use were reflected in the using careers of many controlled subjects. Forty-eight percent of them had one or more past periods in their using careers when they were clearly using opiates compulsively (e.g., 86% of these formerly-compulsive-now-controlled users had been addicted to opiates, defined as having been a daily user for at least 30 days coupled with the subject's self-report that they had a "habit"). The existence of these formerly-compulsive-now-controlled subjects (FCNCs) raised the issue of whether their present period of control represented a brief remission period. Analyses did not substantiate this view. For example, FCNCs had been continuous controlled users for a significantly greater number of years (3.5 years) that the total of all their past periods of compulsive use (1.8) years.

Controlled illicit drug use is also difficult to learn because users cannot rely on drug abuse prevention programs for assistance. Current prevention programs eschew the scare tactics used in programs of the late 1960s and 1970s (Funkhouser & Denniston, 1992), but the information they present is still very biased. Prevention programs concentrate almost exclusively on communicating the dangers of drug use. Their central message is that illicit drug use is harmful, wrong, and that nearly all people who use, or even want to try, illicit drugs suffer from serious personal problems. Until quite recently, "Just Say No" was the federally endorsed approach for youth prevention programs. While most prevention practitioners acknowledge that this approach was too simplistic, they remain unwilling to teach responsible alcohol use, much less methods for using other drugs more safely. One understandable, though debatable, reason for their reluctance is that teaching responsible substance use will promote more drug-taking.

A more troubling reason for not teaching responsible use is that many prevention practitioners are not well informed about substance use, are carriers of cultural misconceptions. When evaluating drug abuse prevention programs, I regularly encounter well-meaning prevention professionals who teach adolescents and adults that post-alcoholic social drinking is impossible, and who have never heard of controlled heroin use. This includes professionals who are operating "state of the art" programs, such as community-based prevention coalitions. Their medium may be modern, but their messages are not. This is not surprising. There is little or no professional training in drug abuse prevention, and publications designed to guide prevention practitioners contain a great deal of inaccurate and biased information. For example, recent issues of a federal publication, *Prevention Pipeline,* contain "Editorial Guidelines" that specify acceptable and unacceptable terminology to be used in prevention messages. These guidelines state that the term "responsible use" should not be used "since there is a risk associated with all use" (Staff, 1993), and that "recreational use of drugs" should not be used because "no drug use is recreational." Prohibition of illicit drugs may also be undermining the transmission and reinforcement of social controls about alcohol use. Several years ago, many parents were relieved to learn that their adolescent child was using alcohol rather than a "bad" illicit drug, and parents generally regarded adolescent experimentation with alcohol as stage leading to adult social drinking (Harding, Apsler & Walsh, 1989a). Now, however, there is a tendency to view adolescent alcohol use as part of the drug problem. This is reflected in new programs and polices. The National Highway Traffic Safety Administration is encouraging states to set the legal limit of intoxication for adolescent drivers at a zero BAC, while the limits for adults are at .08 or .10. The Center for Substance Abuse Prevention advises that designated driver programs and safe ride programs (that offer intoxicated drivers a free or low cost ride home with a sober driver) should not serve adolescents. Many police departments have stepped up enforcement of laws prohibiting possession of alcohol by minors, and sale to minors. Many prevention programs promote alcohol and drug free events for mixed audiences of adolescents and adults, and are opposed to allowing adults to drink on some of these occasions, although this would model responsible alcohol use. These approaches to preventing alcohol abuse have benefits, but they also place adolescent use further more outside moderating social controls, and fail to address the prevention needs of the many adolescents who do drink. In 1993, 51% of students in grade eight (roughly 14 years of age), 69% in grade ten (roughly 16 years of age), and 76% in grade twelve (roughly 18 years of age) reported that they had used alcohol in the past 12 months (Johnston, O'Malley, & Bachman, 1994, p. 8).

TOWARD MORE LIBERAL CONTROLS OVER DRUG USE

Proponents for the legalization of illicit drug use may contend that the preceding discussion supports their position — legalization will eliminate the obstacles that exist to developing controlling norms and rituals and stimulate their dissemination. This argument, however, overlooks the fact that the development of widespread informal social controls, like those that promote controlled alcohol use, appears to take place slowly, over years or perhaps decades. Norms and rituals associated with controlled use emerge from different groups and subcultures, percolate slowly through the culture, and eventually may be melded into precepts and practices that determine the way most people use a drug. Although many more illicit drug users subscribe to norms and rituals for controlled use than is generally appreciated, the abrupt repeal of prohibition would leave current and new users ill-equipped to control their use. It isn't possible to predict what the ratio of abusers to users would be immediately following repeal, but there is a real risk that the number of drug casualties would rise dramatically.

While debates about drug control continue to revolve around prohibition versus legalization, these are not the only choices. Another alternative is to gradually liberalize present controls in ways that will reduce the costs of prohibition and create conditions more conducive to the development of norms and rituals consistent with controlled use of illicit drugs (and of alcohol). The end point of this process may or may not be legalization of all illicit drugs. The process might be halted short of this based on research about how changes in polices and practices affect both the number of users and the consequences of their use.

It is impossible to list in advance all the steps to be taken along the path toward more liberal drug controls. The remainder of this section, however, offers recommendations about initial and near-term changes in drug treatment, prevention, enforcement, and research that will facilitate the establishment of informal social controls.

Changes in Treatment

One pre condition for liberalizing current drug control policies should be an increase in treatment capacity. It would be irresponsible not to assume that as current controls are relaxed, the number of drug-takers and the number of people experiencing problems with drugs will increase. Also, liberalization may help destigmatize participation in treatment, which, in turn, will increase the number of abusers willing to seek help.

Given the serious questions about the efficacy of present treatment programs (Apsler & Harding, 1991), it would be unwise simply to increase treatment capacity without also making a commitment to improving treatment effectiveness. Perhaps improving treatment seems an obvious corollary of liberalizing drug policies, but it is important to emphasize this for two reasons. First, some proponents of legalization neglect this issue because they fear that acknowledging that the need for treatment will increase will undermine their position that legalization is beneficial. Second, and more importantly in this era of scant economic resources, there is a real danger that savings generated by reducing drug enforcement under more liberal control systems, will be reappropriated for programs unrelated to drug use. This would leave treatment programs under-funded just when demand for them is likely to rise.

There are many changes that can be made to improve treatment, some of which are already underway. There is a need for more sophisticated screening procedures of drug treatment programs. These programs need tools to distinguish controlled users from other types of users. This will prevent problems such as admitting controlled opiate users to treatment programs that may addict them to methadone and/or increase their association with compulsive users (Harding, 1992). In addition, better training is needed for medical personnel, teachers, and other gatekeepers who too often both over identify and under identify substance abuse in their clients. For example, at present, school personnel who encounter students who use drugs in a minimal or controlled way tend to regard them as drug abusers who should be punished and/or treated. Many school personnel also explain any other problems the student may be having as a consequence of their drug use, and may fail to provide assistance for serious problems that are, in fact, unrelated to drug use. Medical personnel, on the other hand, often overlook drug problems because they receive little professional training about drug use, although some 25% to 50% of ambulatory patients may have alcohol or drug related problems (Funkhouser, Goperud & Bass, 1992). Another change related to screening and treatment would be to provide the public with better information that they can use to assess their own drug use and to identify sources of assistance if they have a drug problem. This information should distinguish between compulsive use and lesser problems. It should also identify professionals who can provide advice about how to use drugs more safely (when appropriate) along with advice about abstinence. More rigorous research on the outcomes and cost effectiveness of treatment and on matching patients with treatment is long overdue (Apsler & Harding, 1991).

Although such research is expensive, it can generate savings by identifying which treatment modalities work and for what populations. Related to this, there should be more experimentation with treatment programs that use less conventional methods such as acupuncture, new drug therapies, and heroin maintenance. More experimentation should be done with treatment programs that attempt to promote social drinking among problem drinkers and/or alcoholics, and consideration should be given to applying this approach to compulsive users of illicit drugs. The existence of formerly-compulsive-now-controlled heroin users suggests that it might be possible for treatment programs to help opiate addicts become less abusive users (Harding, 1992; Harding & Zinberg, 1983).

Finally, barriers to treatment should be removed. Those experiencing drug-related problems must have easier access to treatment and be encouraged to seek help before their problems become more serious. This will require an increase in treatment capacity, adequate insurance programs to finance treatment, and elimination of explicit and implicit requirements to adopt the stance of a repentant deviant to be accepted for treatment.

Changes in Prevention

Steps toward more liberal drug controls should include greater investment in prevention and the reform of prevention methods. One change that should be made in prevention methods is to increase the channels used to distribute prevention messages. The traditional approaches of distributing messages through the schools and mass media should continue, but messages should also be distributed through religious organizations, government, public and private service organizations, community groups, law enforcement, judicial systems, business, etc. Since drug use is determined by multiple factors (agent, host, and environment), prevention efforts should mobilize and coordinate all systems within a community to change drug use (Benard, 1990).

A systems approach to prevention offers the possibility of creating a consistent, community-wide environment in which norms and rituals promoting controlled use can evolve. It also can reduce the "duplication of efforts and inefficient use of resources" (Gibbs & Bennett, 1990) associated with the poorly coordinated actions of independent agencies and organizations. Although a community-based systems approach makes good sense, empirical evidence for its effectiveness is quite limited (GAO, 1993). Lack of evidence, however, has not deterred implementation of this approach on a large scale. For example, between 1989 and 1992, the federal Center for Substance Abuse Prevention (CSAP) awarded $221 million in grants of three to five years duration to approximately 250 community coalitions formed to prevent substance abuse (GAO, 1993). In 1994, CSAP awarded grants to approximately 20 more coalitions, and at least 100 more awards are planned for 1995. More empirical evidence about the viability and effectiveness of the systems approach will be available as evaluations of these coalitions are completed.

Although prevention programs are usually directed at youth and young adults, it is important to reconceptualize drug prevention as appropriate for all ages. There are at least three reasons for targeting adults: youth model their behavior on adult behavior; many adults have drug problems; and adults, and parents in particular, can have enormous positive impact upon youth drug use through rule-setting, supervision, and the transfer of information and norms (Harding, Apsler & Walsh, 1989a). Prevention should also target all types of drug abuse, rather than concentrating on abuse of illicit drugs. This will help counter the belief that some intoxicants are good and others bad.

Prevention messages about drugs should also be shifted — away from simplistic, drug-centered myths about drug use and drug users, and toward more complex and realistic views. Along with more traditional messages that encourage abstinence as the only certain method for avoiding the risks of drug use, prevention programs should distribute information about strategies for reducing harmful consequences of use. Other examples of information that should be incorporated into prevention messages are: most people find psychoactive drugs pleasurable, many licit and illicit psychoactive drugs have proven or possible medical uses, seeking consciousness change whether through drugs or other means is not abnormal behavior, the way in which drugs are used and their effects vary widely, and some alcoholics and other types of compulsive users can establish patterns of controlled use. I am not recommending that information about how to use drugs safely should be a part of prevention programs aimed at young children. Drug use by children should be actively discouraged. They are least likely to manage it successfully, and very early drug use is associated with an increased risk of later abuse. On the other hand, it is appropriate to distribute some information about how to use drugs more safely to adolescents since this is when many people begin intoxicant use. More specifically, adolescents should be presented with information about how to use drugs more safely at or shortly before the age when they begin nonmedical drug use. National survey data show that this occurs in grades six and seven (Johnston, O'Malley & Bachman, 1994, pp. 136–142). Eleven percent of high school seniors (roughly 18 years of age) report that they initiated alcohol use by the end of grade six (roughly 12 years), and 18% reported that they had tried cigarettes. Illicit drug use begins later: 2% tried marijuana by grade six (12 years), and 7% tried it in grades seven or eight (13 and 14 years respectively).

Although revised prevention programs would continue to disseminate information about the dangers of drug use and the value of abstinence, the content reforms discussed above will stir up much opposition. Some opponents will assert that the "new" information is inaccurate. Some will accept that it is accurate, but argue that should be censored because it will encourage drug use. Some will denounce those who seek revisions as traitors to the cause of preventing drug abuse, or closet drug-takers. Overcoming such resistance to modifying the content of prevention messages will be a very slow process.

As drug controls are liberalized, there will be an increased need for secondary prevention programs that aim to reduce harm to and by drug-takers. Alcohol users, for example, should be encouraged to use designated drivers (Apsler, Harding & Goldfein, 1987). Drinkers who become too intoxicated to drive safely and cannot or will not use a designated driver, can be given a free "safe ride" home by taxi or another conveyance (Harding, Apsler & Goldfein, 1988). Sports stadiums and other public assembly facilities can stop serving alcohol well before events end, and they can also use on site advertising to reduce impaired driving (Apsler & Harding, 1989). Similar harm reduction programs should be applied to illicit drug use. Safe ride services, which are now offered exclusively to drinkers, could be offered to users of other drugs. Needle exchange programs, intended to reduce the transmission of HIV/AIDS, should be disseminated beyond the few sites in which they now are available. Furthermore, the rationale for needle exchange programs should be to prevent the transmission of disease, not just HIV/AIDS. Programs should be offered that test drug samples anonymously submitted by users and provide them with accurate reports about the purity and potency of the sample.

CSAP and other agencies have endorsed the development of drug prevention programs that reduce "risk factors" associated with drug abuse. High risk youth are described as those whose are economically disadvantaged, are runaways or homeless, are school dropouts, have mental health problems, have attempted suicide, are pregnant, are victims of physical, psychological, or sexual abuse, are involved in violent or delinquent acts, etc. (Funkhouser & Denniston, 1992). There are many problems with this approach, but it does raise, perhaps unintentionally, an important fundamental question for prevention (and treatment) programs. To the extent that drug abuse arises from poverty, violence, child abuse, and other social problems, shouldn't prevention efforts be directed at these underlying problems? Discussion of this issue is beyond the scope of this chapter, except to observe that when drug abuse has roots in such social problems, drug abuse prevention may retard efforts to address these problems.

Changes in Drug Laws and Enforcement

The third set of changes in moving toward more liberal controls is a realignment of laws and enforcement programs. Before, identifying some initial steps, I want to emphasize that drug laws and regulations will be necessary even if illicit drugs are legalized. Laws regulating the sale of substances that are now or will become legal must: limit access by minors; discourage black market sales of drugs; define the location, hours of operation, of liquor stores, tobacco sellers, and sellers of other drugs; limit drug advertising; monitor the purity and potency of drugs; and prohibit drunk and drugged driving and other dangerous behavior by intoxicated users, and so on. For example, in the Netherlands, where cannabis is legally sold in "coffee shops," sales of other drugs, and sales of cannabis to persons under 18, and advertising (commercials) are prohibited. Also, local authorities may regulate the number of shops, their closing times, and nuisance behavior associated with them (Netherlands Institute for Alcohol and Drugs, 1995).

How should drugs laws and their enforcement be modified when gradual liberalization, rather than quick transformation, is the goal? One reform that is long overdue, is to reduce penalties for drug possession and to increase the amount of an illicit drug an individual can possess without being charged with trafficking. The guiding principal for this change should be to reduce the penalties for possession to a level where they pose less risk to the well being of the drug user than does use of the drug (Netherlands Institute for Alcohol and Drugs, 1995). Mandatory minimum sentences and for drug offenses and "truth-in-sentencing" measures designed to increase time served in prison or jail should be eliminated. These practices reinforce cultural stereotypes about drug use by ignoring distinctions between users and abusers, and users and traffickers. These practices also have contributed disproportionately to the overcrowding of jails and prisons. Between 1980 and 1989, the number of drug offenders sentenced to federal prison grew 262% while the number of all offenders grew by 99% (Bureau of Justice Statistics, 1992, pp. 190).

Less emphasis should be placed on arrests and prosecution for drug possession. The proportion of arrests for possession of illicit drugs is much higher (68%) than for other drug offenses (sale and manufacture) and this imbalance is much worse for some drugs. In 1992, marijuana arrests constituted 32% of all drug arrests and of these, 26% were for possession of marijuana as compared to 7% for its sale or manufacture (Maguire & Pastore, 1994, p. 458). Because marijuana has a low potential for abuse, criminal penalties now imposed for simple possession should replaced by civil ones that impose fines and/or community service.

More efforts should be made to provide treatment to incarcerated drug abusers. Also, sentencing reform and judicial training programs should encourage the use of community corrections programs as alternatives to incarceration. There is considerable ongoing experimentation with the use of alternative sanctions for drunk driving offenders as a substitute for jail or in combination with reduced jail terms. The alternatives include: victim restitution, intensively supervised probation with drug testing and/or treatment, day reporting centers, use of electronic monitoring to detain offenders at home or limit their movement, use of ignition interlocks that require offenders to pass an alcohol breath test to start their vehicles, and requiring offenders to place special tags or license plates on their vehicles. Although convincing evidence about their effectiveness is lacking, these alternatives have appealing features. They are attractive to offenders, afford a good deal of protection to the public by restricting and/or monitoring the offender's drinking and driving behavior, usually cost less than incarceration, and are supported by the community (Harding, Apsler & Walsh, 1989b). Also, these approaches leave offenders in the community where cultural pressures for reasonable alcohol use continue to operate and can be reinforced by correctional personnel supervising their progress. Jail offers no such support and may reinforce compulsive norms — drug use in jail is not uncommon. Experimentation with alternative sanctions for drunk drivers should be continued.

Experimentation with alternatives sanctions for other drug offenders, should be greatly expanded.

Most drugs laws should be less rigorously enforced than they are now. This applies especially to the enforcement of laws concerning the possession of illicit drugs, to the very costly attempts to suppress drug production in foreign counties, and to efforts to interdict drug smugglers. Law enforcement personnel should not ignore violations of drug laws; they should not turn a blind eye to a drunk or drugged driver. They should, however, give up the hope that drug abuse can be eradicated or sharply reduced through vigorous law enforcement. The goal of enforcement should be to symbolize cultural opposition to drug abuse not to end it.

Reduction in enforcement efforts would free resources that can be redirected to prevention, treatment and research. The President's proposed 1996 national drug control budget allocates approximately 63% of the total 14.6 billion dollars to enforcement, leaving 37% for treatment, prevention and research (Office of National Drug Control Policy, 1995). These resources should be redistributed so that prevention, treatment, and research comprise most of the budget.

Changes in drug laws and enforcement will move slowly because of public attitudes about drug use, crime, and the criminal justice system. In 1989, 58% of Americans identified drugs as the factor most responsible for crime (Bureau of Justice Statistics, 1992, p. 93). Much smaller percentages attributed crime to unemployment (14%), the breakdown of family and societal values (14%), lenient courts (4%), lax punishment (4%), television violence (2%), and other sources (19%). A recent Massachusetts poll ("Public backs," 1995), showed that most Americans do not think that enforcement has been effective: 74% felt that law enforcement is not "winning the war on drugs," 56% that "drugs are more available now," and 78% felt that "mandatory jail terms are getting low-level dealers instead of kingpins." But, their disillusionment does not translate into a willingness to reduce enforcement efforts and legal penalties: 83% favored "long mandatory sentences for convicted drug dealer," and 52% favor "tough sentences even if prisons fill up with low level dealers, not kingpins or violent criminals."

Changes in Research

Commitment to research about drug use/abuse is probably the most important step in liberalizing drug controls. Research should be applied consistently to test the effectiveness of current and proposed programs and polices. Sweeping policy and program changes should be avoided. Instead, changes should be limited to small groups or geographic areas, and the impacts on drug use carefully evaluated before they are disseminated more widely. This approach should be applied to the changes in treatment, prevention, and enforcement recommended above. For example, designated driver and safe ride programs have not been rigorously evaluated. The need to evaluate them is underscored by the fact that, like most programs, they have the potential to produce unintended negative effects. Designated driver programs may increase drinking by the designated driver's companions and safe ride programs may encourage heavy drinking by those using the service (Apsler, Harding & Goldfein, 1987; Harding, Apsler & Goldfein, 1988). Funders should require that treatment and prevention programs set aside a portion of the funds they receive to pay for program evaluation. This practice is becoming more common, but some funders have not followed this trend. The head of one large state agency, for example, funds very little program evaluation based on his belief that the research costs simply detract from agencies ability to fund what they already "know" are good programs. Another problem is that funders who require evaluation frequently do not include sufficient funds to conduct a well designed study.

Basing drug programs and policies on research about what works and what does not, means that movement toward more liberal drug controls will be slow. Research on long-term outcomes and replications of findings frequently take years.

Before research can help depoliticize and rationalize the process of making drug policy, research itself must be depoliticized. The research agendas of government agencies and foundations must be broadened to support investigation of topics that are now treated as off limits. An example is research on possible beneficial aspects of nonmedical drug use, such as enhanced creativity reported by some users, and medical uses for illicit drugs (e.g., psychedelics in conjunction with psychotherapy, marijuana as an appetite stimulant, and heroin as an analgesic). This kind of research may lead to important uses for illicit drugs, and simply undertaking it will help dispel the view that illicit drugs are entirely bad.

Another example of the need to depoliticize research concerns studies of controlled and other styles of use. Very little research has been done on controlled use of opiates or other illicit drugs (Harding, 1992). Information is needed about many issues including: the criteria that should be used to distinguish among different styles of drug use; screening methods for distinguishing among controlled, compulsive and other types of users; factors associated with transitions between using styles; and typical stages in drug-using careers. This information has important practical implications. For example, if treatment and prevention programs cannot distinguish among different styles of use, they may underestimate their success by counting controlled users as failures because they did not achieve abstinence. If programs cannot distinguish among using styles when clients enter, they may overestimate their success if the clients who improve were the most controlled to begin with (Aplser & Harding, 1991).

There are several reasons for the paucity of research about controlled illicit drug use. One is that researchers subscribe to cultural views about the dangers of illicit drugs, tend to dismiss controlled use as a brief, transitional phenomenon leading to abstinence or to increased drug use. Another reason is that some funders assume that interest in such topics indicates that the researcher is biased in favor of liberalizing drug controls. A third is that some researchers may want to avoid controversial issues that might damage their career (Trebach, 1987, pp. 108–109; Peele, 1986).

CONCLUSION

In the United States, public debate about the status of illicit drugs is fixed on the benefits and liabilities of just two positions: maintaining prohibition or legalizing illicit drug use. One goal of this chapter was to increase the productivity of this debate by shifting its focus to a process of gradually liberalizing drug controls. Another goal was to show that planning this process must take account of the variability in the way intoxicants are used and the role played by informal social controls in determining the consequences of their use.

REFERENCES

Apsler, R. and Harding, W.M. (1989) *Responsible alcohol management for public assembly facilities: Guidelines for developing, implementing, and evaluating your program.* Washington, D.C.: U.S. Department of Transportation, National Highway Traffic Safety Administration. (DOT Publication No. HS 807 488).

Apsler, R. and Harding, W.M. (1991) Cost effectiveness analysis of drug abuse treatment: Current status and recommendations for future research. In *Background papers in drug abuse financing and services research* (Drug Abuse Services Research Series No. 1, pp. 58–81). Washington, D.C.: National Institute on Drug Abuse.

Apsler, R., Harding W.M. and Goldfein, J. (1987) *The review and assessment of designated driver programs as an alcohol countermeasure approach.* Washington, D.C.: U.S. Department of Transportation, National Highway Traffic Safety Administration. (DOT Publication No. HS 807 108).

Benard, B. (1990) An overview of community-based prevention. In K. Rey, C. Faegre & P. Lowery (Eds.), *Prevention Research Findings: 1988* (OSAP Prevention Monograph-3, pp. 126–147). Rockville, Maryland: Office for Substance Abuse Prevention. (DHHS Publication No. ADM 89-1615).

Bureau of Justice Statistics (1992) *Drugs, crime and the justice system: A national report from the Bureau of Justice Statistics* (NCJ-133652). Washington, D.C.

Funkhouser, J.E., Goperud, E.N. and Bass, R.O. (1992) 'Current status of prevention strategies'. In M.A. Jansen (Ed.), *A promising future: Alcohol and other drug problem prevention services improvement.* (OSAP Prevention Monograph — 10, pp. 17–82). Rockville, Maryland: Office for Substance Abuse Prevention. (DHHS Publication No. ADM92-1807).

Funkhouser, J.E. and Denniston, R.W. (1992) Historical perspective. In M.A. Jansen (Ed.), *A promising future: Alcohol and other drug problem prevention services improvement.* (OSAP Prevention Monograph — 10, pp. 5–15). Rockville, Maryland: Office for Substance Abuse Prevention. (DHHS Publication No. ADM92-1807).

General Accounting Office (1993) *Community based drug prevention: Comprehensive evaluations of efforts are needed* (GAO/GGD-93-75). Gaithersburg, Maryland.

Gibbs, J. and Bennett, S. (1990) Creating A comprehensive community prevention plan: A leader's guide. Seattle, Washington: Comprehensive Health Education Foundation.

Harding, W.M. (1992) Chipping away at dogma: Policy implications of the existence of formerly-compulsive-now-controlled opiate users (Doctoral Dissertation, Brandeis University), Ann Arbor, Michigan: University Microfilms International.

Harding, W.M. and Apsler, R. (1994) [Survey of high school students]. Unpublished raw data.

Harding, W.M. and Zinberg, N.E. (1983) Occasional opiate use. In N.K. Mello (Ed.), *Advances in substance abuse: Behavioral and Biological Research, Volume 3* (pp. 27–61). Greenwich, Connecticut: JAI Press.

Harding, W.M., Apsler, R. and Goldfein, J. (1988) *The Assessment of Ride Service Programs as an Alcohol Countermeasure.* Washington, D.C.: U.S. Department of Transportation, National Highway Traffic Safety Administration. (DOT Publication No. HS 807 290).

Harding, W.M., Apsler, R. and Walsh, W. (1989a) Identification of parental program structures for deterring adolescent drinking and driving, Volume II: Literature review. Washington, D.C.: *U.S. Department of Transportation,* National Highway Traffic Safety Administration. (DOT Publication No. HS 807 556).

Harding, W.M., Apsler, R. and Walsh, W. (1989b) *Assessment of multiple DWI offender restrictions.* Washington, D.C.: *U.S. Department of Transportation,* National Highway Traffic Safety Administration. (DOT Publication No. HS 807 556).

Johnston, L.D., O'Malley, P.M. and Bachman, J.G. (1994) *National survey results on drug use from the monitoring the future study, 1975–1993, Volume 1 Secondary School Students.* National Institute on Drug Abuse: Rockville, Maryland. (NIH Publication No. 94-3809).

Lender, M.E. and Martin, J.K. (1982) *Drinking in America: A History.* New York: The Free Press.

Maguire, K. and Pastore, A.L. (Eds.). (1994) *Sourcebook of criminal justice statistics — 1993* (NCJ-148211). Washington, D.C.: Bureau of Justice Statistics.

National Highway Traffic Safety Administration (1991) *Fatal accident reporting system 1989.* Washington, D.C.: U.S. Department of Transportation, 1991.

National Institute on Alcohol Abuse and Alcoholism (1994) *Eighth special report to Congress on alcohol and health.* Washington, D.C. (NIH Publication No. 94-3699).

Netherlands Institute for Alcohol and Drugs (1995) *Netherlands alcohol and drug report: Fact report, cannabis policy, number 1.* Utrecht, the Netherlands.

Office of National Drug Control Policy (1995) *Reducing the impact of drugs on American society.* Washington, D.C.

Peele, S. (1986) Denial — of reality and freedom — in addiction research and treatment. *Psychology of Addictive Behaviors,* 5: 149–166.

Public backs heavy penalties (1995, September). *Boston Globe,* p. 11.

Staff (1993, January/February) Editorial guidelines. *Prevention Pipeline,* p. 101.

Szasz, T. (1975) *Ceremonial chemistry: The ritual persecution of drugs, addicts and pushers.* Garden City, New York: Anchor Press/Doubleday.

Trebach, A.S. (1987) *The great drug war.* New York: Mcmillan.

Zinberg, N.E. (1984) *Drug set and setting: The basis for controlled intoxicant use.* New Haven, Connecticut: Yale University Press.

Zinberg, N.E., Harding, W.M. and Winkeller, M. (1977) A study of social regulatory mechanisms in controlled illicit drug users. *Journal of Drug Issues* 7: 117–133.

CHAPTER 13

International Trends in Drug Policy

Richard Hartnoll

INTRODUCTION

This chapter gives an overview of some recent trends in drug policy on the international stage, and looks at the position and future prospects of non-prohibitionist policies within that wider context.

In order to examine trends in non-prohibitionist drug policies on the international stage, it is necessary to clarify the meaning of the terms "non-prohibitionist" and "international stage". Taken literally, "non-prohibitionist" refers to any aspects of policy other than those concerned with banning drugs and drug use. This covers a wide spectrum of policy positions that are rather distinct, from various forms of legalisation of all or selected drugs, through decriminalisation or reduction of penalties for drug use, to demand reduction approaches based on prevention, treatment and rehabilitation, and to the overlapping range of harm reduction interventions such as methadone maintenance or syringe exchange. Although some of the policy changes described in this chapter are a mixture of different elements, an attempt will be made to maintain the distinctions between the different meanings.

The "international stage" also has different meanings. It can refer to the international arena *per se*, for example the international treaties, the activities of international organisations or the conclusions of global or regional conferences. Or it can mean an overview of policies and policy changes observed in different countries, either at national or local level. These policies and trends, both between and within countries, but especially at local level, may be diverse and the rate of change can sometimes be quite rapid. However, these local differences and changes are not necessarily reflected in the international arena in the sense described above. A further distinction must be made between policy as expressed in official statements or legislation, and policy as it is implemented in practice. The gap between these can be large, not just at the level of the difference between what laws say and how they are applied, but also at the much broader level of the gap between public and political discourse and local reality.

The argument put forward in this chapter is that significant tensions are building up over the emphasis and fundamental direction of drug policy. The sources of these tensions are varied. Many could be described in a broad sense as coming from the bottom up, for example from municipal authorities, NGOs, researchers, practitioners, police, journalists, and others. There are also a number states which challenge important aspects of mainstream international policy, and if the adoption of various harm reduction policies are included, a significant and growing number. The issues thrown up by HIV and AIDS, and rising concern about drug trafficking, drug-related crime and public safety, have played a major role in this search for further answers, either through exploring alternative approaches, or through intensifying previous efforts. The key actors at the centre of international policy, supported by a significant number of countries, continue to reinforce the prohibitionist perspective that lies at the core of international drug policy by extending it to incorporate demand reduction approaches in a manner that reaffirms the underlying drug-free philosophy on which that policy is based. However, these tensions should not be seen only as being between the centre and the periphery, but also between actors at the local, national and international level.

Within many countries, tensions can be observed between the local level, where the realities of drug problems are faced and workable approaches have to be negotiated, and the national level, where politics and populist rhetoric often predominate over the need to find solutions to complex problems. Tensions also arise between the national and international levels, when international solidarity and adherence to treaty obligations are invoked to constrain countries seeking to implement alternative policies that they consider to be more appropriate to their situation.

The pressures from the local level are not uniform. Moves to establish non-prohibitionist policies can be observed in some countries, especially at the local level of cities where drugs are most visible and the problems associated with drugs are most acutely experienced. But responses observed at local level are sometimes driven by sharply divergent philosophical and moral perspectives on drugs, as seen for example in the confrontations between supporters of the Frankfurt and Stockholm resolutions.

These different approaches reflect deep differences in core values and moral conceptions of the drug phenomenon, and, at times, in how human behaviour is to be understood and in what are the responsibilities of the state with regard to individual behaviour. On one side, any drug use is defined, *per se*, as wrong and a threat, both to individuals and to society. Policies and interventions may be more or less effective in reducing drug use, but if they do not send the message that drugs are unacceptable, then no amount of evidence is relevant. The drug-free, prohibitionist thrust of international policy is seen as self-evident and not open to question. On the other side, drug use is seen as a part of the human condition, neither right nor wrong in itself. The criteria for judging policies and interventions are whether or not they reduce human suffering or harm, either at individual or societal level. In this perspective, the mainstream policy of prohibition is far from self-evident and is open to question in terms of whether it helps or hinders the goal of minimising damage.

By no means all positions regarding drug policy can be neatly divided into the two conflicting philosophies characterised and to some extent caricatured above. But presenting the issues in a polarised fashion does provide anchor points against which to analyse the conflicting and contradictory trends in international drug policy. The rest of this chapter looks in more detail at some of the developments and tensions that these divergent perspectives generate in the context of international drug policy.

DRUG POLICY IN THE INTERNATIONAL ARENA

The Framework of International Drug Control

International Conventions

The system of international drug control began in 1909 with the first international conference on drugs in Shanghai. This led to the signing of the International Opium Convention at The Hague in 1912. Over the course of the century, international structures, organisations and treaties concerned with the drug field have proliferated, both in number and in complexity. The most important treaties are: the 1961 Single Convention on Narcotic Drugs (amended in 1972), the 1971 Convention on Psychotropic Substances, and the 1988 United Nations Convention against Illicit Traffic in Narcotic Drugs and Psychotropic Substances (for an overview of the United Nations strategy, see Leroy, 1995).

The 1961 Single Convention consolidated most of the previous international instruments for controlling opium, coca, cannabis and their derivatives (such as heroin and cocaine) and established the International Narcotics Control Board (INCB). Although it was mainly concerned with controlling drug manufacture, trade and distribution, it also prohibited practices like opium smoking, chewing coca leaves or smoking cannabis (with transitional periods for states with traditional use). The 1972 amendment to the 1961 Single Convention required countries to take steps to provide health and social measures for drug users as alternatives to imprisonment. The 1971 Convention extended control to manufactured drugs such as amphetamines, hypnotics and hallucinogens. The 1988 Convention extended the scope of measures against trafficking. introduced provisions to control money laundering and seize the assets of drug-traffickers, to allow for extradition of major traffickers and improved legal co-operation between countries, and to regulate the trade in precursors (chemicals used in the production of drugs). It also proposed criminalisation of purchase and possession by users, though it allowed for treatment or rehabilitation as an alternative to a penal sentence.

These Conventions underpin the whole structure of international drug control. They are legally binding on all countries who ratify them, and aim to restrict the supply and use of drugs to scientific or medical purposes only. They oblige signatories to implement a wide variety of measures, including national laws to prohibit non-medical or non-scientific production, distribution, possession and consumption, especially of substances listed in Schedule 1 attached to the 1961 and 1971 Conventions (including heroin, cocaine, cannabis, LSD, etc.). Although they allow some flexibility in terms of interpretation and implementation that enables countries to take account of their needs and circumstances, legalisation of any narcotic drugs as defined in the Conventions is not permitted.

International organisations

The major organisations at world-wide level are linked to the United Nations (UN), notably the United Nations Commission on Narcotic Drugs (CND), which is the central policy-making body, consisting of 53 countries drawn from members of the UN; the International Narcotics Control Board (INCB), which is responsible for monitoring the implementation of the international treaties; and the United Nations Drug Control Programme (UNDCP), which was created in 1990 to co-ordinate all the activities of the United Nations and carry out a wide range of programmes. Other important bodies related to the UN are the World Health Organisation (WHO) which determines which substances should be placed under international control and promotes activities concerning prevention, treatment, training and management of drug problems through its Global Programme on Drug Dependence as well as through its Regional Offices; the International Criminal Police Organisation (Interpol); the World Customs Organisation (WCO, previously CCC, the Customs Co-operation Council); the United Nations Educational, Scientific and Cultural Organisation (UNESCO); and, increasingly, the United Nations Development Programme and a new agency, UNAIDS.

The two main formal statements of international drug policy are to be found in the Declaration of the International Conference on Drug Abuse and Illicit Trafficking and Comprehensive Multi-disciplinary Outline of Future Activities in Drug Abuse Control (United Nations, 1988) adopted by consensus in Vienna in June 1987 at the first UN conference to deal with drugs at ministerial level, and in the Political Declaration and Global Programme of Action, adopted by the General Assembly of the United Nations in March 1990 (United Nations, 1990).

Trends in Policy

At the official, public level of the international arena, it can be hard to discern clear trends or changes. The annual reports of the INCB or the conclusions of inter-governmental conferences contain regular and predictable condemnations and warnings about the evil of drugs and the drugs trade, and frequently reassert the imperative of greater international consensus and action in the struggle against this threat.

Longer-term perspective

From a longer-term perspective, there have been important developments in the emphasis of international control. The concern of treaties in the early part of the 20th. century was to regulate the international trade in drugs, especially opium, through production quotas and import-export regulatory mechanisms. Over the course of the century, and especially since the second world war, the scope has extended in several directions. The range of drugs deemed to be suitable candidates for control and defined by the Conventions as narcotic drugs expanded. For example, the 1961 Single Convention placed particular emphasis on the dangers of cannabis, and the 1971 Convention added a substantial number of other psychotropic substances. Step by step, in addition to regulating production and international trade in narcotic drugs in order to restrict their use to medical and scientific purposes, increased emphasis has been given to ensuring that states take repressive measures to criminalise the illegal supply and the use of narcotic drugs. More recently, reference has been made to prevention, treatment and rehabilitation, and to the need to develop economic, social and cultural alternatives. Currently, many official documents stress the need for a balanced, global approach that encompasses all aspects and causes of both drug demand and drug supply.

This latest extension in the scope of international control does not represent a reduction in the priority given to repression and prohibition. Rather, it adds an additional element to the pre-existing structure. Thus the global approach remains firmly based on a prohibitionist framework and drug-free philosophy of prevention that is constantly reaffirmed. "Only a decade ago, planning towards a society free of drug abuse was thought of as being unrealistic. Many government planners focused instead on how society could learn to live with the effects of drug abuse. Today, it is widely believed that a drug-free society, although far off, is nevertheless possible" (UNDCP, 1992).

However, developments in the international arena are not totally homogenous. Behind the diplomatic conclusions and rhetoric of apparent consensus, there are some real differences and tensions. Some of these are visible from the formal reports or positions of international actors, others are only manifest in more localised disagreements. Indications of change within the international arena, or at least of debate about alternative approaches such non-prohibitionist policies, are more marked for some issues than for others.

Legalisation

The subject of legalisation of drugs has received considerable publicity in many countries over the past few years (see, for example, Reuter & MacCoun, 1995).

These debates have sometimes focused on cannabis, with proponents of legalisation arguing that cannabis is more widely accepted and significantly less dangerous than many other drugs, and that limited resources should be targeted on drugs associated with serious health and social problems rather than on maintaining a failed policy of pursuing and criminalising a broad spectrum of an otherwise law abiding population. Opponents argue that this would legitimise the drug-taking culture and lead to increased consumption of both cannabis and other drugs. At times, this debate has extended to the legalisation of all drugs, on the basis of the argument that current policies to control supply and consumption have not only failed but are counter-productive, for example by stimulating the emergence of an uncontrolled and socially corrupting illicit market.

The debate(s) about legalisation have been reflected in the international arena, for example in recent reports of the INCB. The overwhelming thrust of official opinion at this level is to reject totally all arguments in favour of legalisation, either of cannabis or of all drugs. This response is also seen in the conclusions of inter-governmental conferences and other official reports reflecting policy at an international level.

Decriminalisation and depenalisation

The debate over the related though distinct issue of decriminalisation of drug use has also received considerable attention. The underlying argument put forward by proponents of decriminalisation is that whilst the production and supply of drugs should not be legalised, it is counter-productive to criminalise people who only use them and possess them in small amounts, and that resources should be directed towards prevention, treatment where necessary, and measures to counter the underlying social and individual factors that increase the risks of drug use and drug dependence. Opponents argue that decriminalisation sends the wrong message, and that a legal framework, including the definition of drug taking as an unacceptable behaviour, is an essential part of a comprehensive policy of prevention, treatment and rehabilitation that enables the authorities to intervene in the interests of both society and the individual user.

As with legalisation, the consensus of the large majority of official opinion in the international arena is to reject decriminalisation as a whole. In general, although there are a few well publicised examples of partial decriminalisation, the trend is continued pressure for criminalisation on countries where drug use was not previously criminal (for example in eastern Europe).

However there is a growing recognition that prohibition and law enforcement by themselves are inadequate, especially at the user level, and that imprisonment for drug use per se should be avoided wherever possible. Thus there is increasing support for legislation that provides for alternatives to penal sanctions, for example for treatment or supervision in the community rather than prison. Actual trends appear to contradict this stated goal, since the number and proportion of drug users or drug addicts in prison seems to be increasing in some, and perhaps many countries.

This support for limited depenalisation of drug use, or at least for avoiding the sanction of imprisonment where possible, applies primarily to those who are considered to be "addicts" or 'problematic drug users'. The status of the majority of users who take drugs occasionally, and for whom treatment is not relevant, is not clear. In practice, this situation is resolved, in some countries at least, by the police, prosecutors and/or courts applying the law more or less severely, depending on the type of situation. Thus it seems that whilst the predominant trend at the level of legislation is towards greater repression of drug use, at the level of practice, the opposite trend is observed, at least in Europe and some other regions such as Australasia. Without comparative research on the ways in which laws are applied in practice as opposed to the wording of legislation, it is impossible be more precise.

The other form of limited decriminalisation that is gaining some acceptance within the international arena concerns providing substitutes under medical supervision, though this acceptance is not universal. The discussion of substitution primarily concerns methadone prescribed to opiate addicts within the context of a treatment programme. Although this conflicts with the predominantly abstinence-oriented philosophy of international policy, substitution is increasingly accepted as legitimate medical practice, at least in some circumstances, for example for addicts who are HIV seropositive or who have AIDS, during pregnancy, for long term addicts who have failed in other treatments, or for those who need a period of stabilisation prior to attempting detoxification. The development of long-term methadone maintenance and low threshold methadone programmes is more controversial, though an increasing number of countries are showing interest in these approaches. However, extending these approaches to include providing legal heroin does not find favour within the official international arena. Those few countries who do allow heroin to be prescribed or dispensed as part of a medically-supervised treatment programme (e.g. Britain, Switzerland) or who are considering it (e.g. Australia (Canberra), Netherlands, some German cities) have argued that it is permissible medical or scientific practice under the terms of the international treaties.

Demand reduction

The general concept of demand reduction is unanimously accepted by the international community, but the boundaries of this concept are not always clear. Education and prevention, and especially primary prevention, are clearly included and are being accorded increasing priority in policy documents. Likewise the inclusion of treatment and rehabilitation is unambiguously endorsed, as is training for professionals such as teachers, doctors, nurses and social workers. More controversial is whether certain harm reduction measures should be included. For example, some argue that syringe exchange or education on safe sex are not concerned with reducing the demand for drugs, or that methadone merely substitutes one drug of dependence for another. Others assert that methadone substitution, whilst not necessarily reducing drug use, aims to reduce the demand for illicit drugs. They further argue that 'demand reduction' is not a precisely defined term that is literally restricted to measures that directly reduce drug consumption, but rather that it evolved as a broad concept incorporating a range of responses to drug use and drug problems in the fields of health, social welfare and education. These differences of perspective on what should be the defining characteristics of demand reduction are also seen in disagreements on whether police activities aimed at deterring drug use by arresting drug users should be considered as 'demand reduction'.

Although there is consensus over the core components of demand reduction (education, prevention, treatment, rehabilitation, training) the translation of these concepts into health, education and social policies and concrete interventions is not the responsibility of the international bodies or treaties, but rather of member states and often, within them, of local authorities or nongovernmental organisations. Thus the obligations imposed by the Conventions and the mechanisms established by the international organisations are rather general in nature, leaving the priorities and manner of implementation of drug demand reduction policies to be decided by the countries or local bodies concerned.

Whilst local flexibility is both necessary and desirable, it does mean that the lack of specificity allows countries who do not wish to devote resources to this area to call all manner of existing activities 'demand reduction' whilst taking little action. Thus international policy has much less bite in this area than it does regarding issues of legislation and repression. It would be interesting to look at the extent to which the allocation of budgets and other resources invested by international organisations and the different countries reflect their balance of priorities.

Harm reduction

The main thrust of official international policy as reflected in the Conventions, the CND, INCB and programmes of the UNDCP is to incorporate demand reduction activities to the extent that they are compatible with the overall strategy of moving towards the ideal of a drug-free society, supported by the concept of 'zero tolerance' and legislation to prohibit drug use. Thus it is no surprise that priority is given to primary prevention ("Say No! to Drugs") followed by treatment and rehabilitation.

This means that harm reduction is a controversial issue in the international arena (as well as in some countries). It is a term that is not accepted by the UNDCP and by some other countries such as the United States government, since it is considered that it lacks commitment to a drug-free goal, accepts or condones continued use of drugs, and implies a hidden agenda of decriminalisation or legalisation. Whilst this is partly a matter of terminology, and partly of the associations that the term has acquired rather than of its meaning, this does reflect a substantial range of differences in underlying philosophy between the INCB, UNDCP, some governments and local bodies on the one hand, and a variety of other international organisations, individual countries, local authorities and nongovernmental organisations on the other.

Whilst the idea of harm reduction sits uncomfortably with the predominant philosophy of international control structures, the substantial changes taking place on the ground in many countries, and the pressing need to deal with problems related to public health, crime and public safety, are forcing change.

For example, comments from the Director of UNESCO are based on an analysis that identifies poverty and marginalisation as the broader and fundamental issues to be addressed on a world-wide level, and for greater emphasis to be given to intermediate measures that reduce the cost to the individuals and communities that disproportionately suffer the adverse consequences of drug addiction and other drug-related problems. Whilst this is not of course a call for decriminalisation or legalisation, it does imply a different order of priorities than those reflected in the Conventions or pursued by the UNDCP. Other examples include the public health driven harm-reduction approach followed by the recently created United Nations body for co-ordinating action on AIDS (UNAIDS), and comments by the head of the International Police Organisation (Interpol) questioning the feasibility of controlling illegal production and supply, and the unintended negative consequences of repression.

At more local level, the growing acceptance and implementation in an increasing number of countries of methadone programmes and syringe exchanges in response to HIV and AIDS, the rising pressure to reverse the increasing problems of drug users in prisons, the apparent tendency in some regions to reduce law enforcement directed at drug users or to discuss alternatives to criminalisation are all sources of strain in the search for solidarity on the international stage.

Supply reduction and repressive measures

The above comments should not be taken to imply that international drug policy is about to witness a *volte face*, far from it. Intensified measures to repress illegal cultivation and production, crop-eradication and crop-substitution programmes, control of chemical precursors used in the manufacture of narcotic drugs, new techniques and systems of police co-operation to monitor and interdict traffickers, including, for example, cross-border controlled deliveries, new laws on money laundering and the seizure of assets gained through drug trafficking, extradition treaties for drug traffickers, reversal of burden of proof in cases of suspected financial gains from drug trafficking, economic sanctions on countries that are seen to be uncooperative in the fight against drugs, all these are witness to the continuing momentum of the expanding scope of international drug policy.

The Enduring Principles of International Policy

Thus, despite the developments described above, the guiding principles underlying the framework for international policy have remained those of control, consensus and conservatism.

Control and the legitimisation of the agents of control

The notion of control is central to international drug policy, just as it is to national policies. Whilst almost every party to the debate on drug policy accepts, whatever their orientation, that regulation is necessary, the form that this regulation has assumed reflects the dominant model of "the problem" and thus of "the solution". The roots of this model can be traced in the historical evolution of international bodies and treaties, an evolution that disproportionately reflects the interests and perspective of more powerful countries and interest groups, notably the USA, though also at times European countries such as Britain.

The notion of powerful interests legitimising their role and reinforcing the dominant model of control can also be linked to the implications of the end of cold war. This led to a search for a new role and legitimacy in the new world order by the United States and by West Europeans, and by state organs such as security forces, counter-intelligence, and the armed forces. Thus terrorism, organised crime and immigration have been linked up with drugs into a cluster of issues, and at times a conspiracy of evil forces, that threaten to undermine the authority and stability of civilisation. Thus clustered, the imperative for greater control through a repressive apparatus is deemed to be self-evident.

Consensus

The need for consensus is a powerful force. Once an international structure has been established, especially one with a dominant mission of control (rather than, for example, as a forum for exchange of information and mutual benefits so as to learn from a diversity of different points of view and experiences) there is an inevitable tendency towards standardisation, justified in terms of "a global problem requires a global solution".

The most recent example in Europe is the conflict between the Netherlands and several other countries, notably France, though also Germany, Sweden and the United States, concerning its drug policy, for example the tolerance of cannabis sales in coffee shops. It does not necessarily matter that closing the coffee shops would probably have a minimal effect on cannabis availability and use in France or Germany. Rather, this pressure to conform can be seen as intolerance of deviance from the international norm. One might further suggest that examples of 'deviants' such as the Netherlands are useful to the majority as examples that allow reaffirmation of the norm.

On an international scale, this consensus is reinforced by pressure from more powerful countries. A clear example is the use of economic sanctions by the United States on countries such as Colombia which do not play the game — though these threats should also be seen in the wider context of US foreign policy. The Action Plan on Drugs currently under discussion in the European Union also foresees drug control clauses being included in trade agreements with third countries.

Conservatism

Conservatism can be seen in institutionalisation of the direction and momentum of international treaties, in the goals and administrative structures of international bodies and their national counterparts, and in the development of vested interests in the apparatus of making, monitoring and implementing policies, treaties and programmes that have built up over the course of this century. Complex structures such as this are slow to change, both collectively and within their individual components. Furthermore, they tend to be reactive and unlikely to initiate change.

These are constraints on the possibilities for change. Pressures for change largely come from outside the international organisations, and usually from the bottom up, though in the longer term it is possible that a growing gap between official goals and the apparent reality could lead to radical re-alignments. At the moment it is hard to see how and where such a radical shift would come from within the international stage, despite the strains that have been described above.

In the next section, we look at examples of developments at local and national level, with an emphasis on Europe, though with brief mentions of other regions.

NATIONAL TRENDS AND POLICY DIFFERENCES

Western Europe

Drug policies in different countries of western Europe are neither uniform nor static. Whilst there are similarities, there are also marked differences in underlying philosophies and expressions of policy objectives, in legislation and in the types of interventions that are found. Thus the stated goal of drug policy in countries such as Norway and Sweden is a drug-free society, and the use of any and all drugs is strongly stigmatised. Primary prevention and police intervention against users as well as traffickers are given high priority. Interventions that appear to accept continued drug use, such as methadone maintenance or needle exchange, have traditionally been viewed with suspicion. In contrast, Dutch policy explicitly refers to the priority of reducing the damage caused by drugs rather than to eliminating drug use *per se*. Thus they adopt an approach that includes "normalising" rather than stigmatising and marginalising drug users, and that differentiates between drugs such as cannabis and higher-risk drugs such as heroin.

However, it would be a mistake to try to place European countries on a single dimension with regard to drug policy. For example, although the Dutch and Swedish policy statements contrast with respect to stated policy goals, both countries have placed a high priority on providing a comprehensive network of treatment and social care facilities within the broader context of a strong welfare state.

Harm reduction and changes in policy

Furthermore, the situation in several European countries has changed markedly over the past ten years. For example, Swiss drug policy, especially in the German speaking areas, has swung from an approach based primarily on police enforcement and drug-free treatment to one that emphasises low-threshold programmes, outreach, methadone maintenance, and, most recently the provision of heroin for addicts. A similar trend can be observed in Germany, especially in cities such as Frankfurt, Hamburg and Bremen, and though the Federal Government has adopted a more cautious position, it has dropped its opposition to methadone and has encouraged other measures to reduce the risk of HIV infection amongst drug injectors.

Less dramatic changes are seen in countries such as France, Belgium, Austria, or Greece that traditionally have pursued a repressive and drug-free oriented approach, though issues such as methadone remain controversial. In Britain, where measures such as prescribing opiate substitutes (mainly methadone, though also heroin) or outreach have a longer history, the tone of official pronouncements on drug policy have fluctuated with the ministers involved, but the practice on the ground has remained firmly pragmatic and eclectic. In several countries (e.g. Spain or Ireland) methadone maintenance has expanded rapidly in recent years, whereas others are being much more cautious (e.g. Norway).

Trends in legislation

In terms of legislation, the general tendency in Europe has been toward increased severity of sanctions for traffick or supply related offences and drug-related crime. The situation and trends regarding drug use and possession for personal use varies. For example, possession of small amounts of cannabis has effectively been decriminalised in the Netherlands, and in 1994 the German Constitutional Court ruled in 1994 that possessing a small amount of cannabis should no longer be punishable, though this has not been implemented in all the German Lander. Conversely, drug use has recently been made an imprisonable offence in Sweden. In other countries, such as Spain and Italy, drug legislation has fluctuated over the past decade. In the former, a relaxation of the law in 1983, which included the removal of drug use from the list of punishable offences, was partly reversed by 1988 reforms to the Penal Code (though drug use *per se* remains unpunished) and by the introduction of administrative sanctions against drug use in public in 1992. In Italy, the law of 1975 did not punish drug use or possession of small amounts. In 1990, drug use was prohibited, though administrative sanctions such as suspension of driving licence or passport were applied for the first two or three offences, and only for subsequent offences did punitive sanctions come into effect. The referendum of 1993 overturned this, and since then, the use of drugs is no longer prohibited. Whilst drug use itself is not illegal in several other countries, it is in effect criminalised through legislation prohibiting posses-sion. Systematic analyses of legislation on drugs in European countries can be found in several recent reports (Cervello, 1989, Albrecht & van Kalmthout, 1989; Leroy, 1995, De Ruyver, 1995).

Common themes

Despite differences between European countries, several common themes can be identified. Some of these have been discussed in recent major European confer-ences (for example in Florence in December 1993, and a second in Brussels in December 1995, involving the 15 Member States of the European Union, the European Commission and the Parliament)

There is a growing recognition of the importance of a global multi-disciplinary, multi-agency approach. This is reflected in, for example, the emergence of inter-ministerial commissions, or of local co-operation structures. However, the contra-dictions that can arise between the different strands of policy are not always (publicly) acknowledged, for example tensions between police and public health priorities regarding syringe exchange or fixing rooms. This suggests that the dif-ferences in underlying philosophies and conceptions of drug use are not resolved simply by creating a multi-disciplinary model. Increased emphasis on prevention is another clear trend, though the message ("Say No! to drugs" or, "It's best not to use, but if you do use, use safely") also depends on the wider context of the phi-losophy underlying drug policy.

Differences in legislation and penalties conceal a trend towards much homo-geneity in terms of the application of the law. Thus in almost all European coun-tries, possession of small amounts of drugs, especially by first offenders, are increasingly dealt with by warnings or fines rather than by more severe sanc-tions. Even where the law makes no distinction, cannabis cases are dealt with more leniently than drugs such as heroin, and all countries have provisions for enabling addicts to undergo treatment rather than imprisonment. However, state-ments of intent are contradicted by the increasing number and proportion of drug users and drug addicts in prisons in many European countries.

Various harm reduction measures have expanded markedly in almost all countries. The major driving force behind these changes has been concern about HIV and AIDS. This is most notable concerning methadone, though syringe exchange, outreach, low threshold projects, peer education have all gained higher priority across Europe. Similarly, concern is rising about the number of drug users, and in particular drug addicts, in prison, though changes here tend to be slower.

A comprehensive overview of European policies and strategies on drugs within the framework of the Treaty of European Union (Maastricht) is provided in a recent book by the Director of the new European Monitoring Centre on Drugs and Drug Addiction (Estievenart, 1995).

Other Regions

Eastern Europe

Prior to the political changes that swept the countries of Central and Eastern Europe in 1989, national laws often did not criminalise drug use, though there were various provisions for taking action, including compulsory treatment or measures related to criminal behaviour or intoxication. Since that time, intensive efforts by the international community, especially the UNDCP, the United States, supported by European countries such as Sweden, have been under way to ensure ratification and implementation of the international Conventions. Given that most of the countries concerned have willingly taken steps to integrate into western political and economic institutions, and given the efforts of the international organisations, they have also, at governmental level at least, also been willing to bring their legislation on drugs into line with mainstream international policy.

This led in countries such as Poland or the Czech Republic to a strong debate on the balance between repression and tolerance regarding drug use, and between drug free and harm reduction approaches. Opponents of criminalisation have, by and large, failed to prevent the process of harmonisation of legislation in conformity with international policy, though as with western Europe, there are variations in how legislation on drug use is being implemented. In the area of harm reduction approaches, however, the situation remains open. On the one hand, in many countries, the predominant concept of drug use was either formulated in terms of social deviance or medical pathology. Although public health institutes existed, they were not conceptually equipped to deal with drug use as a social phenomena. Thus the idea of harm reduction was not one which could be readily assimilated into the framework of existing health and social institutions, nor one which could easily gain political and public acceptance in the context of fear and stigmatisation of drug users. This had potentially serious implications regarding the possible spread of AIDS amongst drug injectors. However, over the past few years, there has been a significant level of contact and exchange of experience between professionals working in the field in Eastern and Central Europe and their colleagues in western countries. This has stimulated a variety of initiatives, including outreach and peer education, methadone, syringe exchange, ethnographic research and other activities falling under the broad heading of harm reduction. Currently, these are reinforced through the activities of the Lindesmith Foundation in the United States.

United States of America

The recent evolution of drug policy in the United States has been described and discussed in numerous publications. Over the 1980s, drug policy at national level became increasingly committed to a drug-free ideology combined with repression against drug use and a war against drugs at national and international level.

Harm reduction measures such as syringe exchange were condemned as encouraging drug use. Across the country, this was also reflected at local level, especially amongst predominantly white and middle-class communities. However, within inner-city areas most affected by high levels of drug addiction and AIDS, many local initiatives were launched to implement harm-reduction interventions, including outreach, efforts to persuade injectors to sterilise syringes with bleach, semi-illegal syringe exchanges and so on. Despite expectations, the election of Clinton had relatively little effect on the overall direction of drug policy, and harm reduction strategies still struggle to achieve acceptance or support.

In the international arena, the United States continues to play a major role, for example within the United Nations and in parts of the world where it has strong foreign policy interests, especially Latin America and the Caribbean.

Other regions

Some of the most striking initiatives in drug policy have been taking place in Australia. Several states have moved in the direction of decriminalising the use and possession of cannabis, a wide range of harm reduction interventions have been launched, and in Canberra, proposals for a substantial heroin maintenance programme are being carried forward. The situation in some of their relative neighbours in Southeast Asia is the reverse. Several countries have implemented strong measures against drug use, including imprisonment and the extensive use of compulsory treatment, as well as draconian measures against drug trafficking. In South America, proposals from some countries to explore alternative policies have met strong opposition and direct interventions from the United States.

UNDERLYING ISSUES AND TENSIONS

Between Countries and Regions

On the one hand, the goal of international policy as reflected in the Conventions is to achieve a united and unitary approach. On the other, the social, economic and political interests of different countries and regions are not always consistent with the same approach.

Some years ago, received wisdom divided the world into producer countries, usually third world or developing nations, where there might be "traditional" patterns of drug consumption (opium smoking, coca leaf chewing, marijuana smoking) but relatively few drug-related problems, and consumer countries, typically North American or Western European, where there was relatively little production, but a high level of use and related problems.

This simple division is no longer valid, even if it ever was. Substantial problems related to drug consumption have become manifest in many Asian countries (urban heroin addiction replacing rural opium smoking) parts of South

America (cocaine use replacing coca leaf chewing) and more recently in other regions such as Africa. Conversely, countries that were previously seen as importers and consumers are now seen also as major producers and exporters, for example of amphetamines or other manufactured drugs.

However, the conclusion that is sometimes drawn from this blurring of the producer/consumer distinction, that everyone is now in the same boat and so the same rules should apply equally to all, is misleading. In North America and Europe, illicit drug production remains a marginal activity in the context of rich and diversified economies and stable political systems. In many of the countries that were previously designated as producers, drug production is an important area of activity in what are often poor and under-developed economies, perhaps more so since there is now a domestic market as well as an international one. In a significant number of cases, the political system is not stable, at times aggravated by wars or civil conflict.

There is not space here to pursue this point, since it requires analysis on a region by region, country by country, issue by issue basis. However it cannot be assumed that the interests of each region or country are identical or even in the same direction as the framework laid down in international treaties. For example, it has been argued that the emergence of heroin use in some Asian countries or of cocaine use in some South American nations was in part at least a consequence of the requirement of the 1961 Single Convention to ban (progressively) traditional patterns of drug consumption. It is not intended here to examine the arguments on these particular cases. It is the intention to argue that what is in the interests of the more powerful actors on the international stage in the call for solidarity is not necessarily in the interests of the less powerful.

Between Different Levels

A similar line of argument is put forward regarding the convergence or divergence of interests between local, national and international level. At local level, where circumstances vary considerably, diversity implies the need for flexibility. At international level, standardisation and consensus are major driving forces.

At national level, both forces come into play — centrally, there is often pressure for uniformity within the country, which creates tension with local authorities and nongovernmental organisations who desire greater autonomy (though this varies with degree of centralisation or federalism). At the same time, international norms can also threaten national sovereignty and national interests, leading to tensions that in a general sense mirror those between national and local bodies within countries.

Between Sectors

There are important tensions between the different sectors that are reflected in international policy, though they are equally found at national and local level as well.

Political needs, professional experience

There are at least two levels at which tensions between political needs and professional knowledge hinders the development of rational drug policies.

The first is that of politicians' need for popular and appealing messages regardless of the evidence. Emotive populism, the political attractiveness of short term, simple-sounding solutions, and the fear of appearing to be 'soft on drugs' are often at odds with longer term, rational though usually complex analyses based on evidence.

The second is a dislocation arising from the turnover of political figures and the longer term accumulation of scientific knowledge and professional experience. It is all too common for a new minister to take office, having little knowledge of the subject but yet wishing to make his or her distinctive mark. This can mean ignoring what has been or was being done, initiating yet another review of the situation, listening to a different group of experts, or launching another 'new' initiative, before being transferred to another department or removed from office. This process may be more or less marked in different countries, and the stability of public administrations may ensure some continuity and development in policy, but the result is that the easy to recycle clichés tend to be recycled, with only a passing reference to evidence when convenient.

Repression, public health, prevention and treatment

In many countries, and in particular in the larger cities, crime, public nuisance and community safety related to drug use and drug dealing has become a major issue. This is perhaps the most acute example of the tensions between the different strands of drug policy noted above (for example, see Dorn, Jepsen & Savona, 1996). Thus actions aimed at 'cleaning up the streets' or 'cracking down on drug-related crime' implies pursuing drug users as well as local drug retailers and driving them out of sight, either underground, into prison or into other communities or countries. Whilst increased law enforcement may also drive some drug users to seek treatment in the short term, the overall effect can all too easily be in direct contradiction to the goals of public health policy, especially in the context of HIV and AIDS, to reduce stigmatisation and marginalisation, to increase contact with hidden populations, and to increase the accessibility of services.

As with crime-reduction and community safety policies, prevention policy can easily conflict with the goals of public health approaches. Strategies and campaigns to increase awareness and inculcate anti-drug attitudes can readily elicit hostility and rejection of drug users, widening further the gap between those who use and those who do not.

The relationship between demand reduction and law enforcement also poses questions which can be resolved, if they are resolved, in different ways. For example, some NGOs evolve to serve and protect the interests of certain vulnerable groups, including drug users. Since those groups tend to be in conflict with the police or are suspicious of official authorities, then those NGOs cannot at the same time collude with a repressive approach, though they may negotiate on behalf of their client group. In other cases, however, demand reduction approaches to prevention or therapy sit comfortably within a broadly repressive context. A coercive framework is seen as being valuable to deter use, to provide pressure to go into treatment, or to give a clear message.

Drug policy and the wider context

Drug policy should be seen in the wider context of international social and economic trends. These include an increasing polarisation in wealth between richer and poorer regions of the world, and in some cases within countries as well. This has far-reaching implications not only for reducing cultivation and production, but also for the distribution of drug-related problems. It might be possible to foresee endemic and intractable drug problems in poorer, marginalised communities, whilst resources are concentrated in the wealthier areas, protected by geographical distance as well as the police from 'contamination'. Such a pattern can be observed in the United States, where over the 1980s, drug use across much of the country was declining, whilst indicators of the casualties of drug dependence, hospital emergencies, demands, and above all prison admissions increased within poorer, often ethnic minority inner-city areas. Within many European countries, cutbacks in welfare and services, and growing anxieties about crime that are sometimes linked to racist perceptions, also threaten a further shift towards polarisation and exclusion of unpopular minorities, including drug users.

Another important trend that is observed in different parts of the world is a shift of power from the centralised nation state towards either decentralisation or regionalisation, or towards multi-national corporations or organisations (legal or illegal). The increasing economic and hence political influence of major cities, of regional groupings that may cut across national boundaries, and of international structures and communication networks that are not directly accountable to governments may produce profound though unpredictable changes in a range of policies, including those concerned with drugs.

CONCLUSIONS AND IMPLICATIONS FOR THE FUTURE

This chapter has covered some of the issues and current trends in international drug policy. It should be clear that although there are some consistent themes, there are also contradictory tendencies. This makes it difficult to anticipate the direction that drug policy will take in the future. It is also clear, that whatever developments do take place, there is unlikely to be any tidy or definitive resolution of these tensions in the foreseeable future.

Do the changes described above represent a sea-change or not? The short answer in the sense of a reversal of prohibition as a legal fact is no, they do not. However, in some regions, for example in an increasing number of European countries and in Australia, use and possession for personal use, especially though not only of cannabis, is now rarely dealt with through imprisonment. And in terms of the growing priority given to harm reduction approaches, they do constitute a significant change of course, at least in some parts of the world. More significant still may be the struggle to formulate drug policies within a wider context of policies on public health, social welfare, urban security and quality of life, and more broadly still, on local and regional development.

Pressure for a change in the direction of drug policy is unlikely to come from the top or from official drug control agencies. The potential for change driven from the bottom, or perhaps from an unexpected sideways direction, is probably greater than might appear. The gap between official policy pronouncements and the reality on the ground, between the letter of law and the application of the law, between the conflicting interests of the different parties described above, and between the narrow preoccupations of drug policy and the profound social, economic and political changes taking place across the international community, raises the possibility that major realignments in the dynamics of drug policy could well occur. The main possibilities for the immediate future lie in part with the development of harm reduction, including treatment and other approaches to minimising risks to individual users. In the longer term, they lie in the evolution of policies that are not based on narrow arguments about drugs, but are integrated into a broader framework.

It might help in the future if a better term were found for 'harm reduction', since it is now difficult to use it without the risk of confusing the debate about the legal status of drugs with concrete public health measures to save lives. There may well be a link between whether drug use is legal or illegal and the costs associated with drug use, but it would be a tragedy if progress in implementing concrete measures were delayed indefinitely by ideological debate about the direction of that link. One question for the future is whether reason, based on scientific evidence, day-by day reality, and a willingness to think clearly and imaginatively about a complex issue can play even a slightly larger role than it has on a topic dominated by unthinking reaction based on moralistic rhetoric.

REFERENCES

Leroy, B. (1995) The United Nations strategy, in Estievenart (Ed.) *Policies and Strategies to Combat Drugs in Europe: The Treaty on European Union: Framework for a New European Strategy to Combat Drugs?* (Florence: European University Institute, Martinus Nijhoff Publishers) pp. 27–38.

UNDCP (1992) *The United Nations and Drug Abuse Control* (New York & Geneva, United Nations Dept. of Public Information) p. 47.

Reuter, P. and MacCoun, R. (1995) Assessing the legalisation debate, in Estievenart (Ed.) *Policies and Strategies to Combat Drugs in Europe: The Treaty on European Union: Framework for a New European Strategy to Combat Drugs?* (Florence: European University Institute, Martinus Nijhoff Publishers) pp. 39–49.

Albrecht, H.-J. and van Kalmthout, A. (1989) *Drug Policies in Western Europe*, Kriminologische Forschungberichte aus dem Max-Planck Institut für ausländisches und internationales Strafrecht (Frieburg im Br., Max-Planck Institut)

Cervello, C. (1989) Rapport sur les concepts pénaux de base des pays membres du Groupe Pompidou en matière de lutte contre le trafic et la consommation de drogue (Strasbourg: Council of Europe, Pompidou Group).

De Ruyver, B. (1995) *Drug Policy in the European Union: Identification of Differences in Drug Penal Legislation in the Member States of the European Union* (Ghent, University of Ghent).

Leroy, B. (1995) European legislative systems in relation to the demand in 1993: recent developments and comparative study, in Estievenart (Ed.) *Policies and Strategies to Combat Drugs in Europe: The Treaty on European Union: Framework for a New European Strategy to Combat Drugs?* (Florence: European University Institute, Martinus Nijhoff Publishers) pp. 112–130.

Estievenart, G. (Ed.) (1995) *Policies and Strategies to Combat Drugs in Europe: The Treaty on European Union: Framework for a New European Strategy to Combat Drugs?* (Florence: European University Institute, Martinus Nijhoff Publishers).

Dorn, N. Jepsen, J. and Savona, E. (1996) *European Drug Policies and Enforcement* (London: MacMillan Press Ltd.).

INDEX